Hockey Karma

By
Howard Shapiro

Art & Color
Andres J. Mossa

Animal Media Group, LLC
Pittsburgh

Hockey Karma

Animal Media Group books may be ordered through booksellers, or by contacting:

Animal Media Group
100 1st Ave suite 1100
Pittsburgh, PA 15222
www.animalmediagroup.com
412-566-5656

ISBN: 978-0-9861489-3-4 (pbk)
ISBN: 978-0-9861489-4-1 (ebk)

Acknowledgements

Thanks to all of my friends at Animal Inc. and Animal Media Group LLC you guys made this all possible and for that I will always be grateful and appreciative! Bruce Springsteen, Big Country, Rush, U2, Pete Townshend, The Who, Bob Dylan, The Rolling Stones, The Clash, Rancid, Green Day, Eric Clapton, Ray Davies, Stan Lee, Bob Kane, Jeff Jones, Gary Craig, Davide DiRenzo, Kenny Greer, (the great) Jimmy Holmstrom, Scott Morrison, Keith Primeau, Joel Bloom (along with Carmel and Clarence), the Catanzarite Family, Jean Vallesteros, Bryant & Barbra Dillon, Andrew Cosby, Katharine Kan, Sean McIndoe, Barry Petchesky, John Branch, Greg Wyshynski, the hockey and YA and Graphic Novel book blogging communities (too many to name but thank you for all you do!) Anthony Brooks, Esq., Joe Migliozzi, Greg Schell, Cindy Himes, Mark Shuttleworth, Karen Ford, everyone at Total Hockey, Dave Hanson, Blaine Buterbaugh and Paul Harrington.

Very special thanks to my all-star team of the great, great, great Andres Mossa, Ryan Ferrier, Kris Boban, Michael Killen, Gavin Kosco and Idil Gozde for their creativity, vision and hard work bringing this story to life. It was a long haul my friends, but I wouldn't have wanted to make the journey without you guys by my side. Also, special thanks to Brianne Halverson and Autumn Van Gunten for their work on the publicity, marketing and social media fronts. You two did the equivalent of raising the dead and I cannot thank you enough! I also wanted to single out and say thanks to my good friend Christina Ahn. If it wasn't for you, Christina, this book would not exist. You are a great friend and collaborator and thank you for all that you have done for me and my writing! A huge shout out to Tom Cochrane for his friendship, inspiration and the kindness extended to me over the years… you're the best, my friend! To my sister Jody Shapiro and my mom Alice Shapiro whose strength and character are second to none. I love you so much.

Extra special thanks to Gina, Sasha and Nikita, I love you three more than anything in the world.

This book is dedicated to the loving and everlasting memory of my dad, Arnold Shapiro (7/21/31 – 11/11/05),

Mi manchi ogni giorno e io ti amo mio caro amico

Hockey Karma, A Supersonic Storybook and Animal Media Group LLC Production was filmed on location in Pittsburgh, PA, St. Louis, MO, Milan, Italy, Calgary, Alberta, London, England, Austin, TX, Los Angeles, CA and Toronto, Ontario.

For more information please log onto www.animalmediagroup.com or www.howardshapiro.net. Please send your comments, questions or feedback to info@animalmediagroup.com or hockeyplayer4life@gmail.com. Please check out my pages on Facebook http://www.facebook.com/hockeyplayer4life and http://www.facebook.com/pages/Howard-Shapiro/296610707017204?ref=ts. Please also look for me on Goodreads, Instagram and on Twitter (@hockeyplayer).

CHAPTER 1
Tick Tock (Part 1)

RECOMMENDED LISTENING:

"MY OWN WORST ENEMY"
LIT

"BORN TOO LATE"
THE CLARKS

"MOTHER'S LITTLE HELPER"
THE ROLLING STONES

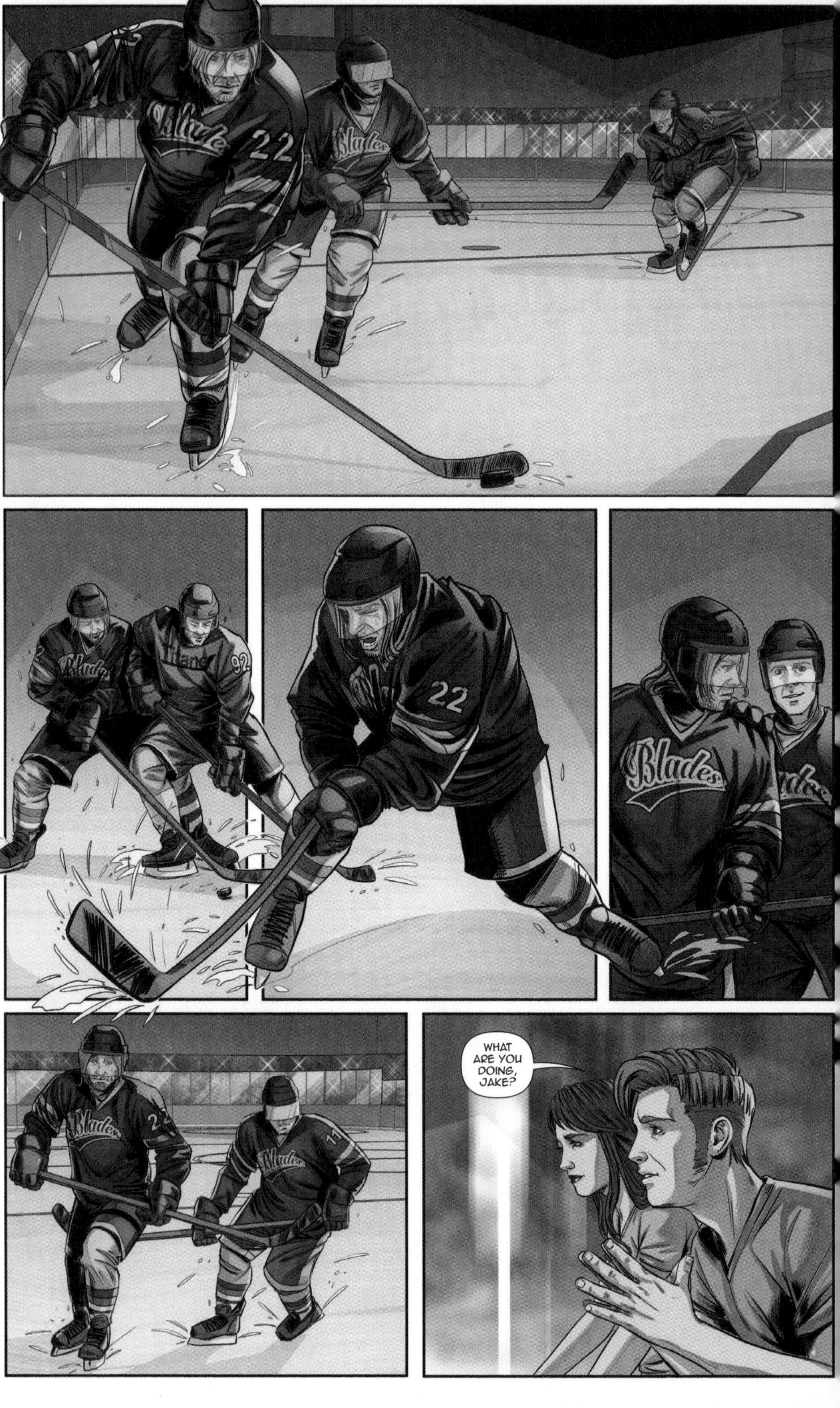
WHAT ARE YOU DOING, JAKE?

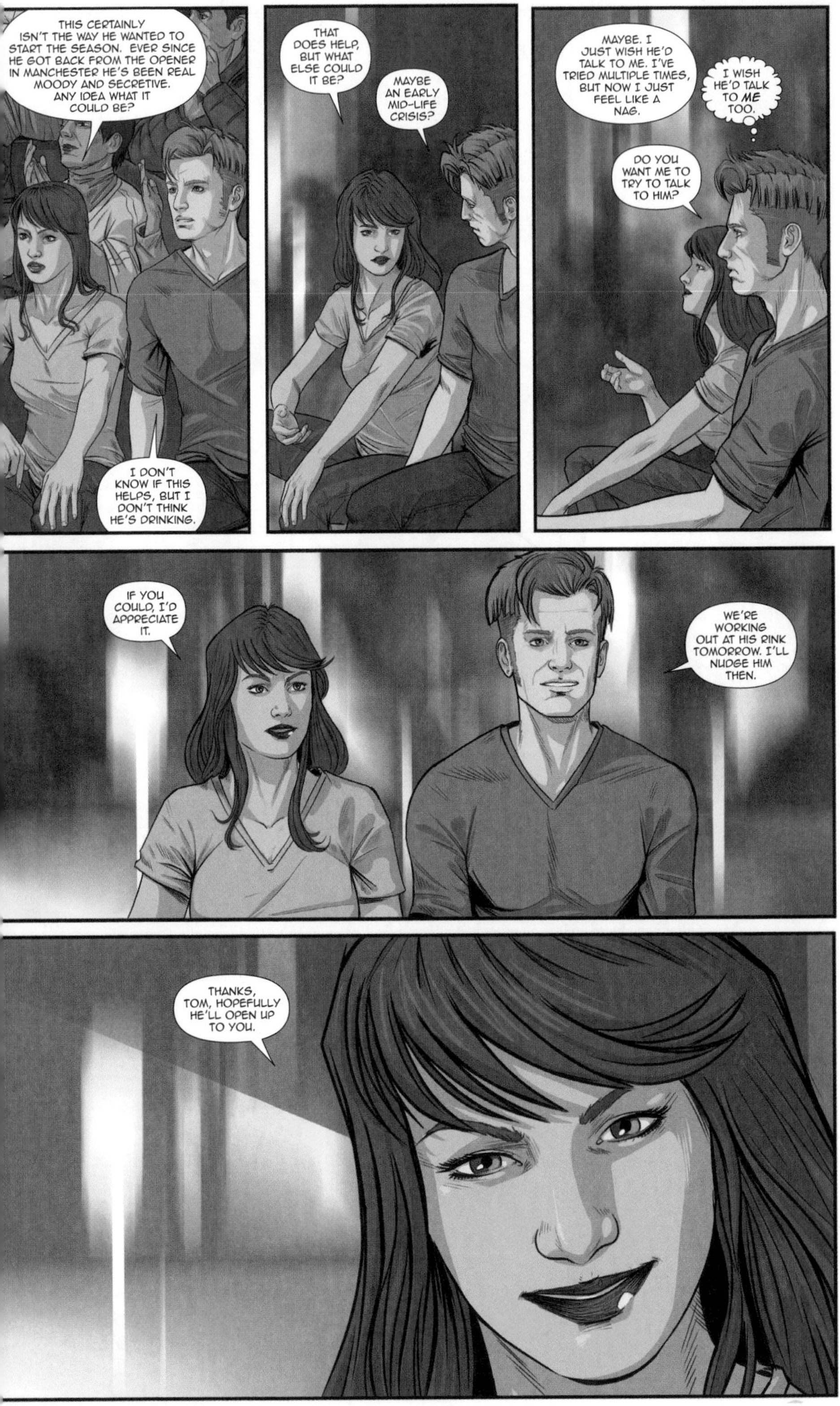
THIS CERTAINLY ISN'T THE WAY HE WANTED TO START THE SEASON. EVER SINCE HE GOT BACK FROM THE OPENER IN MANCHESTER HE'S BEEN REAL MOODY AND SECRETIVE. ANY IDEA WHAT IT COULD BE?
I DON'T KNOW IF THIS HELPS, BUT I DON'T THINK HE'S DRINKING.
THAT DOES HELP, BUT WHAT ELSE COULD IT BE?
MAYBE AN EARLY MID-LIFE CRISIS?
MAYBE. I JUST WISH HE'D TALK TO ME. I'VE TRIED MULTIPLE TIMES, BUT NOW I JUST FEEL LIKE A NAG.
I WISH HE'D TALK TO *ME* TOO.
DO YOU WANT ME TO TRY TO TALK TO HIM?
IF YOU COULD, I'D APPRECIATE IT.
WE'RE WORKING OUT AT HIS RINK TOMORROW. I'LL NUDGE HIM THEN.
THANKS, TOM, HOPEFULLY HE'LL OPEN UP TO YOU.

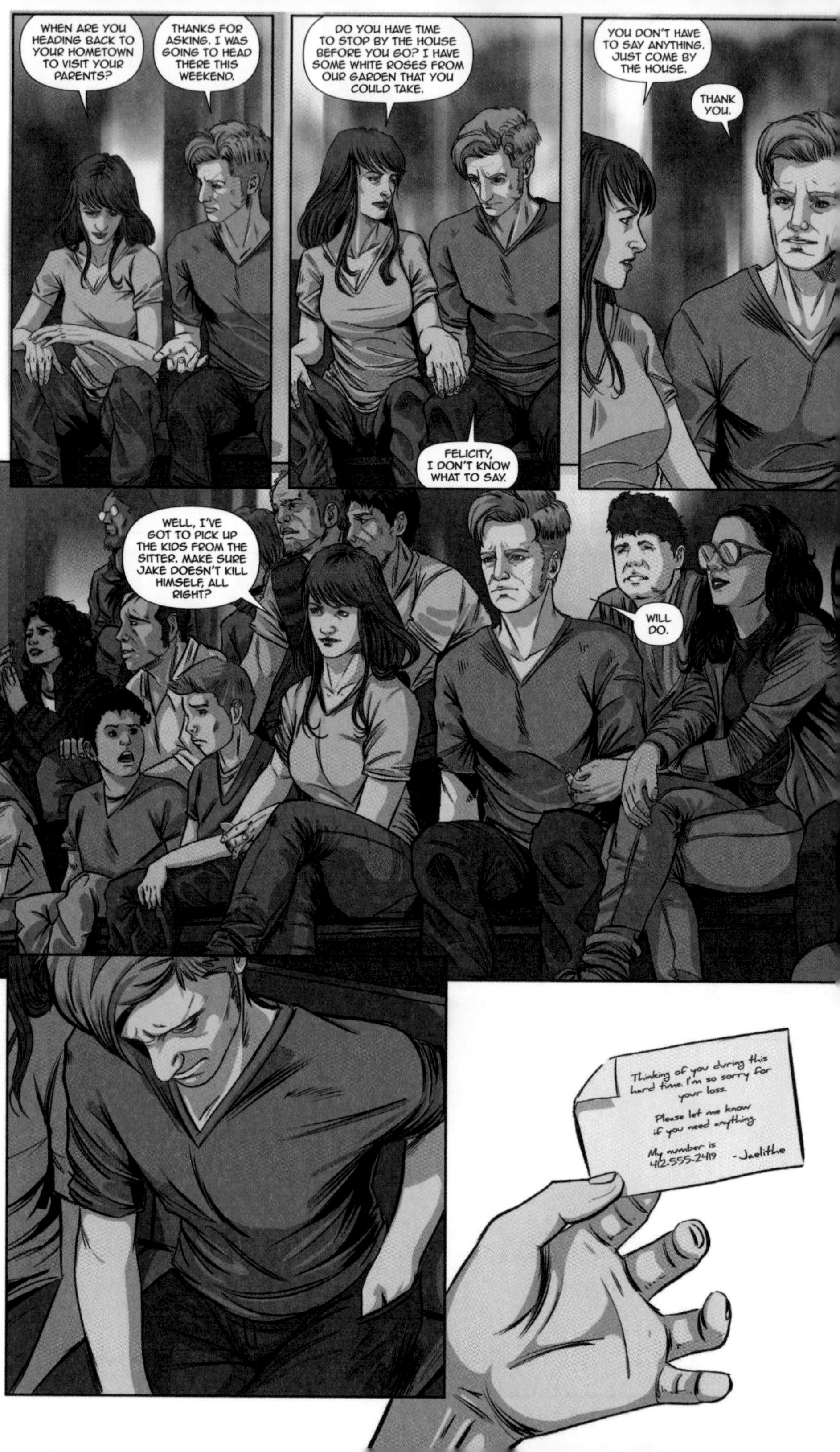
WHEN ARE YOU HEADING BACK TO YOUR HOMETOWN TO VISIT YOUR PARENTS?
THANKS FOR ASKING. I WAS GOING TO HEAD THERE THIS WEEKEND.
DO YOU HAVE TIME TO STOP BY THE HOUSE BEFORE YOU GO? I HAVE SOME WHITE ROSES FROM OUR GARDEN THAT YOU COULD TAKE.
FELICITY, I DON'T KNOW WHAT TO SAY.
YOU DON'T HAVE TO SAY ANYTHING. JUST COME BY THE HOUSE.
THANK YOU.
WELL, I'VE GOT TO PICK UP THE KIDS FROM THE SITTER. MAKE SURE JAKE DOESN'T KILL HIMSELF, ALL RIGHT?
WILL DO.
Thinking of you during this hard time. I'm so sorry for your loss.
Please let me know if you need anything.
My number is 412-555-2419
-Jaelithe

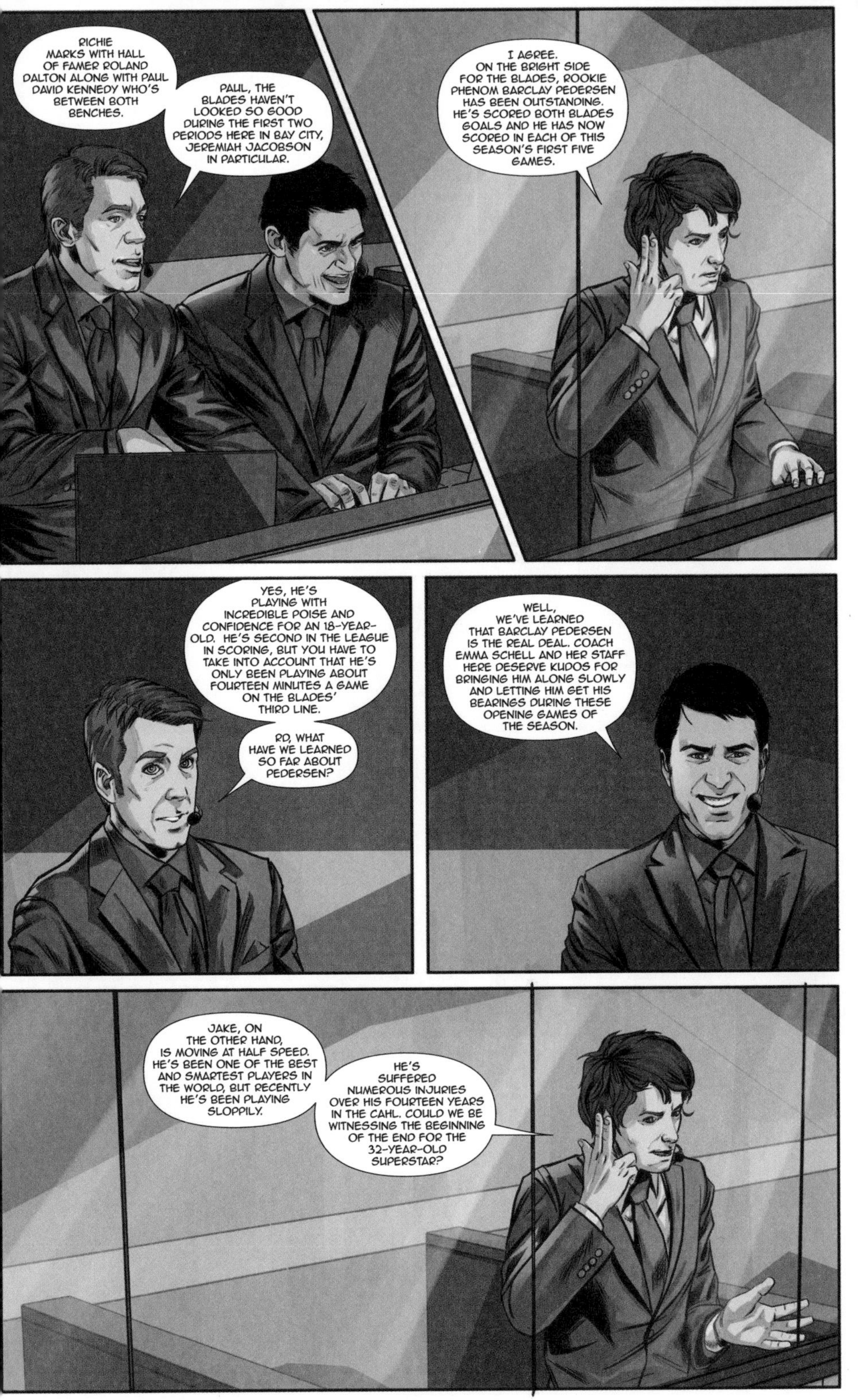
RICHIE MARKS WITH HALL OF FAMER ROLAND DALTON ALONG WITH PAUL DAVID KENNEDY WHO'S BETWEEN BOTH BENCHES.
PAUL, THE BLADES HAVEN'T LOOKED SO GOOD DURING THE FIRST TWO PERIODS HERE IN BAY CITY, JEREMIAH JACOBSON IN PARTICULAR.
I AGREE. ON THE BRIGHT SIDE FOR THE BLADES, ROOKIE PHENOM BARCLAY PEDERSEN HAS BEEN OUTSTANDING. HE'S SCORED BOTH BLADES GOALS AND HE HAS NOW SCORED IN EACH OF THIS SEASON'S FIRST FIVE GAMES.
YES, HE'S PLAYING WITH INCREDIBLE POISE AND CONFIDENCE FOR AN 18-YEAR-OLD. HE'S SECOND IN THE LEAGUE IN SCORING, BUT YOU HAVE TO TAKE INTO ACCOUNT THAT HE'S ONLY BEEN PLAYING ABOUT FOURTEEN MINUTES A GAME ON THE BLADES' THIRD LINE.
RD, WHAT HAVE WE LEARNED SO FAR ABOUT PEDERSEN?
WELL, WE'VE LEARNED THAT BARCLAY PEDERSEN IS THE REAL DEAL. COACH EMMA SCHELL AND HER STAFF HERE DESERVE KUDOS FOR BRINGING HIM ALONG SLOWLY AND LETTING HIM GET HIS BEARINGS DURING THESE OPENING GAMES OF THE SEASON.
JAKE, ON THE OTHER HAND, IS MOVING AT HALF SPEED. HE'S BEEN ONE OF THE BEST AND SMARTEST PLAYERS IN THE WORLD, BUT RECENTLY HE'S BEEN PLAYING SLOPPILY.
HE'S SUFFERED NUMEROUS INJURIES OVER HIS FOURTEEN YEARS IN THE CAHL. COULD WE BE WITNESSING THE BEGINNING OF THE END FOR THE 32-YEAR-OLD SUPERSTAR?

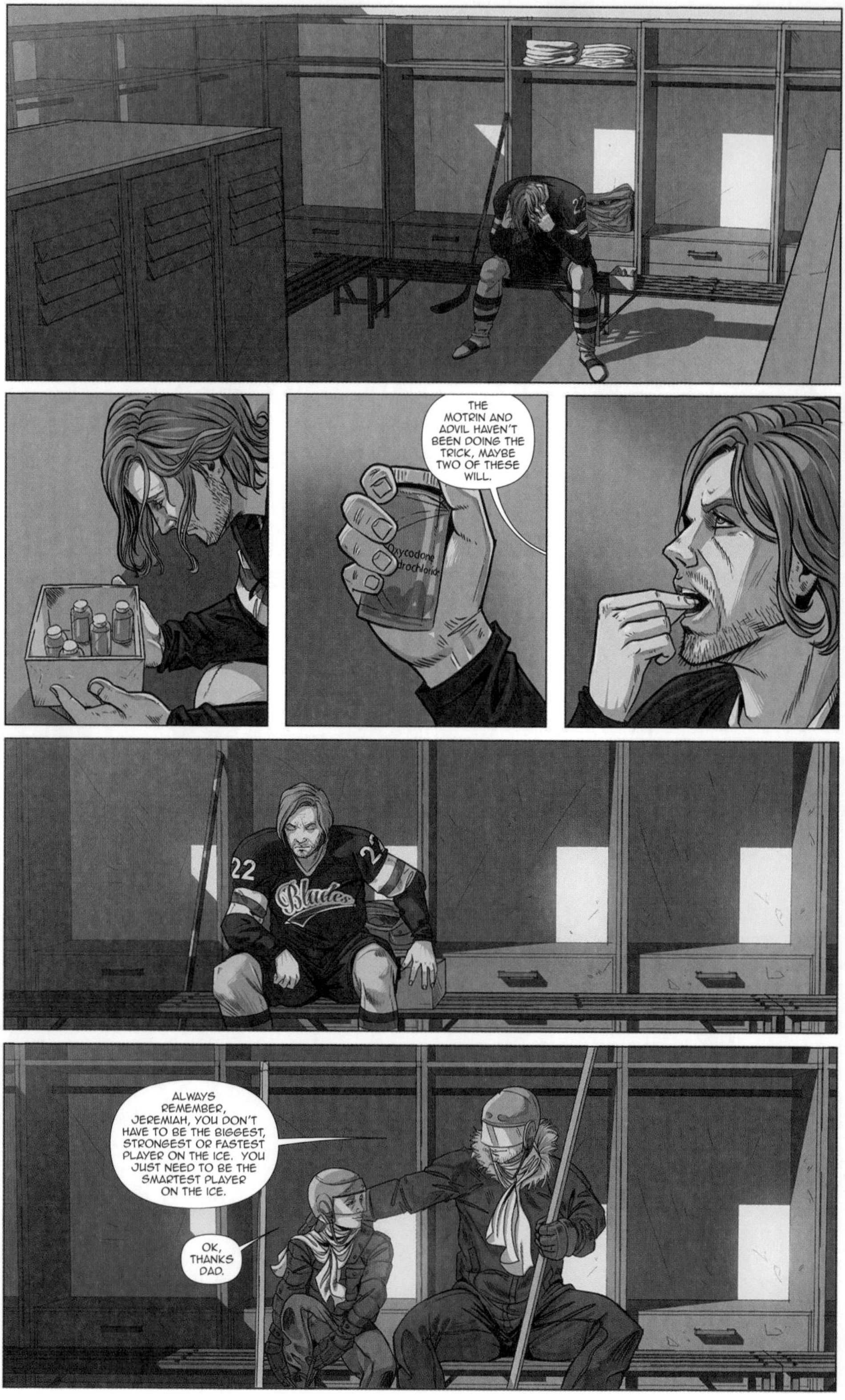
THE MOTRIN AND ADVIL HAVEN'T BEEN DOING THE TRICK, MAYBE TWO OF THESE WILL.
Oxycodone
drochloride
22
22
Blades
ALWAYS REMEMBER, JEREMIAH, YOU DON'T HAVE TO BE THE BIGGEST, STRONGEST OR FASTEST PLAYER ON THE ICE. YOU JUST NEED TO BE THE SMARTEST PLAYER ON THE ICE.
OK, THANKS DAD.

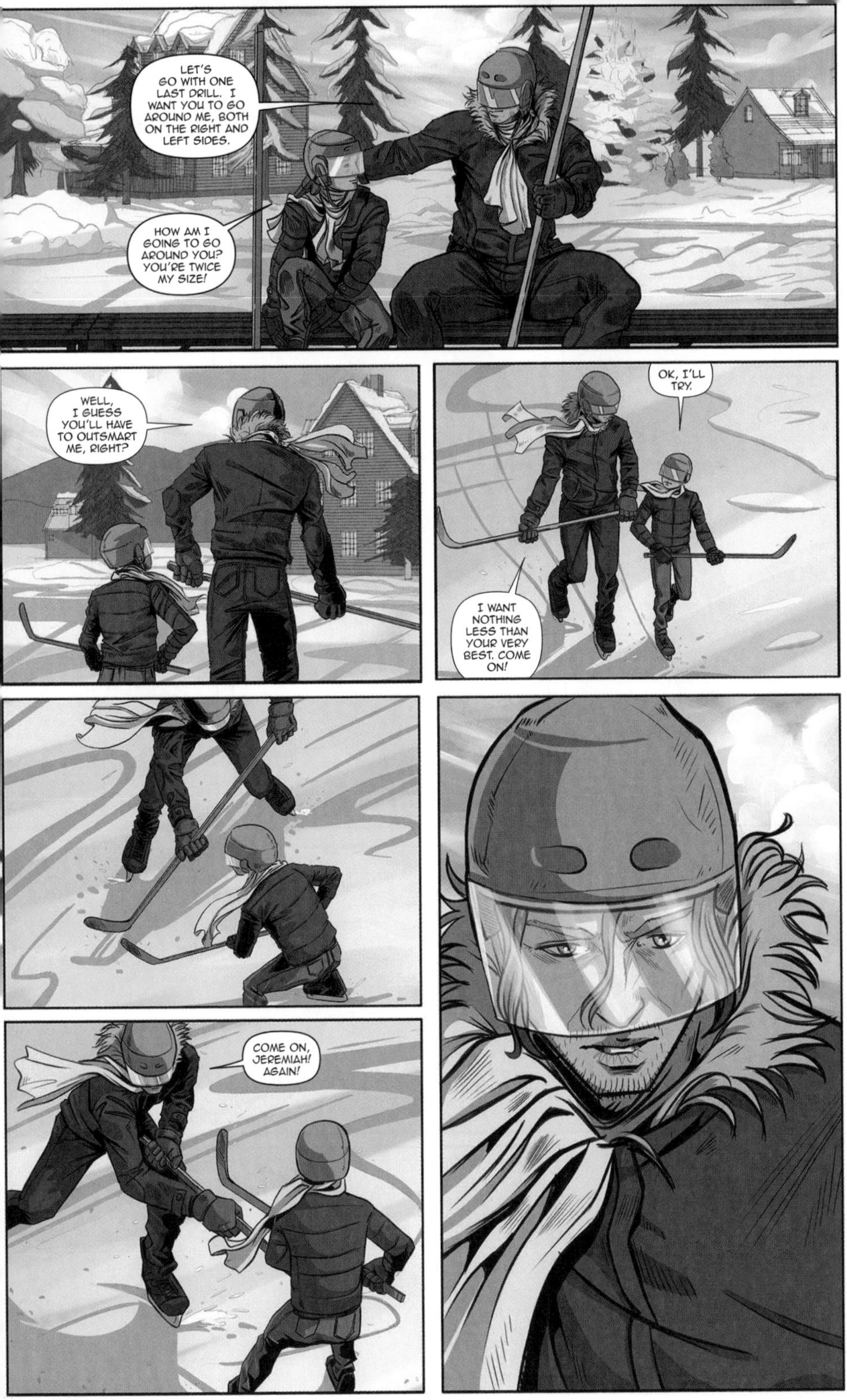
LET'S GO WITH ONE LAST DRILL. I WANT YOU TO GO AROUND ME, BOTH ON THE RIGHT AND LEFT SIDES.
HOW AM I GOING TO GO AROUND YOU? YOU'RE TWICE MY SIZE!
WELL, I GUESS YOU'LL HAVE TO OUTSMART ME, RIGHT?
OK, I'LL TRY.
I WANT NOTHING LESS THAN YOUR VERY BEST. COME ON!
COME ON, JEREMIAH! AGAIN!

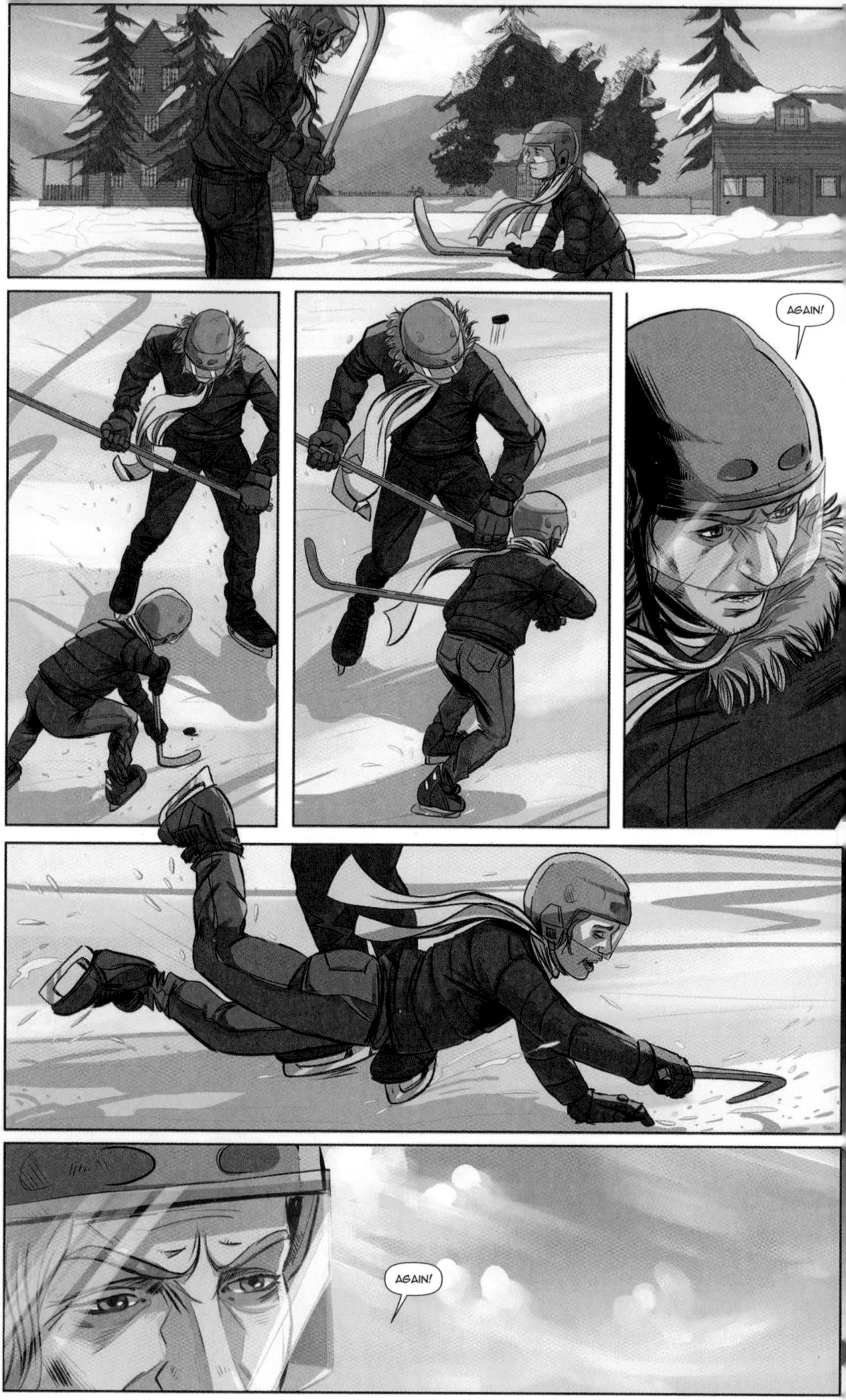
AGAIN!
AGAIN!

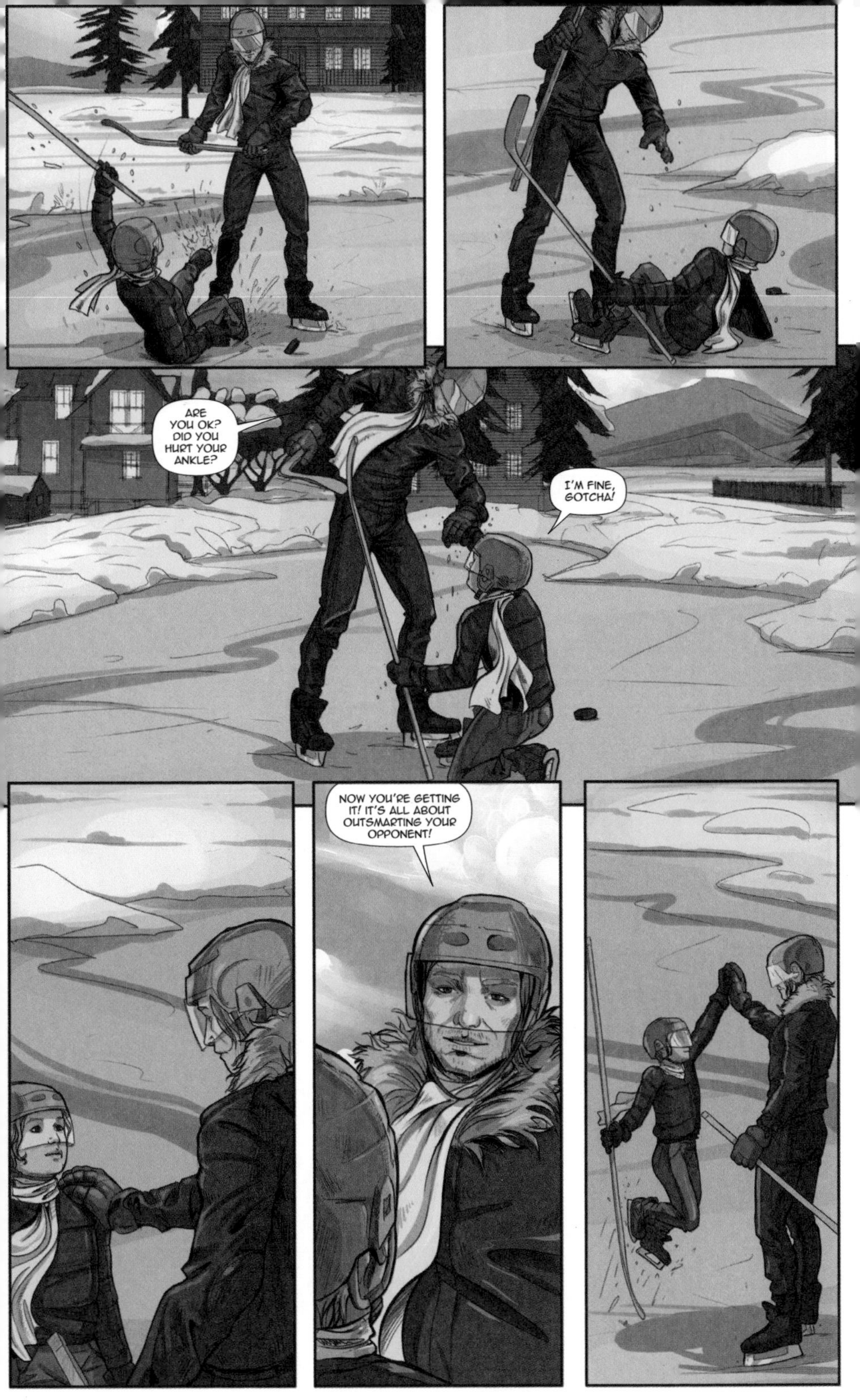
ARE YOU OK? DID YOU HURT YOUR ANKLE?
I'M FINE, GOTCHA!
NOW YOU'RE GETTING IT! IT'S ALL ABOUT OUTSMARTING YOUR OPPONENT!

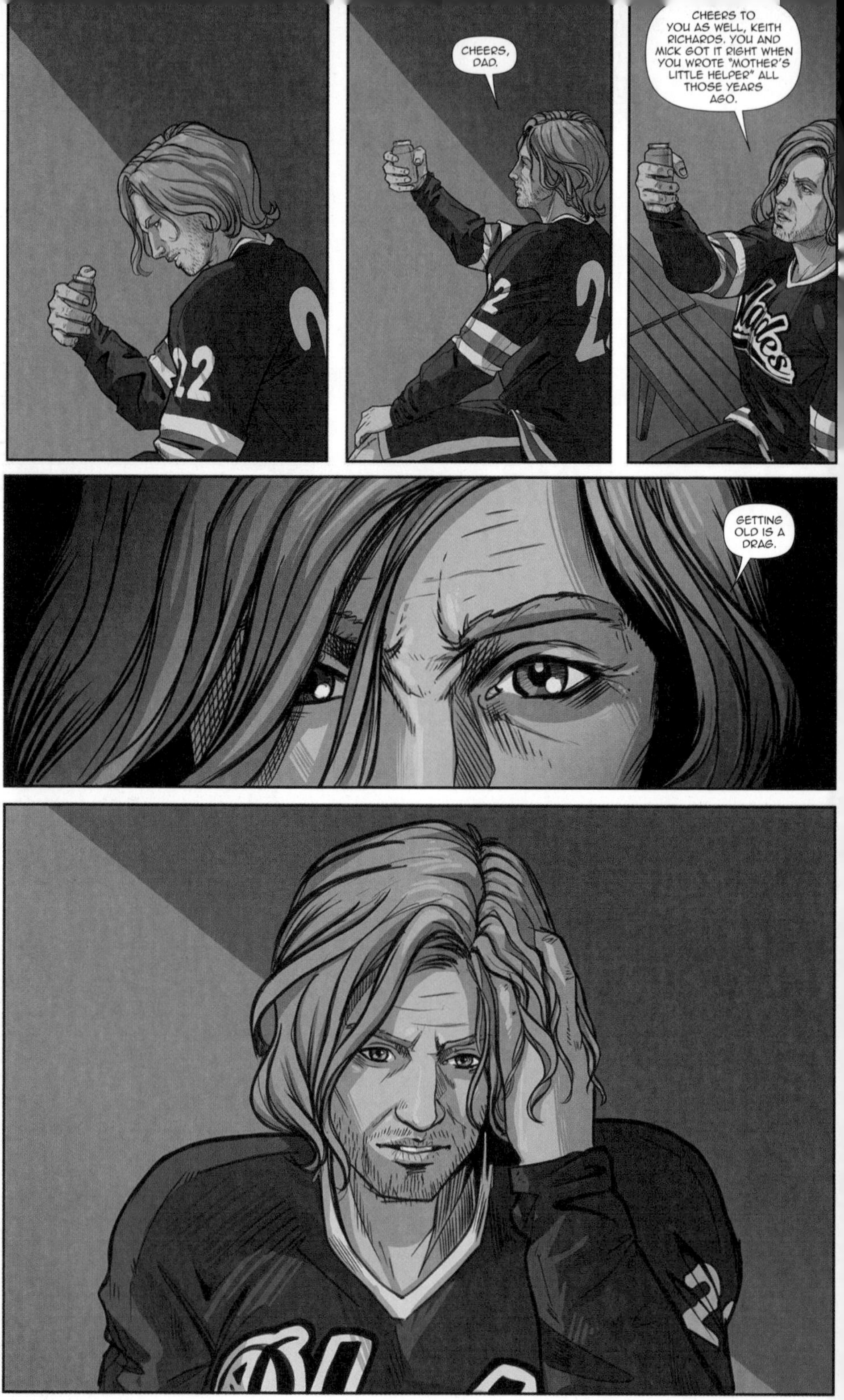
CHEERS, DAD.
CHEERS TO YOU AS WELL, KEITH RICHARDS. YOU AND MICK GOT IT RIGHT WHEN YOU WROTE "MOTHER'S LITTLE HELPER" ALL THOSE YEARS AGO.
GETTING OLD IS A DRAG.

CHAPTER 2
Keeping the Wolves at Bay

RECOMMENDED LISTENING:

"TRAIN IN VAIN"
THE CLASH

"WAR ON THE EAST COAST"
THE NEW PORNOGRAPHERS

"HEROES"
DAVID BOWIE

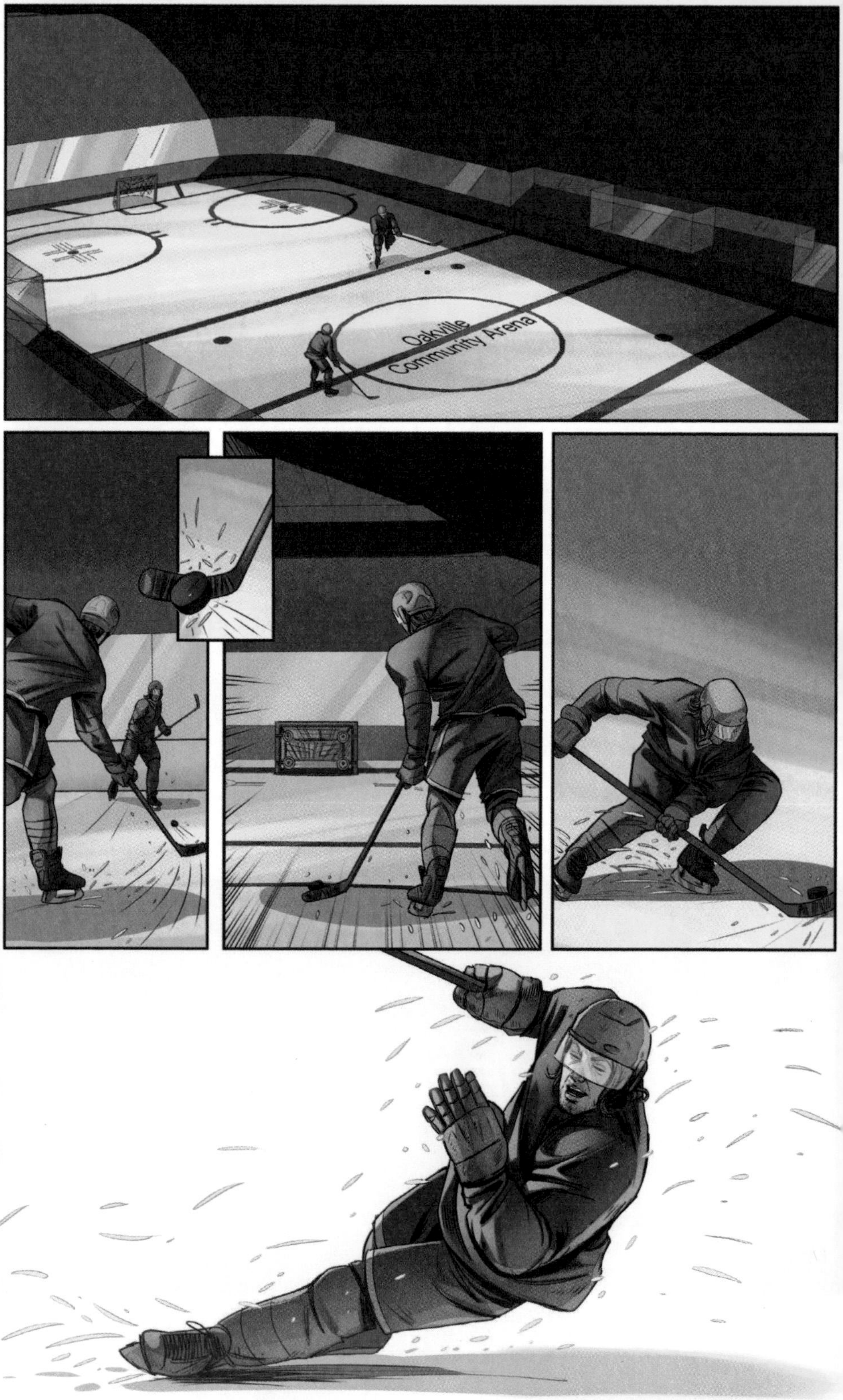
Oakville
Community Arena

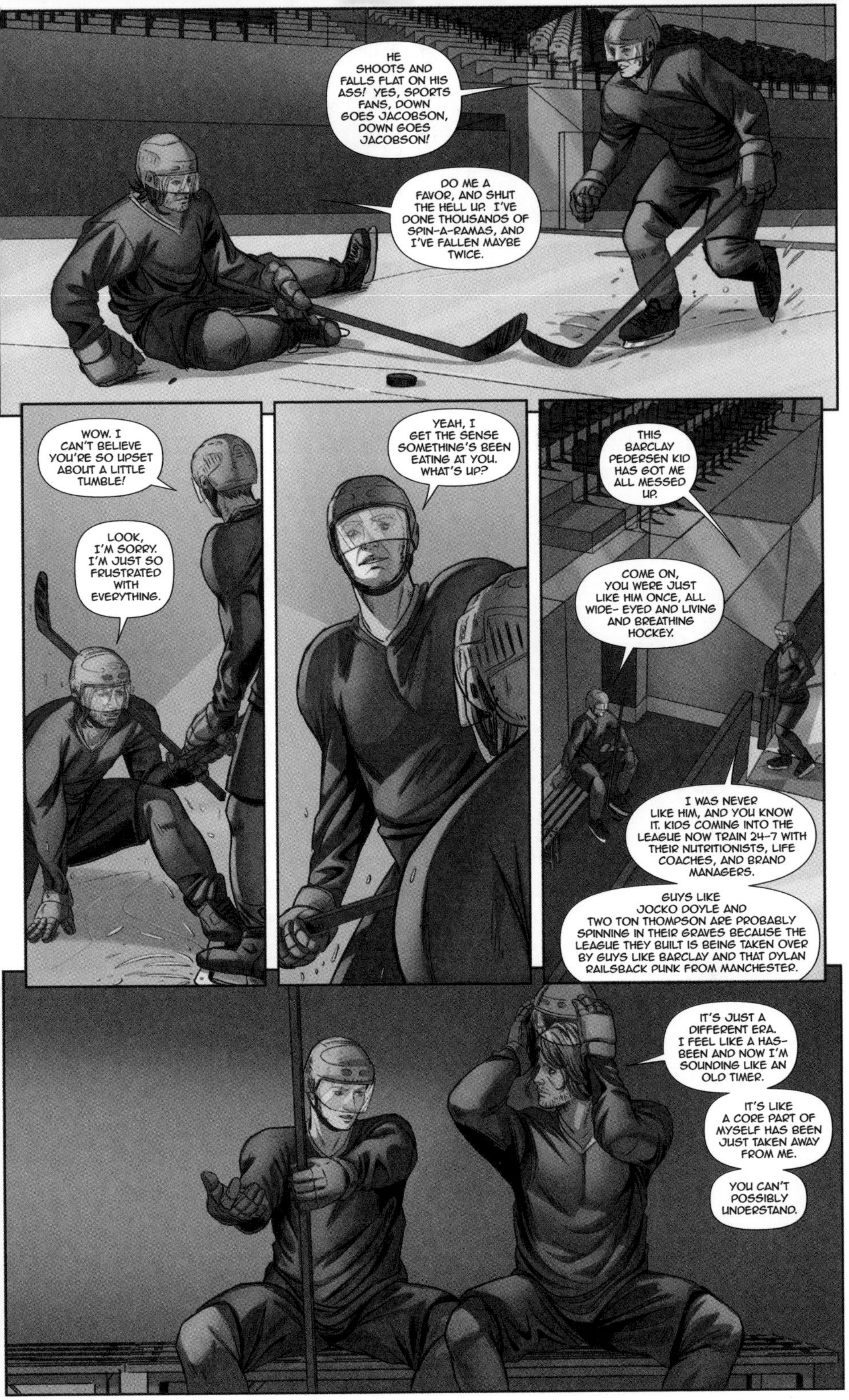
HE SHOOTS AND FALLS FLAT ON HIS ASS! YES, SPORTS FANS, DOWN GOES JACOBSON, DOWN GOES JACOBSON!
DO ME A FAVOR, AND SHUT THE HELL UP. I'VE DONE THOUSANDS OF SPIN-A-RAMAS, AND I'VE FALLEN MAYBE TWICE.
WOW. I CAN'T BELIEVE YOU'RE SO UPSET ABOUT A LITTLE TUMBLE!
LOOK, I'M SORRY. I'M JUST SO FRUSTRATED WITH EVERYTHING.
YEAH, I GET THE SENSE SOMETHING'S BEEN EATING AT YOU. WHAT'S UP?
THIS BARCLAY PEDERSEN KID HAS GOT ME ALL MESSED UP.
COME ON, YOU WERE JUST LIKE HIM ONCE, ALL WIDE- EYED AND LIVING AND BREATHING HOCKEY.
I WAS NEVER LIKE HIM, AND YOU KNOW IT. KIDS COMING INTO THE LEAGUE NOW TRAIN 24-7 WITH THEIR NUTRITIONISTS, LIFE COACHES, AND BRAND MANAGERS.
GUYS LIKE JOCKO DOYLE AND TWO TON THOMPSON ARE PROBABLY SPINNING IN THEIR GRAVES BECAUSE THE LEAGUE THEY BUILT IS BEING TAKEN OVER BY GUYS LIKE BARCLAY AND THAT DYLAN RAILSBACK PUNK FROM MANCHESTER.
IT'S JUST A DIFFERENT ERA. I FEEL LIKE A HAS-BEEN AND NOW I'M SOUNDING LIKE AN OLD TIMER.
IT'S LIKE A CORE PART OF MYSELF HAS BEEN JUST TAKEN AWAY FROM ME.
YOU CAN'T POSSIBLY UNDERSTAND.

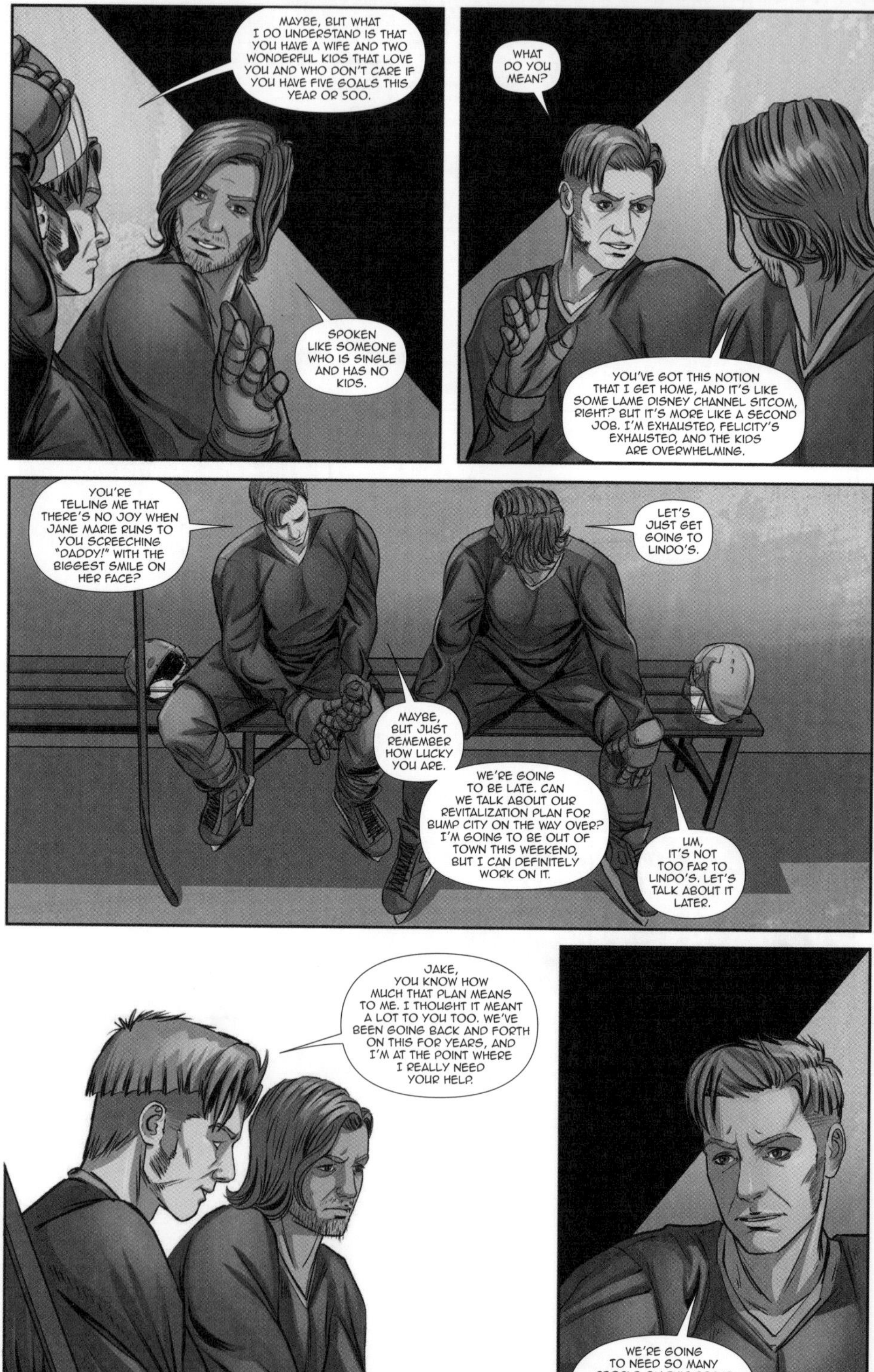
MAYBE, BUT WHAT I DO UNDERSTAND IS THAT YOU HAVE A WIFE AND TWO WONDERFUL KIDS THAT LOVE YOU AND WHO DON'T CARE IF YOU HAVE FIVE GOALS THIS YEAR OR 500.
SPOKEN LIKE SOMEONE WHO IS SINGLE AND HAS NO KIDS.
WHAT DO YOU MEAN?
YOU'VE GOT THIS NOTION THAT I GET HOME, AND IT'S LIKE SOME LAME DISNEY CHANNEL SITCOM, RIGHT? BUT IT'S MORE LIKE A SECOND JOB. I'M EXHAUSTED, FELICITY'S EXHAUSTED, AND THE KIDS ARE OVERWHELMING.
YOU'RE TELLING ME THAT THERE'S NO JOY WHEN JANE MARIE RUNS TO YOU SCREECHING "DADDY!" WITH THE BIGGEST SMILE ON HER FACE?
LET'S JUST GET GOING TO LINDO'S.
MAYBE, BUT JUST REMEMBER HOW LUCKY YOU ARE.
WE'RE GOING TO BE LATE. CAN WE TALK ABOUT OUR REVITALIZATION PLAN FOR BUMP CITY ON THE WAY OVER? I'M GOING TO BE OUT OF TOWN THIS WEEKEND, BUT I CAN DEFINITELY WORK ON IT.
UM, IT'S NOT TOO FAR TO LINDO'S. LET'S TALK ABOUT IT LATER.
JAKE, YOU KNOW HOW MUCH THAT PLAN MEANS TO ME. I THOUGHT IT MEANT A LOT TO YOU TOO. WE'VE BEEN GOING BACK AND FORTH ON THIS FOR YEARS, AND I'M AT THE POINT WHERE I REALLY NEED YOUR HELP.
WE'RE GOING TO NEED SO MANY PEOPLE ON THIS FOR IT EVEN TO BE FEASIBLE, AND I FEEL OUT OF MY ELEMENT. I DON'T HAVE YOUR STAR POWER.

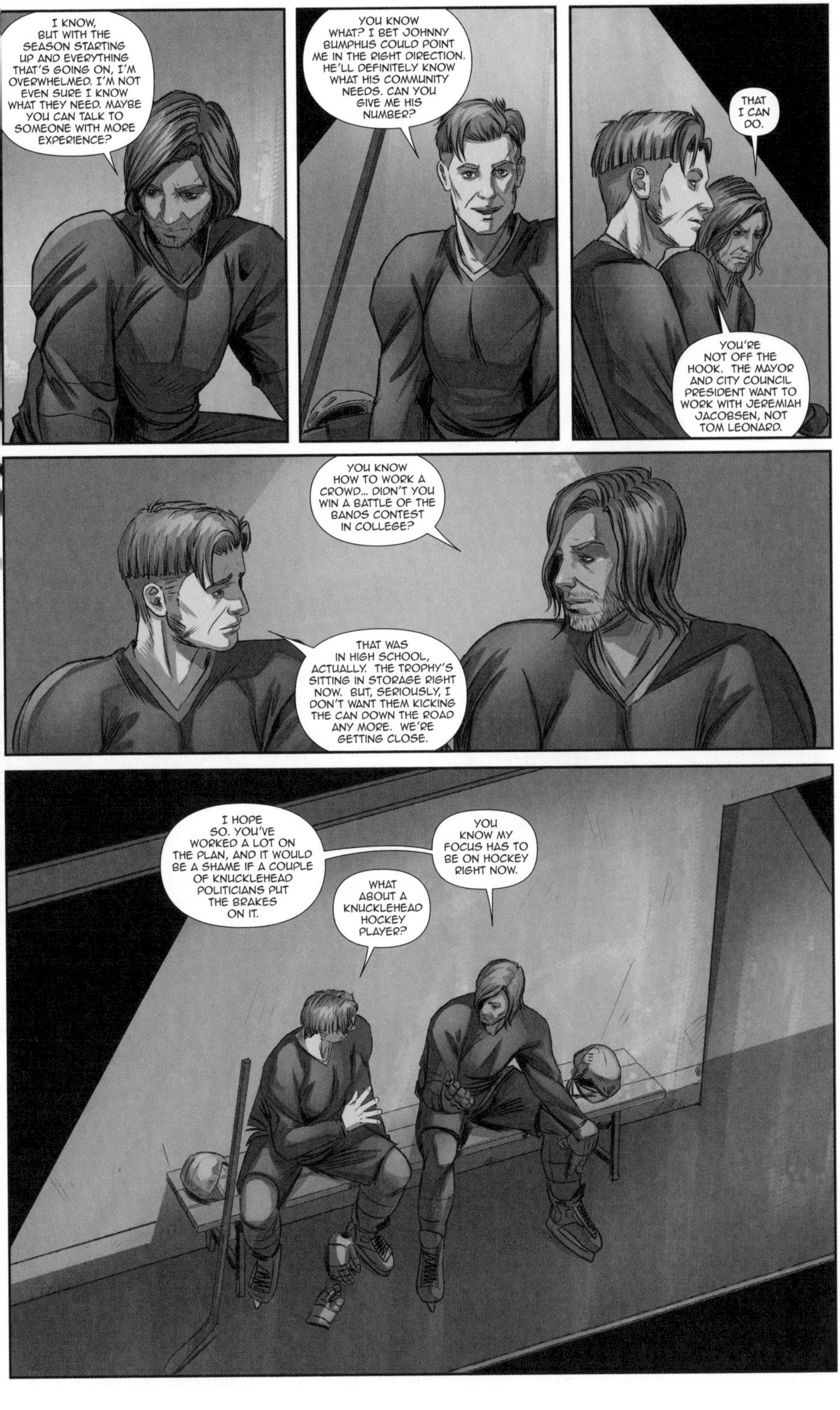
I KNOW, BUT WITH THE SEASON STARTING UP AND EVERYTHING THAT'S GOING ON, I'M OVERWHELMED. I'M NOT EVEN SURE I KNOW WHAT THEY NEED. MAYBE YOU CAN TALK TO SOMEONE WITH MORE EXPERIENCE?
YOU KNOW WHAT? I BET JOHNNY BUMPHUS COULD POINT ME IN THE RIGHT DIRECTION. HE'LL DEFINITELY KNOW WHAT HIS COMMUNITY NEEDS. CAN YOU GIVE ME HIS NUMBER?
THAT I CAN DO.
YOU'RE NOT OFF THE HOOK. THE MAYOR AND CITY COUNCIL PRESIDENT WANT TO WORK WITH JEREMIAH JACOBSEN, NOT TOM LEONARD.
YOU KNOW HOW TO WORK A CROWD... DIDN'T YOU WIN A BATTLE OF THE BANDS CONTEST IN COLLEGE?
THAT WAS IN HIGH SCHOOL, ACTUALLY. THE TROPHY'S SITTING IN STORAGE RIGHT NOW. BUT, SERIOUSLY, I DON'T WANT THEM KICKING THE CAN DOWN THE ROAD ANY MORE. WE'RE GETTING CLOSE.
I HOPE SO. YOU'VE WORKED A LOT ON THE PLAN, AND IT WOULD BE A SHAME IF A COUPLE OF KNUCKLEHEAD POLITICIANS PUT THE BRAKES ON IT.
YOU KNOW MY FOCUS HAS TO BE ON HOCKEY RIGHT NOW.
WHAT ABOUT A KNUCKLEHEAD HOCKEY PLAYER?

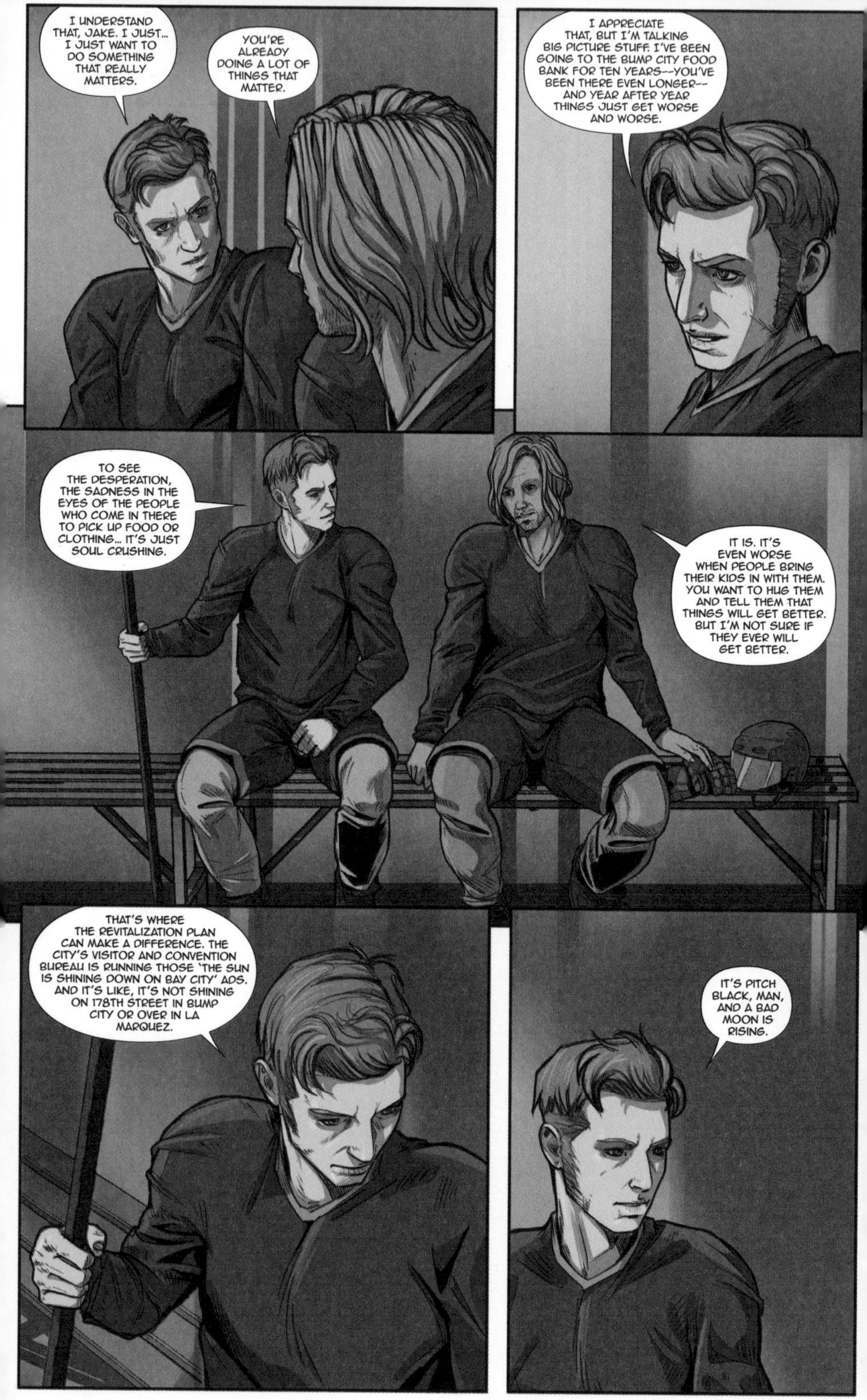
I UNDERSTAND THAT, JAKE. I JUST... I JUST WANT TO DO SOMETHING THAT REALLY MATTERS.
YOU'RE ALREADY DOING A LOT OF THINGS THAT MATTER.
I APPRECIATE THAT, BUT I'M TALKING BIG PICTURE STUFF. I'VE BEEN GOING TO THE BUMP CITY FOOD BANK FOR TEN YEARS--YOU'VE BEEN THERE EVEN LONGER--AND YEAR AFTER YEAR THINGS JUST GET WORSE AND WORSE.
TO SEE THE DESPERATION, THE SADNESS IN THE EYES OF THE PEOPLE WHO COME IN THERE TO PICK UP FOOD OR CLOTHING... IT'S JUST SOUL CRUSHING.
IT IS. IT'S EVEN WORSE WHEN PEOPLE BRING THEIR KIDS IN WITH THEM. YOU WANT TO HUG THEM AND TELL THEM THAT THINGS WILL GET BETTER. BUT I'M NOT SURE IF THEY EVER WILL GET BETTER.
THAT'S WHERE THE REVITALIZATION PLAN CAN MAKE A DIFFERENCE. THE CITY'S VISITOR AND CONVENTION BUREAU IS RUNNING THOSE 'THE SUN IS SHINING DOWN ON BAY CITY' ADS. AND IT'S LIKE, IT'S NOT SHINING ON 178TH STREET IN BUMP CITY OR OVER IN LA MARQUEZ.
IT'S PITCH BLACK, MAN, AND A BAD MOON IS RISING.

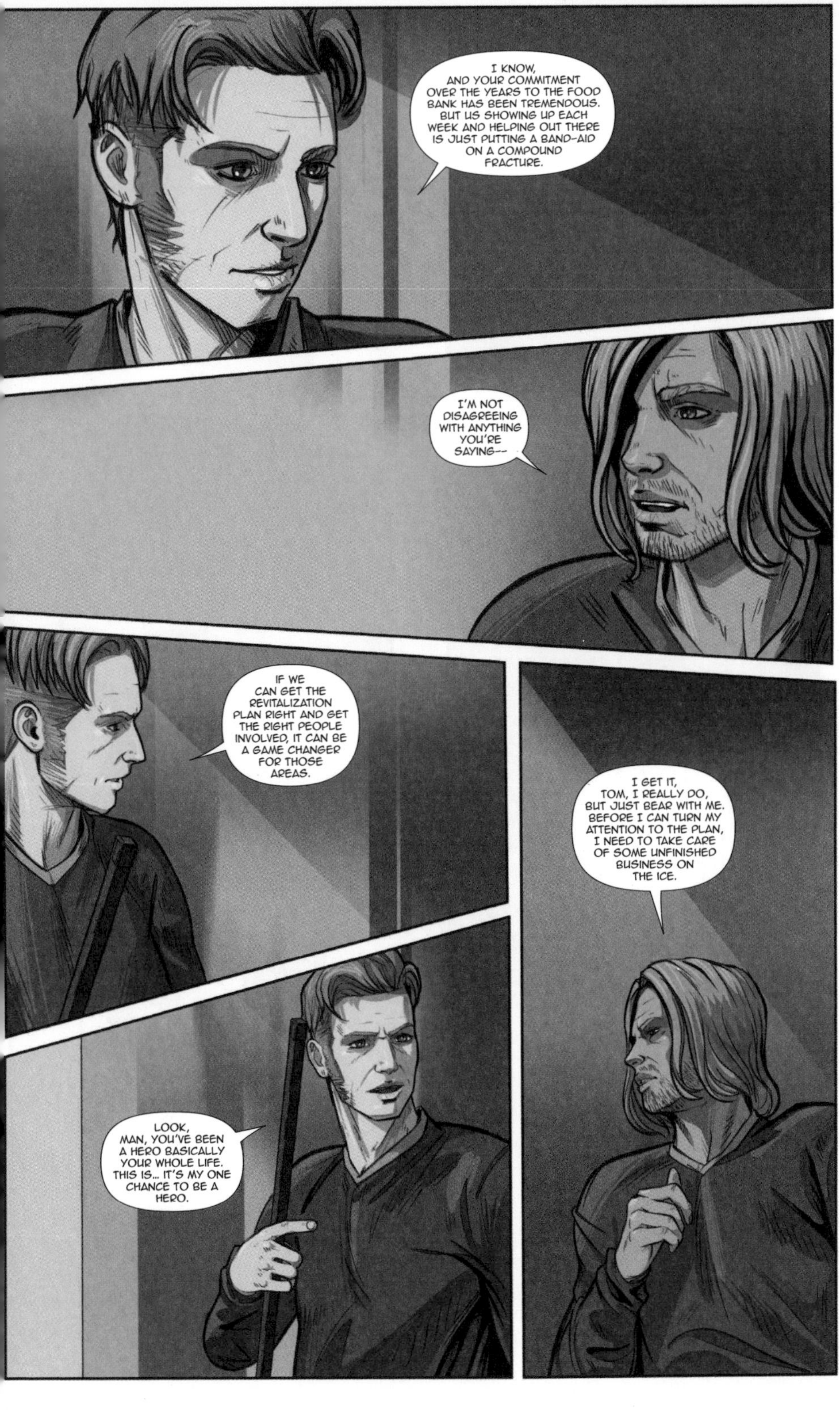
I KNOW, AND YOUR COMMITMENT OVER THE YEARS TO THE FOOD BANK HAS BEEN TREMENDOUS. BUT US SHOWING UP EACH WEEK AND HELPING OUT THERE IS JUST PUTTING A BAND-AID ON A COMPOUND FRACTURE.
I'M NOT DISAGREEING WITH ANYTHING YOU'RE SAYING--
IF WE CAN GET THE REVITALIZATION PLAN RIGHT AND GET THE RIGHT PEOPLE INVOLVED, IT CAN BE A GAME CHANGER FOR THOSE AREAS.
I GET IT, TOM, I REALLY DO, BUT JUST BEAR WITH ME. BEFORE I CAN TURN MY ATTENTION TO THE PLAN, I NEED TO TAKE CARE OF SOME UNFINISHED BUSINESS ON THE ICE.
LOOK, MAN, YOU'VE BEEN A HERO BASICALLY YOUR WHOLE LIFE. THIS IS... IT'S MY ONE CHANCE TO BE A HERO.

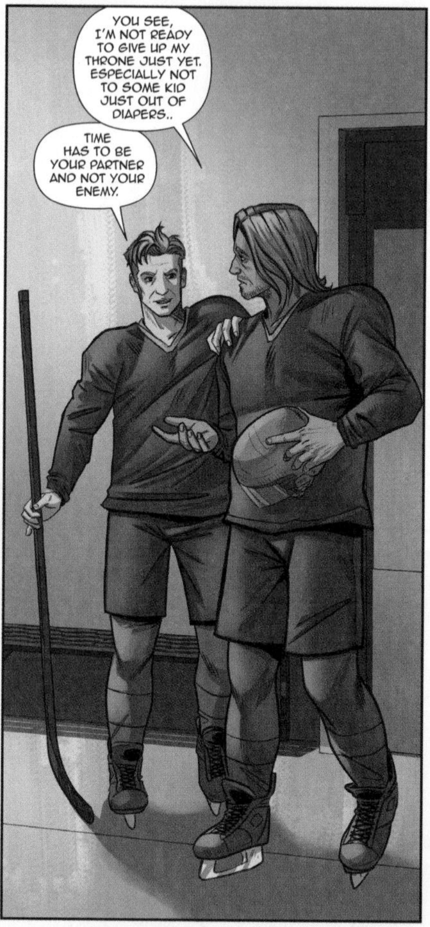
YOU SEE, I'M NOT READY TO GIVE UP MY THRONE JUST YET. ESPECIALLY NOT TO SOME KID JUST OUT OF DIAPERS..
TIME HAS TO BE YOUR PARTNER AND NOT YOUR ENEMY.

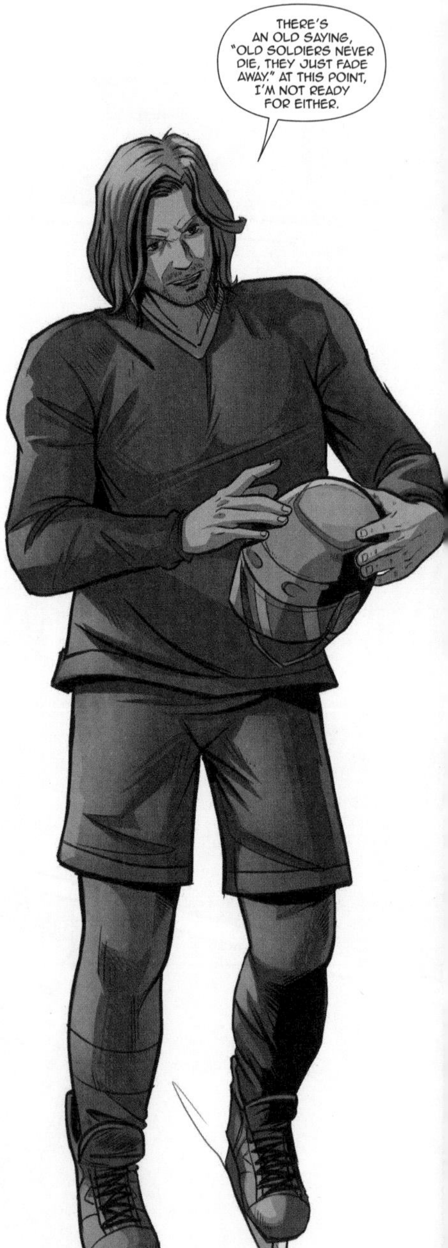
THERE'S AN OLD SAYING, "OLD SOLDIERS NEVER DIE, THEY JUST FADE AWAY." AT THIS POINT, I'M NOT READY FOR EITHER.

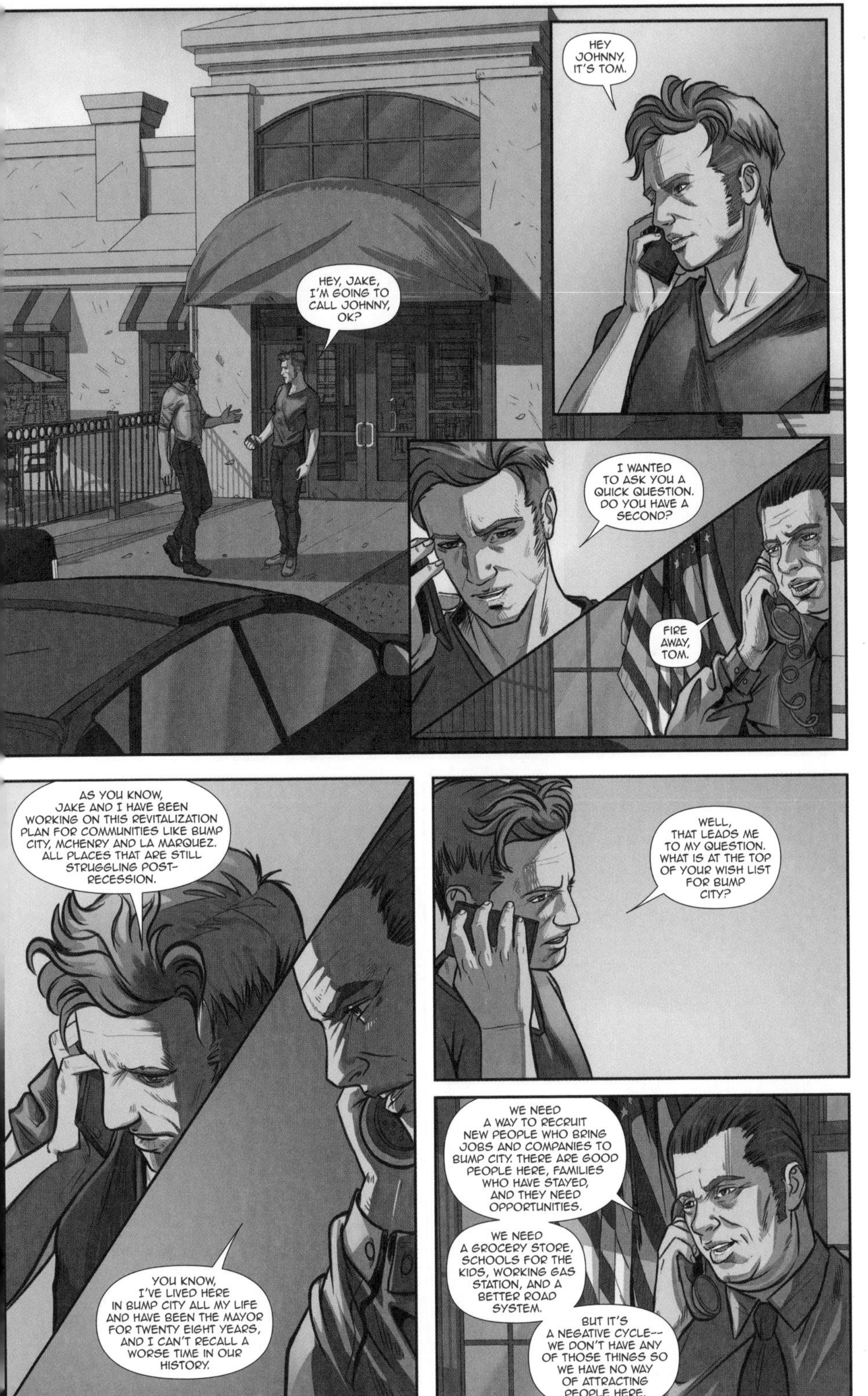
HEY, JAKE, I'M GOING TO CALL JOHNNY, OK?
HEY JOHNNY, IT'S TOM.
I WANTED TO ASK YOU A QUICK QUESTION. DO YOU HAVE A SECOND?
FIRE AWAY, TOM.
AS YOU KNOW, JAKE AND I HAVE BEEN WORKING ON THIS REVITALIZATION PLAN FOR COMMUNITIES LIKE BUMP CITY, MCHENRY AND LA MARQUEZ. ALL PLACES THAT ARE STILL STRUGGLING POST-RECESSION.
YOU KNOW, I'VE LIVED HERE IN BUMP CITY ALL MY LIFE AND HAVE BEEN THE MAYOR FOR TWENTY EIGHT YEARS, AND I CAN'T RECALL A WORSE TIME IN OUR HISTORY.
WELL, THAT LEADS ME TO MY QUESTION. WHAT IS AT THE TOP OF YOUR WISH LIST FOR BUMP CITY?
WE NEED A WAY TO RECRUIT NEW PEOPLE WHO BRING JOBS AND COMPANIES TO BUMP CITY. THERE ARE GOOD PEOPLE HERE, FAMILIES WHO HAVE STAYED, AND THEY NEED OPPORTUNITIES.
WE NEED A GROCERY STORE, SCHOOLS FOR THE KIDS, WORKING GAS STATION, AND A BETTER ROAD SYSTEM.
BUT IT'S A NEGATIVE CYCLE-- WE DON'T HAVE ANY OF THOSE THINGS SO WE HAVE NO WAY OF ATTRACTING PEOPLE HERE.

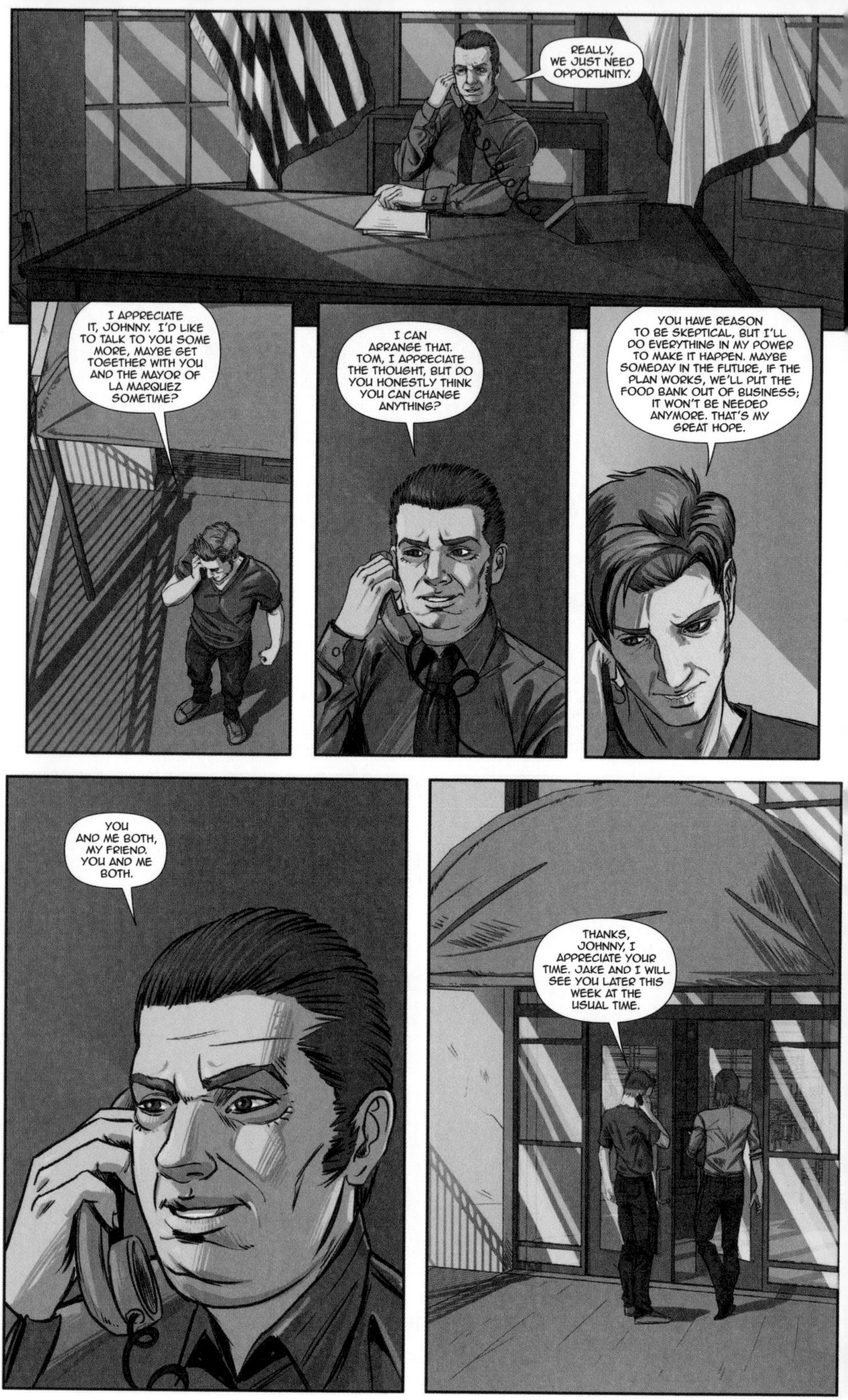
REALLY, WE JUST NEED OPPORTUNITY.
I APPRECIATE IT, JOHNNY. I'D LIKE TO TALK TO YOU SOME MORE, MAYBE GET TOGETHER WITH YOU AND THE MAYOR OF LA MARQUEZ SOMETIME?
I CAN ARRANGE THAT. TOM, I APPRECIATE THE THOUGHT, BUT DO YOU HONESTLY THINK YOU CAN CHANGE ANYTHING?
YOU HAVE REASON TO BE SKEPTICAL, BUT I'LL DO EVERYTHING IN MY POWER TO MAKE IT HAPPEN. MAYBE SOMEDAY IN THE FUTURE, IF THE PLAN WORKS, WE'LL PUT THE FOOD BANK OUT OF BUSINESS; IT WON'T BE NEEDED ANYMORE. THAT'S MY GREAT HOPE.
YOU AND ME BOTH, MY FRIEND. YOU AND ME BOTH.
THANKS, JOHNNY, I APPRECIATE YOUR TIME. JAKE AND I WILL SEE YOU LATER THIS WEEK AT THE USUAL TIME.

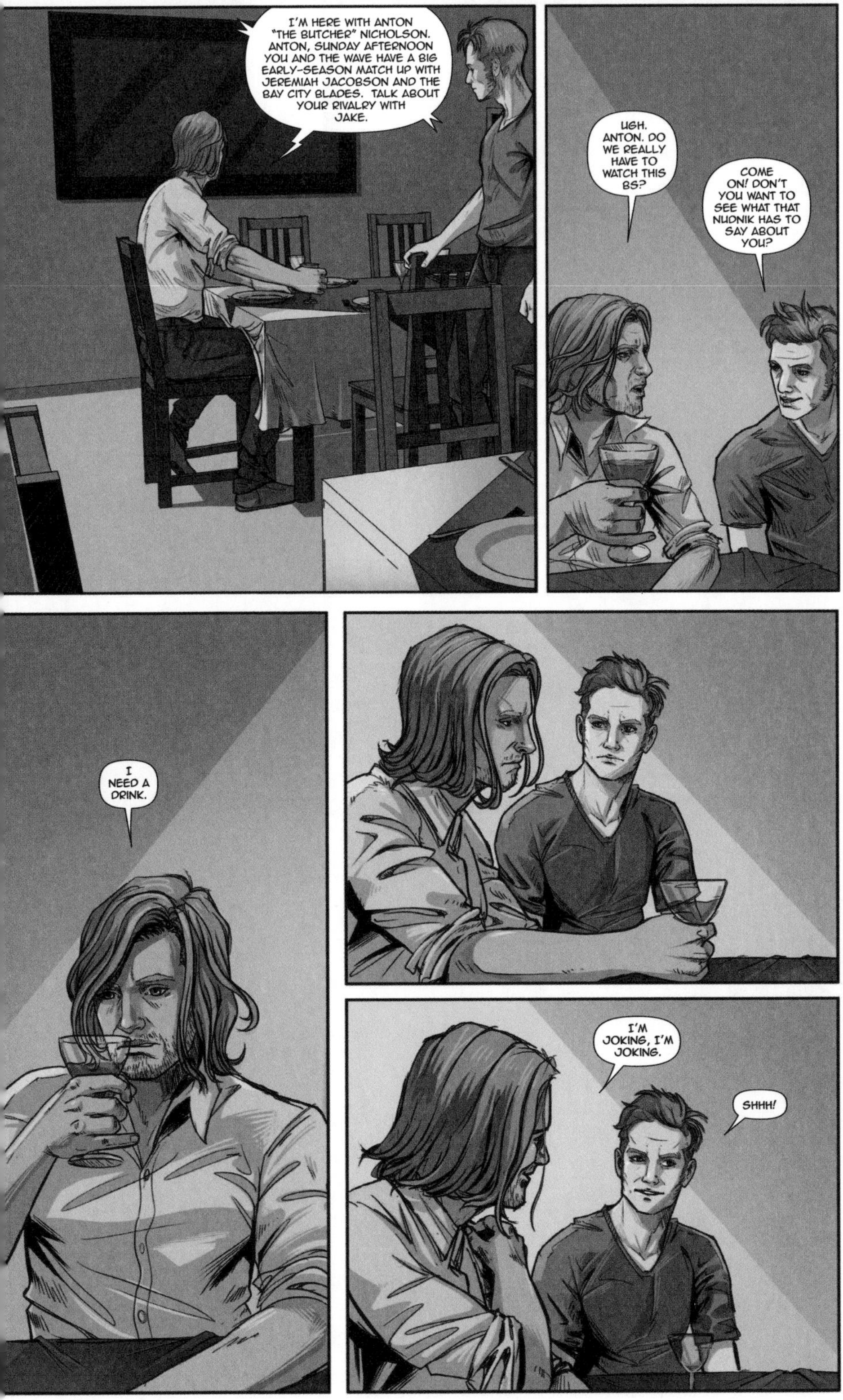
I'M HERE WITH ANTON "THE BUTCHER" NICHOLSON. ANTON, SUNDAY AFTERNOON YOU AND THE WAVE HAVE A BIG EARLY-SEASON MATCH UP WITH JEREMIAH JACOBSON AND THE BAY CITY BLADES. TALK ABOUT YOUR RIVALRY WITH JAKE.
UGH. ANTON. DO WE REALLY HAVE TO WATCH THIS BS?
COME ON! DON'T YOU WANT TO SEE WHAT THAT NUDNIK HAS TO SAY ABOUT YOU?
I NEED A DRINK.
I'M JOKING, I'M JOKING.
SHHH!

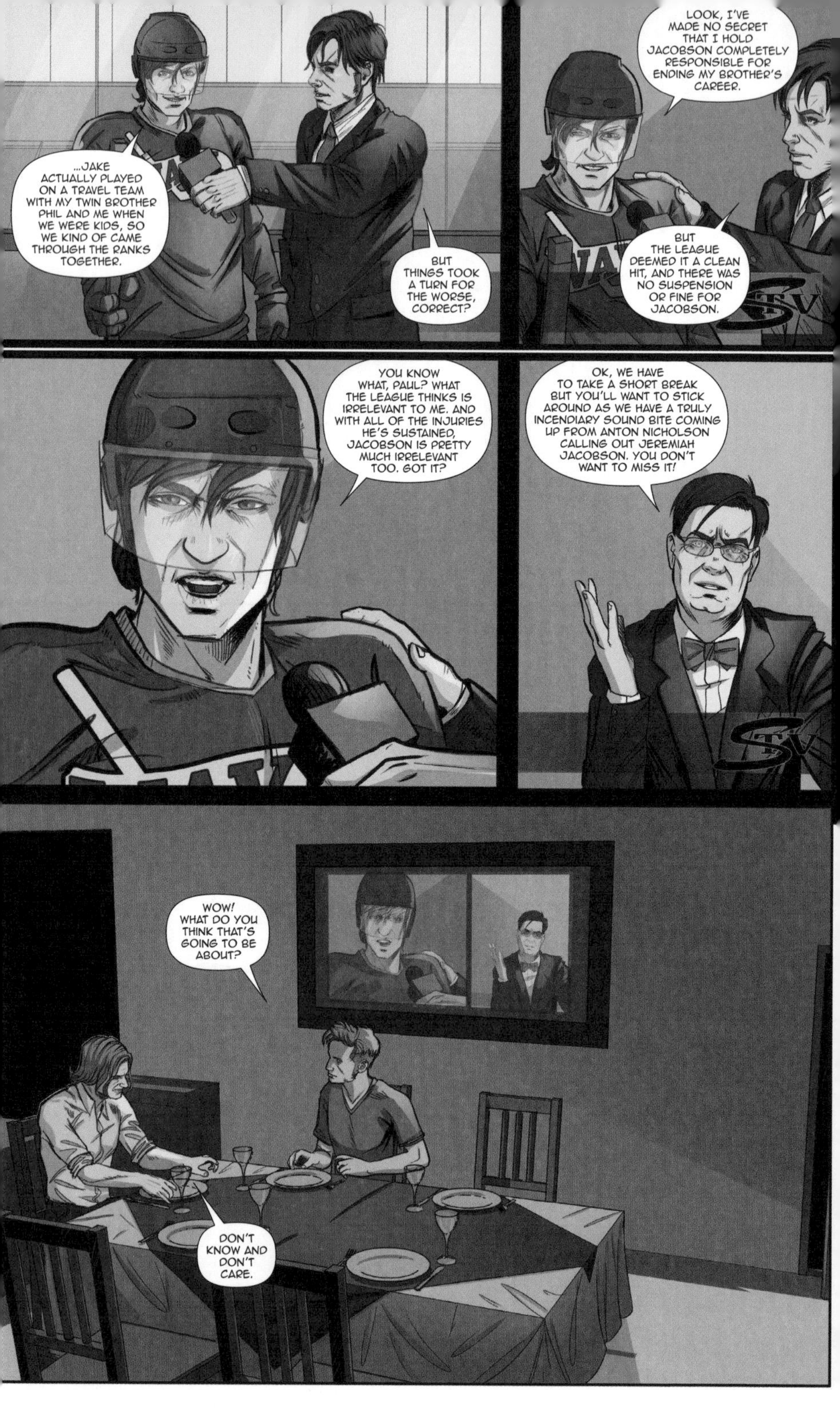
...JAKE ACTUALLY PLAYED ON A TRAVEL TEAM WITH MY TWIN BROTHER PHIL AND ME WHEN WE WERE KIDS, SO WE KIND OF CAME THROUGH THE RANKS TOGETHER.
BUT THINGS TOOK A TURN FOR THE WORSE, CORRECT?
LOOK, I'VE MADE NO SECRET THAT I HOLD JACOBSON COMPLETELY RESPONSIBLE FOR ENDING MY BROTHER'S CAREER.
BUT THE LEAGUE DEEMED IT A CLEAN HIT, AND THERE WAS NO SUSPENSION OR FINE FOR JACOBSON.
YOU KNOW WHAT, PAUL? WHAT THE LEAGUE THINKS IS IRRELEVANT TO ME. AND WITH ALL OF THE INJURIES HE'S SUSTAINED, JACOBSON IS PRETTY MUCH IRRELEVANT TOO. GOT IT?
OK, WE HAVE TO TAKE A SHORT BREAK BUT YOU'LL WANT TO STICK AROUND AS WE HAVE A TRULY INCENDIARY SOUND BITE COMING UP FROM ANTON NICHOLSON CALLING OUT JEREMIAH JACOBSON. YOU DON'T WANT TO MISS IT!
WOW! WHAT DO YOU THINK THAT'S GOING TO BE ABOUT?
DON'T KNOW AND DON'T CARE.

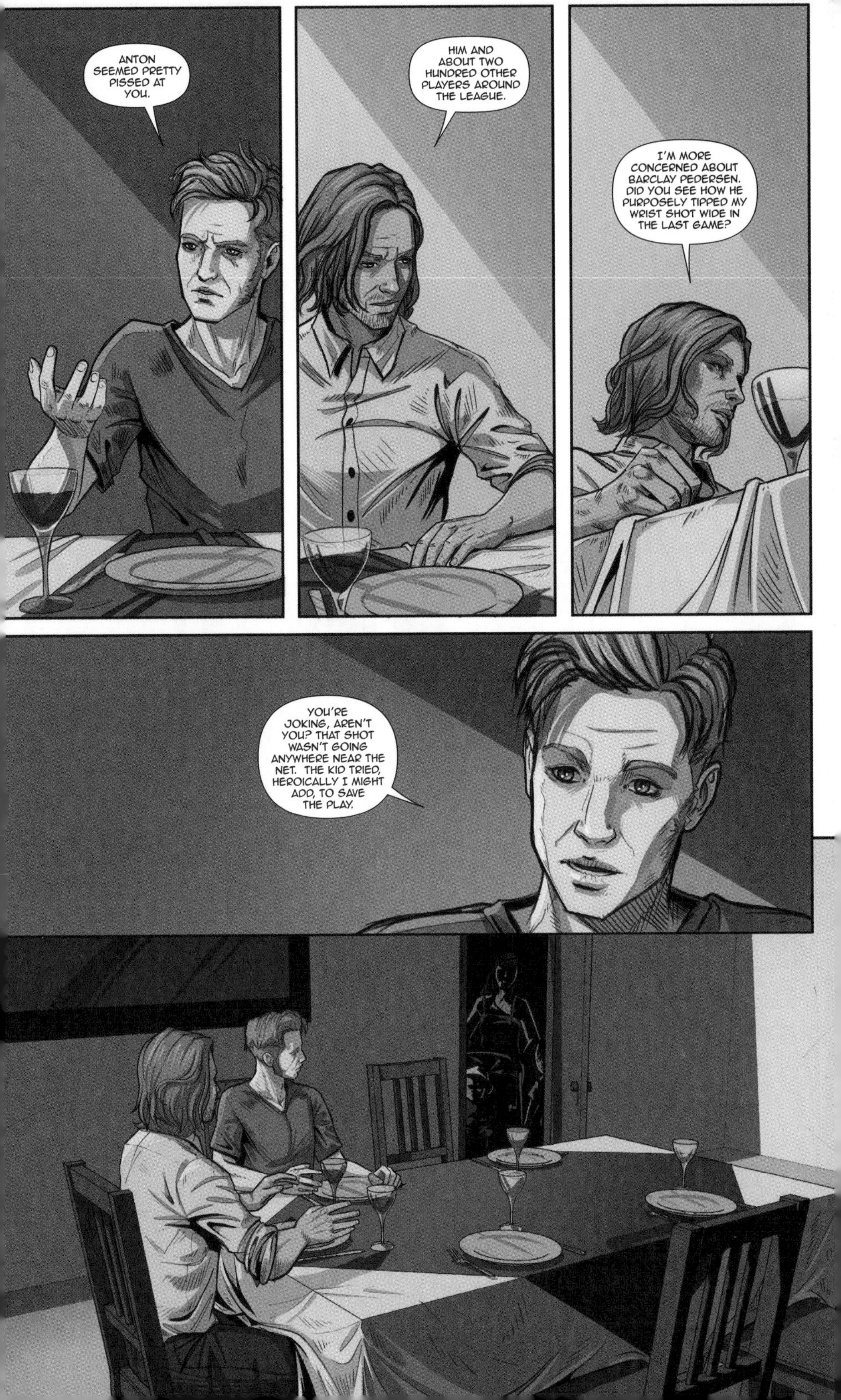
ANTON SEEMED PRETTY PISSED AT YOU.
HIM AND ABOUT TWO HUNDRED OTHER PLAYERS AROUND THE LEAGUE.
I'M MORE CONCERNED ABOUT BARCLAY PEDERSEN. DID YOU SEE HOW HE PURPOSELY TIPPED MY WRIST SHOT WIDE IN THE LAST GAME?
YOU'RE JOKING, AREN'T YOU? THAT SHOT WASN'T GOING ANYWHERE NEAR THE NET. THE KID TRIED, HEROICALLY I MIGHT ADD, TO SAVE THE PLAY.

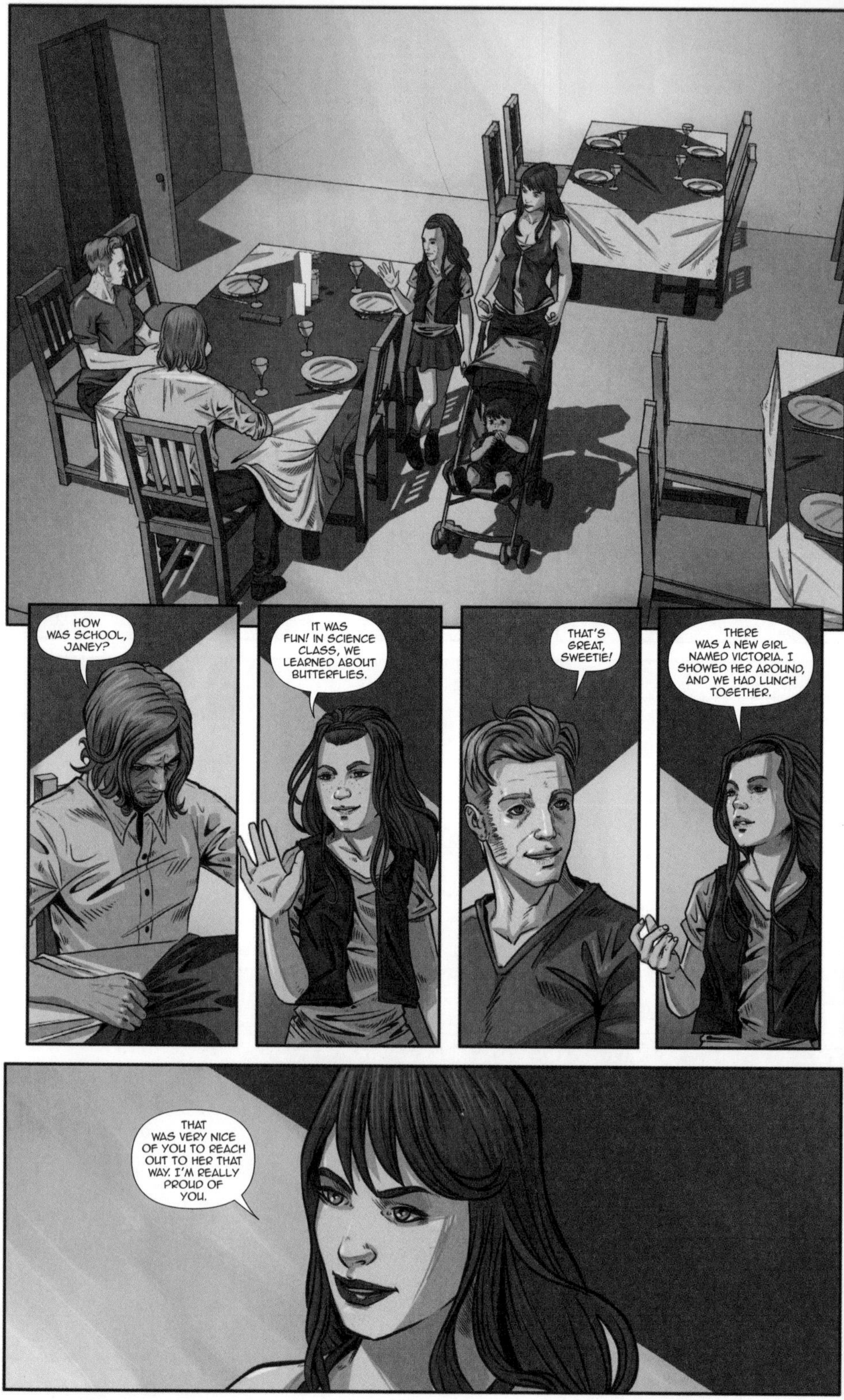
HOW WAS SCHOOL, JANEY?
IT WAS FUN! IN SCIENCE CLASS, WE LEARNED ABOUT BUTTERFLIES.
THAT'S GREAT, SWEETIE!
THERE WAS A NEW GIRL NAMED VICTORIA. I SHOWED HER AROUND, AND WE HAD LUNCH TOGETHER.
THAT WAS VERY NICE OF YOU TO REACH OUT TO HER THAT WAY. I'M REALLY PROUD OF YOU.

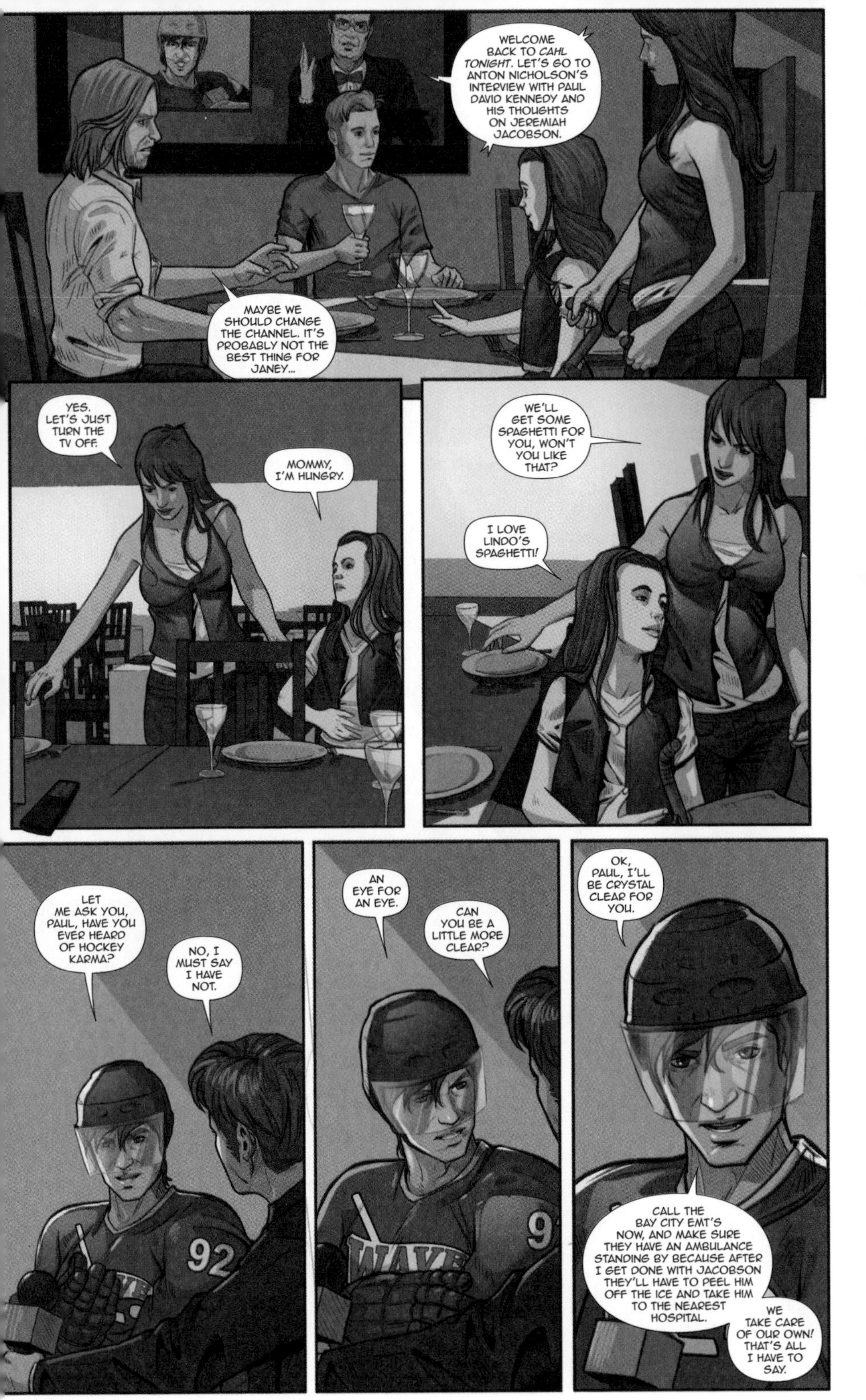
WELCOME BACK TO CAHL TONIGHT. LET'S GO TO ANTON NICHOLSON'S INTERVIEW WITH PAUL DAVID KENNEDY AND HIS THOUGHTS ON JEREMIAH JACOBSON.
MAYBE WE SHOULD CHANGE THE CHANNEL. IT'S PROBABLY NOT THE BEST THING FOR JANEY...
YES. LET'S JUST TURN THE TV OFF.
MOMMY, I'M HUNGRY.
WE'LL GET SOME SPAGHETTI FOR YOU, WON'T YOU LIKE THAT?
I LOVE LINDO'S SPAGHETTI!
LET ME ASK YOU, PAUL, HAVE YOU EVER HEARD OF HOCKEY KARMA?
NO, I MUST SAY I HAVE NOT.
92
AN EYE FOR AN EYE.
CAN YOU BE A LITTLE MORE CLEAR?
WAVE
OK, PAUL, I'LL BE CRYSTAL CLEAR FOR YOU.
CALL THE BAY CITY EMT'S NOW, AND MAKE SURE THEY HAVE AN AMBULANCE STANDING BY BECAUSE AFTER I GET DONE WITH JACOBSON THEY'LL HAVE TO PEEL HIM OFF THE ICE AND TAKE HIM TO THE NEAREST HOSPITAL.
WE TAKE CARE OF OUR OWN! THAT'S ALL I HAVE TO SAY.

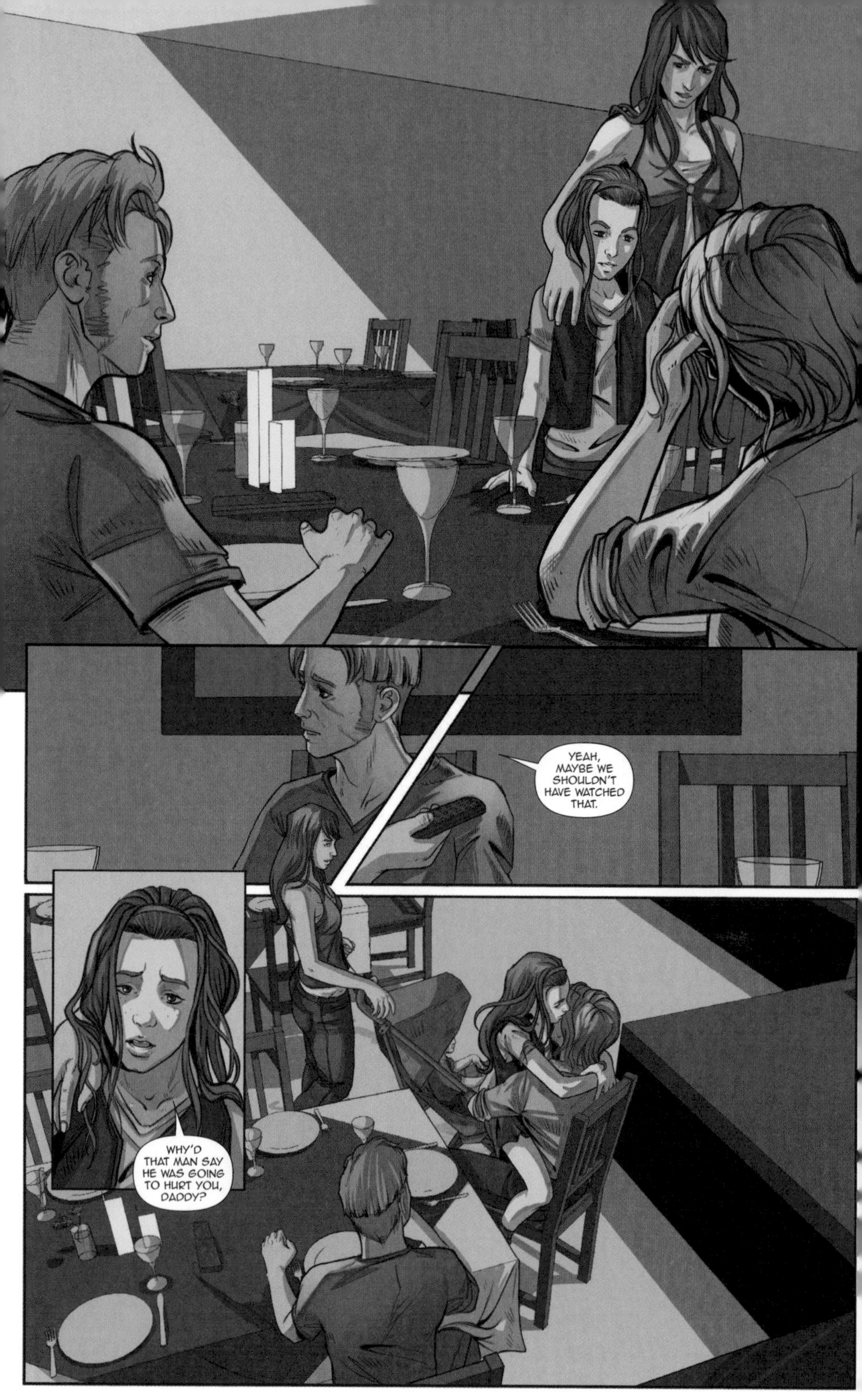
YEAH, MAYBE WE SHOULDN'T HAVE WATCHED THAT.
WHY'D THAT MAN SAY HE WAS GOING TO HURT YOU, DADDY?

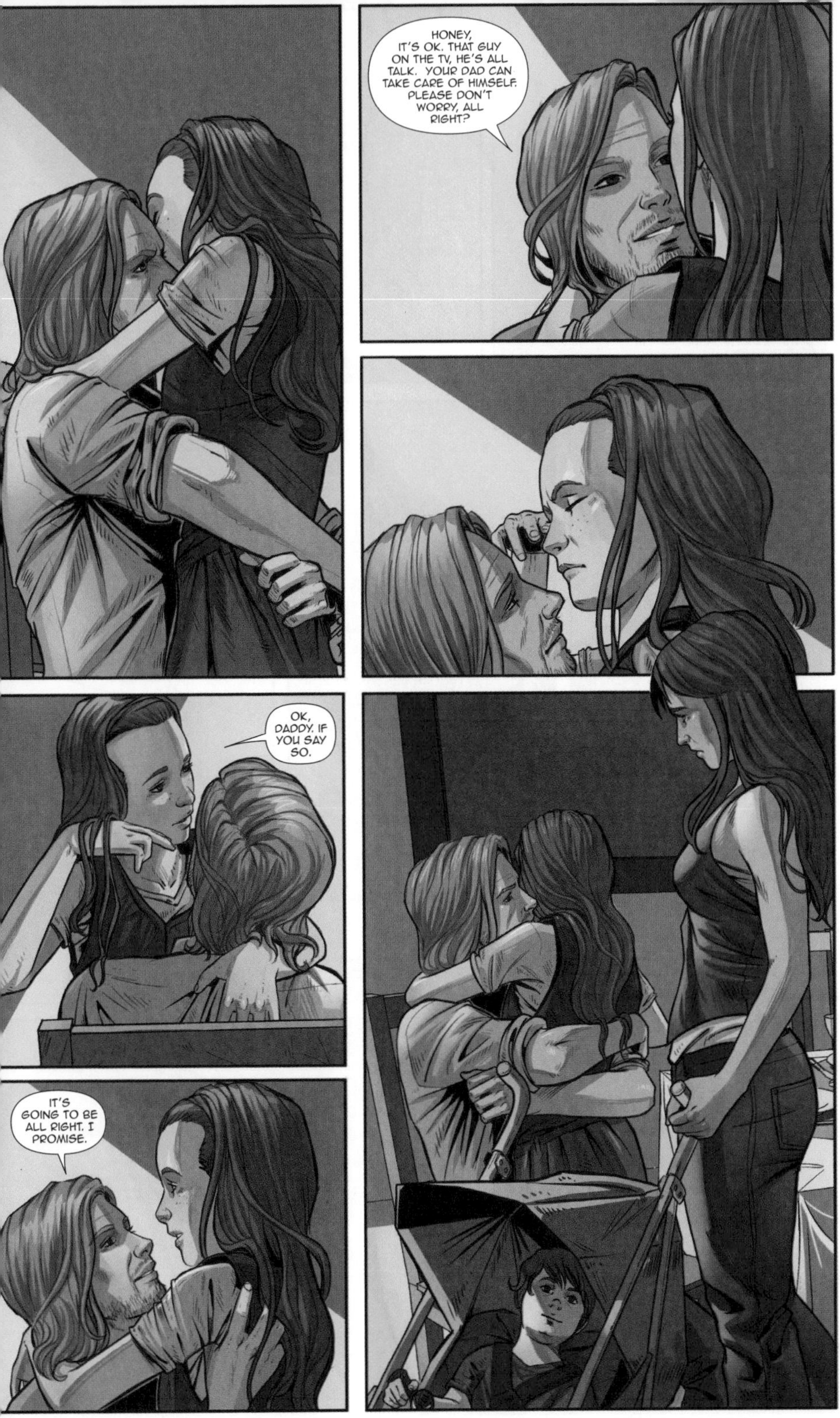
HONEY, IT'S OK. THAT GUY ON THE TV, HE'S ALL TALK. YOUR DAD CAN TAKE CARE OF HIMSELF. PLEASE DON'T WORRY, ALL RIGHT?
OK, DADDY. IF YOU SAY SO.
IT'S GOING TO BE ALL RIGHT. I PROMISE.

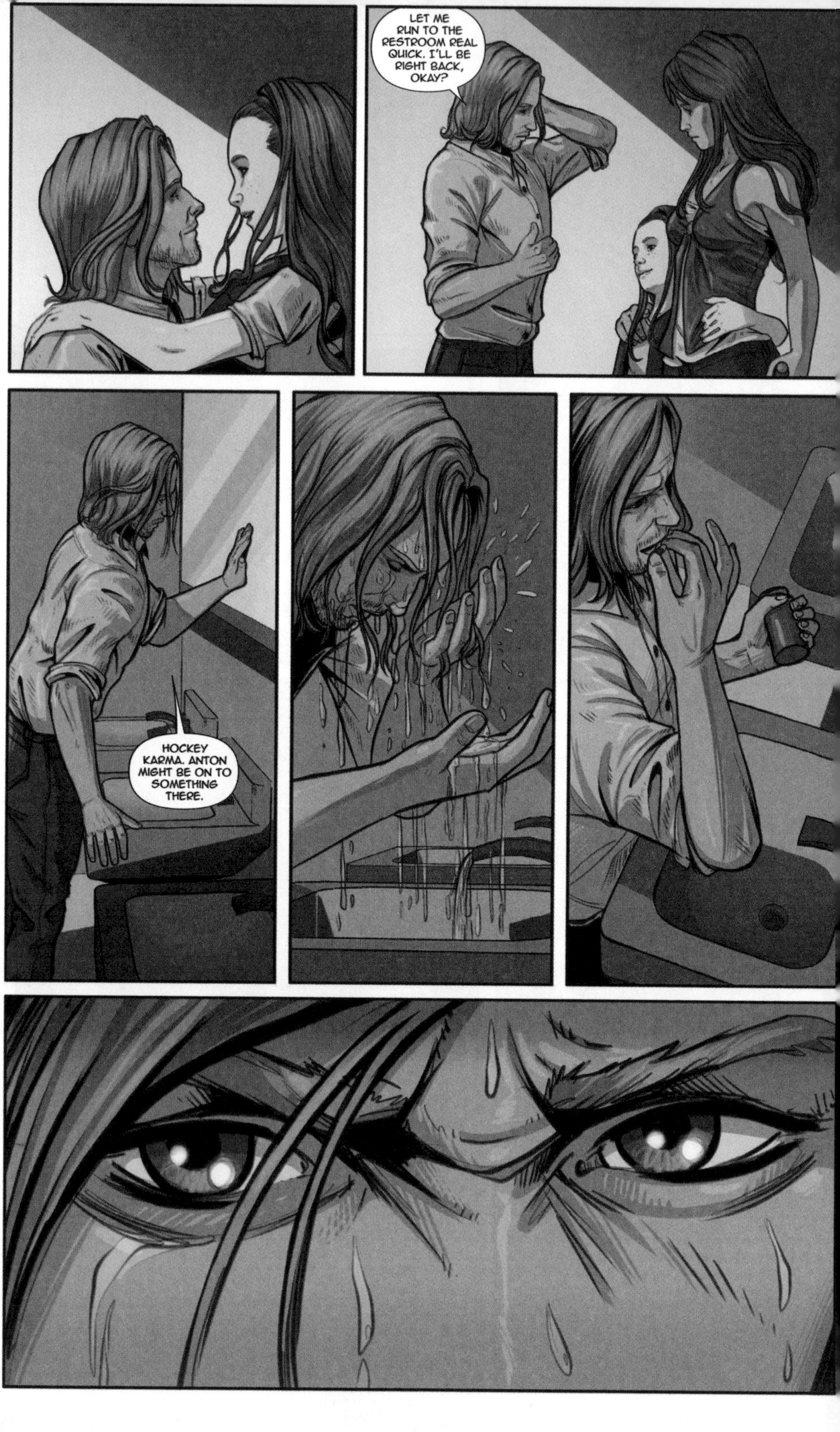
LET ME RUN TO THE RESTROOM REAL QUICK. I'LL BE RIGHT BACK, OKAY?
HOCKEY KARMA. ANTON MIGHT BE ON TO SOMETHING THERE.

CHAPTER 3
The (Less Than) Magnificent Twenty Two

RECOMMENDED LISTENING:

"WHAT'S THE FREQUENCY, KENNETH?"
REM

"MERCY NOW"
MIKE FARRIS

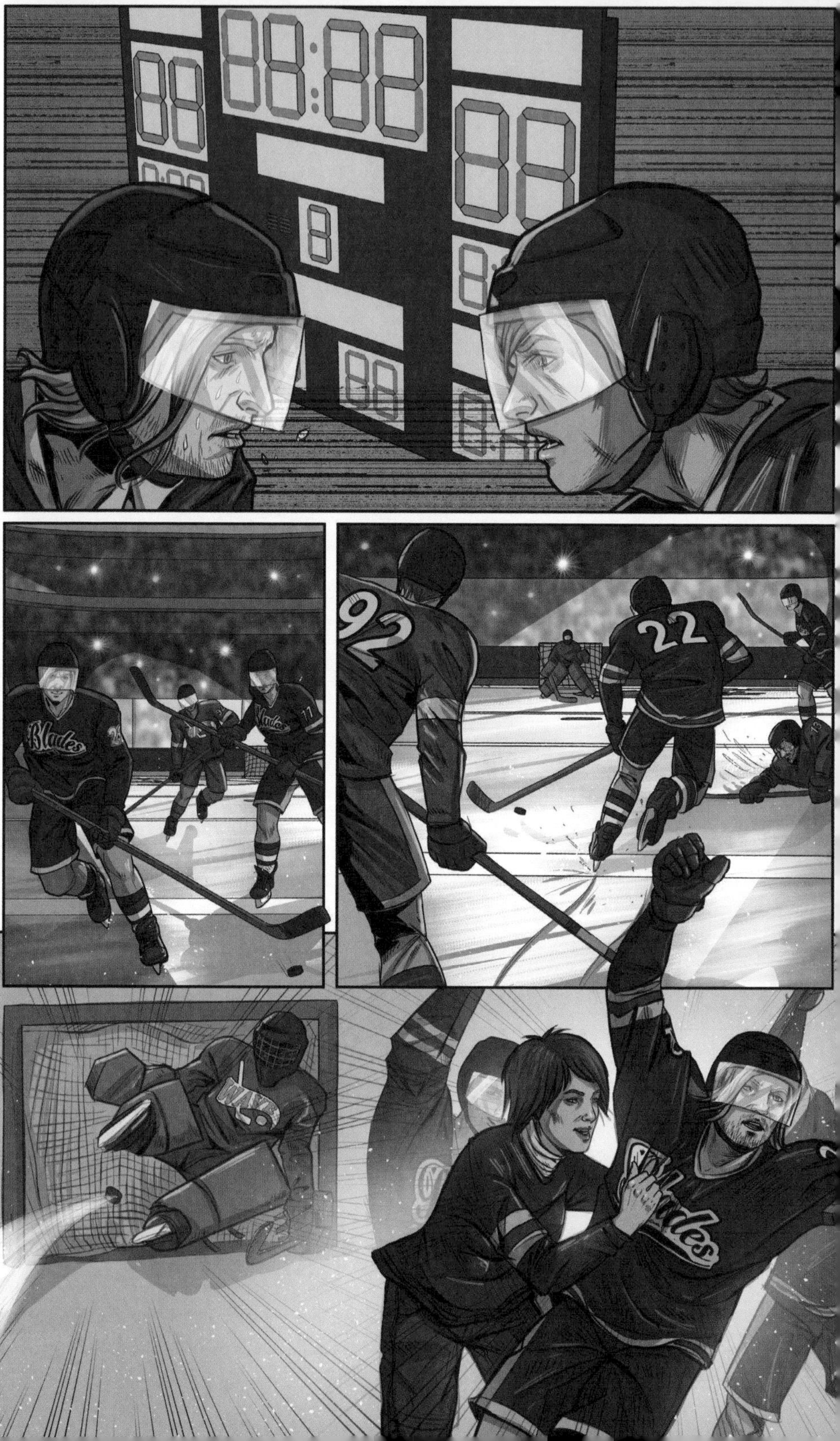
Blades
92
22
Blades
Blades

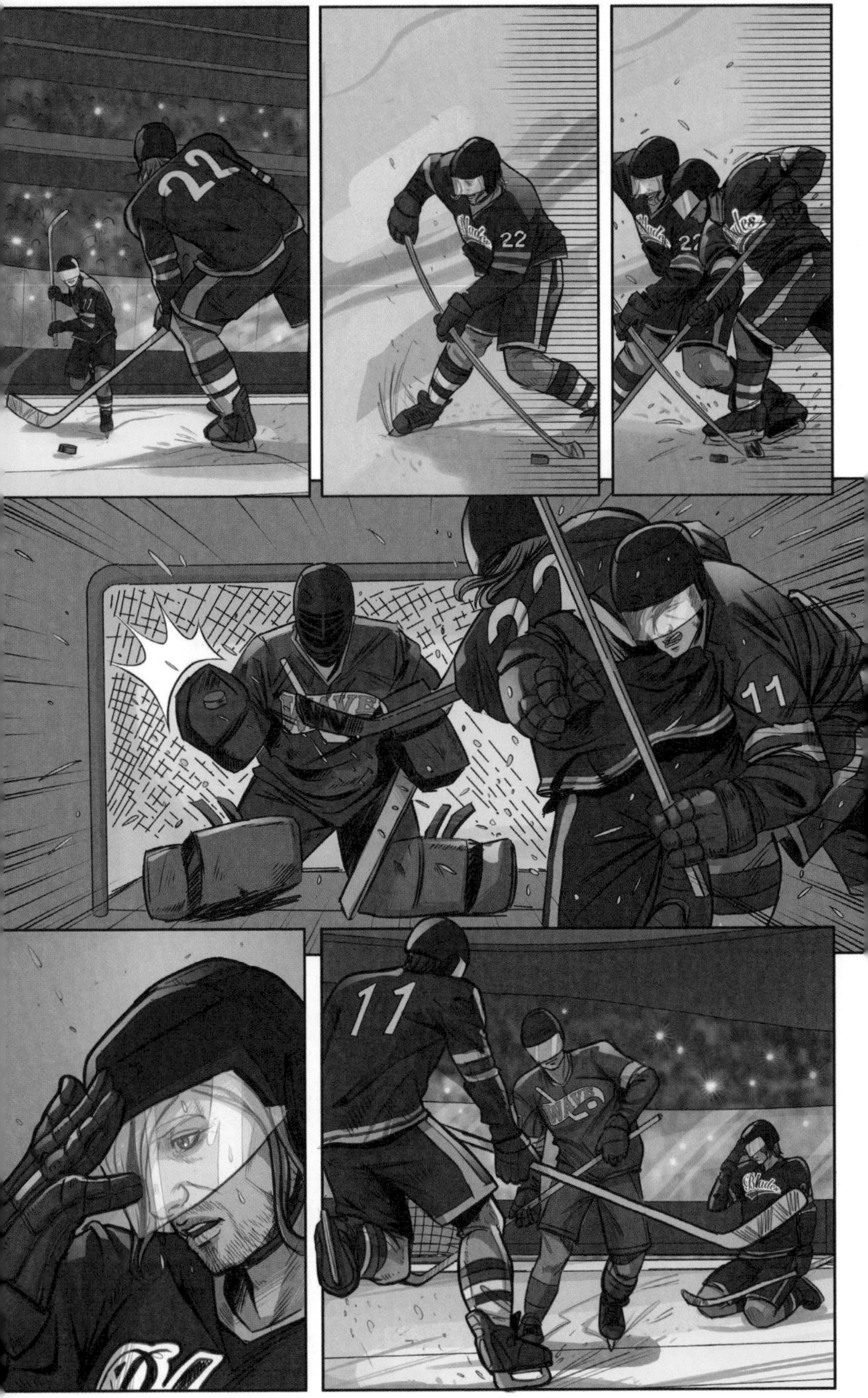

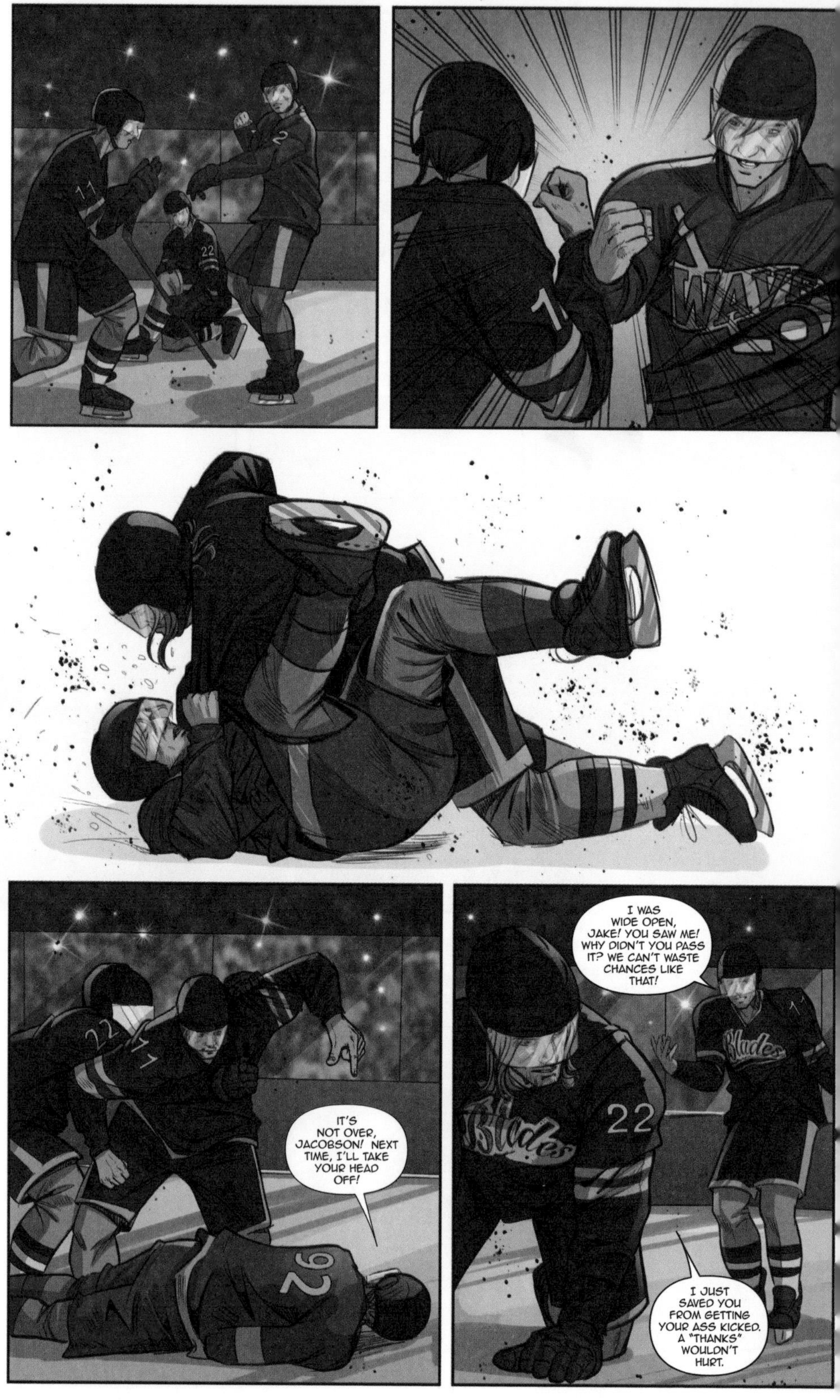
IT'S NOT OVER, JACOBSON! NEXT TIME, I'LL TAKE YOUR HEAD OFF!
I WAS WIDE OPEN, JAKE! YOU SAW ME! WHY DIDN'T YOU PASS IT? WE CAN'T WASTE CHANCES LIKE THAT!
I JUST SAVED YOU FROM GETTING YOUR ASS KICKED. A "THANKS" WOULDN'T HURT.

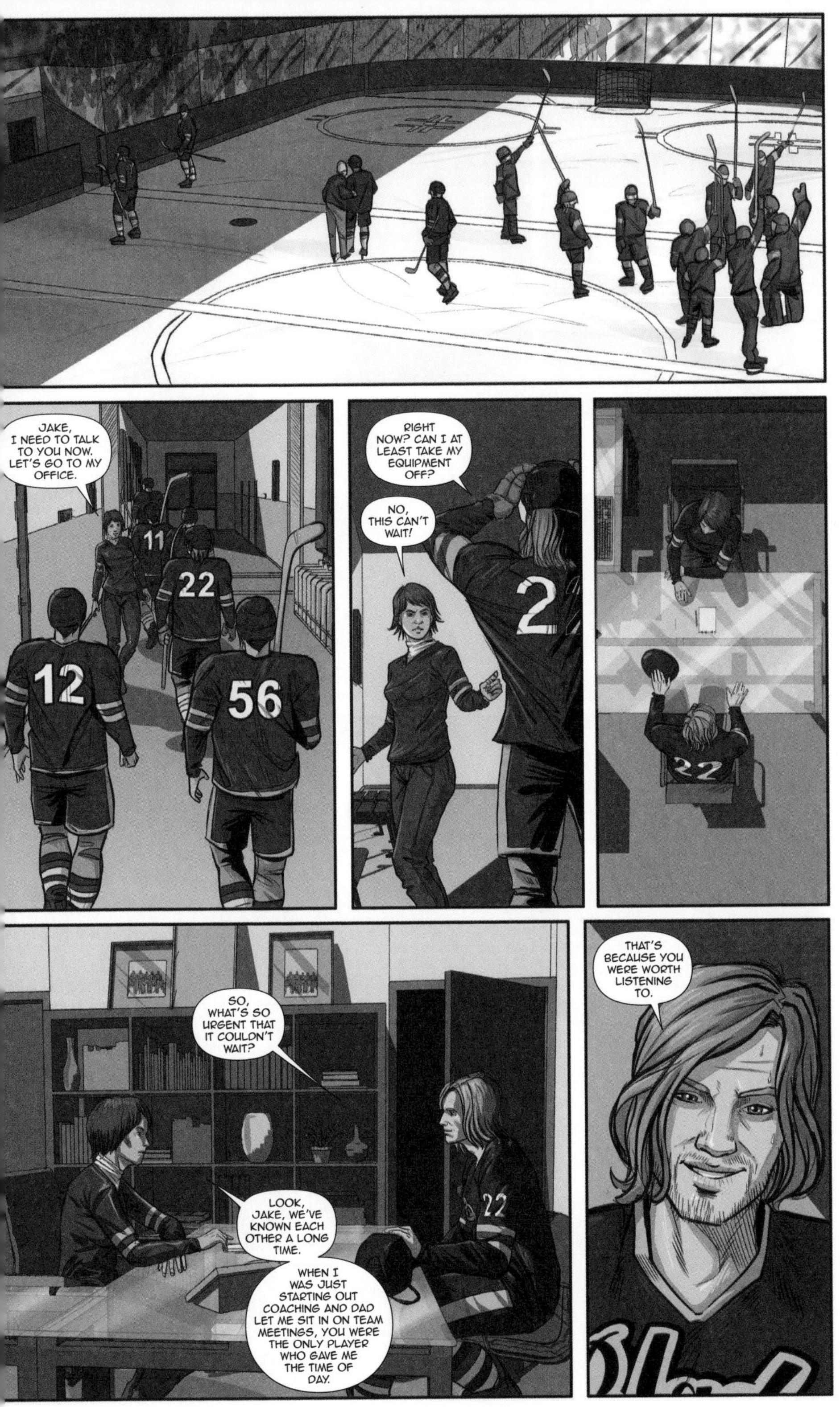
JAKE, I NEED TO TALK TO YOU NOW. LET'S GO TO MY OFFICE.
RIGHT NOW? CAN I AT LEAST TAKE MY EQUIPMENT OFF?
NO, THIS CAN'T WAIT!
SO, WHAT'S SO URGENT THAT IT COULDN'T WAIT?
LOOK, JAKE, WE'VE KNOWN EACH OTHER A LONG TIME.
WHEN I WAS JUST STARTING OUT COACHING AND DAD LET ME SIT IN ON TEAM MEETINGS, YOU WERE THE ONLY PLAYER WHO GAVE ME THE TIME OF DAY.
THAT'S BECAUSE YOU WERE WORTH LISTENING TO.

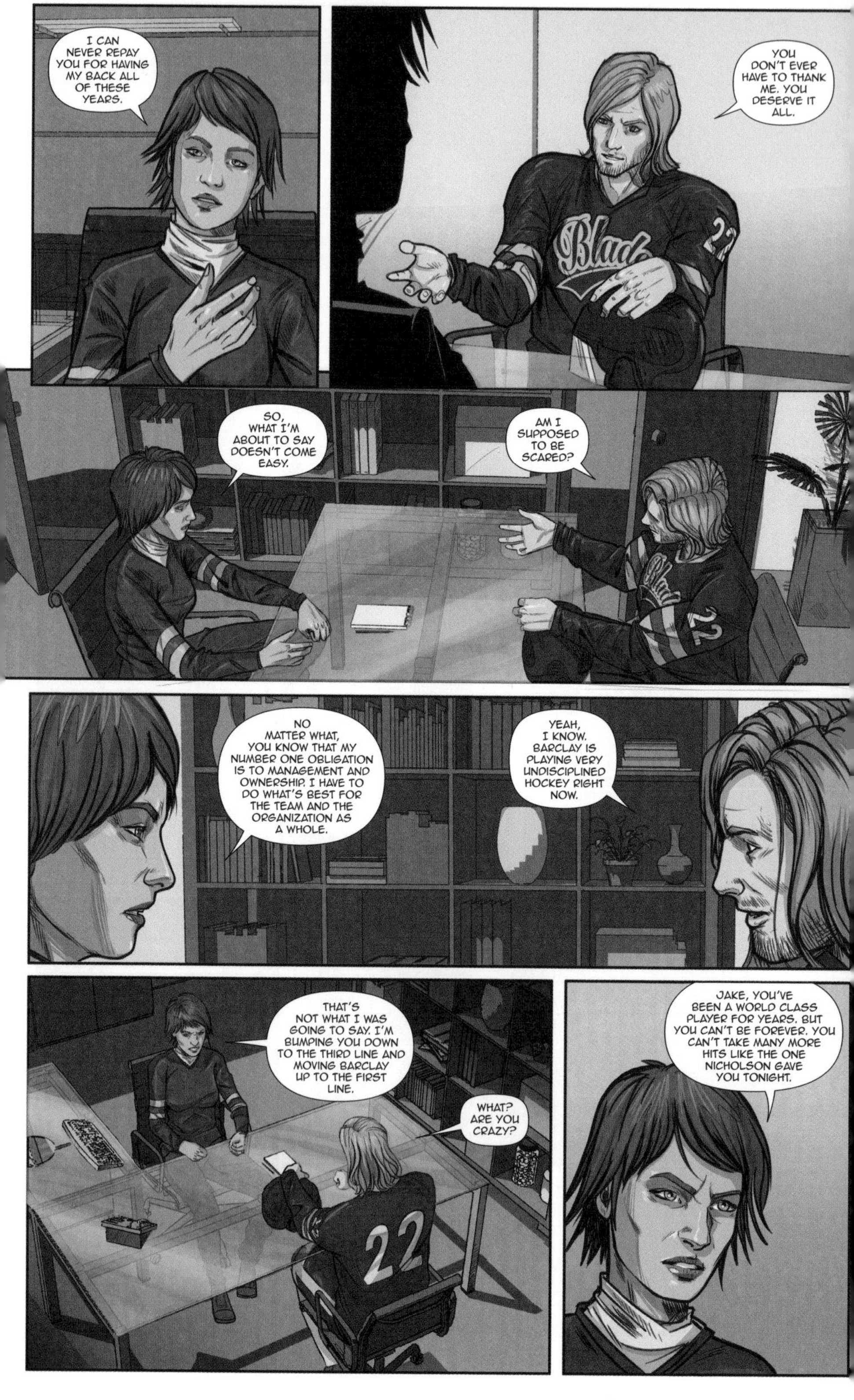
I CAN NEVER REPAY YOU FOR HAVING MY BACK ALL OF THESE YEARS.
YOU DON'T EVER HAVE TO THANK ME. YOU DESERVE IT ALL.
SO, WHAT I'M ABOUT TO SAY DOESN'T COME EASY.
AM I SUPPOSED TO BE SCARED?
NO MATTER WHAT, YOU KNOW THAT MY NUMBER ONE OBLIGATION IS TO MANAGEMENT AND OWNERSHIP. I HAVE TO DO WHAT'S BEST FOR THE TEAM AND THE ORGANIZATION AS A WHOLE.
YEAH, I KNOW. BARCLAY IS PLAYING VERY UNDISCIPLINED HOCKEY RIGHT NOW.
THAT'S NOT WHAT I WAS GOING TO SAY. I'M BUMPING YOU DOWN TO THE THIRD LINE AND MOVING BARCLAY UP TO THE FIRST LINE.
WHAT? ARE YOU CRAZY?
JAKE, YOU'VE BEEN A WORLD CLASS PLAYER FOR YEARS. BUT YOU CAN'T BE FOREVER. YOU CAN'T TAKE MANY MORE HITS LIKE THE ONE NICHOLSON GAVE YOU TONIGHT.

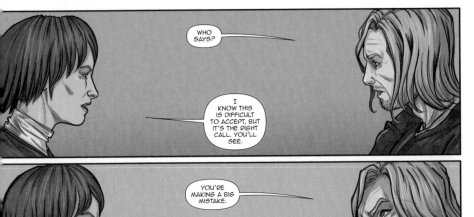

WHO SAYS?

I KNOW THIS IS DIFFICULT TO ACCEPT, BUT IT'S THE RIGHT CALL. YOU'LL SEE.

YOU'RE MAKING A BIG MISTAKE.

WHAT'D YOU SAY? I THOUGHT I HEARD YOU SAY I WAS MAKING A BIG MISTAKE WHICH WOULD MEAN THAT YOU'RE TRYING TO TELL ME HOW TO RUN THE TEAM, RIGHT?

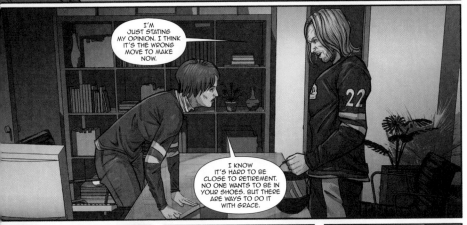

I'M JUST STATING MY OPINION. I THINK IT'S THE WRONG MOVE TO MAKE NOW.

I KNOW IT'S HARD TO BE CLOSE TO RETIREMENT. NO ONE WANTS TO BE IN YOUR SHOES. BUT THERE ARE WAYS TO DO IT WITH GRACE.

EMMA, THAT'S BS. I'M NOWHERE NEAR CLOSE TO RETIREMENT. PEDERSEN IS GOING TO BRING THIS TEAM DOWN. YOU CAN'T DO THIS WITHOUT ME.

WHAT IS YOUR DEAL WITH HIM?

HE'S TOO YOUNG. HIS TALENT WILL ONLY TAKE HIM SO FAR AND HE DOESN'T HAVE HOCKEY SMARTS...

THE KID IS LIKE A SPONGE. YOU SHOULD SIT DOWN AND TALK WITH HIM.

THAT'S YOUR JOB, NOT MINE. MY JOB IS TO SCORE GOALS, GET IN FIGHTS, AND WIN HOCKEY GAMES.

FUNNY. I SEEM TO RECALL ANDRE LAMBERT BEING LIKE A BIG BROTHER TO YOU WHEN YOU WERE A ROOKIE.

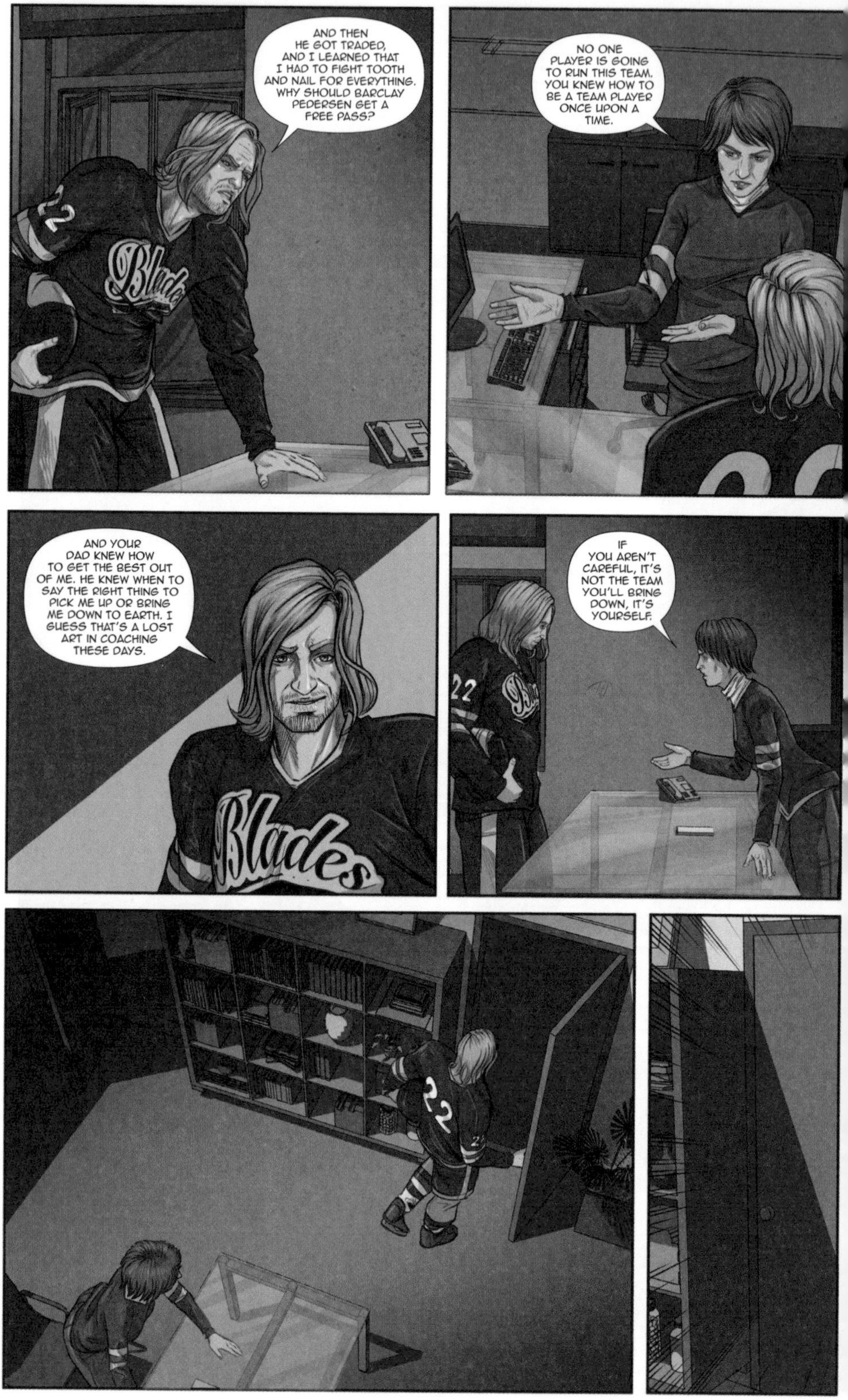
AND THEN HE GOT TRADED, AND I LEARNED THAT I HAD TO FIGHT TOOTH AND NAIL FOR EVERYTHING. WHY SHOULD BARCLAY PEDERSEN GET A FREE PASS?
NO ONE PLAYER IS GOING TO RUN THIS TEAM. YOU KNEW HOW TO BE A TEAM PLAYER ONCE UPON A TIME.
AND YOUR DAD KNEW HOW TO GET THE BEST OUT OF ME. HE KNEW WHEN TO SAY THE RIGHT THING TO PICK ME UP OR BRING ME DOWN TO EARTH. I GUESS THAT'S A LOST ART IN COACHING THESE DAYS.
IF YOU AREN'T CAREFUL, IT'S NOT THE TEAM YOU'LL BRING DOWN, IT'S YOURSELF.

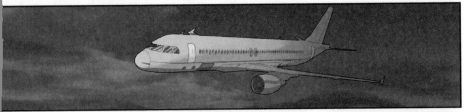

CAHL.COM
PEDERSEN SHINES BUT B
LADES FALL TO THE WAVE
4 — 3

ARE YOU A HOCKEY FAN?

YEAH, I'M A BIG BLADES FAN.

I DON'T KNOW ABOUT THEM THIS YEAR. JACOBSON STINKS AND THEY SHOULD FIRE THE COACH AND GM TOO.

YEAH... RIGHT. I BET YOU LISTEN TO A LOT OF SPORTS TALK RADIO WITH HOT TAKES LIKE THAT.

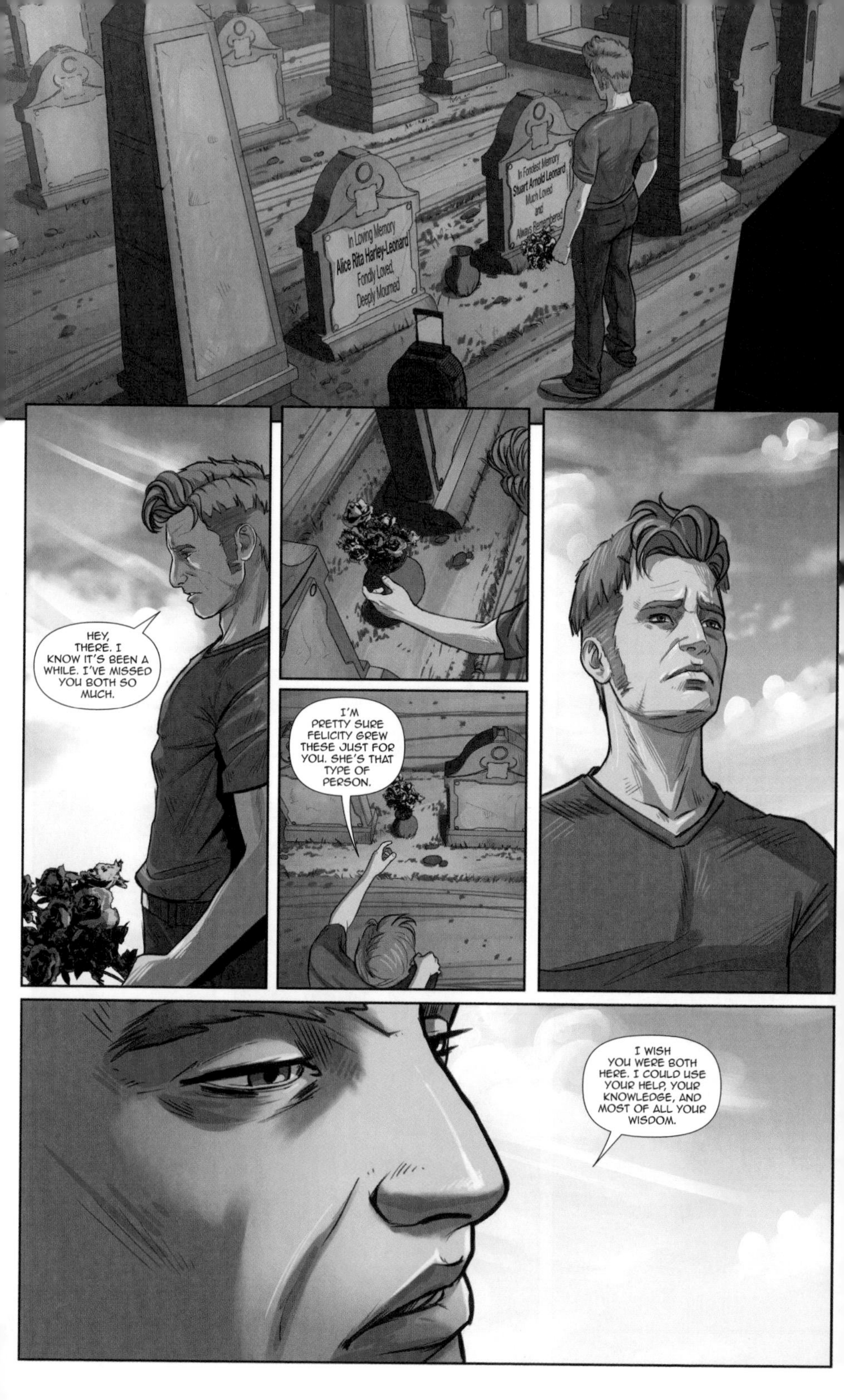
In Loving Memory
Alice Rita Harley-Leonard
Fondly Loved,
Deeply Mourned
In Fondest Memory
Stuart Arnold Leonard
Much Loved
and
Always Remembered
HEY, THERE. I KNOW IT'S BEEN A WHILE. I'VE MISSED YOU BOTH SO MUCH.
I'M PRETTY SURE FELICITY GREW THESE JUST FOR YOU. SHE'S THAT TYPE OF PERSON.
I WISH YOU WERE BOTH HERE. I COULD USE YOUR HELP, YOUR KNOWLEDGE, AND MOST OF ALL YOUR WISDOM.

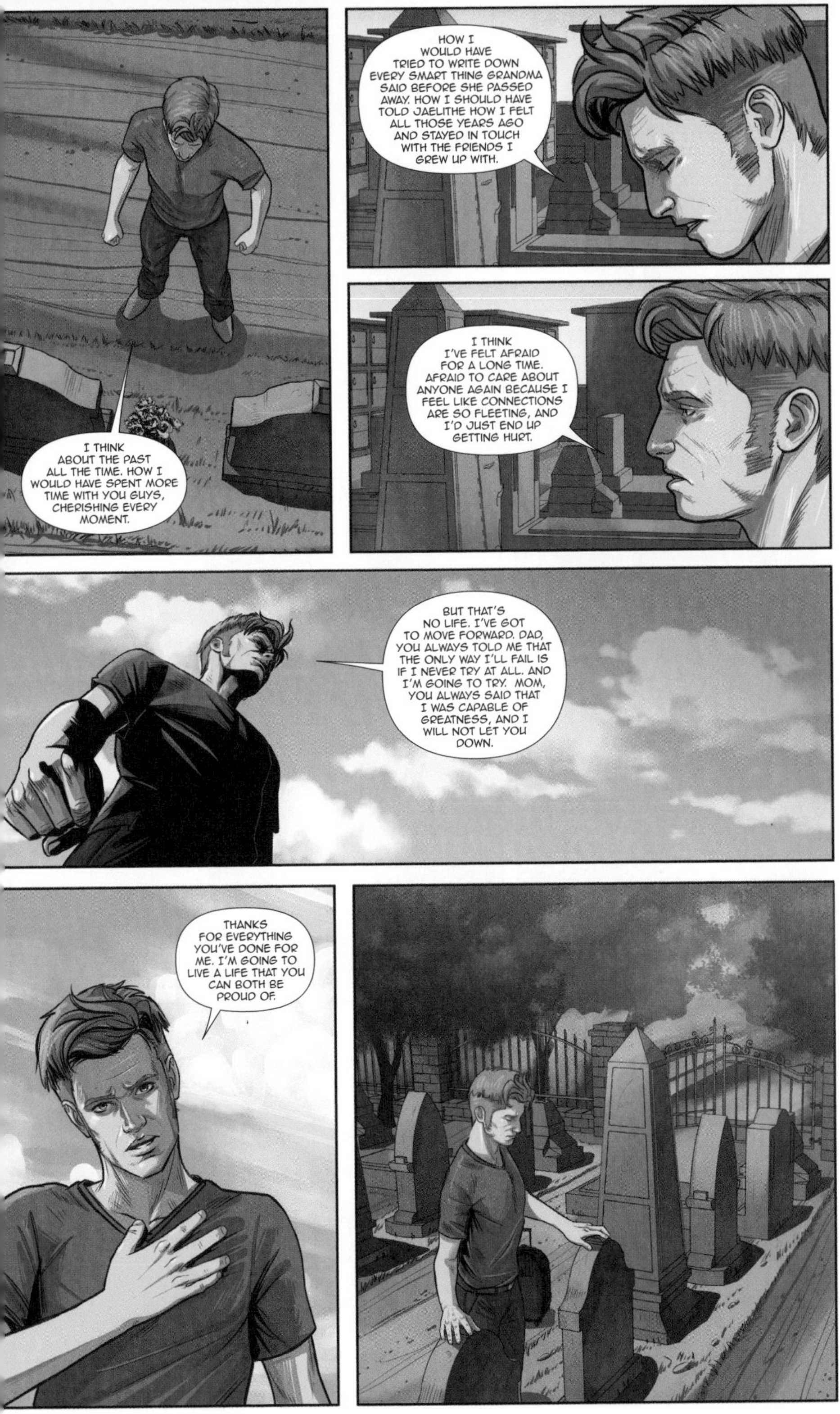
I THINK ABOUT THE PAST ALL THE TIME. HOW I WOULD HAVE SPENT MORE TIME WITH YOU GUYS, CHERISHING EVERY MOMENT.
HOW I WOULD HAVE TRIED TO WRITE DOWN EVERY SMART THING GRANDMA SAID BEFORE SHE PASSED AWAY. HOW I SHOULD HAVE TOLD JAELITHE HOW I FELT ALL THOSE YEARS AGO AND STAYED IN TOUCH WITH THE FRIENDS I GREW UP WITH.
I THINK I'VE FELT AFRAID FOR A LONG TIME. AFRAID TO CARE ABOUT ANYONE AGAIN BECAUSE I FEEL LIKE CONNECTIONS ARE SO FLEETING, AND I'D JUST END UP GETTING HURT.
BUT THAT'S NO LIFE. I'VE GOT TO MOVE FORWARD. DAD, YOU ALWAYS TOLD ME THAT THE ONLY WAY I'LL FAIL IS IF I NEVER TRY AT ALL. AND I'M GOING TO TRY. MOM, YOU ALWAYS SAID THAT I WAS CAPABLE OF GREATNESS, AND I WILL NOT LET YOU DOWN.
THANKS FOR EVERYTHING YOU'VE DONE FOR ME. I'M GOING TO LIVE A LIFE THAT YOU CAN BOTH BE PROUD OF.

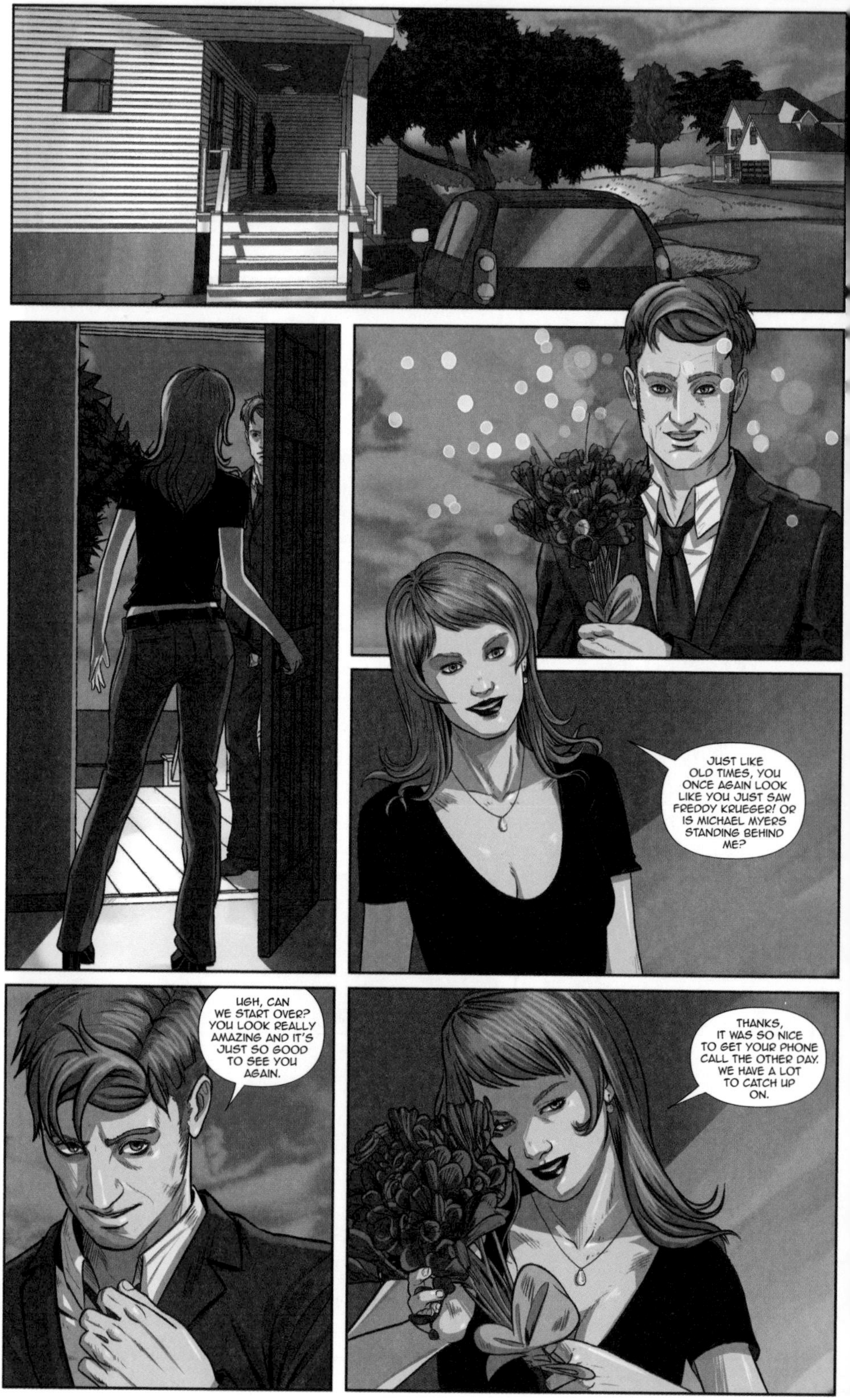

JUST LIKE OLD TIMES, YOU ONCE AGAIN LOOK LIKE YOU JUST SAW FREDDY KRUEGER! OR IS MICHAEL MYERS STANDING BEHIND ME?
UGH, CAN WE START OVER? YOU LOOK REALLY AMAZING AND IT'S JUST SO GOOD TO SEE YOU AGAIN.
THANKS, IT WAS SO NICE TO GET YOUR PHONE CALL THE OTHER DAY. WE HAVE A LOT TO CATCH UP ON.

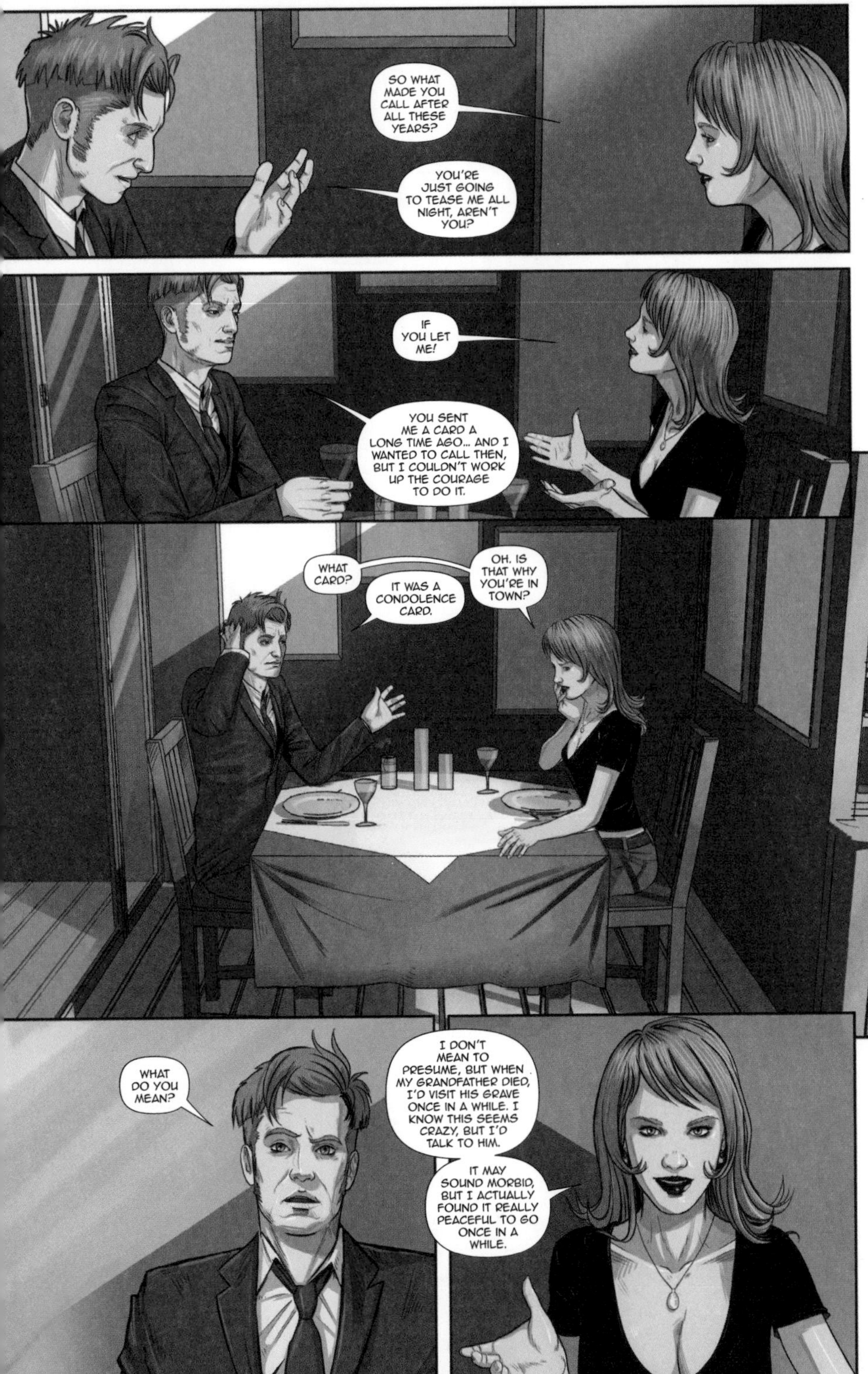
SO WHAT MADE YOU CALL AFTER ALL THESE YEARS?
YOU'RE JUST GOING TO TEASE ME ALL NIGHT, AREN'T YOU?
IF YOU LET ME!
YOU SENT ME A CARD A LONG TIME AGO... AND I WANTED TO CALL THEN, BUT I COULDN'T WORK UP THE COURAGE TO DO IT.
WHAT CARD?
IT WAS A CONDOLENCE CARD.
OH. IS THAT WHY YOU'RE IN TOWN?
WHAT DO YOU MEAN?
I DON'T MEAN TO PRESUME, BUT WHEN MY GRANDFATHER DIED, I'D VISIT HIS GRAVE ONCE IN A WHILE. I KNOW THIS SEEMS CRAZY, BUT I'D TALK TO HIM.
IT MAY SOUND MORBID, BUT I ACTUALLY FOUND IT REALLY PEACEFUL TO GO ONCE IN A WHILE.

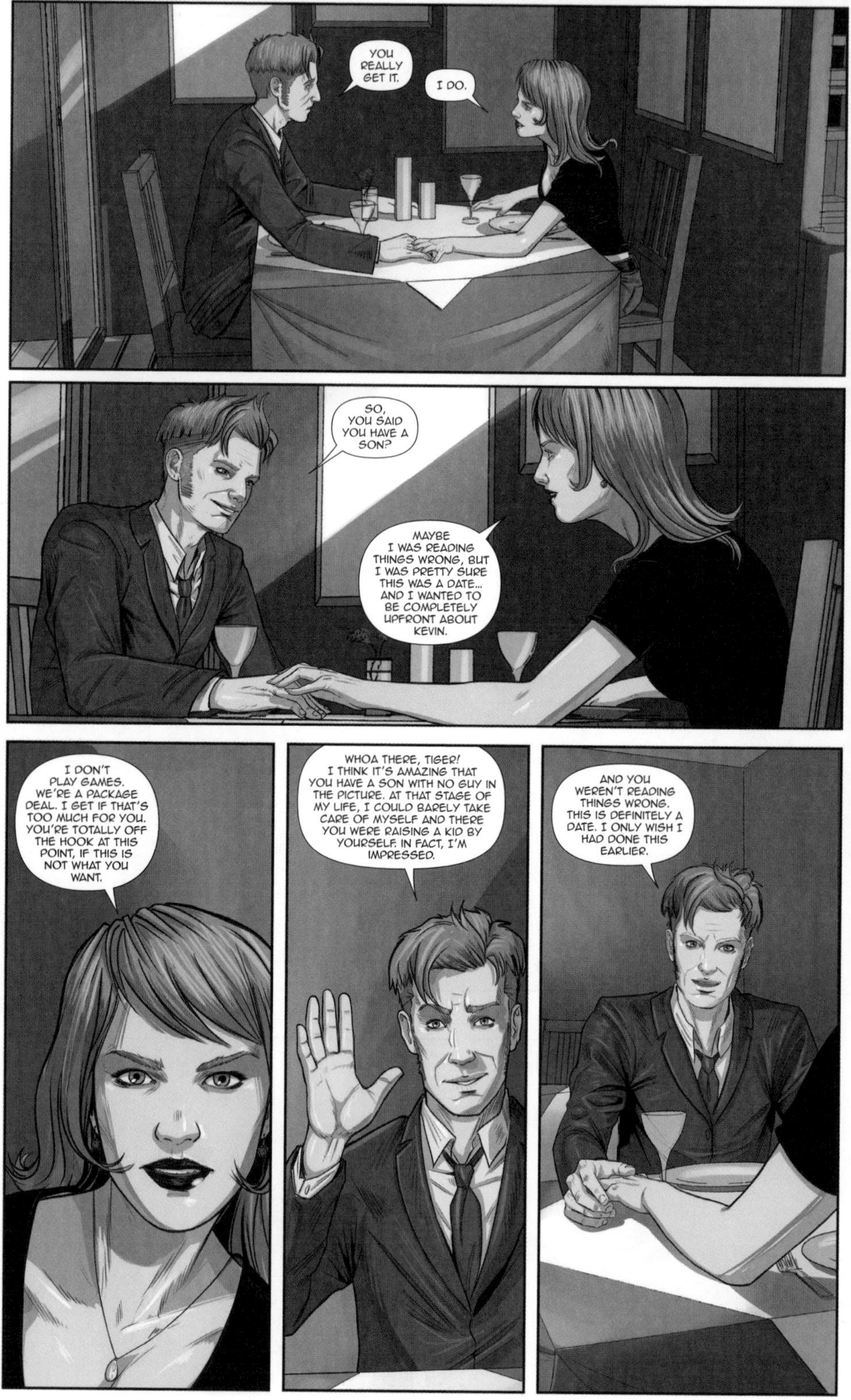
YOU REALLY GET IT.
I DO.
SO, YOU SAID YOU HAVE A SON?
MAYBE I WAS READING THINGS WRONG, BUT I WAS PRETTY SURE THIS WAS A DATE... AND I WANTED TO BE COMPLETELY UPFRONT ABOUT KEVIN.
I DON'T PLAY GAMES. WE'RE A PACKAGE DEAL. I GET IF THAT'S TOO MUCH FOR YOU. YOU'RE TOTALLY OFF THE HOOK AT THIS POINT, IF THIS IS NOT WHAT YOU WANT.
WHOA THERE, TIGER! I THINK IT'S AMAZING THAT YOU HAVE A SON WITH NO GUY IN THE PICTURE. AT THAT STAGE OF MY LIFE, I COULD BARELY TAKE CARE OF MYSELF AND THERE YOU WERE RAISING A KID BY YOURSELF. IN FACT, I'M IMPRESSED.
AND YOU WEREN'T READING THINGS WRONG. THIS IS DEFINITELY A DATE. I ONLY WISH I HAD DONE THIS EARLIER.

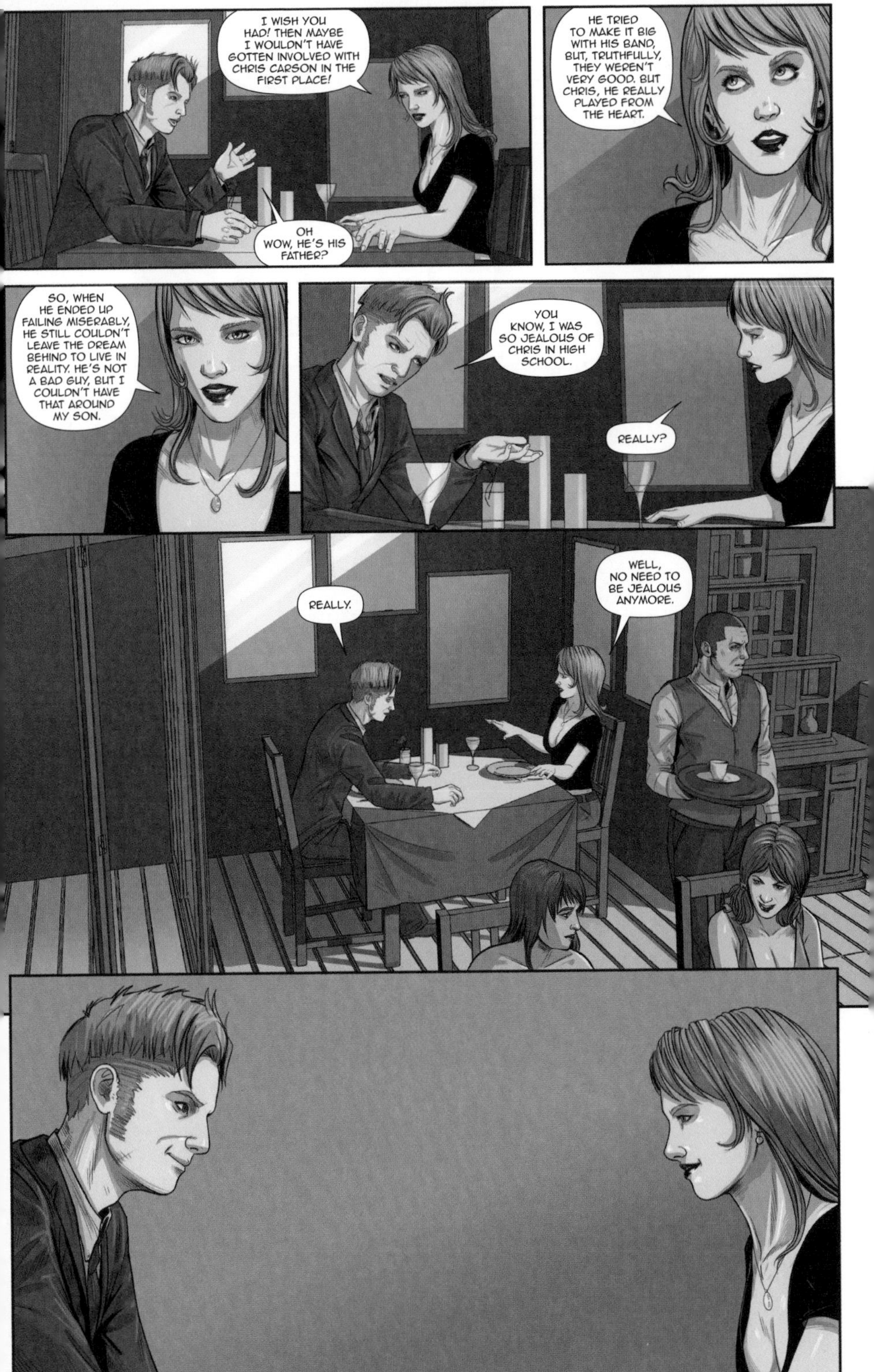
I WISH YOU HAD! THEN MAYBE I WOULDN'T HAVE GOTTEN INVOLVED WITH CHRIS CARSON IN THE FIRST PLACE!
OH WOW, HE'S HIS FATHER?
HE TRIED TO MAKE IT BIG WITH HIS BAND, BUT, TRUTHFULLY, THEY WEREN'T VERY GOOD. BUT CHRIS, HE REALLY PLAYED FROM THE HEART.
SO, WHEN HE ENDED UP FAILING MISERABLY, HE STILL COULDN'T LEAVE THE DREAM BEHIND TO LIVE IN REALITY. HE'S NOT A BAD GUY, BUT I COULDN'T HAVE THAT AROUND MY SON.
YOU KNOW, I WAS SO JEALOUS OF CHRIS IN HIGH SCHOOL.
REALLY?
REALLY.
WELL, NO NEED TO BE JEALOUS ANYMORE.

CHAPTER 4
TEMPTATION

RECOMMENDED LISTENING:

"HEAVEN KNOWS
I'M MISERABLE NOW"
THE SMITHS

"EVERYONE'S AT IT"
LILY ALLEN

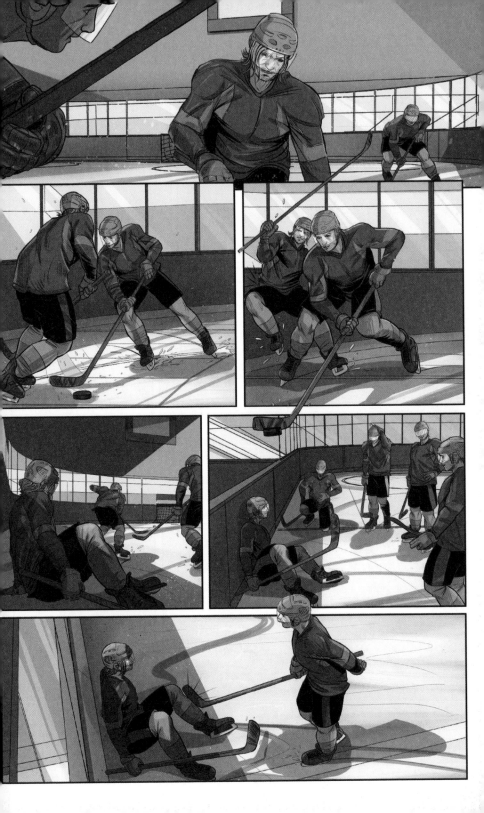

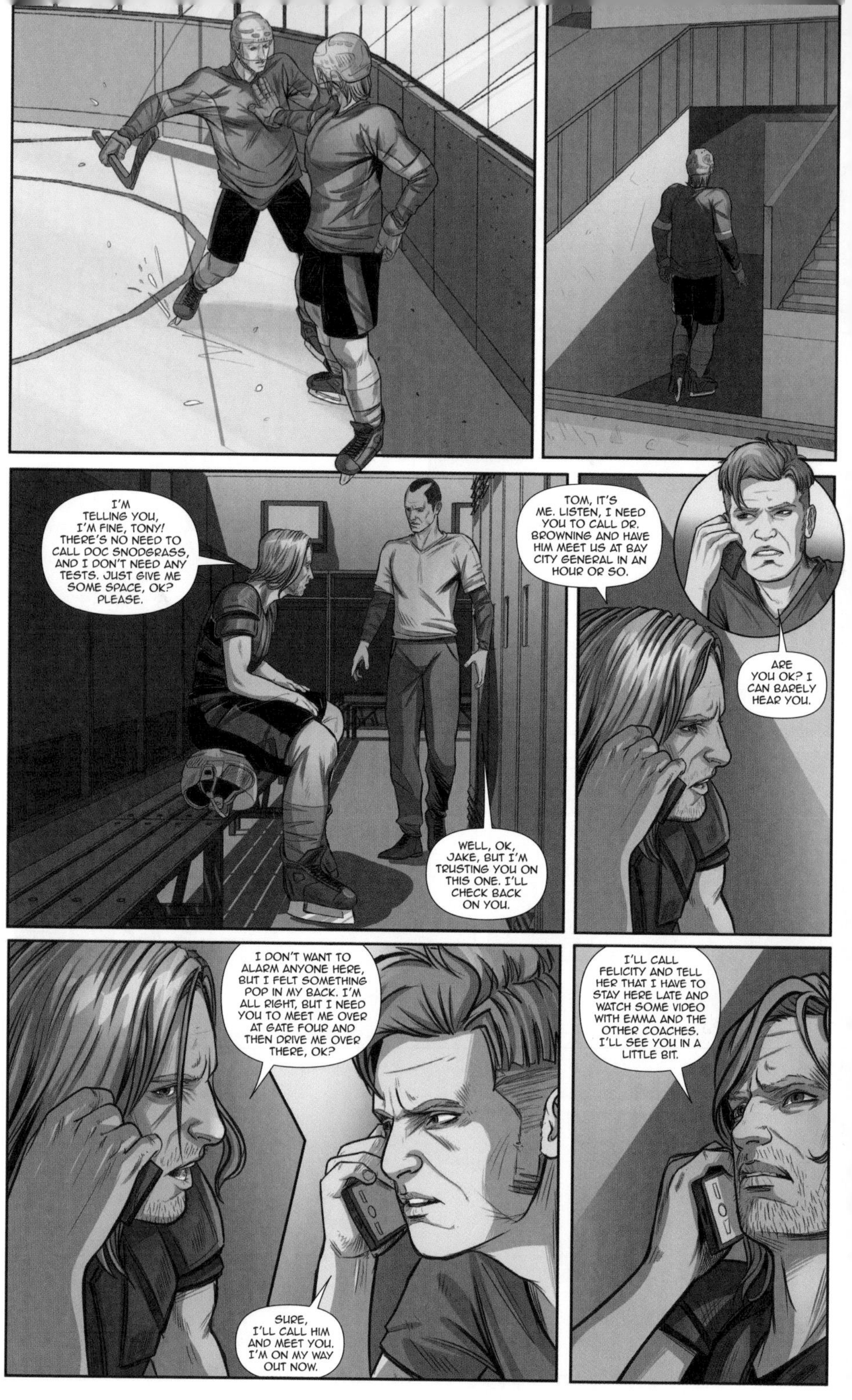
I'M TELLING YOU, I'M FINE, TONY! THERE'S NO NEED TO CALL DOC SNODGRASS, AND I DON'T NEED ANY TESTS. JUST GIVE ME SOME SPACE, OK? PLEASE.
WELL, OK, JAKE, BUT I'M TRUSTING YOU ON THIS ONE. I'LL CHECK BACK ON YOU.
TOM, IT'S ME. LISTEN, I NEED YOU TO CALL DR. BROWNING AND HAVE HIM MEET US AT BAY CITY GENERAL IN AN HOUR OR SO.
ARE YOU OK? I CAN BARELY HEAR YOU.
I DON'T WANT TO ALARM ANYONE HERE, BUT I FELT SOMETHING POP IN MY BACK. I'M ALL RIGHT, BUT I NEED YOU TO MEET ME OVER AT GATE FOUR AND THEN DRIVE ME OVER THERE, OK?
SURE, I'LL CALL HIM AND MEET YOU. I'M ON MY WAY OUT NOW.
I'LL CALL FELICITY AND TELL HER THAT I HAVE TO STAY HERE LATE AND WATCH SOME VIDEO WITH EMMA AND THE OTHER COACHES. I'LL SEE YOU IN A LITTLE BIT.

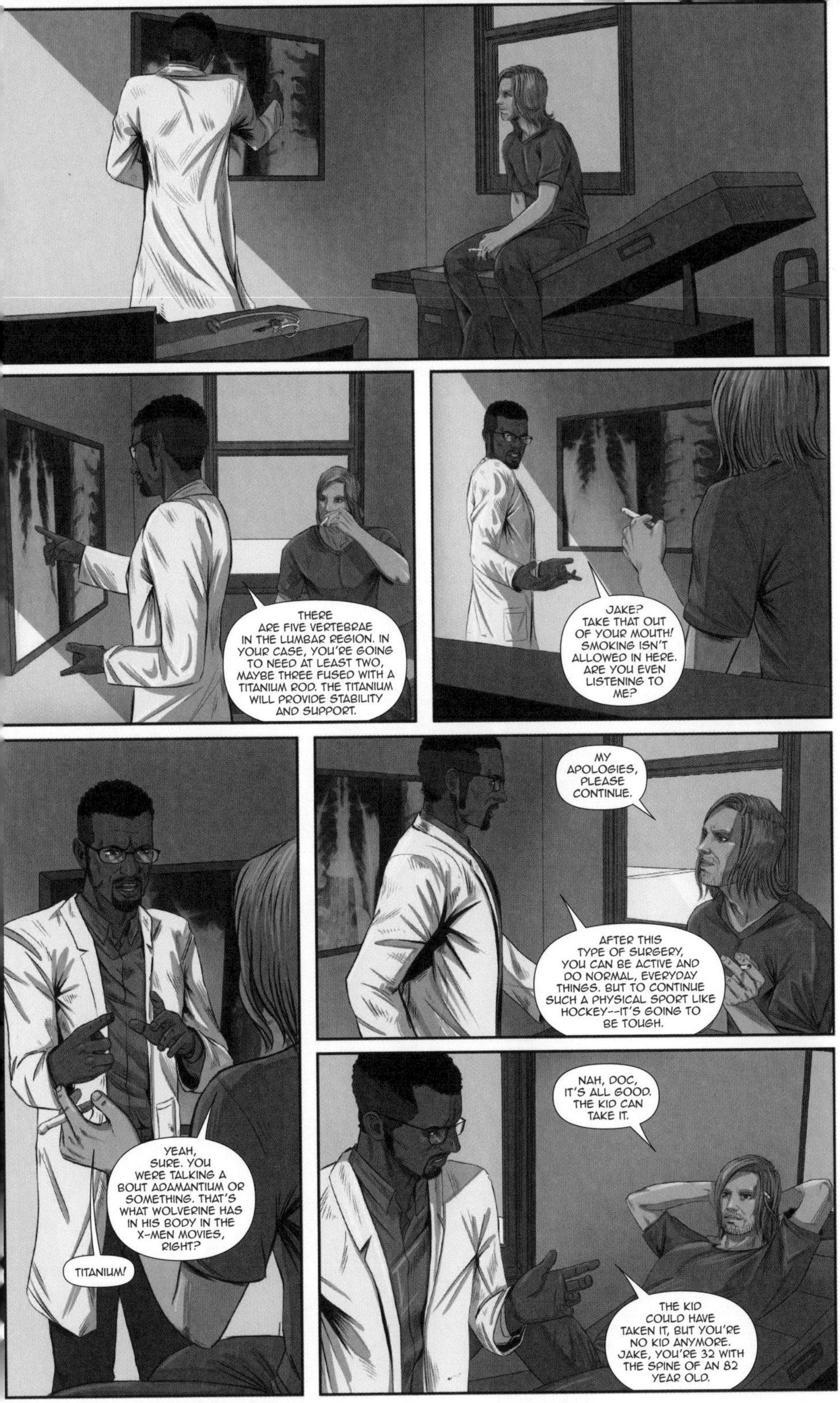
THERE ARE FIVE VERTEBRAE IN THE LUMBAR REGION. IN YOUR CASE, YOU'RE GOING TO NEED AT LEAST TWO, MAYBE THREE FUSED WITH A TITANIUM ROD. THE TITANIUM WILL PROVIDE STABILITY AND SUPPORT.
JAKE? TAKE THAT OUT OF YOUR MOUTH! SMOKING ISN'T ALLOWED IN HERE. ARE YOU EVEN LISTENING TO ME?
YEAH, SURE. YOU WERE TALKING A BOUT ADAMANTIUM OR SOMETHING. THAT'S WHAT WOLVERINE HAS IN HIS BODY IN THE X-MEN MOVIES, RIGHT?
TITANIUM!
MY APOLOGIES, PLEASE CONTINUE.
AFTER THIS TYPE OF SURGERY, YOU CAN BE ACTIVE AND DO NORMAL, EVERYDAY THINGS. BUT TO CONTINUE SUCH A PHYSICAL SPORT LIKE HOCKEY--IT'S GOING TO BE TOUGH.
NAH, DOC, IT'S ALL GOOD. THE KID CAN TAKE IT.
THE KID COULD HAVE TAKEN IT, BUT YOU'RE NO KID ANYMORE. JAKE, YOU'RE 32 WITH THE SPINE OF AN 82 YEAR OLD.

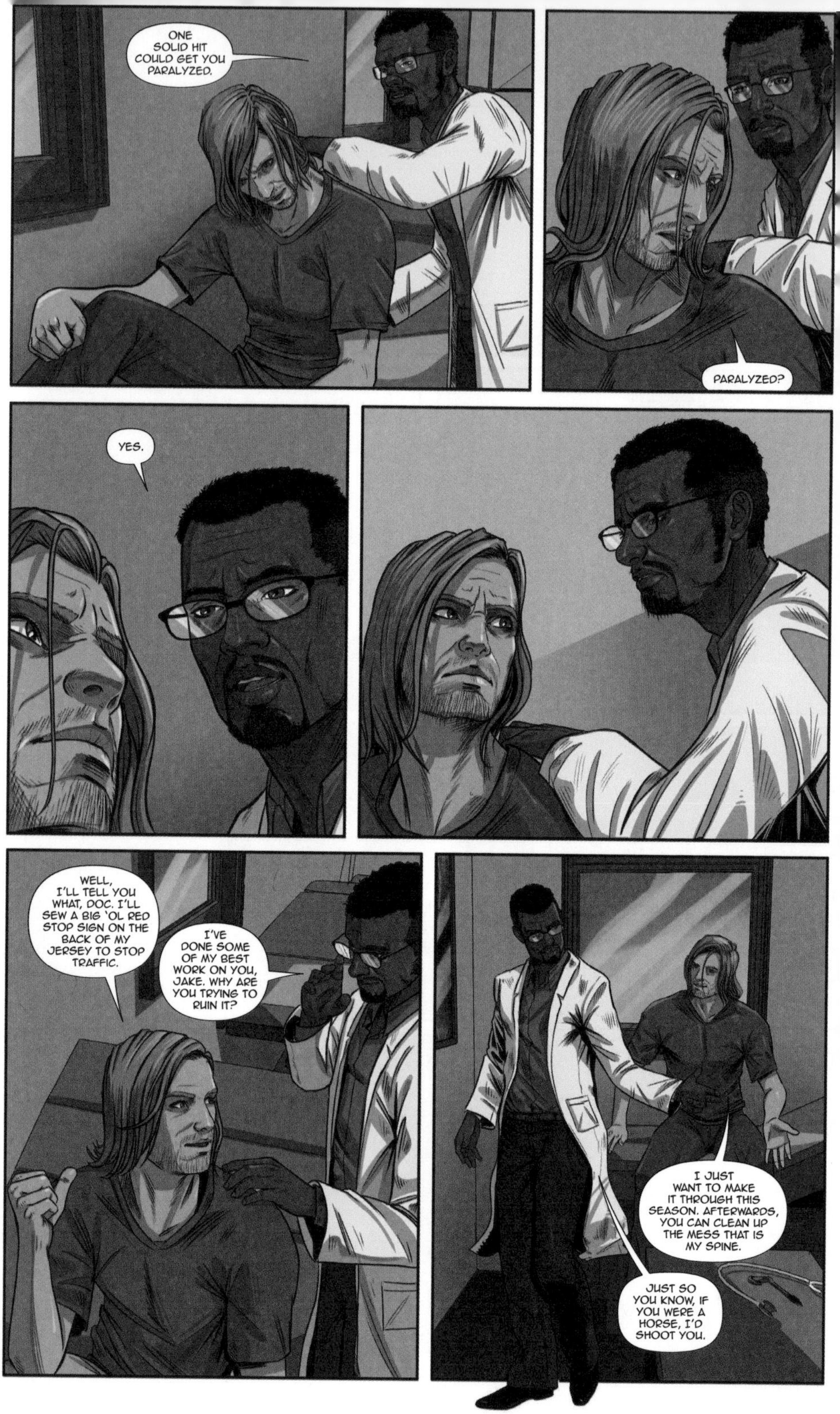

ONE SOLID HIT COULD GET YOU PARALYZED.
PARALYZED?
YES.
WELL, I'LL TELL YOU WHAT, DOC. I'LL SEW A BIG 'OL RED STOP SIGN ON THE BACK OF MY JERSEY TO STOP TRAFFIC.
I'VE DONE SOME OF MY BEST WORK ON YOU, JAKE. WHY ARE YOU TRYING TO RUIN IT?
I JUST WANT TO MAKE IT THROUGH THIS SEASON. AFTERWARDS, YOU CAN CLEAN UP THE MESS THAT IS MY SPINE.
JUST SO YOU KNOW, IF YOU WERE A HORSE, I'D SHOOT YOU.

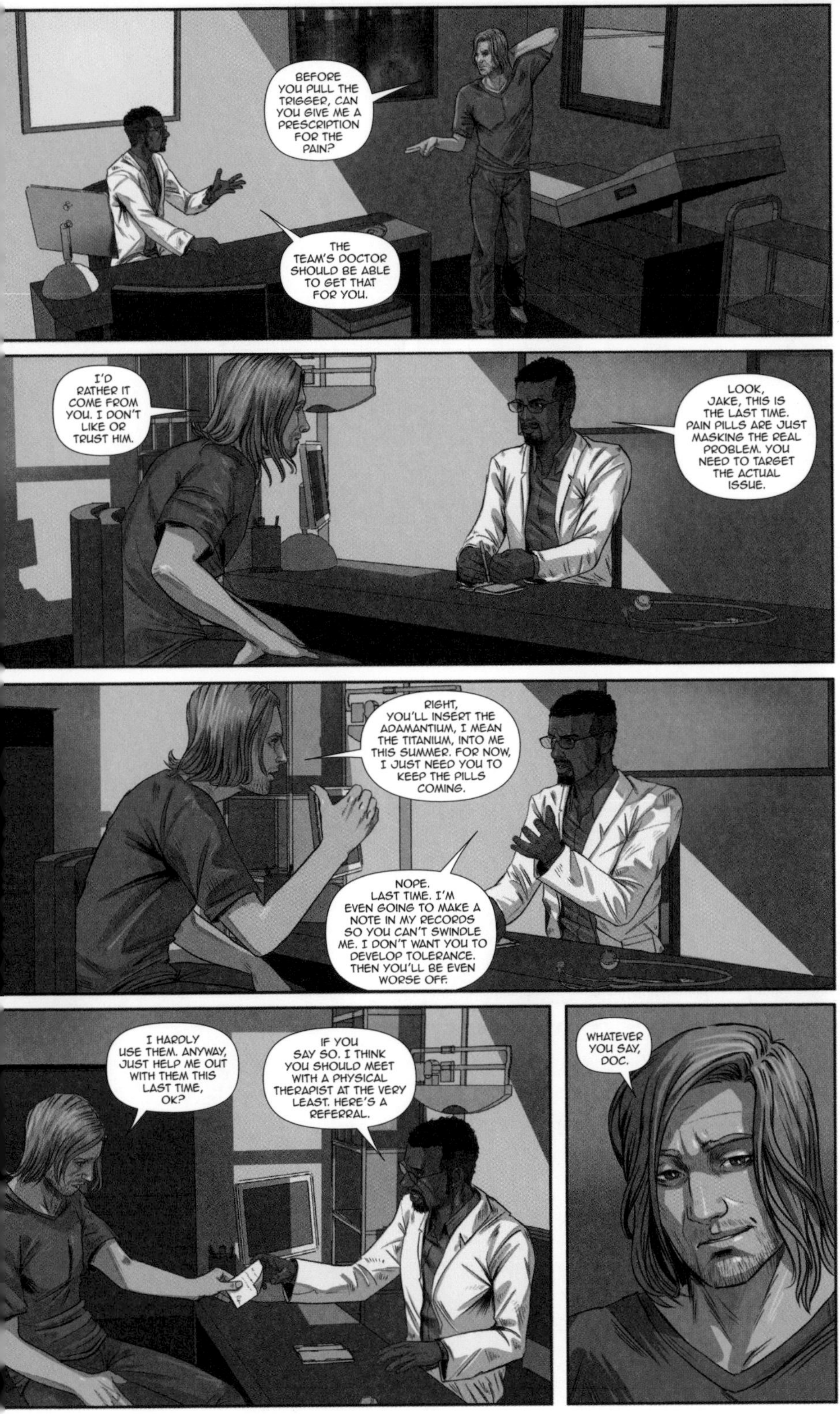
BEFORE YOU PULL THE TRIGGER, CAN YOU GIVE ME A PRESCRIPTION FOR THE PAIN?
THE TEAM'S DOCTOR SHOULD BE ABLE TO GET THAT FOR YOU.
I'D RATHER IT COME FROM YOU. I DON'T LIKE OR TRUST HIM.
LOOK, JAKE, THIS IS THE LAST TIME. PAIN PILLS ARE JUST MASKING THE REAL PROBLEM. YOU NEED TO TARGET THE ACTUAL ISSUE.
RIGHT, YOU'LL INSERT THE ADAMANTIUM, I MEAN THE TITANIUM, INTO ME THIS SUMMER. FOR NOW, I JUST NEED YOU TO KEEP THE PILLS COMING.
NOPE. LAST TIME. I'M EVEN GOING TO MAKE A NOTE IN MY RECORDS SO YOU CAN'T SWINDLE ME. I DON'T WANT YOU TO DEVELOP TOLERANCE. THEN YOU'LL BE EVEN WORSE OFF.
I HARDLY USE THEM. ANYWAY, JUST HELP ME OUT WITH THEM THIS LAST TIME, OK?
IF YOU SAY SO. I THINK YOU SHOULD MEET WITH A PHYSICAL THERAPIST AT THE VERY LEAST. HERE'S A REFERRAL.
WHATEVER YOU SAY, DOC.

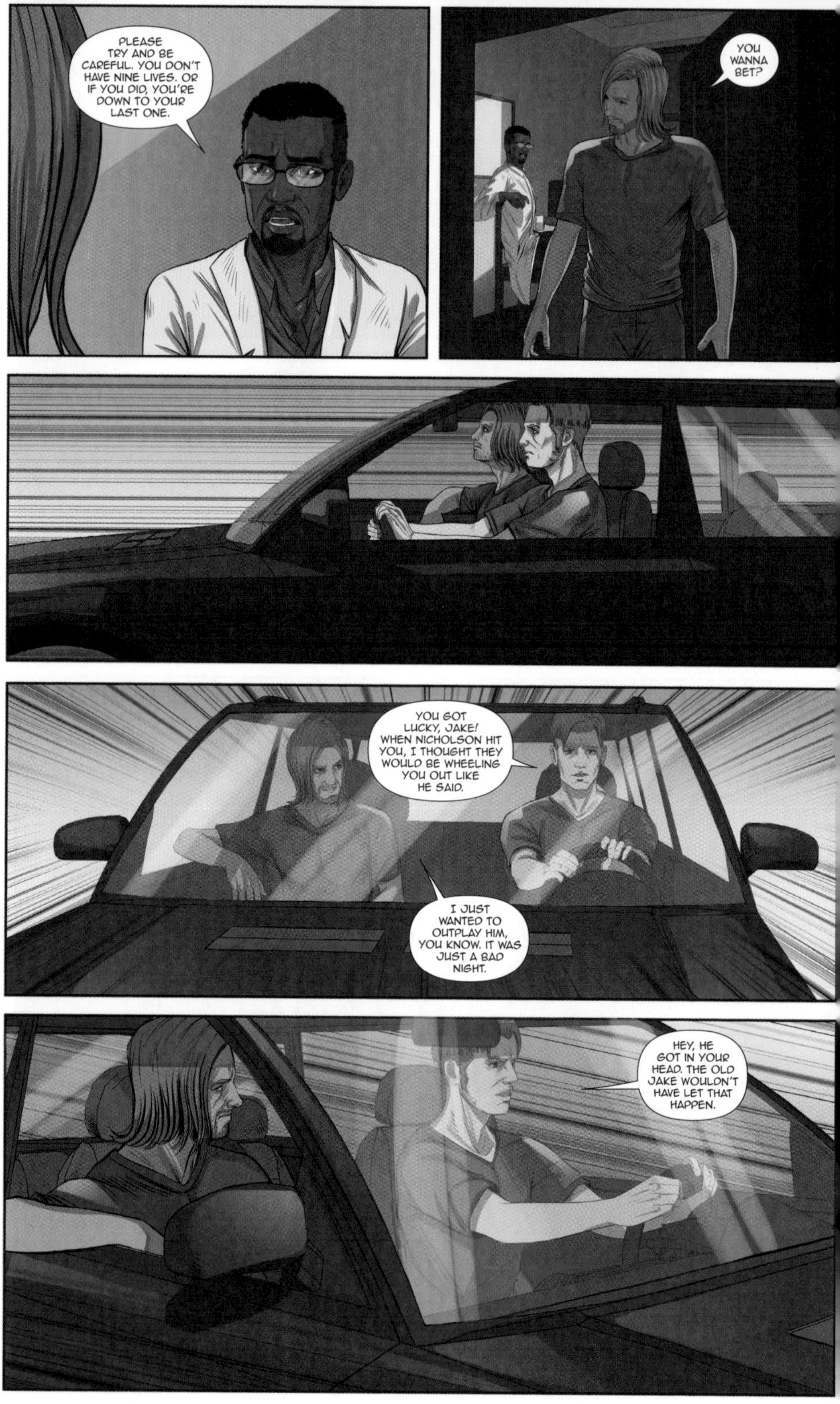
PLEASE TRY AND BE CAREFUL. YOU DON'T HAVE NINE LIVES. OR IF YOU DID, YOU'RE DOWN TO YOUR LAST ONE.
YOU WANNA BET?
YOU GOT LUCKY, JAKE! WHEN NICHOLSON HIT YOU, I THOUGHT THEY WOULD BE WHEELING YOU OUT LIKE HE SAID.
I JUST WANTED TO OUTPLAY HIM, YOU KNOW. IT WAS JUST A BAD NIGHT.
HEY, HE GOT IN YOUR HEAD. THE OLD JAKE WOULDN'T HAVE LET THAT HAPPEN.

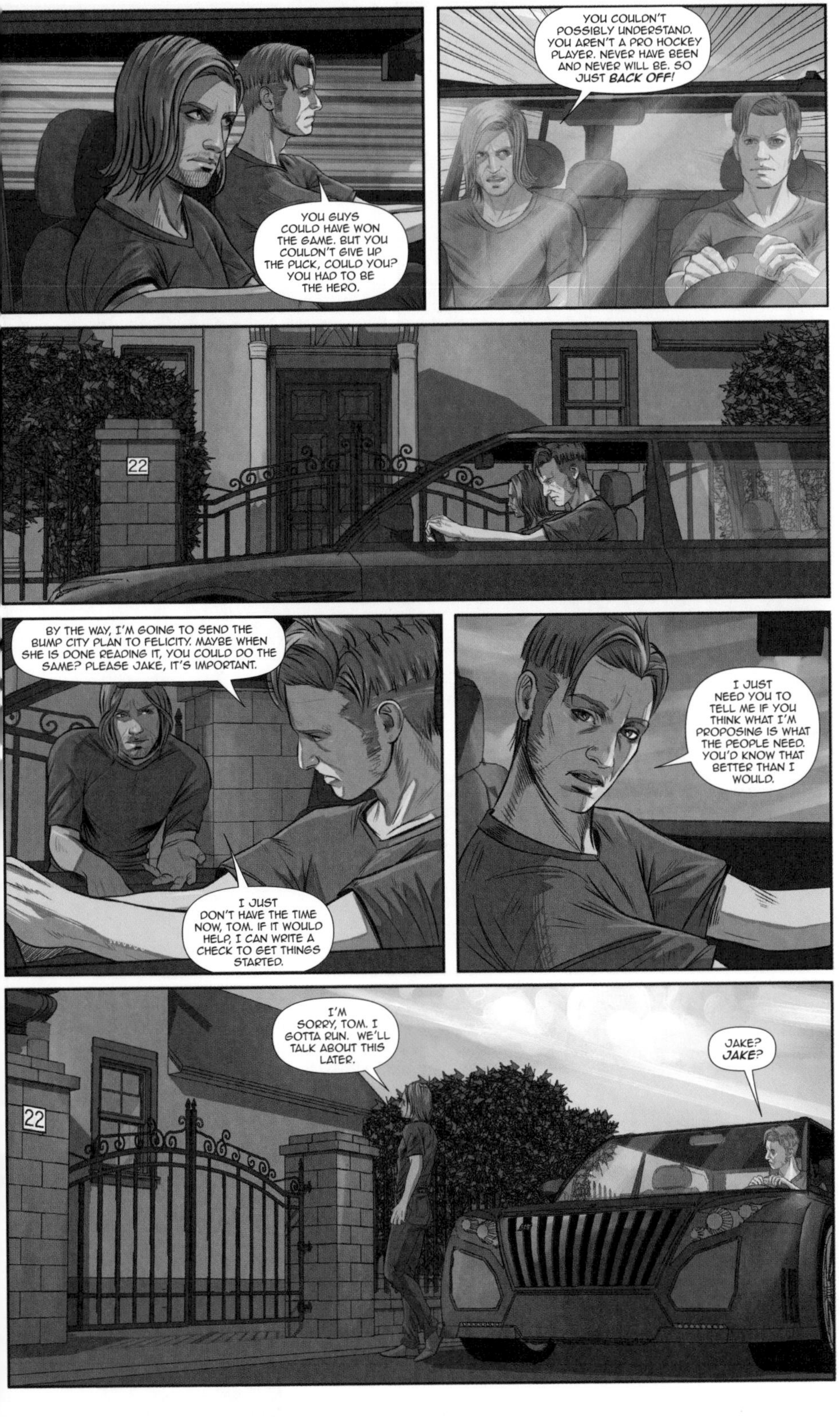
YOU GUYS COULD HAVE WON THE GAME. BUT YOU COULDN'T GIVE UP THE PUCK, COULD YOU? YOU HAD TO BE THE HERO.
YOU COULDN'T POSSIBLY UNDERSTAND. YOU AREN'T A PRO HOCKEY PLAYER. NEVER HAVE BEEN AND NEVER WILL BE. SO JUST BACK OFF!
22
BY THE WAY, I'M GOING TO SEND THE BUMP CITY PLAN TO FELICITY. MAYBE WHEN SHE IS DONE READING IT, YOU COULD DO THE SAME? PLEASE JAKE, IT'S IMPORTANT.
I JUST DON'T HAVE THE TIME NOW, TOM. IF IT WOULD HELP, I CAN WRITE A CHECK TO GET THINGS STARTED.
I JUST NEED YOU TO TELL ME IF YOU THINK WHAT I'M PROPOSING IS WHAT THE PEOPLE NEED. YOU'D KNOW THAT BETTER THAN I WOULD.
I'M SORRY, TOM. I GOTTA RUN. WE'LL TALK ABOUT THIS LATER.
JAKE? JAKE?
22

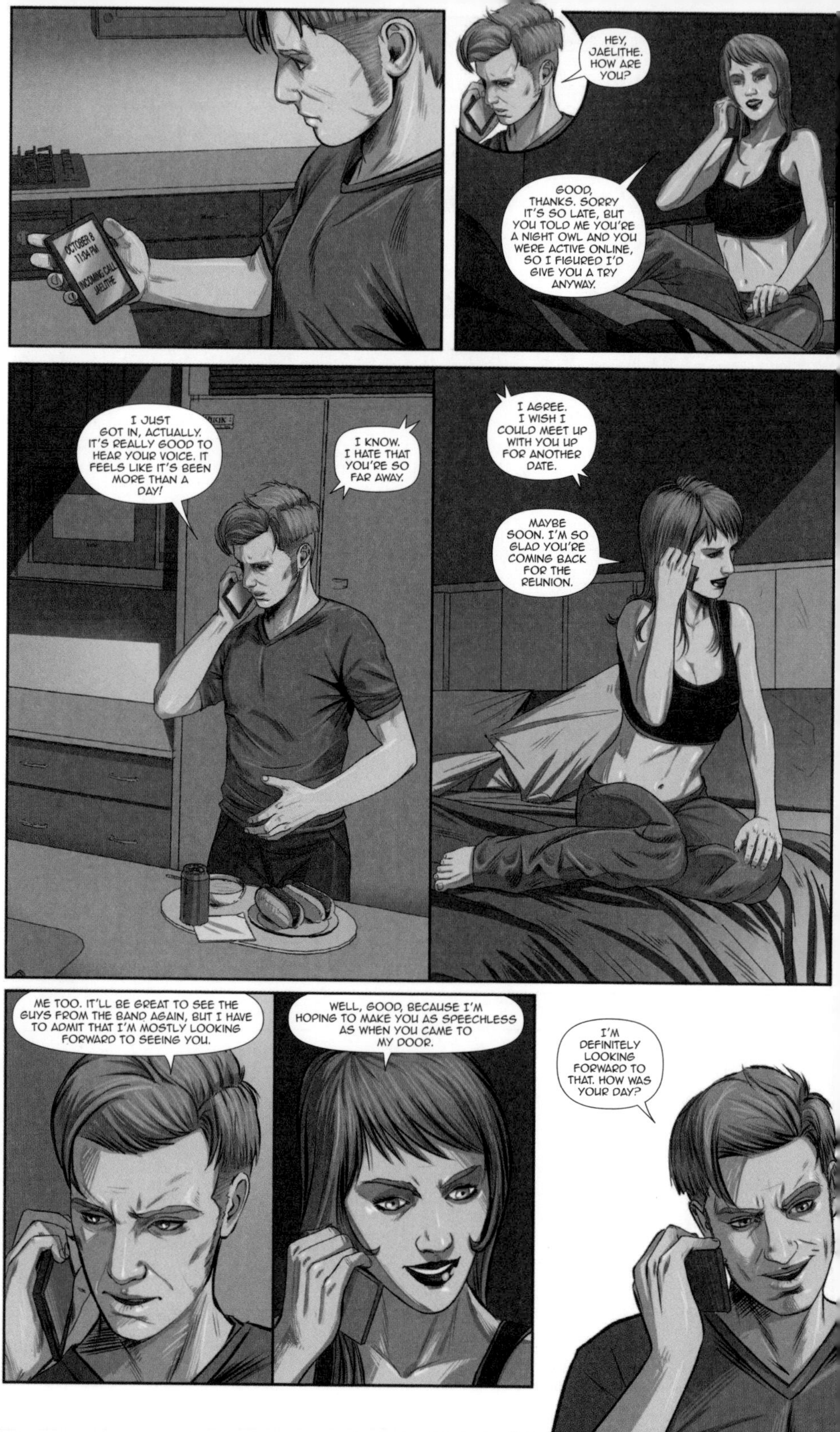
OCTOBER 8 11:04 PM INCOMING CALL JAELITHE
HEY, JAELITHE. HOW ARE YOU?
GOOD, THANKS. SORRY IT'S SO LATE, BUT YOU TOLD ME YOU'RE A NIGHT OWL AND YOU WERE ACTIVE ONLINE, SO I FIGURED I'D GIVE YOU A TRY ANYWAY.
I JUST GOT IN, ACTUALLY. IT'S REALLY GOOD TO HEAR YOUR VOICE. IT FEELS LIKE IT'S BEEN MORE THAN A DAY!
I KNOW. I HATE THAT YOU'RE SO FAR AWAY.
I AGREE. I WISH I COULD MEET UP WITH YOU UP FOR ANOTHER DATE.
MAYBE SOON. I'M SO GLAD YOU'RE COMING BACK FOR THE REUNION.
ME TOO. IT'LL BE GREAT TO SEE THE GUYS FROM THE BAND AGAIN, BUT I HAVE TO ADMIT THAT I'M MOSTLY LOOKING FORWARD TO SEEING YOU.
WELL, GOOD, BECAUSE I'M HOPING TO MAKE YOU AS SPEECHLESS AS WHEN YOU CAME TO MY DOOR.
I'M DEFINITELY LOOKING FORWARD TO THAT. HOW WAS YOUR DAY?

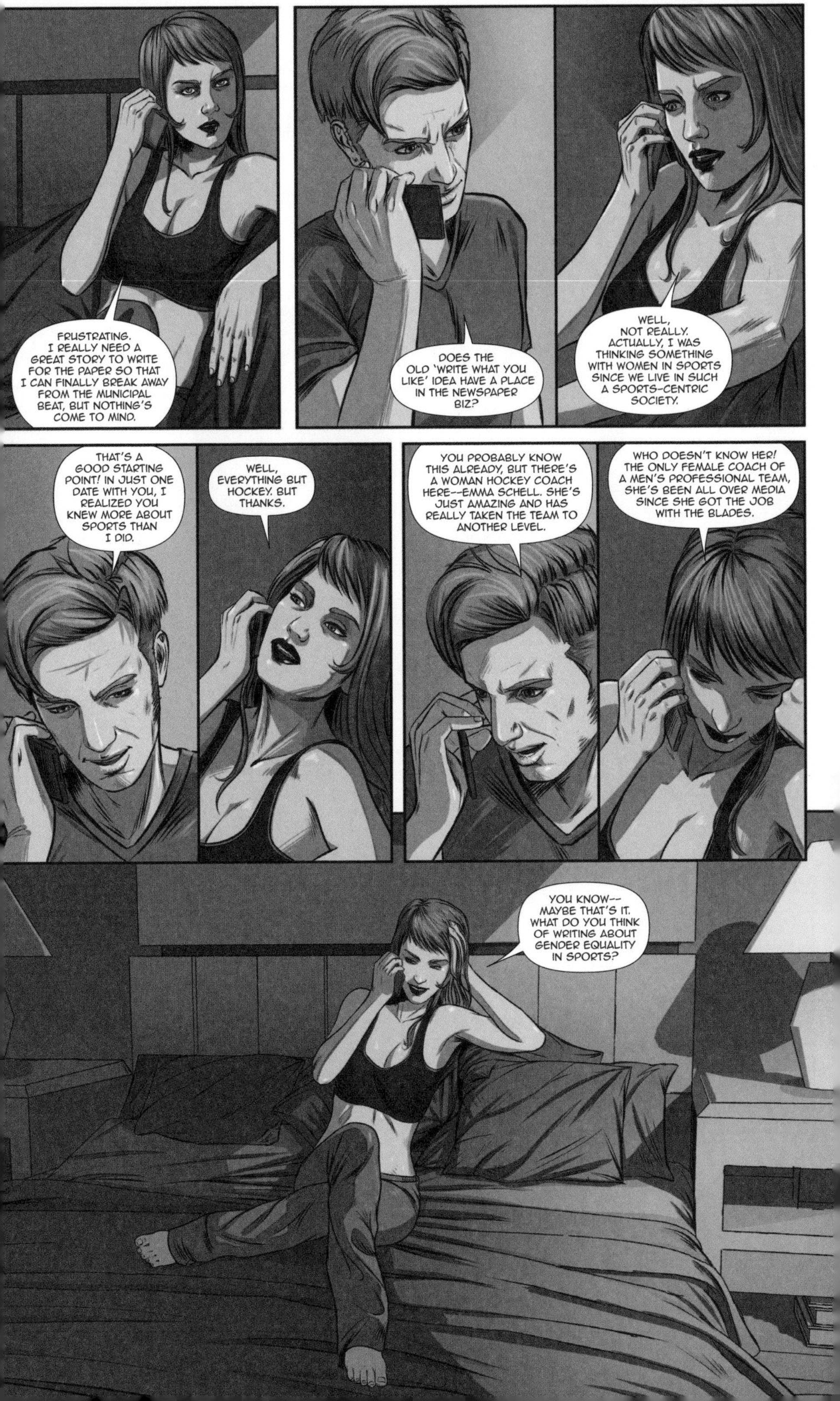
FRUSTRATING. I REALLY NEED A GREAT STORY TO WRITE FOR THE PAPER SO THAT I CAN FINALLY BREAK AWAY FROM THE MUNICIPAL BEAT, BUT NOTHING'S COME TO MIND.
DOES THE OLD 'WRITE WHAT YOU LIKE' IDEA HAVE A PLACE IN THE NEWSPAPER BIZ?
WELL, NOT REALLY. ACTUALLY, I WAS THINKING SOMETHING WITH WOMEN IN SPORTS SINCE WE LIVE IN SUCH A SPORTS-CENTRIC SOCIETY.
THAT'S A GOOD STARTING POINT! IN JUST ONE DATE WITH YOU, I REALIZED YOU KNEW MORE ABOUT SPORTS THAN I DID.
WELL, EVERYTHING BUT HOCKEY. BUT THANKS.
YOU PROBABLY KNOW THIS ALREADY, BUT THERE'S A WOMAN HOCKEY COACH HERE--EMMA SCHELL. SHE'S JUST AMAZING AND HAS REALLY TAKEN THE TEAM TO ANOTHER LEVEL.
WHO DOESN'T KNOW HER! THE ONLY FEMALE COACH OF A MEN'S PROFESSIONAL TEAM, SHE'S BEEN ALL OVER MEDIA SINCE SHE GOT THE JOB WITH THE BLADES.
YOU KNOW-- MAYBE THAT'S IT. WHAT DO YOU THINK OF WRITING ABOUT GENDER EQUALITY IN SPORTS?

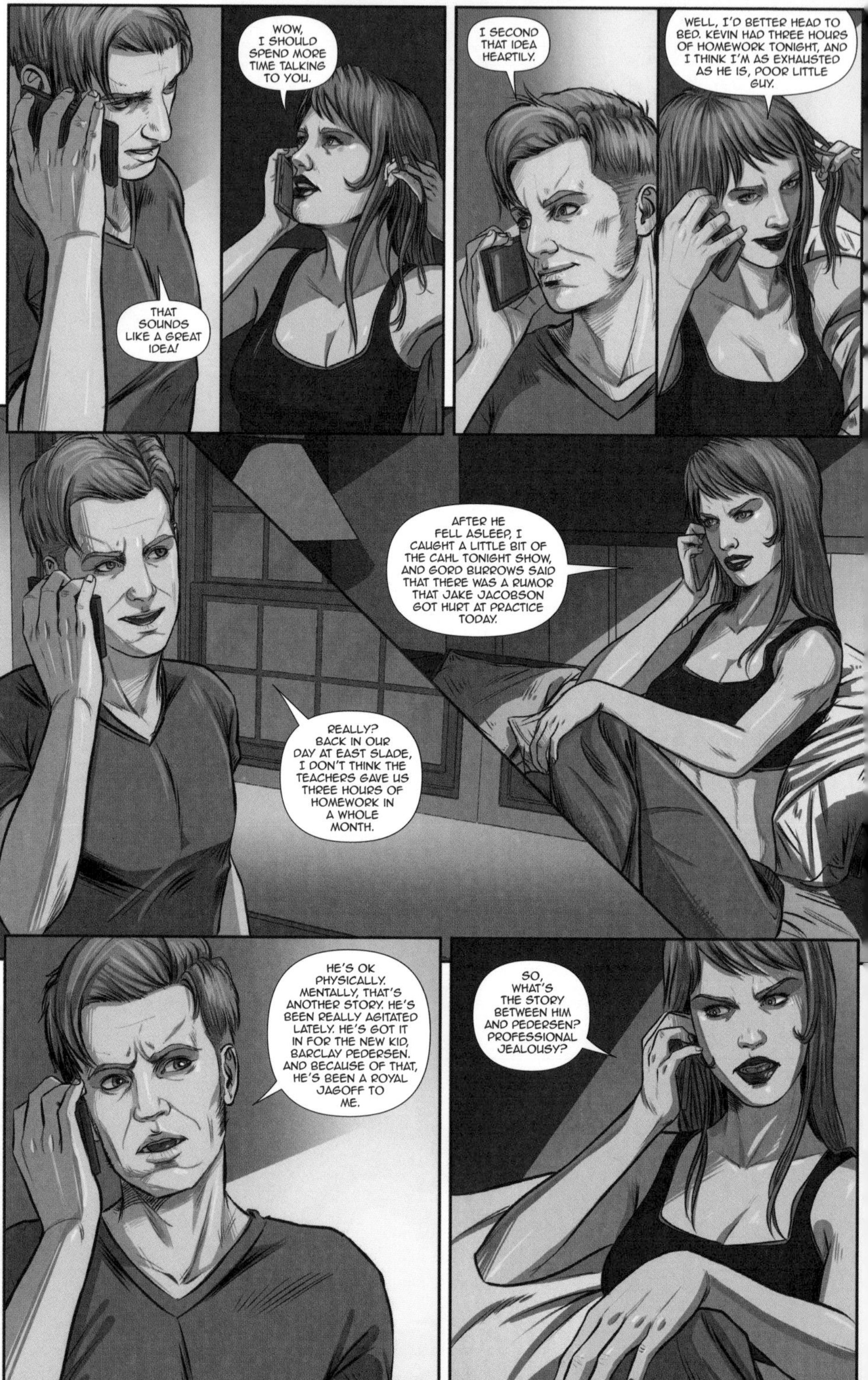
WOW, I SHOULD SPEND MORE TIME TALKING TO YOU.
THAT SOUNDS LIKE A GREAT IDEA!
I SECOND THAT IDEA HEARTILY.
WELL, I'D BETTER HEAD TO BED. KEVIN HAD THREE HOURS OF HOMEWORK TONIGHT, AND I THINK I'M AS EXHAUSTED AS HE IS, POOR LITTLE GUY.
REALLY? BACK IN OUR DAY AT EAST SLADE, I DON'T THINK THE TEACHERS GAVE US THREE HOURS OF HOMEWORK IN A WHOLE MONTH.
AFTER HE FELL ASLEEP, I CAUGHT A LITTLE BIT OF THE CAHL TONIGHT SHOW, AND GORD BURROWS SAID THAT THERE WAS A RUMOR THAT JAKE JACOBSON GOT HURT AT PRACTICE TODAY.
HE'S OK PHYSICALLY. MENTALLY, THAT'S ANOTHER STORY. HE'S BEEN REALLY AGITATED LATELY. HE'S GOT IT IN FOR THE NEW KID, BARCLAY PEDERSEN. AND BECAUSE OF THAT, HE'S BEEN A ROYAL JAGOFF TO ME.
SO, WHAT'S THE STORY BETWEEN HIM AND PEDERSEN? PROFESSIONAL JEALOUSY?

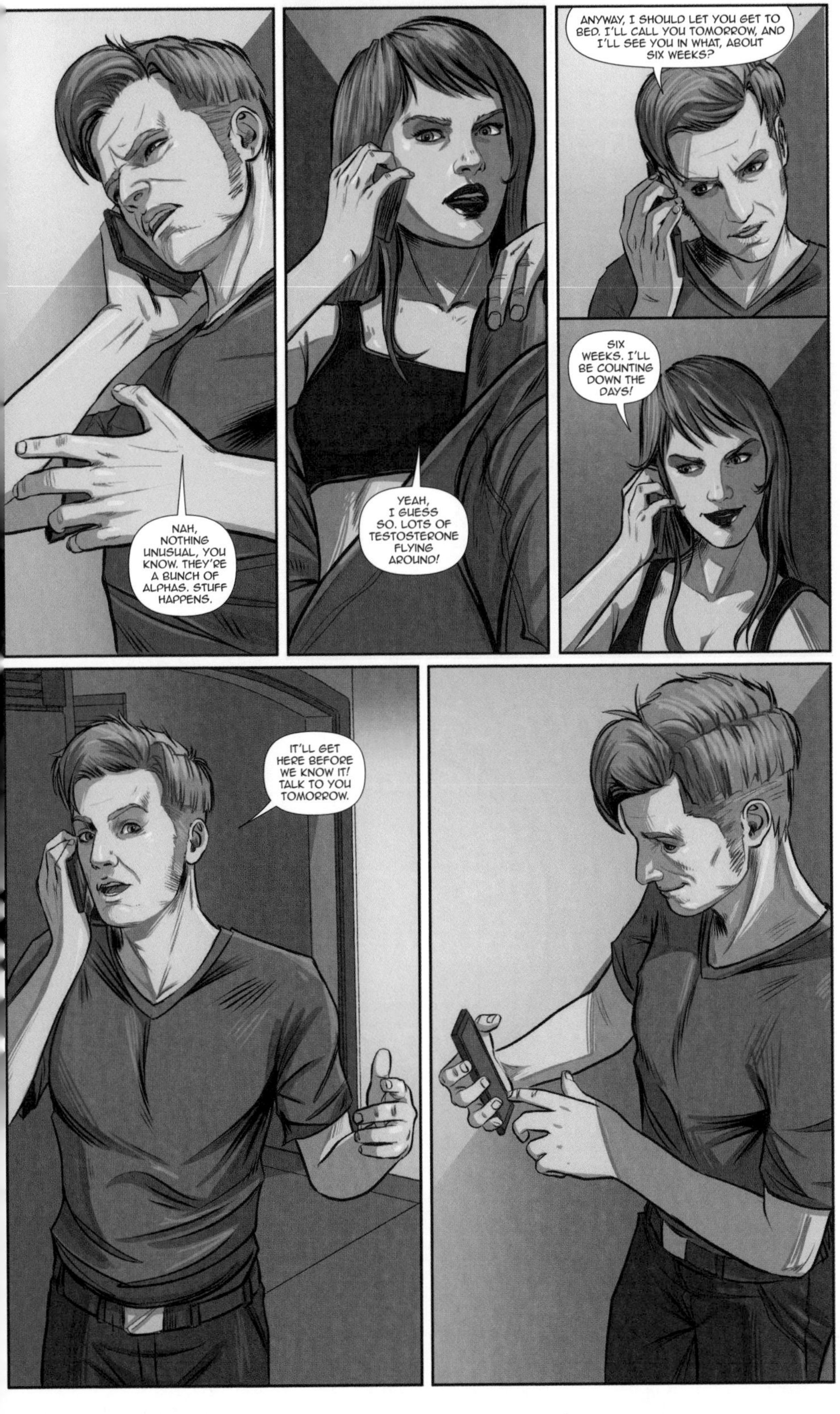
NAH, NOTHING UNUSUAL, YOU KNOW. THEY'RE A BUNCH OF ALPHAS. STUFF HAPPENS.
YEAH, I GUESS SO. LOTS OF TESTOSTERONE FLYING AROUND!
ANYWAY, I SHOULD LET YOU GET TO BED. I'LL CALL YOU TOMORROW, AND I'LL SEE YOU IN WHAT, ABOUT SIX WEEKS?
SIX WEEKS. I'LL BE COUNTING DOWN THE DAYS!
IT'LL GET HERE BEFORE WE KNOW IT! TALK TO YOU TOMORROW.

CHAPTER 5
LIVING WITH SHAME

RECOMMENDED LISTENING:

"EVEN HERE WE ARE"
PAUL WESTERBERG

"TIME WAITS FOR NO ONE"
THE ROLLING STONES

"YOU AND I WILL MEET AGAIN"
TOM PETTY AND THE HEARTBREAKERS

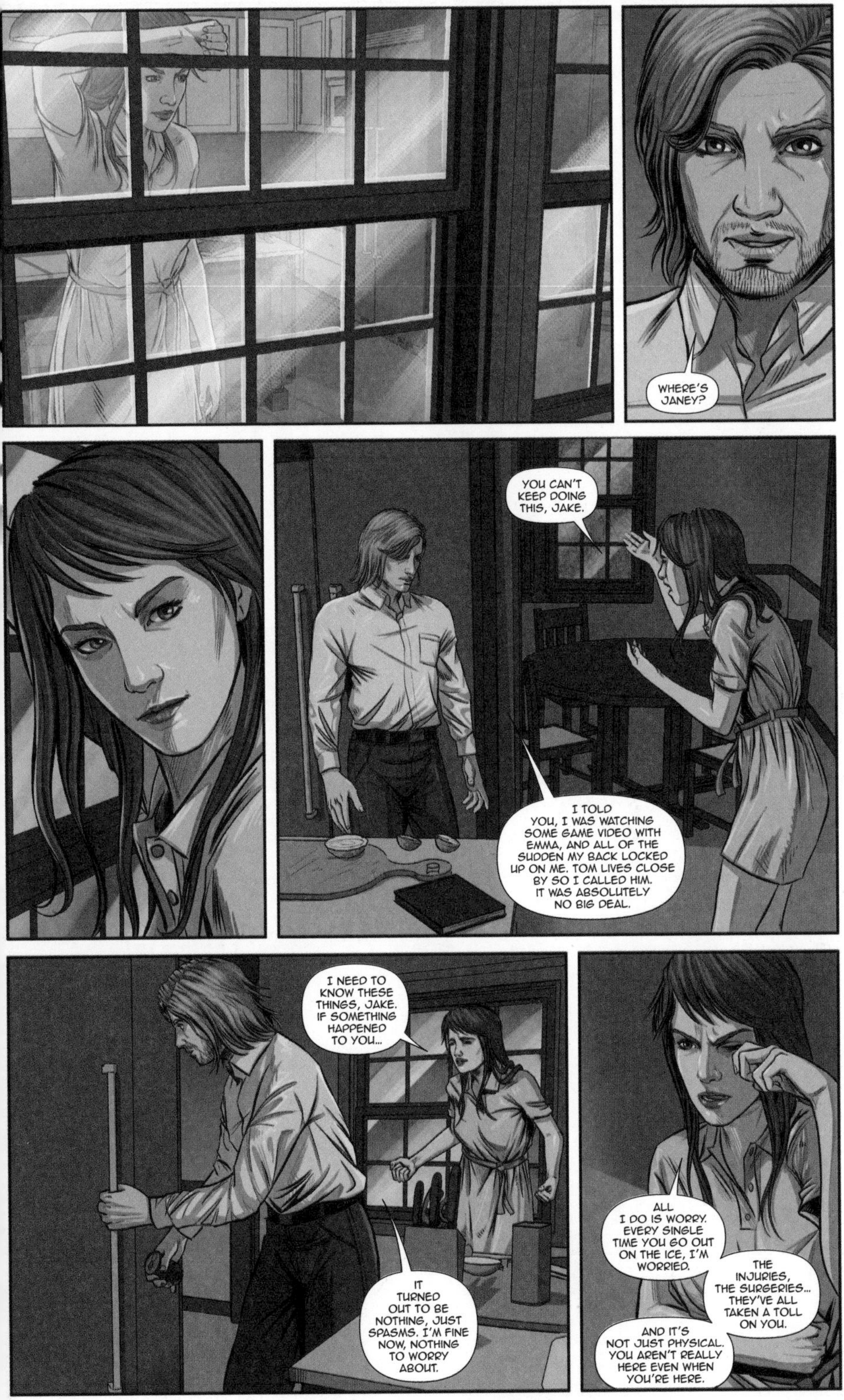
WHERE'S JANEY?
YOU CAN'T KEEP DOING THIS, JAKE.
I TOLD YOU, I WAS WATCHING SOME GAME VIDEO WITH EMMA, AND ALL OF THE SUDDEN MY BACK LOCKED UP ON ME. TOM LIVES CLOSE BY SO I CALLED HIM. IT WAS ABSOLUTELY NO BIG DEAL.
I NEED TO KNOW THESE THINGS, JAKE. IF SOMETHING HAPPENED TO YOU...
IT TURNED OUT TO BE NOTHING, JUST SPASMS. I'M FINE NOW, NOTHING TO WORRY ABOUT.
ALL I DO IS WORRY. EVERY SINGLE TIME YOU GO OUT ON THE ICE, I'M WORRIED.
THE INJURIES, THE SURGERIES... THEY'VE ALL TAKEN A TOLL ON YOU.
AND IT'S NOT JUST PHYSICAL. YOU AREN'T REALLY HERE EVEN WHEN YOU'RE HERE.

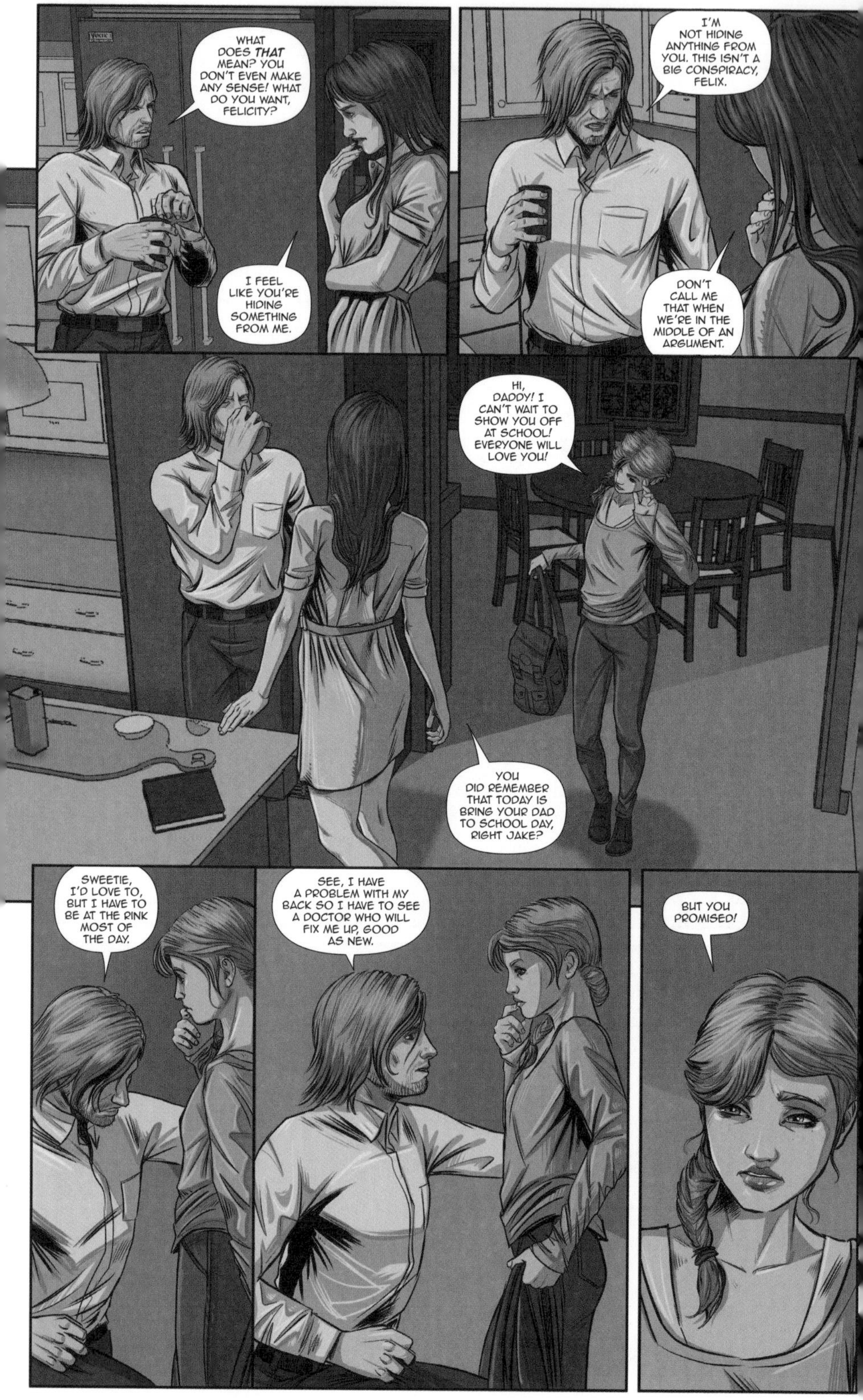
WHAT DOES *THAT* MEAN? YOU DON'T EVEN MAKE ANY SENSE! WHAT DO YOU WANT, FELICITY?
I FEEL LIKE YOU'RE HIDING SOMETHING FROM ME.
I'M NOT HIDING ANYTHING FROM YOU. THIS ISN'T A BIG CONSPIRACY, FELIX.
DON'T CALL ME THAT WHEN WE'RE IN THE MIDDLE OF AN ARGUMENT.
HI, DADDY! I CAN'T WAIT TO SHOW YOU OFF AT SCHOOL! EVERYONE WILL LOVE YOU!
YOU DID REMEMBER THAT TODAY IS BRING YOUR DAD TO SCHOOL DAY, RIGHT JAKE?
SWEETIE, I'D LOVE TO, BUT I HAVE TO BE AT THE RINK MOST OF THE DAY.
SEE, I HAVE A PROBLEM WITH MY BACK SO I HAVE TO SEE A DOCTOR WHO WILL FIX ME UP, GOOD AS NEW.
BUT YOU PROMISED!

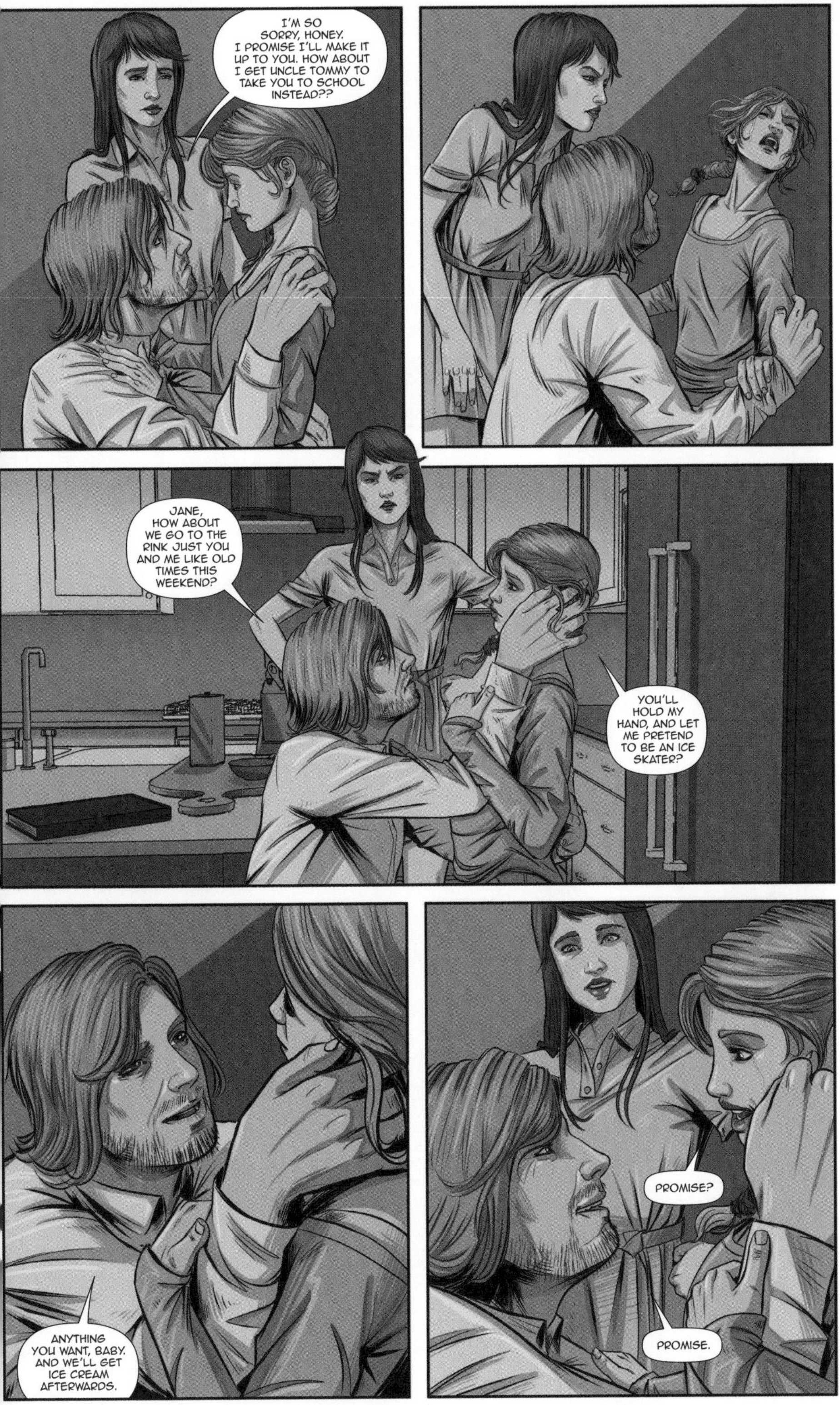
I'M SO SORRY, HONEY. I PROMISE I'LL MAKE IT UP TO YOU. HOW ABOUT I GET UNCLE TOMMY TO TAKE YOU TO SCHOOL INSTEAD??
JANE, HOW ABOUT WE GO TO THE RINK JUST YOU AND ME LIKE OLD TIMES THIS WEEKEND?
YOU'LL HOLD MY HAND, AND LET ME PRETEND TO BE AN ICE SKATER?
ANYTHING YOU WANT, BABY. AND WE'LL GET ICE CREAM AFTERWARDS.
PROMISE?
PROMISE.

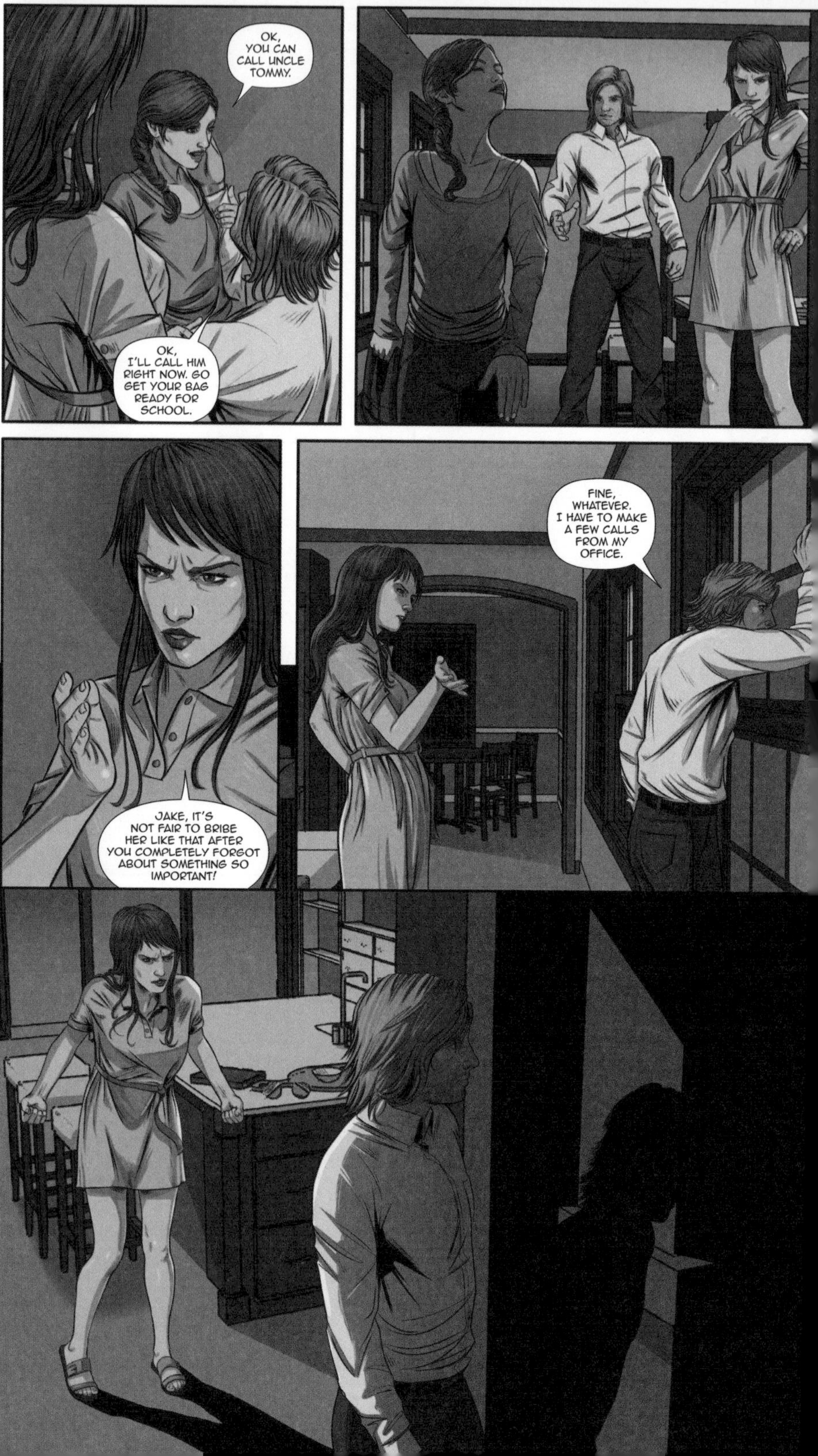
OK, YOU CAN CALL UNCLE TOMMY.
OK, I'LL CALL HIM RIGHT NOW. GO GET YOUR BAG READY FOR SCHOOL.
JAKE, IT'S NOT FAIR TO BRIBE HER LIKE THAT AFTER YOU COMPLETELY FORGOT ABOUT SOMETHING SO IMPORTANT!
FINE, WHATEVER. I HAVE TO MAKE A FEW CALLS FROM MY OFFICE.

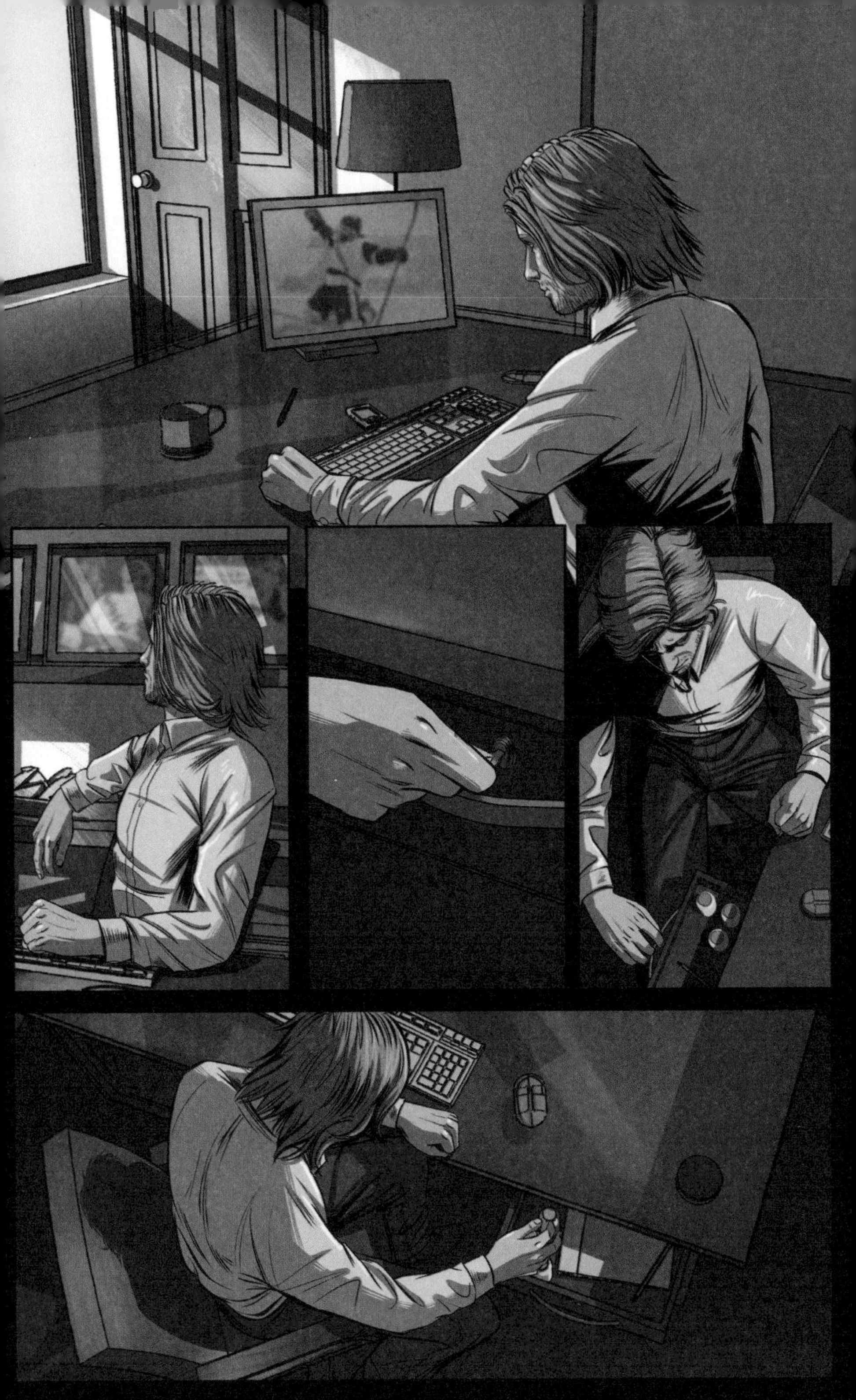

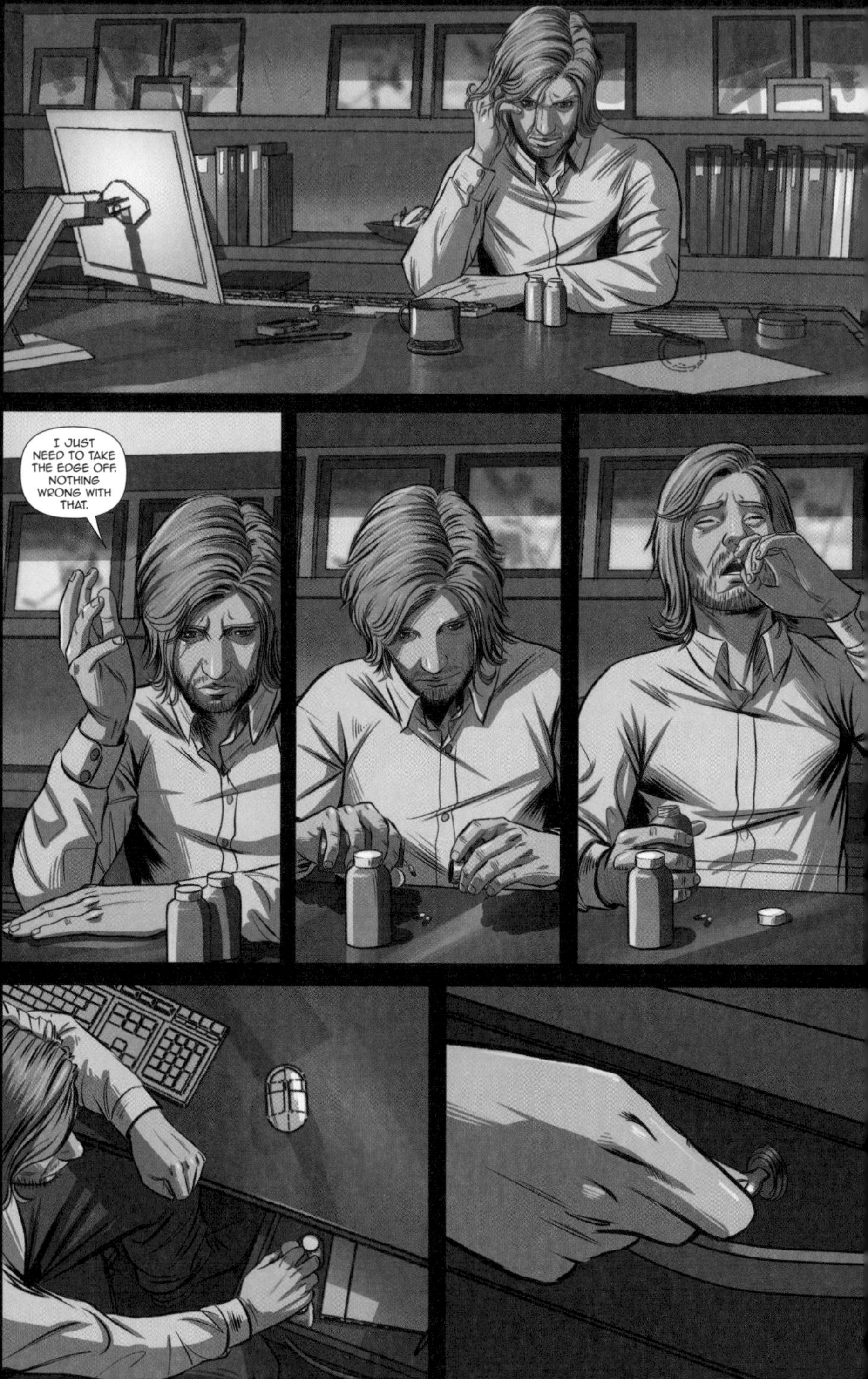
I JUST NEED TO TAKE THE EDGE OFF. NOTHING WRONG WITH THAT.

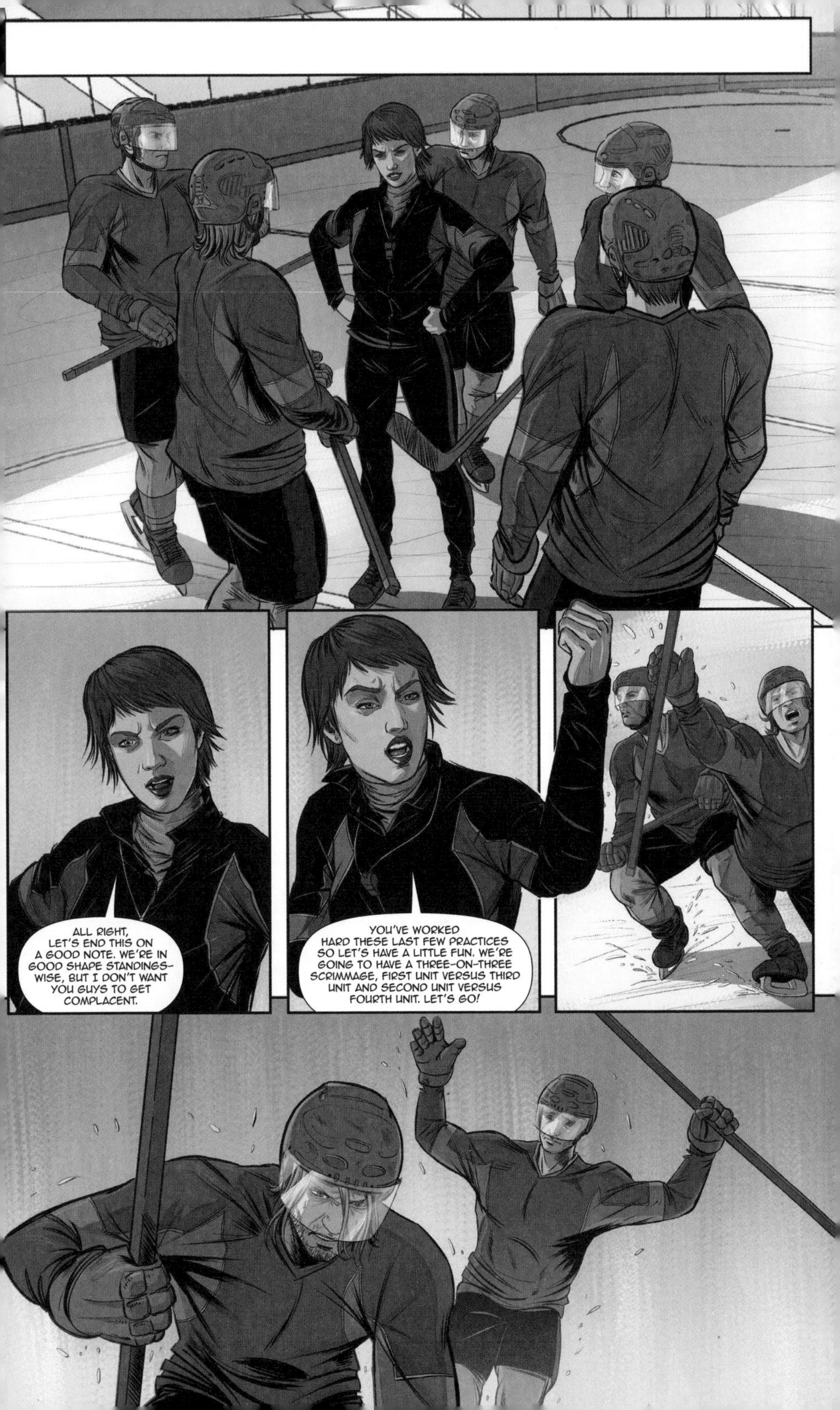
ALL RIGHT, LET'S END THIS ON A GOOD NOTE. WE'RE IN GOOD SHAPE STANDINGS-WISE, BUT I DON'T WANT YOU GUYS TO GET COMPLACENT.
YOU'VE WORKED HARD THESE LAST FEW PRACTICES SO LET'S HAVE A LITTLE FUN. WE'RE GOING TO HAVE A THREE-ON-THREE SCRIMMAGE, FIRST UNIT VERSUS THIRD UNIT AND SECOND UNIT VERSUS FOURTH UNIT. LET'S GO!

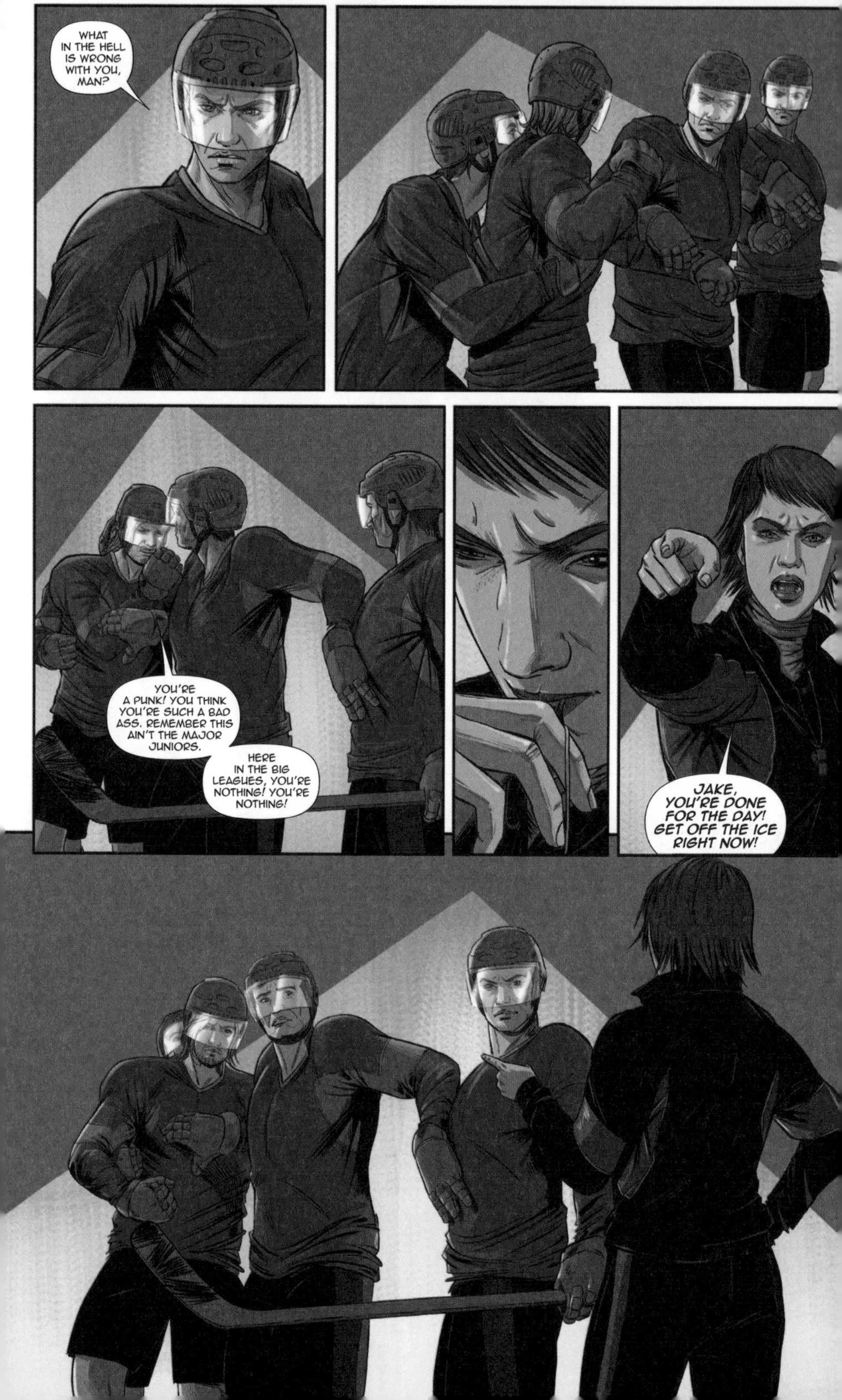
WHAT IN THE HELL IS WRONG WITH YOU, MAN?
YOU'RE A PUNK! YOU THINK YOU'RE SUCH A BAD ASS. REMEMBER THIS AIN'T THE MAJOR JUNIORS.
HERE IN THE BIG LEAGUES, YOU'RE NOTHING! YOU'RE NOTHING!
JAKE, YOU'RE DONE FOR THE DAY! GET OFF THE ICE RIGHT NOW!

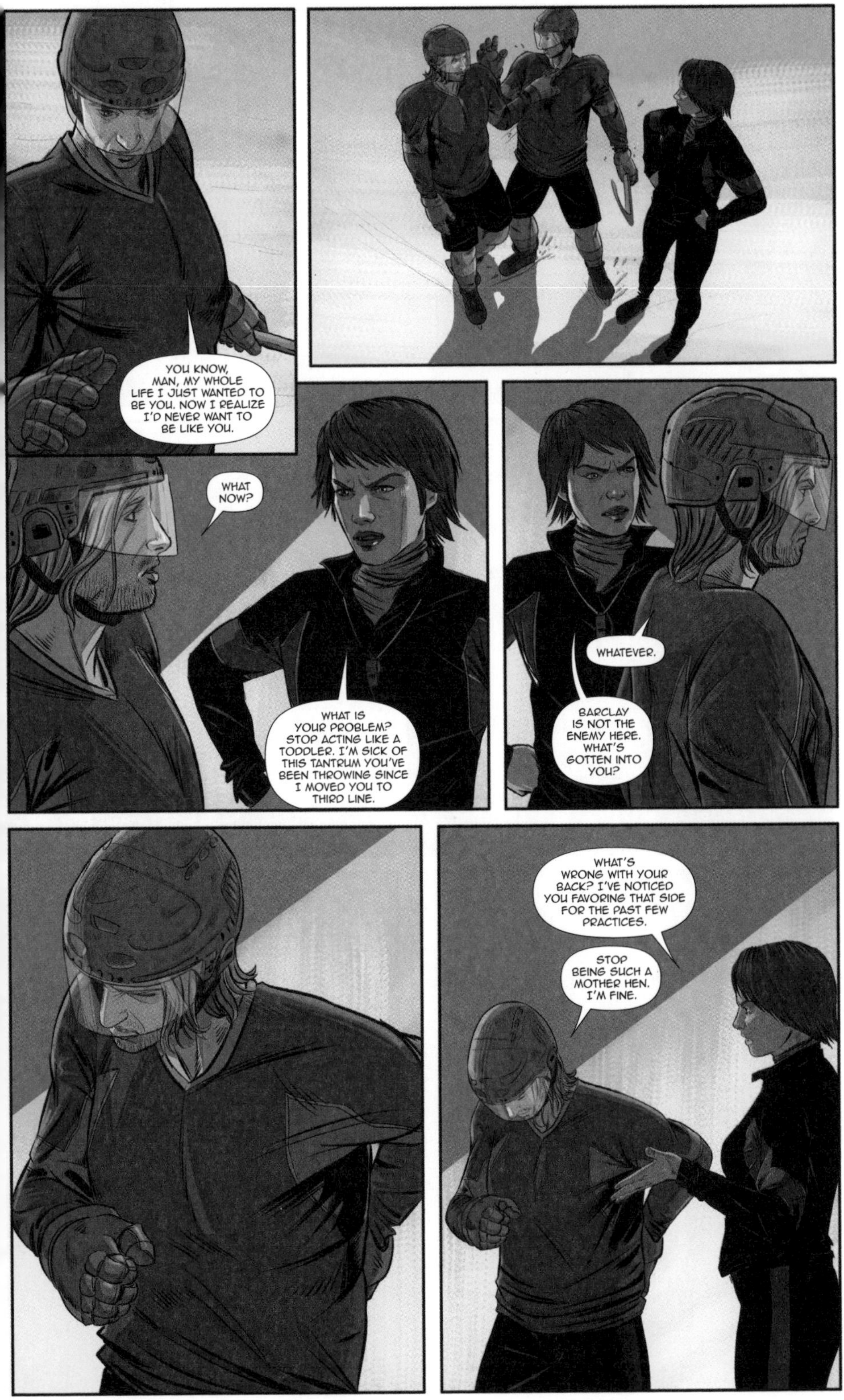
YOU KNOW, MAN, MY WHOLE LIFE I JUST WANTED TO BE YOU. NOW I REALIZE I'D NEVER WANT TO BE LIKE YOU.
WHAT NOW?
WHAT IS YOUR PROBLEM? STOP ACTING LIKE A TODDLER. I'M SICK OF THIS TANTRUM YOU'VE BEEN THROWING SINCE I MOVED YOU TO THIRD LINE.
WHATEVER.
BARCLAY IS NOT THE ENEMY HERE. WHAT'S GOTTEN INTO YOU?
WHAT'S WRONG WITH YOUR BACK? I'VE NOTICED YOU FAVORING THAT SIDE FOR THE PAST FEW PRACTICES.
STOP BEING SUCH A MOTHER HEN. I'M FINE.

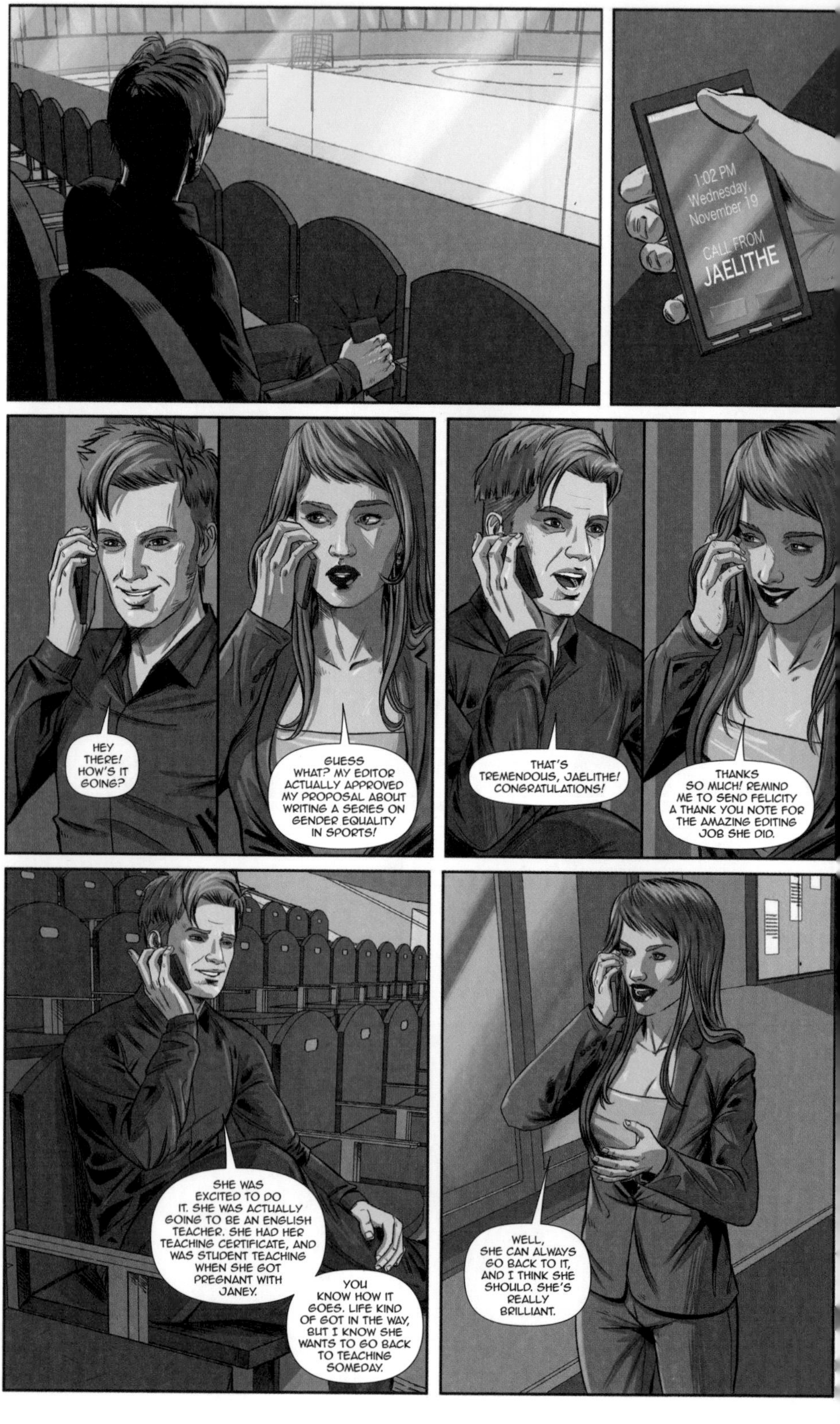
1:02 PM
Wednesday,
November 19
CALL FROM
JAELITHE
HEY THERE! HOW'S IT GOING?
GUESS WHAT? MY EDITOR ACTUALLY APPROVED MY PROPOSAL ABOUT WRITING A SERIES ON GENDER EQUALITY IN SPORTS!
THAT'S TREMENDOUS, JAELITHE! CONGRATULATIONS!
THANKS SO MUCH! REMIND ME TO SEND FELICITY A THANK YOU NOTE FOR THE AMAZING EDITING JOB SHE DID.
SHE WAS EXCITED TO DO IT. SHE WAS ACTUALLY GOING TO BE AN ENGLISH TEACHER. SHE HAD HER TEACHING CERTIFICATE, AND WAS STUDENT TEACHING WHEN SHE GOT PREGNANT WITH JANEY.
YOU KNOW HOW IT GOES. LIFE KIND OF GOT IN THE WAY, BUT I KNOW SHE WANTS TO GO BACK TO TEACHING SOMEDAY.
WELL, SHE CAN ALWAYS GO BACK TO IT, AND I THINK SHE SHOULD. SHE'S REALLY BRILLIANT.

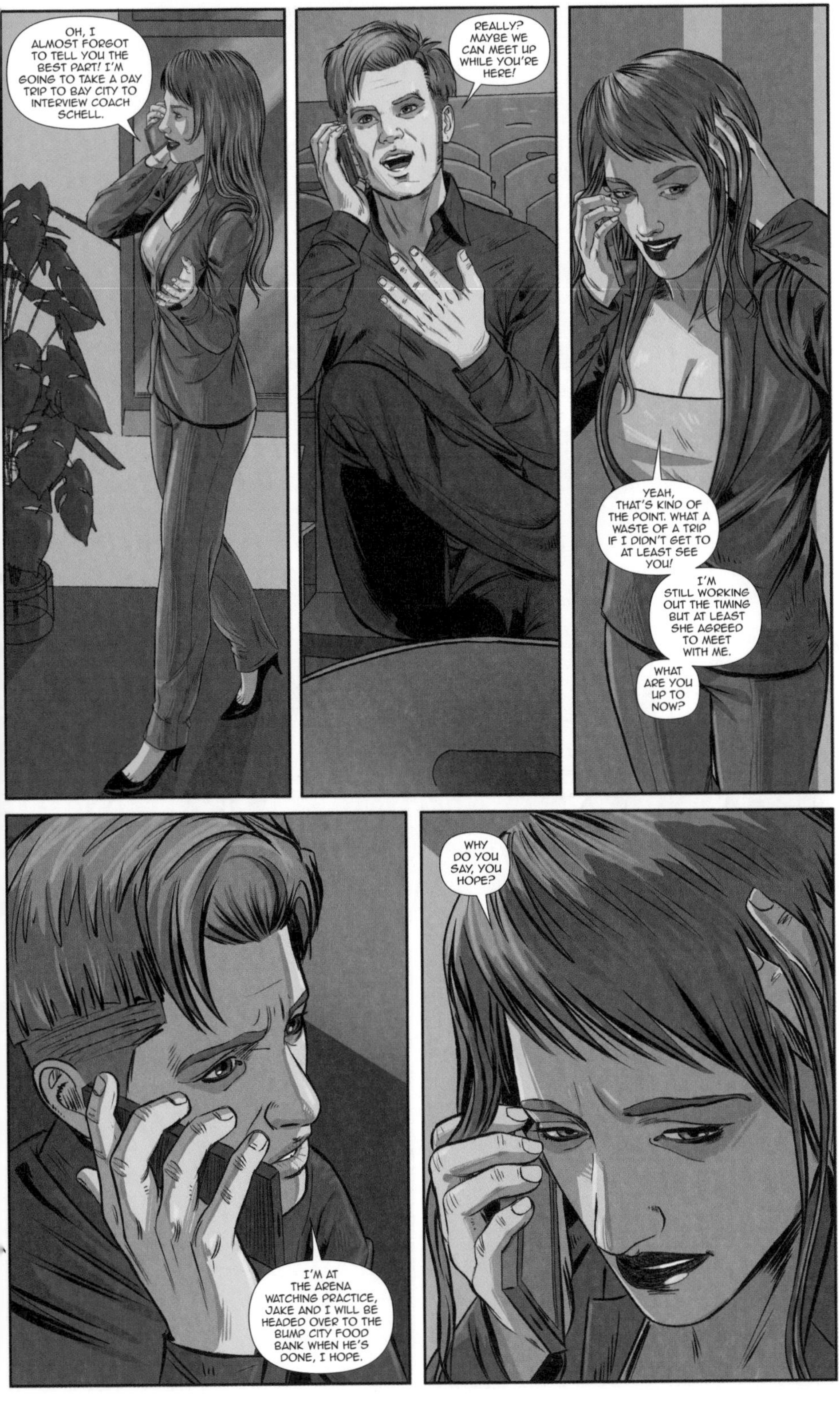
OH, I ALMOST FORGOT TO TELL YOU THE BEST PART! I'M GOING TO TAKE A DAY TRIP TO BAY CITY TO INTERVIEW COACH SCHELL.
REALLY? MAYBE WE CAN MEET UP WHILE YOU'RE HERE!
YEAH, THAT'S KIND OF THE POINT. WHAT A WASTE OF A TRIP IF I DIDN'T GET TO AT LEAST SEE YOU!
I'M STILL WORKING OUT THE TIMING BUT AT LEAST SHE AGREED TO MEET WITH ME.
WHAT ARE YOU UP TO NOW?
I'M AT THE ARENA WATCHING PRACTICE, JAKE AND I WILL BE HEADED OVER TO THE BUMP CITY FOOD BANK WHEN HE'S DONE, I HOPE.
WHY DO YOU SAY, YOU HOPE?

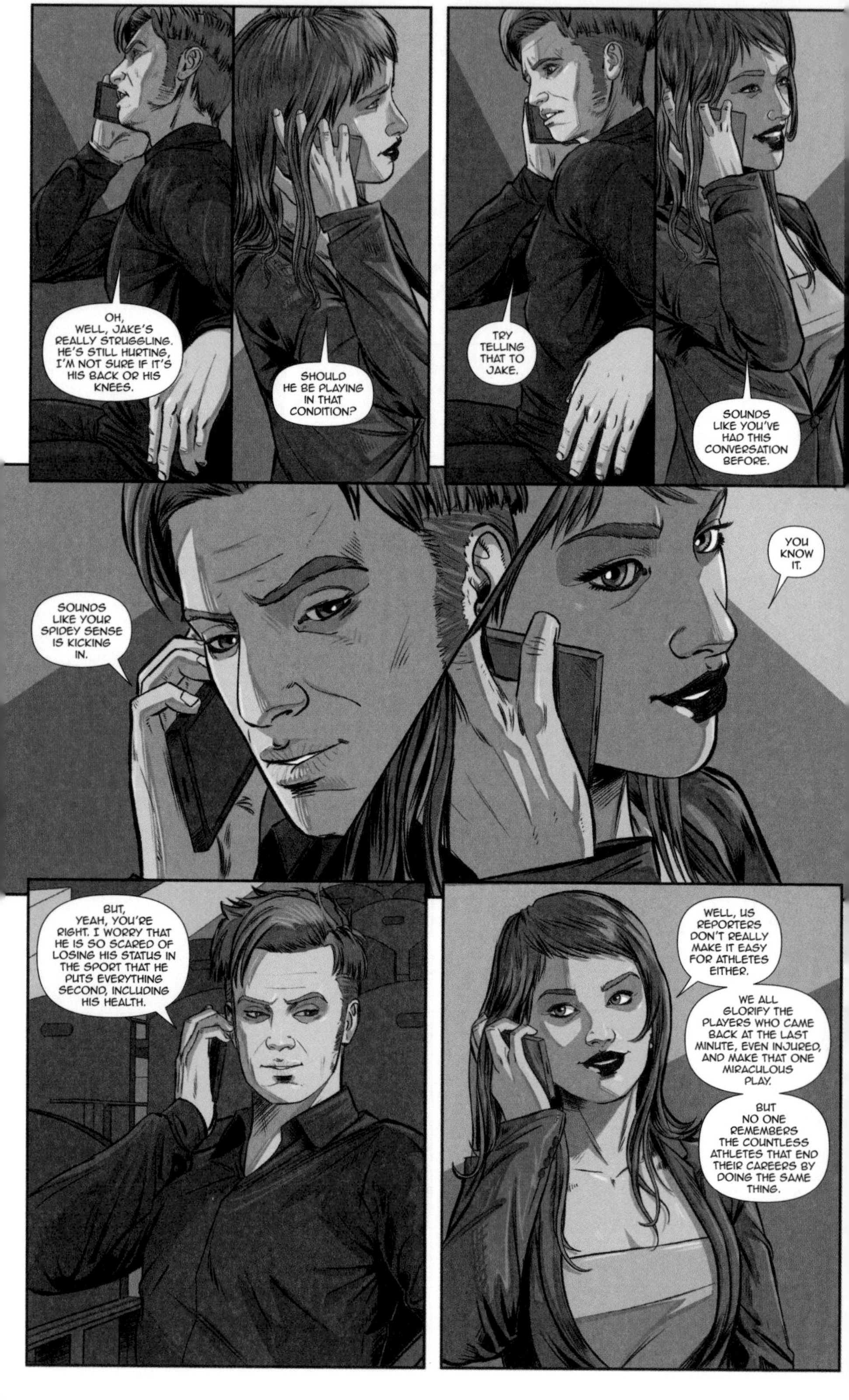
OH, WELL, JAKE'S REALLY STRUGGLING. HE'S STILL HURTING, I'M NOT SURE IF IT'S HIS BACK OR HIS KNEES.
SHOULD HE BE PLAYING IN THAT CONDITION?
TRY TELLING THAT TO JAKE.
SOUNDS LIKE YOU'VE HAD THIS CONVERSATION BEFORE.
SOUNDS LIKE YOUR SPIDEY SENSE IS KICKING IN.
YOU KNOW IT.
BUT, YEAH, YOU'RE RIGHT. I WORRY THAT HE IS SO SCARED OF LOSING HIS STATUS IN THE SPORT THAT HE PUTS EVERYTHING SECOND, INCLUDING HIS HEALTH.
WELL, US REPORTERS DON'T REALLY MAKE IT EASY FOR ATHLETES EITHER.
WE ALL GLORIFY THE PLAYERS WHO CAME BACK AT THE LAST MINUTE, EVEN INJURED, AND MAKE THAT ONE MIRACULOUS PLAY.
BUT NO ONE REMEMBERS THE COUNTLESS ATHLETES THAT END THEIR CAREERS BY DOING THE SAME THING.

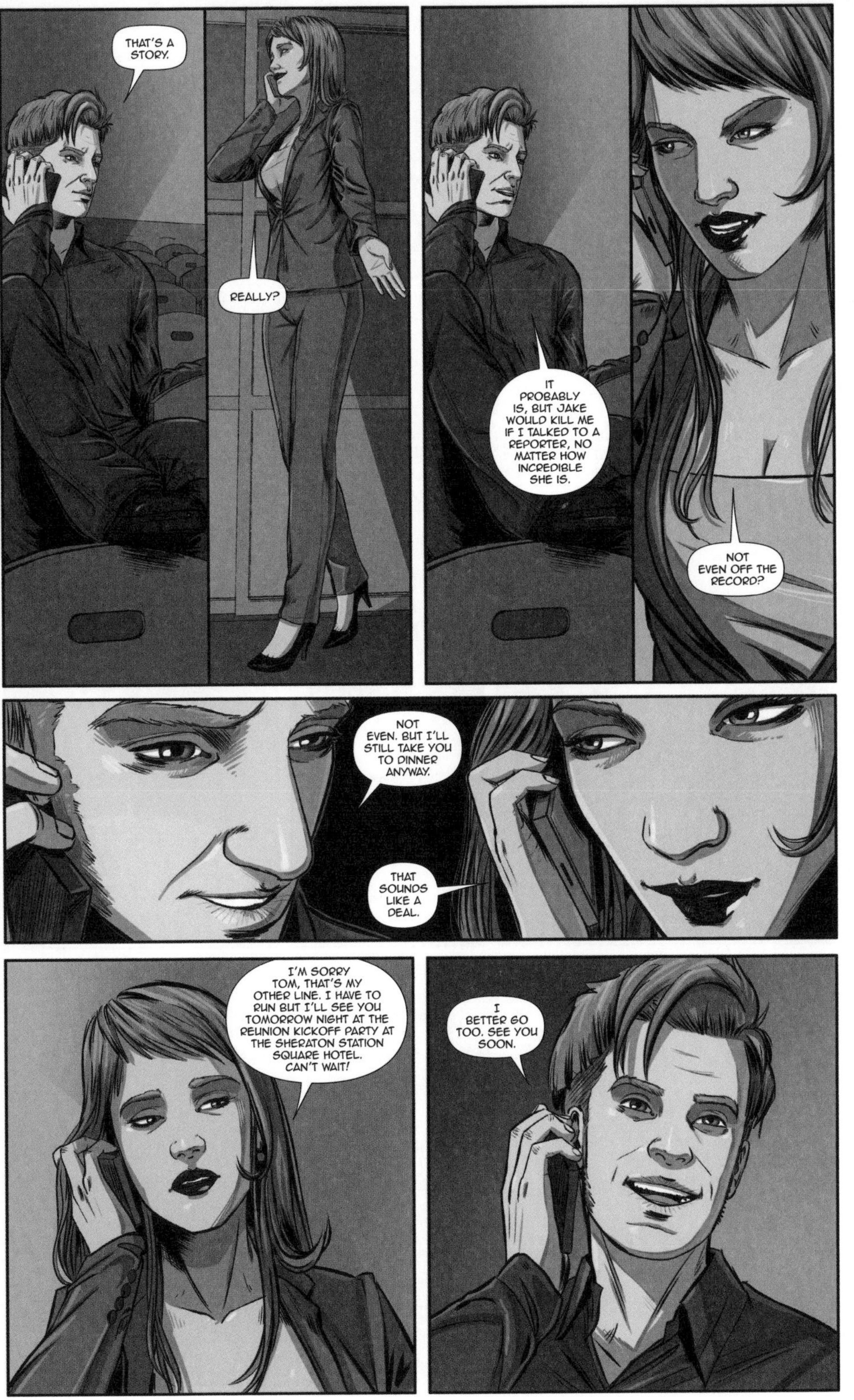
THAT'S A STORY.
REALLY?
IT PROBABLY IS, BUT JAKE WOULD KILL ME IF I TALKED TO A REPORTER, NO MATTER HOW INCREDIBLE SHE IS.
NOT EVEN OFF THE RECORD?
NOT EVEN. BUT I'LL STILL TAKE YOU TO DINNER ANYWAY.
THAT SOUNDS LIKE A DEAL.
I'M SORRY TOM, THAT'S MY OTHER LINE. I HAVE TO RUN BUT I'LL SEE YOU TOMORROW NIGHT AT THE REUNION KICKOFF PARTY AT THE SHERATON STATION SQUARE HOTEL. CAN'T WAIT!
I BETTER GO TOO. SEE YOU SOON.

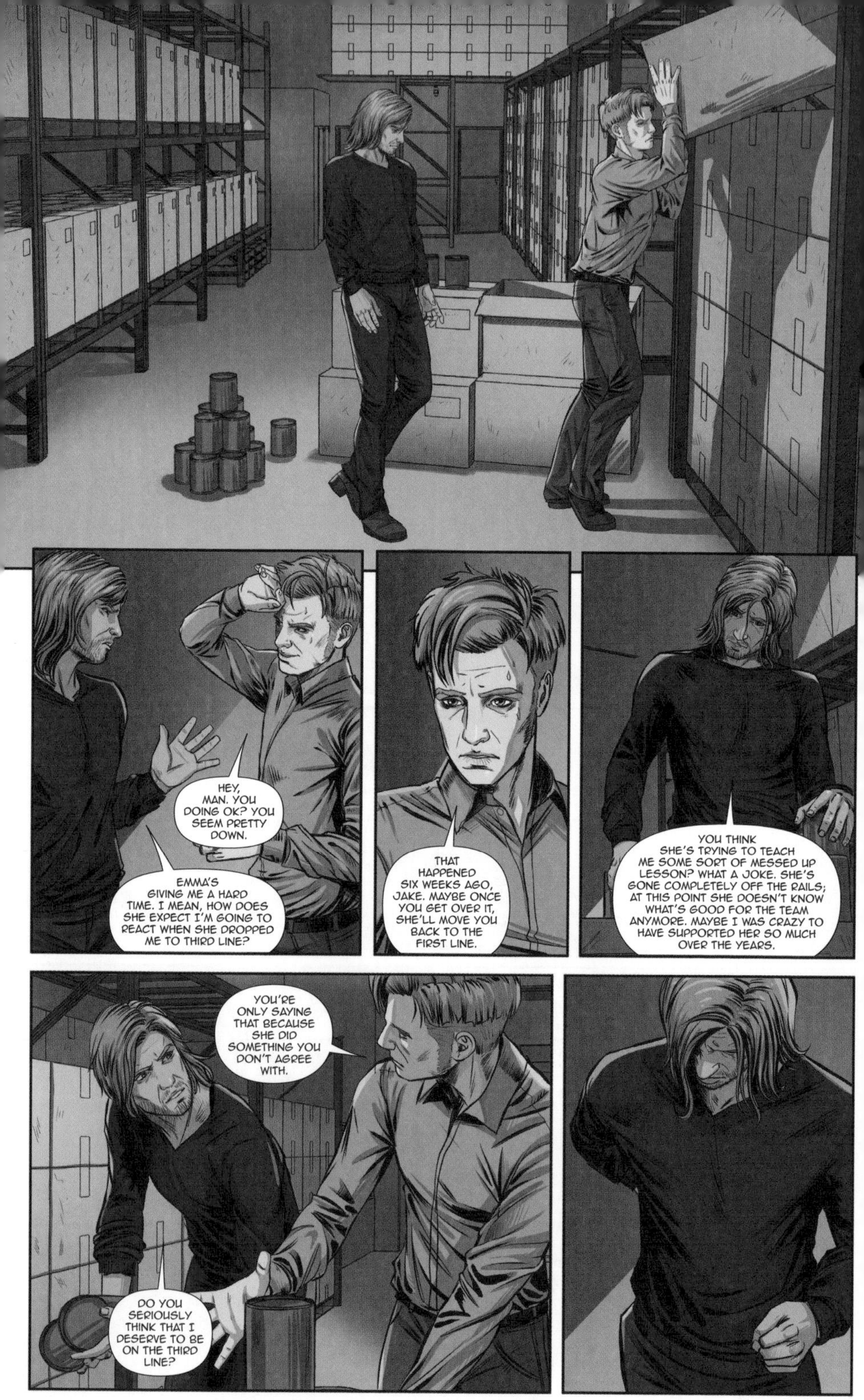
HEY, MAN. YOU DOING OK? YOU SEEM PRETTY DOWN.
EMMA'S GIVING ME A HARD TIME. I MEAN, HOW DOES SHE EXPECT I'M GOING TO REACT WHEN SHE DROPPED ME TO THIRD LINE?
THAT HAPPENED SIX WEEKS AGO, JAKE. MAYBE ONCE YOU GET OVER IT, SHE'LL MOVE YOU BACK TO THE FIRST LINE.
YOU THINK SHE'S TRYING TO TEACH ME SOME SORT OF MESSED UP LESSON? WHAT A JOKE. SHE'S GONE COMPLETELY OFF THE RAILS; AT THIS POINT SHE DOESN'T KNOW WHAT'S GOOD FOR THE TEAM ANYMORE. MAYBE I WAS CRAZY TO HAVE SUPPORTED HER SO MUCH OVER THE YEARS.
YOU'RE ONLY SAYING THAT BECAUSE SHE DID SOMETHING YOU DON'T AGREE WITH.
DO YOU SERIOUSLY THINK THAT I DESERVE TO BE ON THE THIRD LINE?

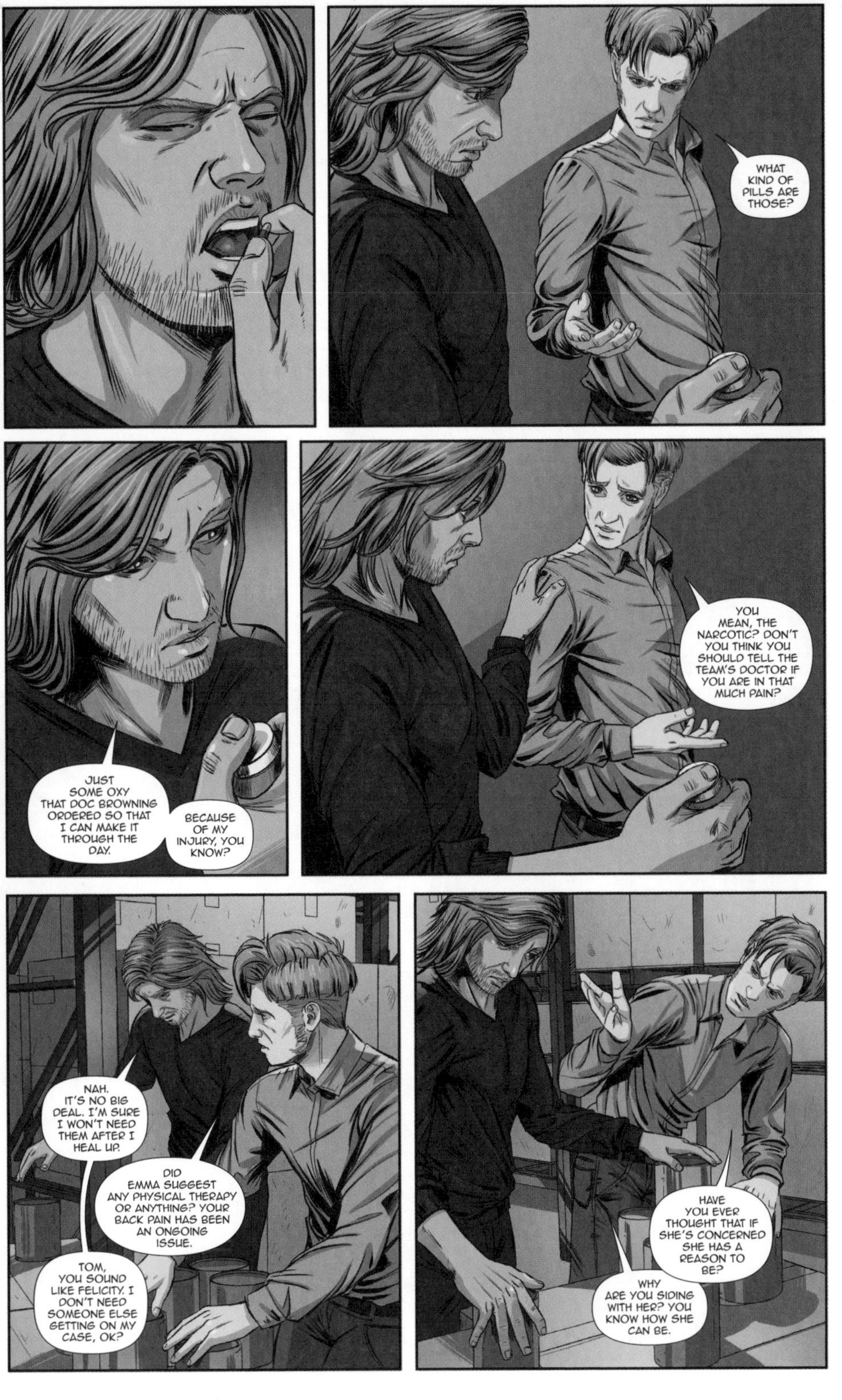
WHAT KIND OF PILLS ARE THOSE?
JUST SOME OXY THAT DOC BROWNING ORDERED SO THAT I CAN MAKE IT THROUGH THE DAY.
BECAUSE OF MY INJURY, YOU KNOW?
YOU MEAN, THE NARCOTIC? DON'T YOU THINK YOU SHOULD TELL THE TEAM'S DOCTOR IF YOU ARE IN THAT MUCH PAIN?
NAH. IT'S NO BIG DEAL. I'M SURE I WON'T NEED THEM AFTER I HEAL UP.
DID EMMA SUGGEST ANY PHYSICAL THERAPY OR ANYTHING? YOUR BACK PAIN HAS BEEN AN ONGOING ISSUE.
TOM, YOU SOUND LIKE FELICITY. I DON'T NEED SOMEONE ELSE GETTING ON MY CASE, OK?
HAVE YOU EVER THOUGHT THAT IF SHE'S CONCERNED SHE HAS A REASON TO BE?
WHY ARE YOU SIDING WITH HER? YOU KNOW HOW SHE CAN BE.

I KNOW THAT SHE'S STUCK WITH YOU THROUGH THICK AND THIN.
I DON'T WANT TO TALK ABOUT THIS ANYMORE.
YOU'RE SUCH A SELF-INVOLVED JERK RIGHT NOW. THERE'S STUFF GOING ON WITH ME, AND YOU JUST HAVE NO IDEA.
GIVE ME A BREAK. THE BUMP CITY PLAN?
NO, JAKE. I DO HAVE A LIFE OUTSIDE OF WORK. DO YOU EVEN KNOW WHERE I WENT A FEW WEEKS AGO?
AM I SUPPOSED TO REMEMBER?
I TOLD YOU I WAS GOING OUT OF TOWN, AND THAT DIDN'T EVEN REGISTER WITH YOU. I WENT TO VISIT MY PARENTS.
OH MY GOD, TOM. I'M SORRY.
IT'S OKAY. FELICITY DID THE REMEMBERING FOR YOU, AS SHE ALWAYS DOES.
THE WHITE ROSES.
THE WHITE ROSES.
FELIX SURE IS SOMETHING.
YES, SHE IS. SO, I MET A GIRL.
YOU STEPPED UP YOUR GAME, FINALLY!

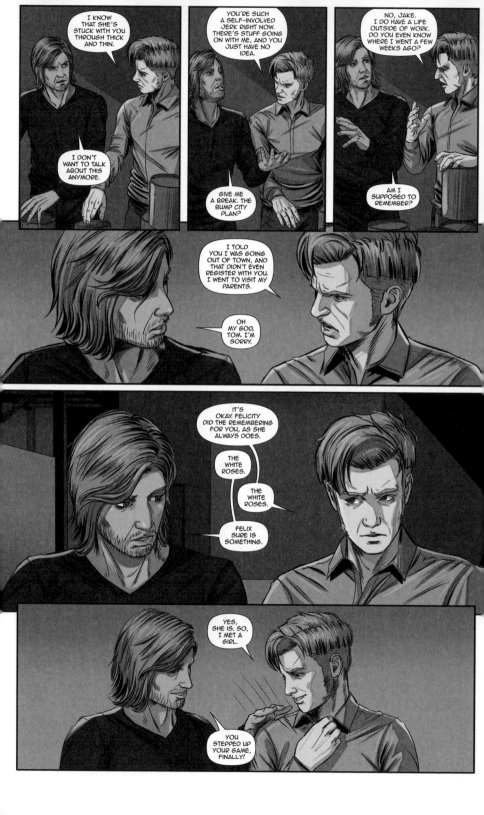

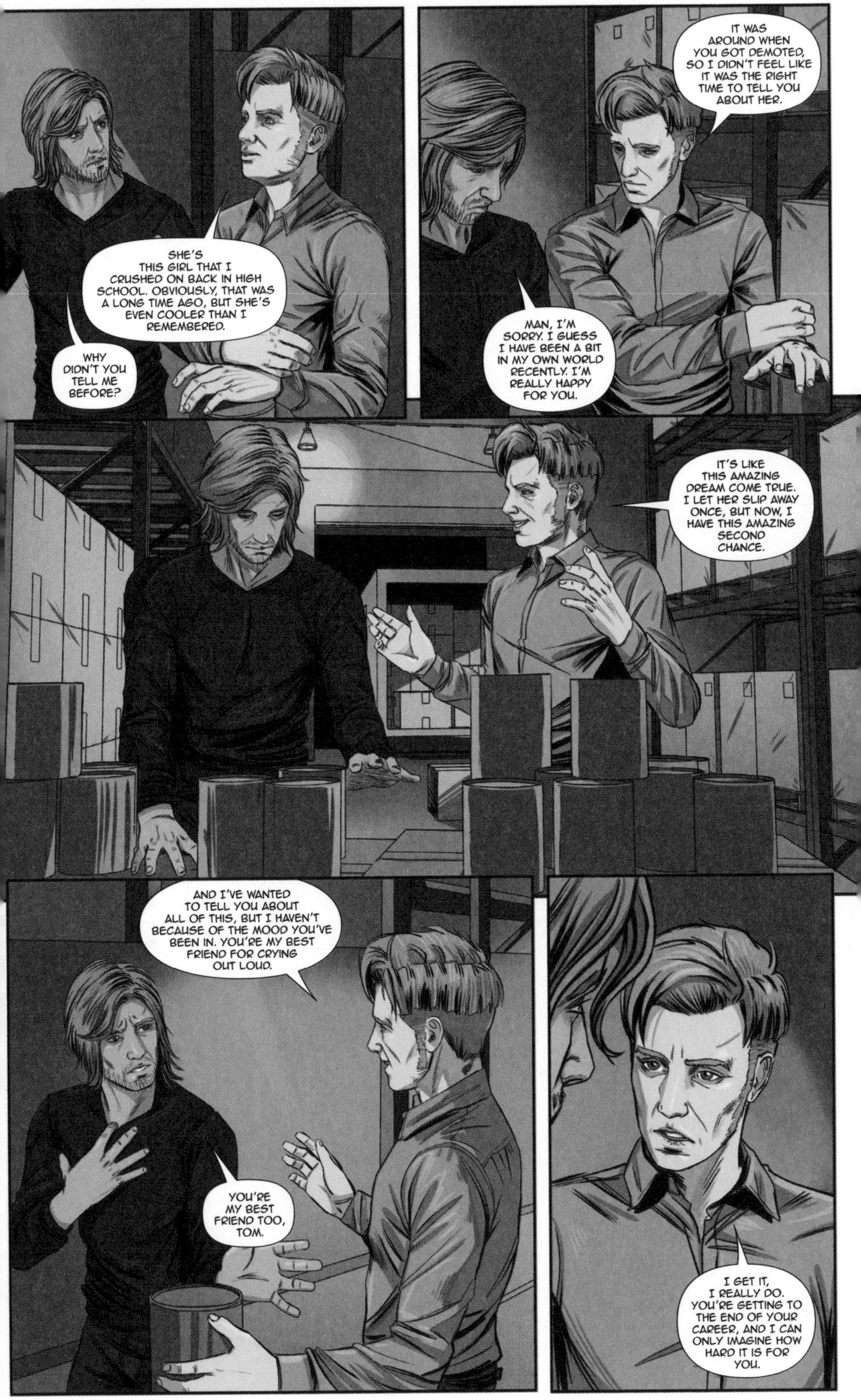
SHE'S THIS GIRL THAT I CRUSHED ON BACK IN HIGH SCHOOL. OBVIOUSLY, THAT WAS A LONG TIME AGO, BUT SHE'S EVEN COOLER THAN I REMEMBERED.
WHY DIDN'T YOU TELL ME BEFORE?
IT WAS AROUND WHEN YOU GOT DEMOTED, SO I DIDN'T FEEL LIKE IT WAS THE RIGHT TIME TO TELL YOU ABOUT HER.
MAN, I'M SORRY. I GUESS I HAVE BEEN A BIT IN MY OWN WORLD RECENTLY. I'M REALLY HAPPY FOR YOU.
IT'S LIKE THIS AMAZING DREAM COME TRUE. I LET HER SLIP AWAY ONCE, BUT NOW, I HAVE THIS AMAZING SECOND CHANCE.
AND I'VE WANTED TO TELL YOU ABOUT ALL OF THIS, BUT I HAVEN'T BECAUSE OF THE MOOD YOU'VE BEEN IN. YOU'RE MY BEST FRIEND FOR CRYING OUT LOUD.
YOU'RE MY BEST FRIEND TOO, TOM.
I GET IT, I REALLY DO. YOU'RE GETTING TO THE END OF YOUR CAREER, AND I CAN ONLY IMAGINE HOW HARD IT IS FOR YOU.

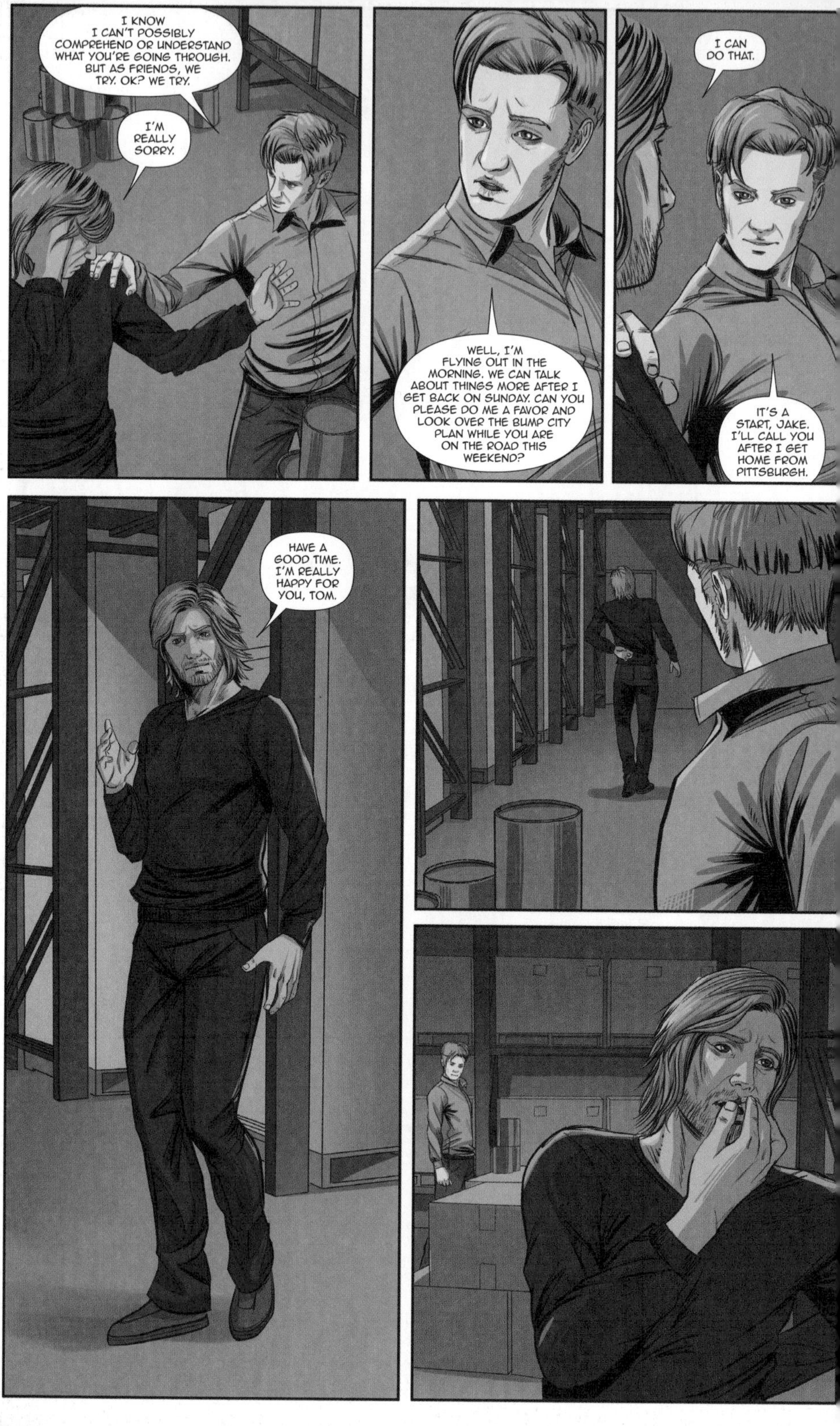
I KNOW I CAN'T POSSIBLY COMPREHEND OR UNDERSTAND WHAT YOU'RE GOING THROUGH. BUT AS FRIENDS, WE TRY. OK? WE TRY.
I'M REALLY SORRY.
WELL, I'M FLYING OUT IN THE MORNING. WE CAN TALK ABOUT THINGS MORE AFTER I GET BACK ON SUNDAY. CAN YOU PLEASE DO ME A FAVOR AND LOOK OVER THE BUMP CITY PLAN WHILE YOU ARE ON THE ROAD THIS WEEKEND?
I CAN DO THAT.
IT'S A START, JAKE. I'LL CALL YOU AFTER I GET HOME FROM PITTSBURGH.
HAVE A GOOD TIME. I'M REALLY HAPPY FOR YOU, TOM.

CHAPTER 6
EXIT THE DRAGON

RECOMMENDED LISTENING:

"NOT IF YOU WERE
THE LAST JUNKIE
ON EARTH"
THE DANDY WARHOLS

"I REMEMBER YOU"
SKID ROW

"ONE"
U2

"PRINCE JOHNNY"
ST. VINCENT

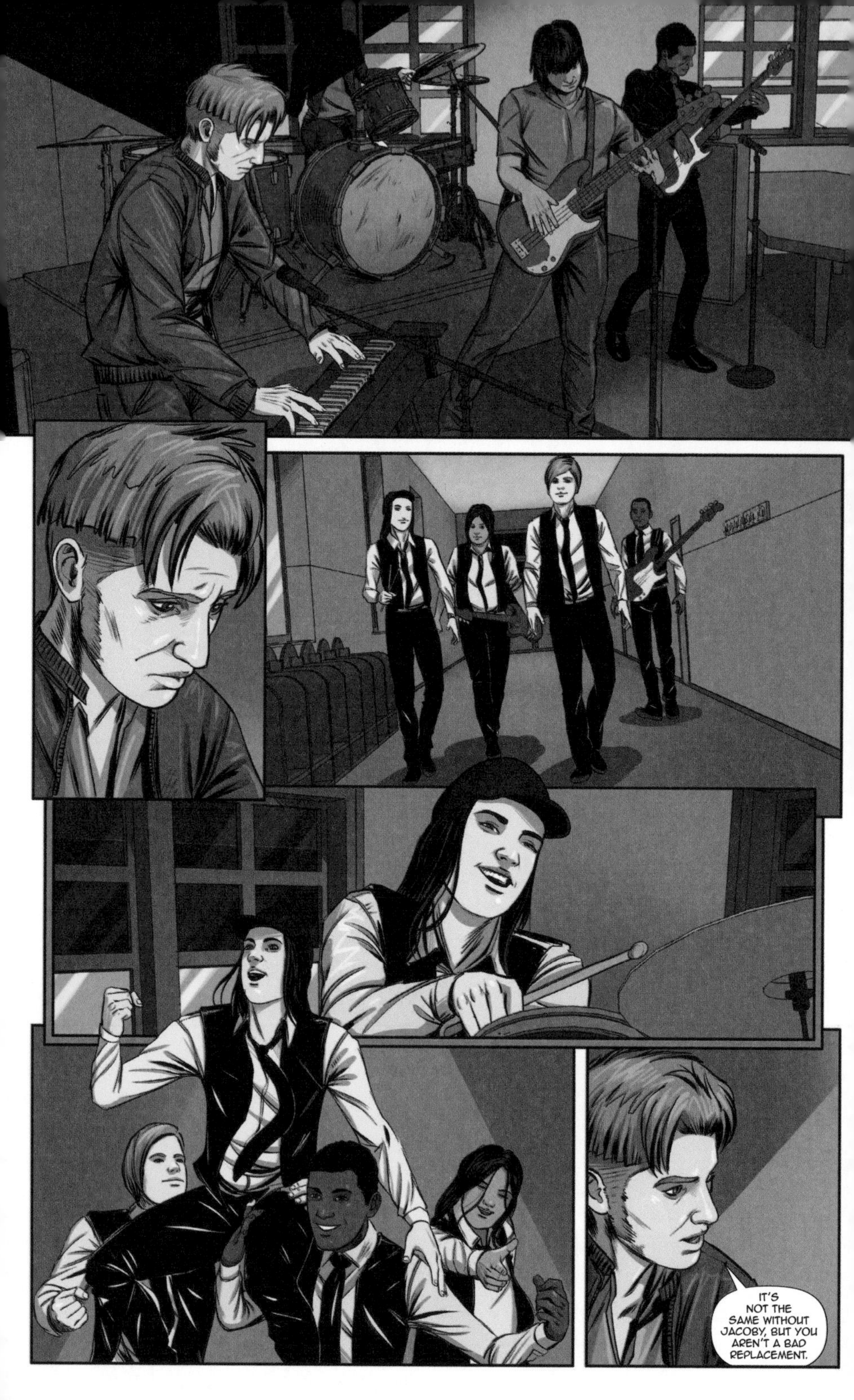
IT'S NOT THE SAME WITHOUT JACOBY, BUT YOU AREN'T A BAD REPLACEMENT.

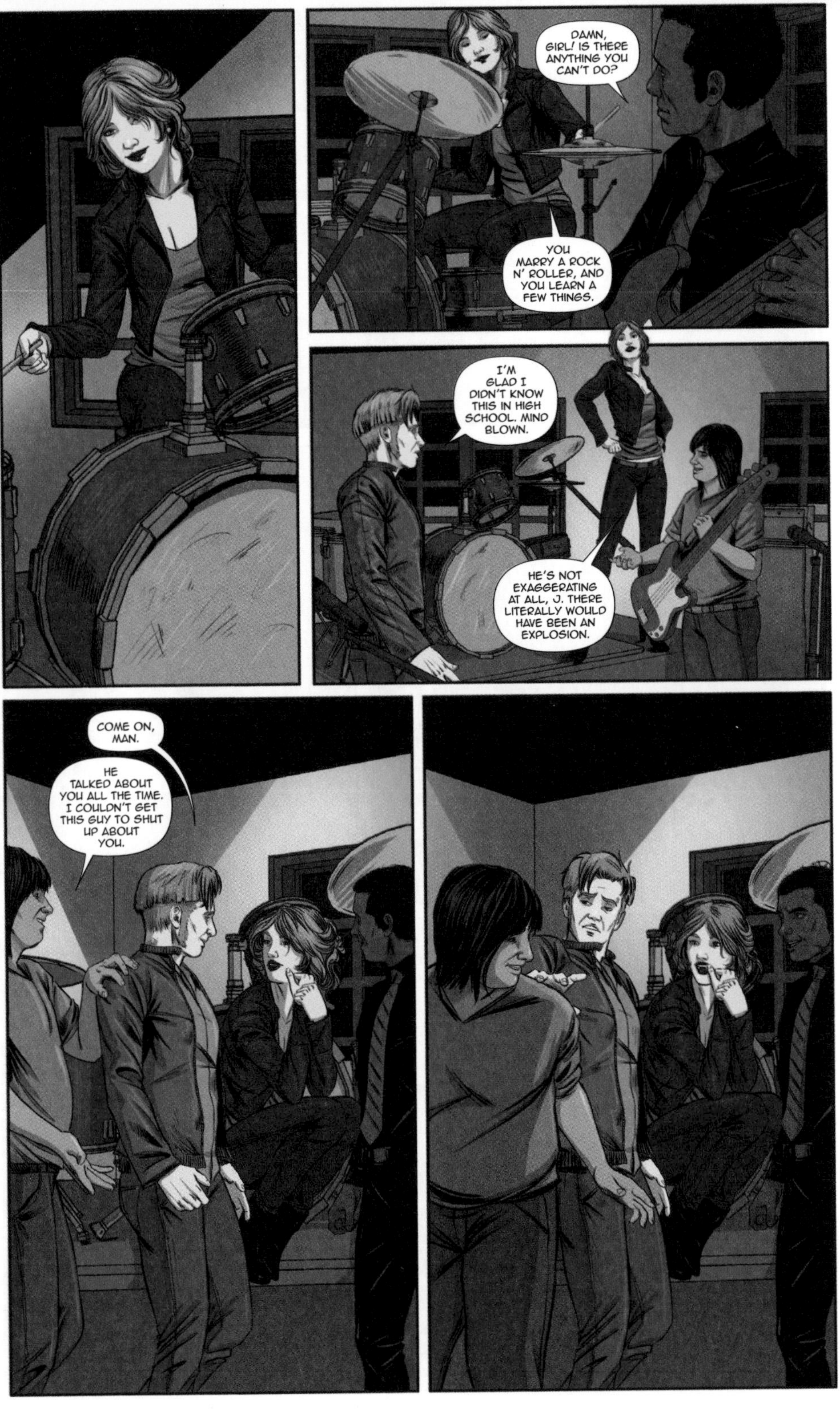
DAMN, GIRL! IS THERE ANYTHING YOU CAN'T DO?
YOU MARRY A ROCK N' ROLLER, AND YOU LEARN A FEW THINGS.
I'M GLAD I DIDN'T KNOW THIS IN HIGH SCHOOL. MIND BLOWN.
HE'S NOT EXAGGERATING AT ALL, J. THERE LITERALLY WOULD HAVE BEEN AN EXPLOSION.
COME ON, MAN.
HE TALKED ABOUT YOU ALL THE TIME. I COULDN'T GET THIS GUY TO SHUT UP ABOUT YOU.

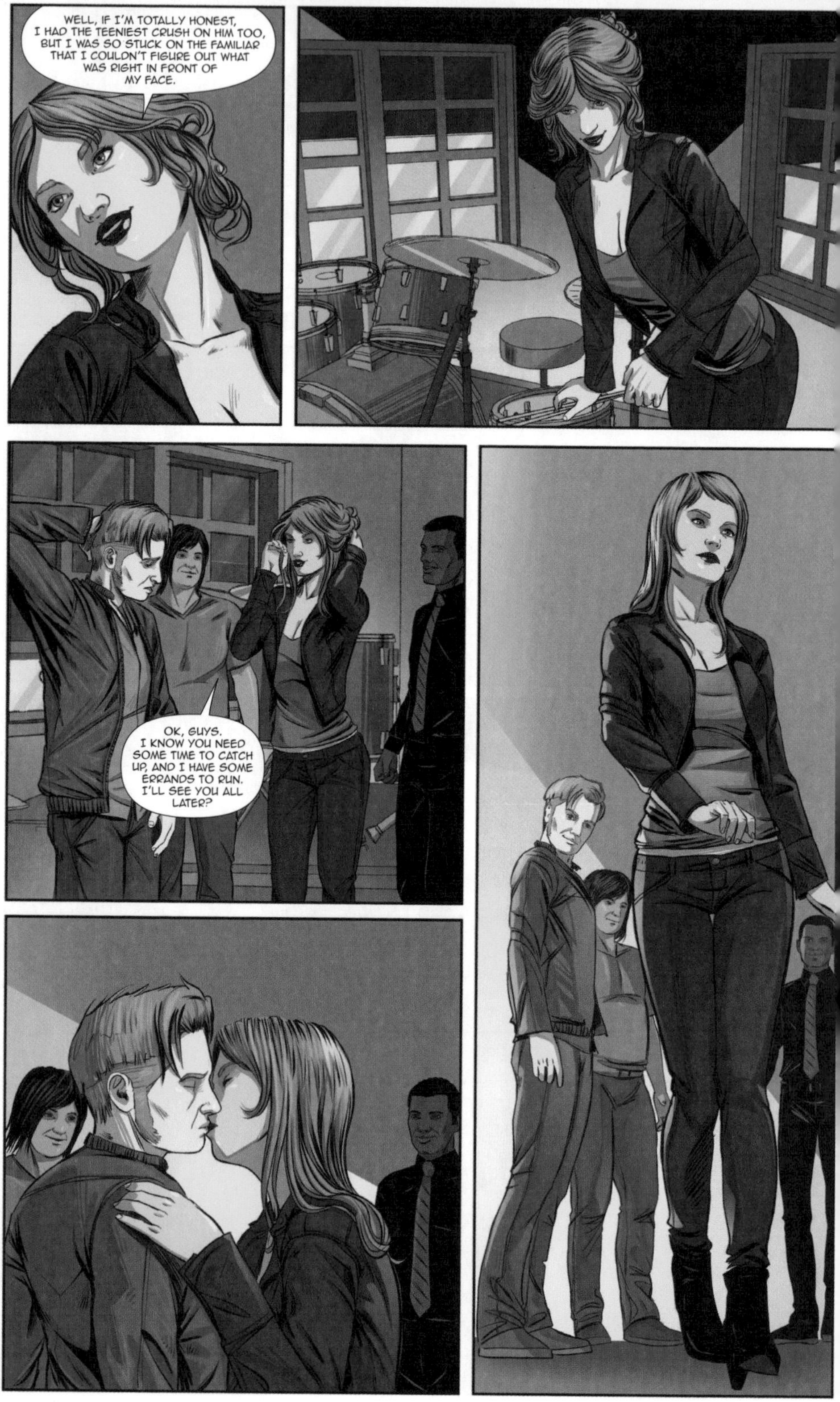
WELL, IF I'M TOTALLY HONEST, I HAD THE TEENIEST CRUSH ON HIM TOO, BUT I WAS SO STUCK ON THE FAMILIAR THAT I COULDN'T FIGURE OUT WHAT WAS RIGHT IN FRONT OF MY FACE.
OK, GUYS. I KNOW YOU NEED SOME TIME TO CATCH UP, AND I HAVE SOME ERRANDS TO RUN. I'LL SEE YOU ALL LATER?

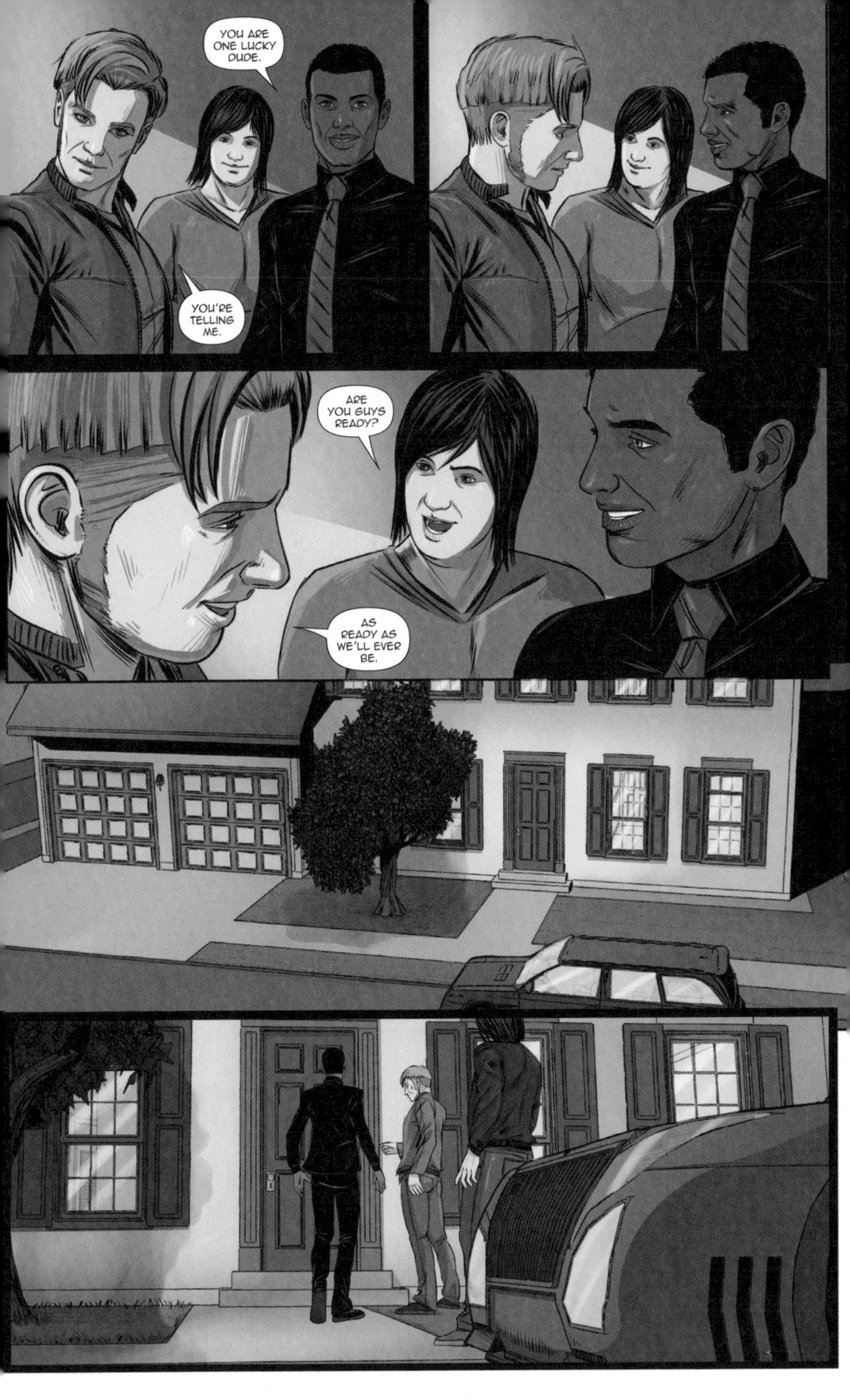
YOU ARE ONE LUCKY DUDE.
YOU'RE TELLING ME.
ARE YOU GUYS READY?
AS READY AS WE'LL EVER BE.

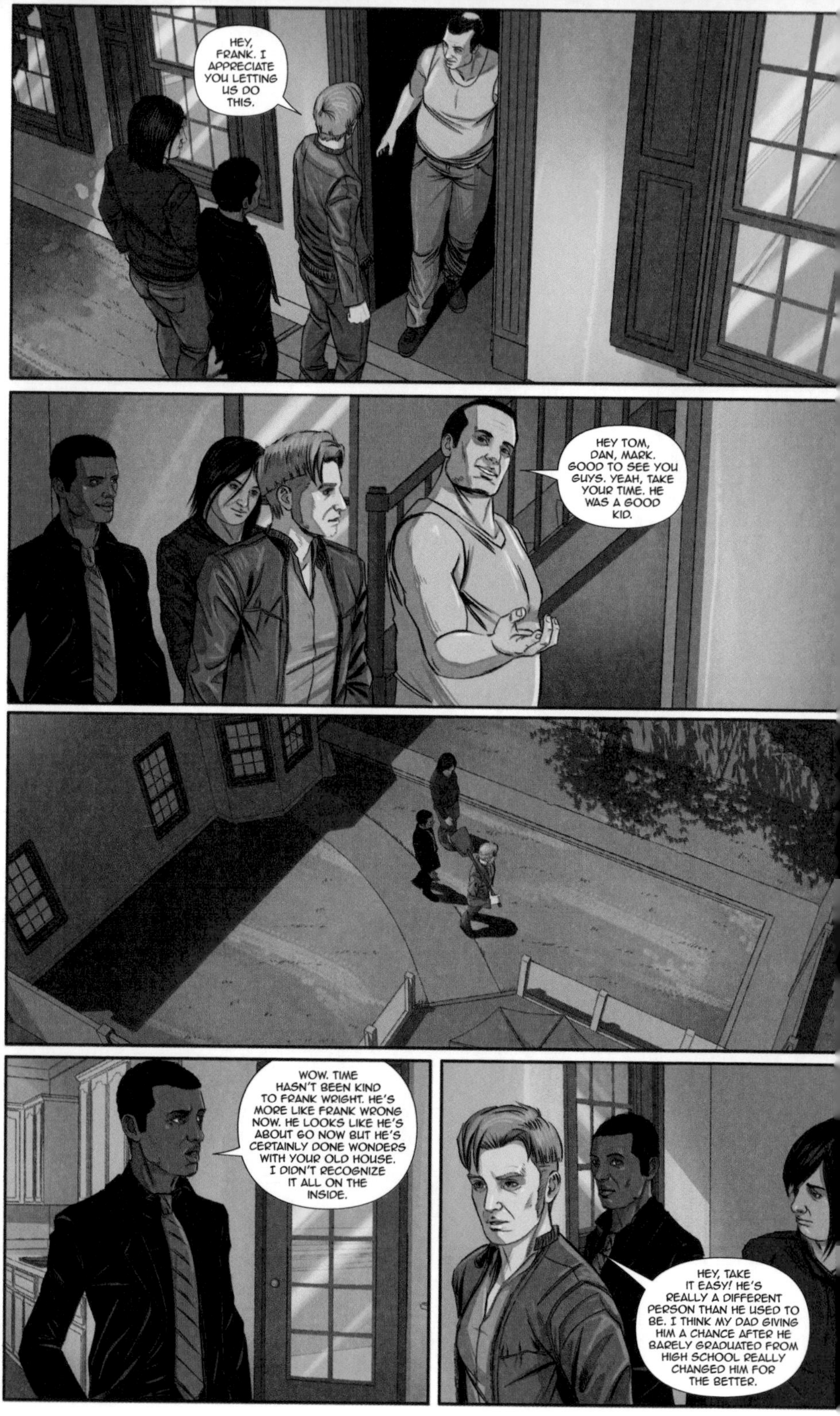
HEY, FRANK. I APPRECIATE YOU LETTING US DO THIS.
HEY TOM, DAN, MARK. GOOD TO SEE YOU GUYS. YEAH, TAKE YOUR TIME. HE WAS A GOOD KID.
WOW. TIME HASN'T BEEN KIND TO FRANK WRIGHT. HE'S MORE LIKE FRANK WRONG NOW. HE LOOKS LIKE HE'S ABOUT 60 NOW BUT HE'S CERTAINLY DONE WONDERS WITH YOUR OLD HOUSE. I DIDN'T RECOGNIZE IT ALL ON THE INSIDE.
HEY, TAKE IT EASY! HE'S REALLY A DIFFERENT PERSON THAN HE USED TO BE. I THINK MY DAD GIVING HIM A CHANCE AFTER HE BARELY GRADUATED FROM HIGH SCHOOL REALLY CHANGED HIM FOR THE BETTER.

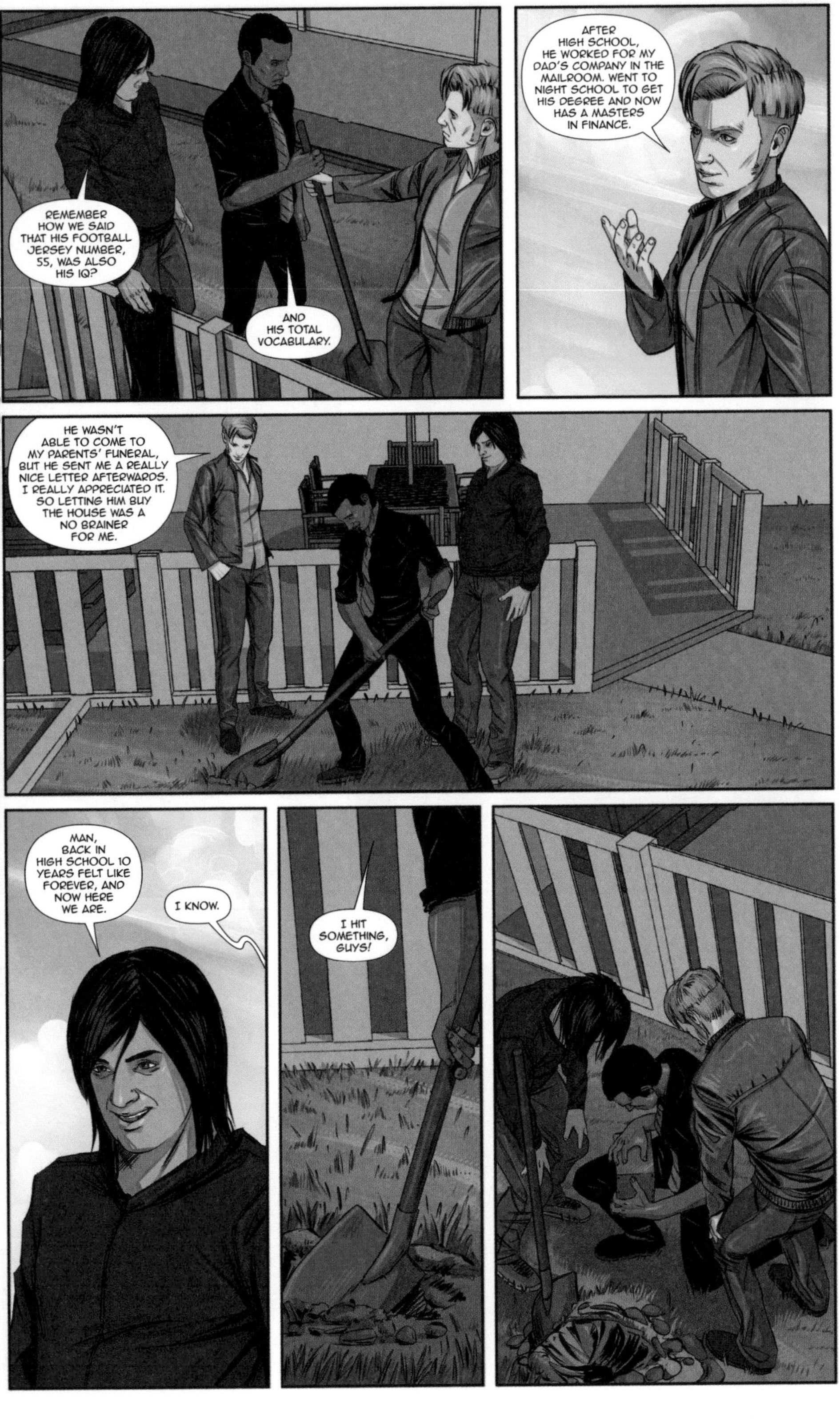
REMEMBER HOW WE SAID THAT HIS FOOTBALL JERSEY NUMBER, 55, WAS ALSO HIS IQ?
AND HIS TOTAL VOCABULARY.
AFTER HIGH SCHOOL, HE WORKED FOR MY DAD'S COMPANY IN THE MAILROOM. WENT TO NIGHT SCHOOL TO GET HIS DEGREE AND NOW HAS A MASTERS IN FINANCE.
HE WASN'T ABLE TO COME TO MY PARENTS' FUNERAL, BUT HE SENT ME A REALLY NICE LETTER AFTERWARDS. I REALLY APPRECIATED IT. SO LETTING HIM BUY THE HOUSE WAS A NO BRAINER FOR ME.
MAN, BACK IN HIGH SCHOOL 10 YEARS FELT LIKE FOREVER, AND NOW HERE WE ARE.
I KNOW.
I HIT SOMETHING, GUYS!

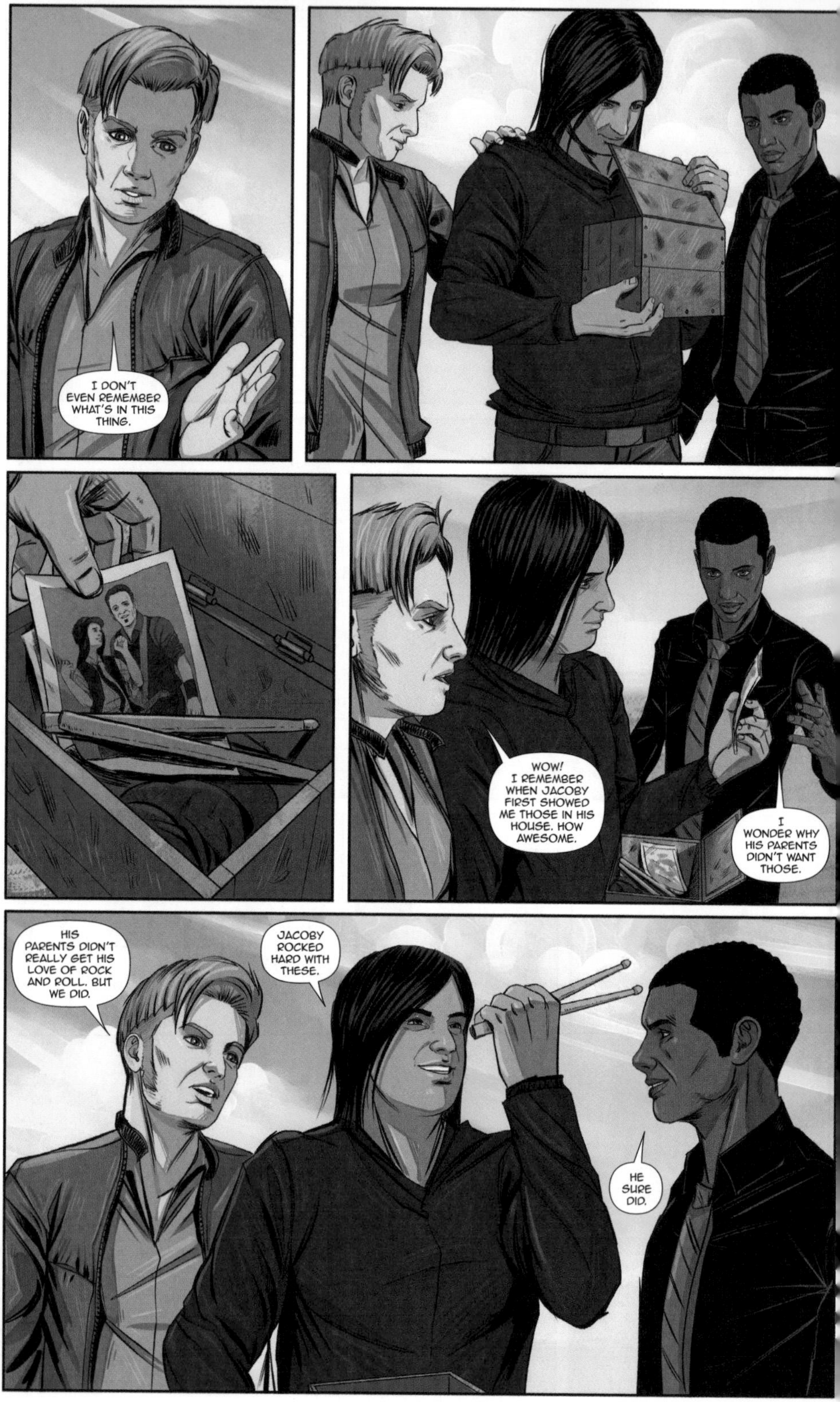
I DON'T EVEN REMEMBER WHAT'S IN THIS THING.
WOW! I REMEMBER WHEN JACOBY FIRST SHOWED ME THOSE IN HIS HOUSE. HOW AWESOME.
I WONDER WHY HIS PARENTS DIDN'T WANT THOSE.
HIS PARENTS DIDN'T REALLY GET HIS LOVE OF ROCK AND ROLL. BUT WE DID.
JACOBY ROCKED HARD WITH THESE.
HE SURE DID.

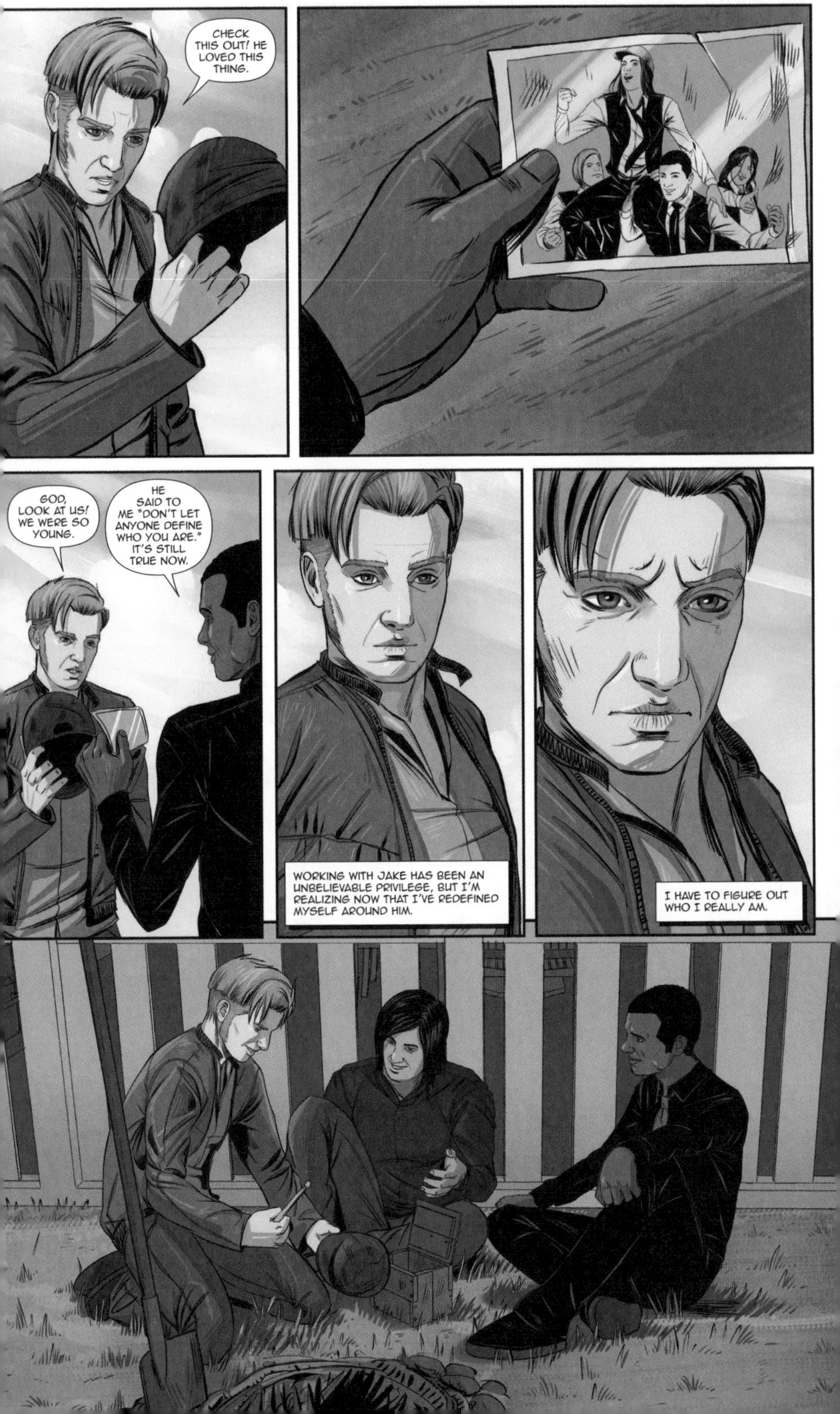
CHECK THIS OUT! HE LOVED THIS THING.
GOD, LOOK AT US! WE WERE SO YOUNG.
HE SAID TO ME "DON'T LET ANYONE DEFINE WHO YOU ARE." IT'S STILL TRUE NOW.
WORKING WITH JAKE HAS BEEN AN UNBELIEVABLE PRIVILEGE, BUT I'M REALIZING NOW THAT I'VE REDEFINED MYSELF AROUND HIM.
I HAVE TO FIGURE OUT WHO I REALLY AM.

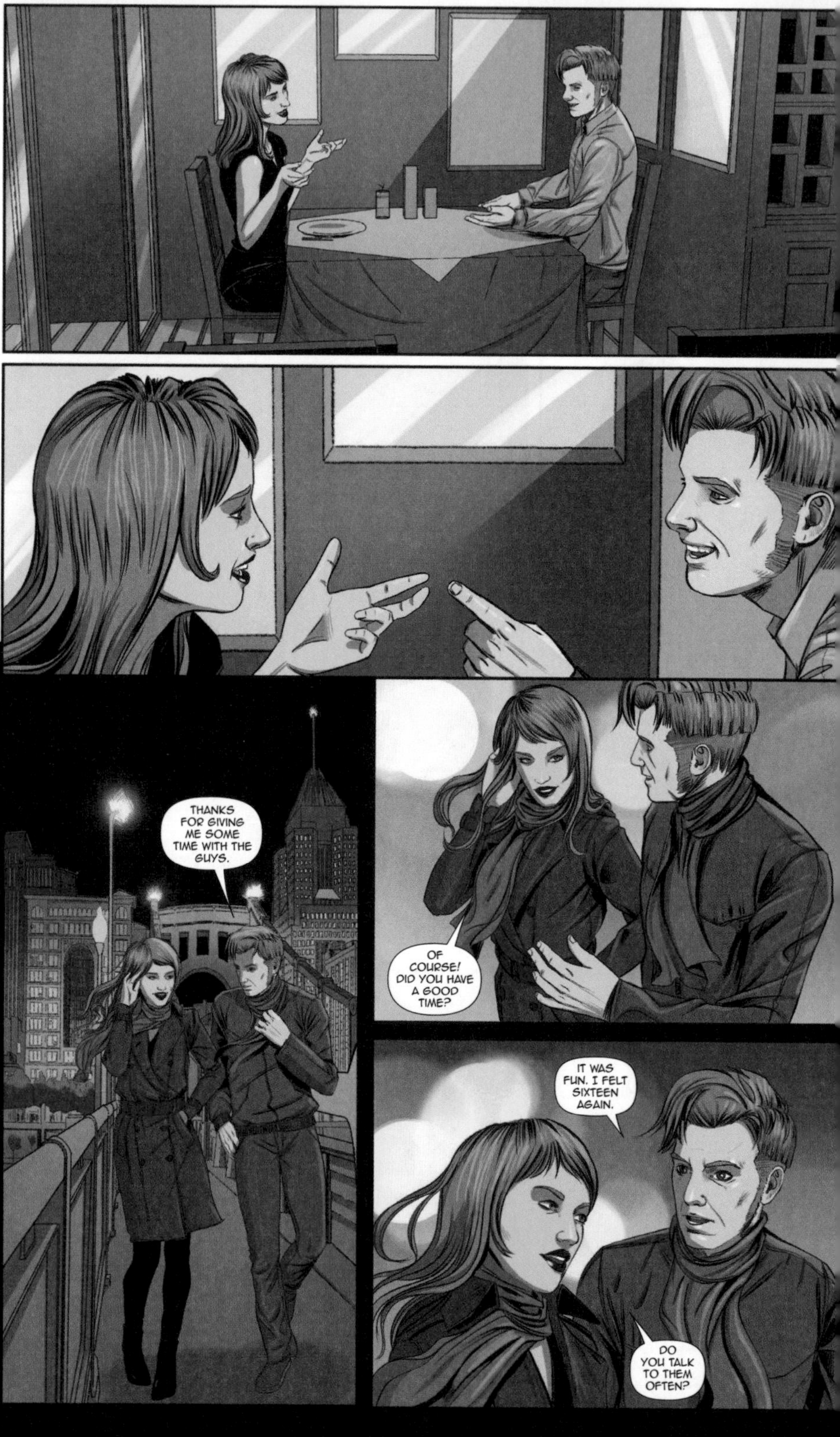
THANKS FOR GIVING ME SOME TIME WITH THE GUYS.
OF COURSE! DID YOU HAVE A GOOD TIME?
IT WAS FUN. I FELT SIXTEEN AGAIN.
DO YOU TALK TO THEM OFTEN?

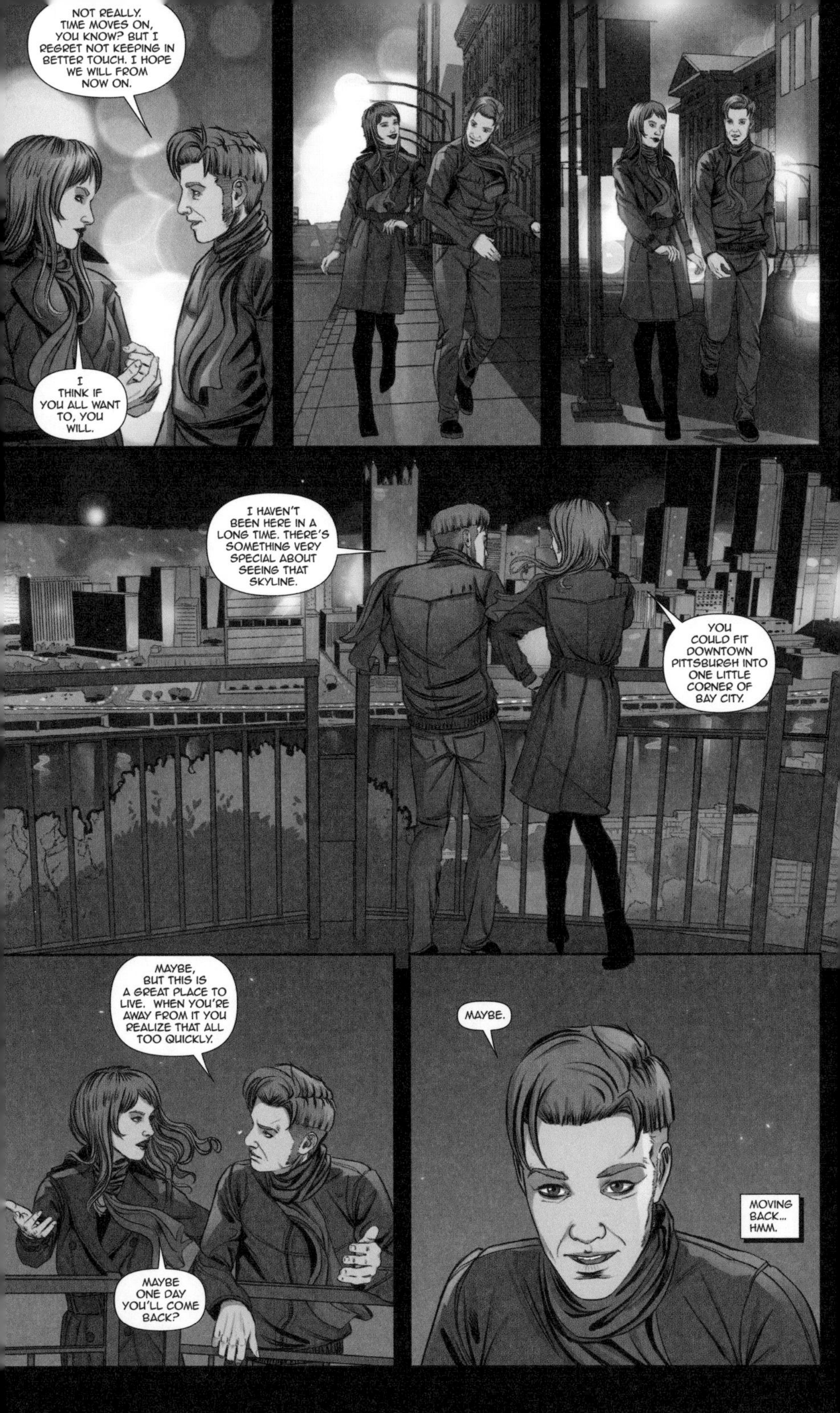

NOT REALLY. TIME MOVES ON, YOU KNOW? BUT I REGRET NOT KEEPING IN BETTER TOUCH. I HOPE WE WILL FROM NOW ON.
I THINK IF YOU ALL WANT TO, YOU WILL.
I HAVEN'T BEEN HERE IN A LONG TIME. THERE'S SOMETHING VERY SPECIAL ABOUT SEEING THAT SKYLINE.
YOU COULD FIT DOWNTOWN PITTSBURGH INTO ONE LITTLE CORNER OF BAY CITY.
MAYBE, BUT THIS IS A GREAT PLACE TO LIVE. WHEN YOU'RE AWAY FROM IT YOU REALIZE THAT ALL TOO QUICKLY.
MAYBE ONE DAY YOU'LL COME BACK?
MAYBE.
MOVING BACK... HMM.

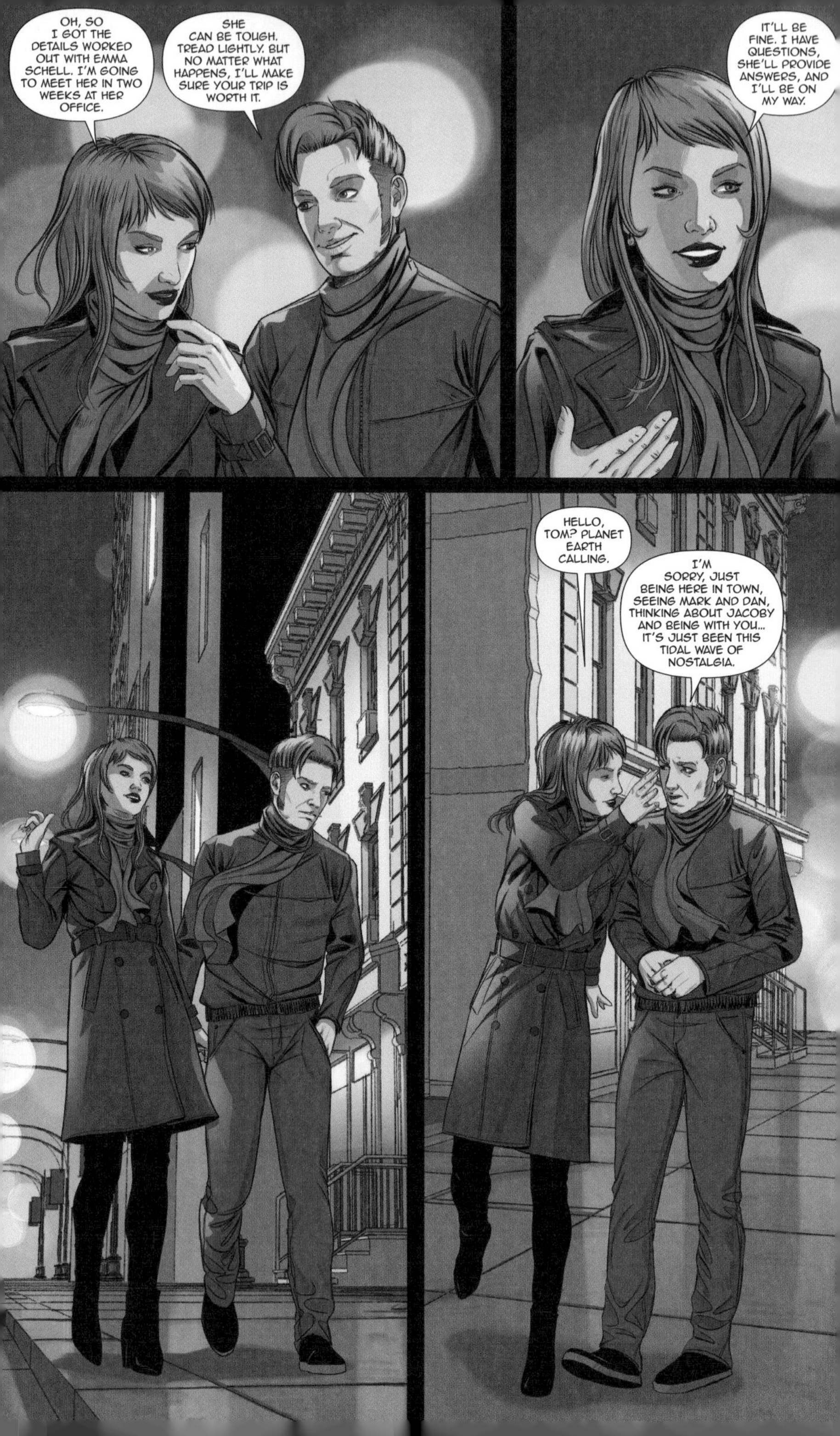
OH, SO I GOT THE DETAILS WORKED OUT WITH EMMA SCHELL. I'M GOING TO MEET HER IN TWO WEEKS AT HER OFFICE.
SHE CAN BE TOUGH. TREAD LIGHTLY. BUT NO MATTER WHAT HAPPENS, I'LL MAKE SURE YOUR TRIP IS WORTH IT.
IT'LL BE FINE. I HAVE QUESTIONS, SHE'LL PROVIDE ANSWERS, AND I'LL BE ON MY WAY.
HELLO, TOM? PLANET EARTH CALLING.
I'M SORRY, JUST BEING HERE IN TOWN, SEEING MARK AND DAN, THINKING ABOUT JACOBY AND BEING WITH YOU... IT'S JUST BEEN THIS TIDAL WAVE OF NOSTALGIA.

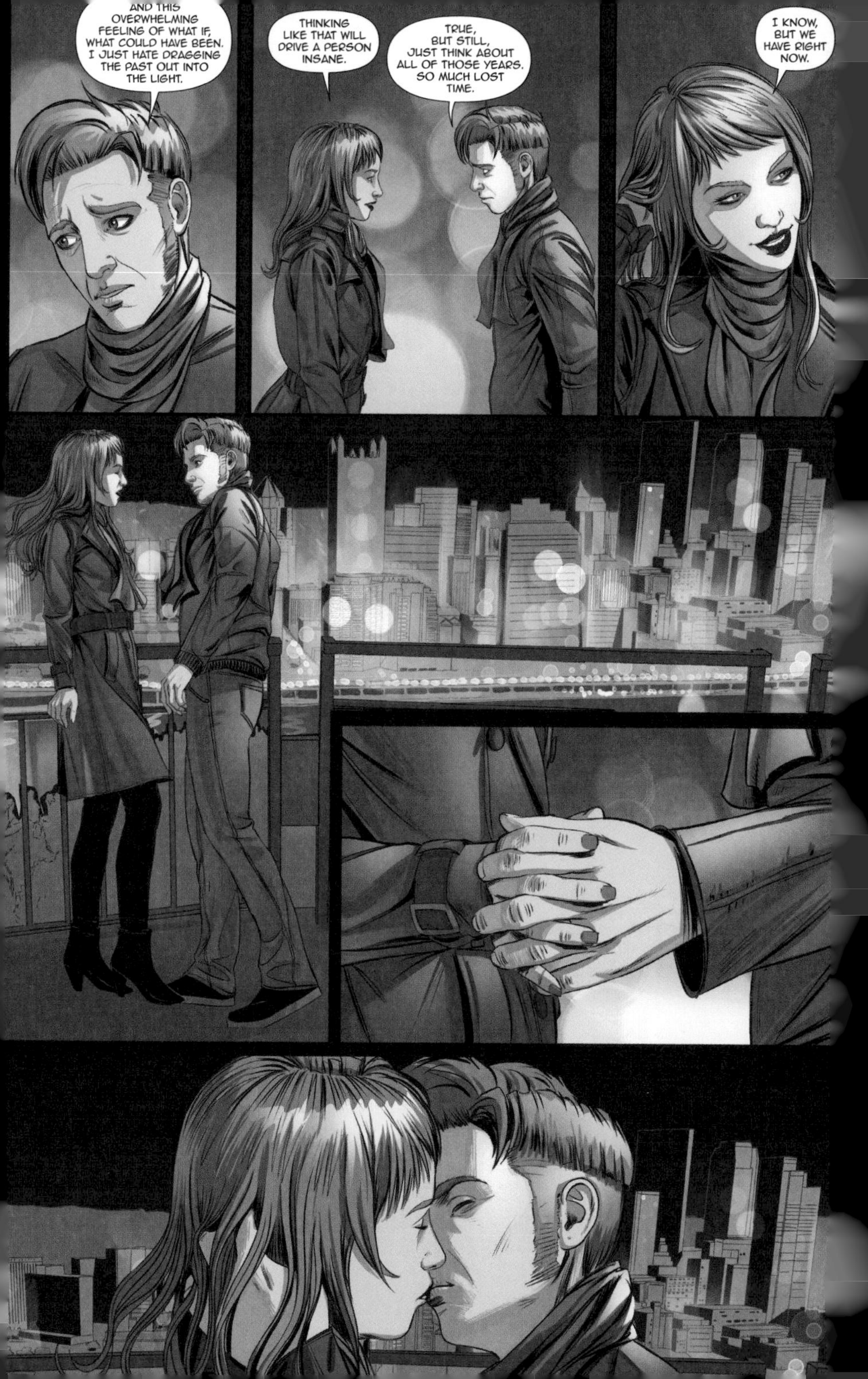
AND THIS OVERWHELMING FEELING OF WHAT IF, WHAT COULD HAVE BEEN. I JUST HATE DRAGGING THE PAST OUT INTO THE LIGHT.
THINKING LIKE THAT WILL DRIVE A PERSON INSANE.
TRUE, BUT STILL, JUST THINK ABOUT ALL OF THOSE YEARS. SO MUCH LOST TIME.
I KNOW, BUT WE HAVE RIGHT NOW.

CHAPTER 7
FOLLOW THAT DREAM

RECOMMENDED LISTENING:

"FRIDAY I'M IN LOVE"
THE CURE

"BEST DAY OF MY LIFE"
AMERICAN AUTHORS

"DELIVER ME"
TOM PETTY AND THE HEARTBREAKERS

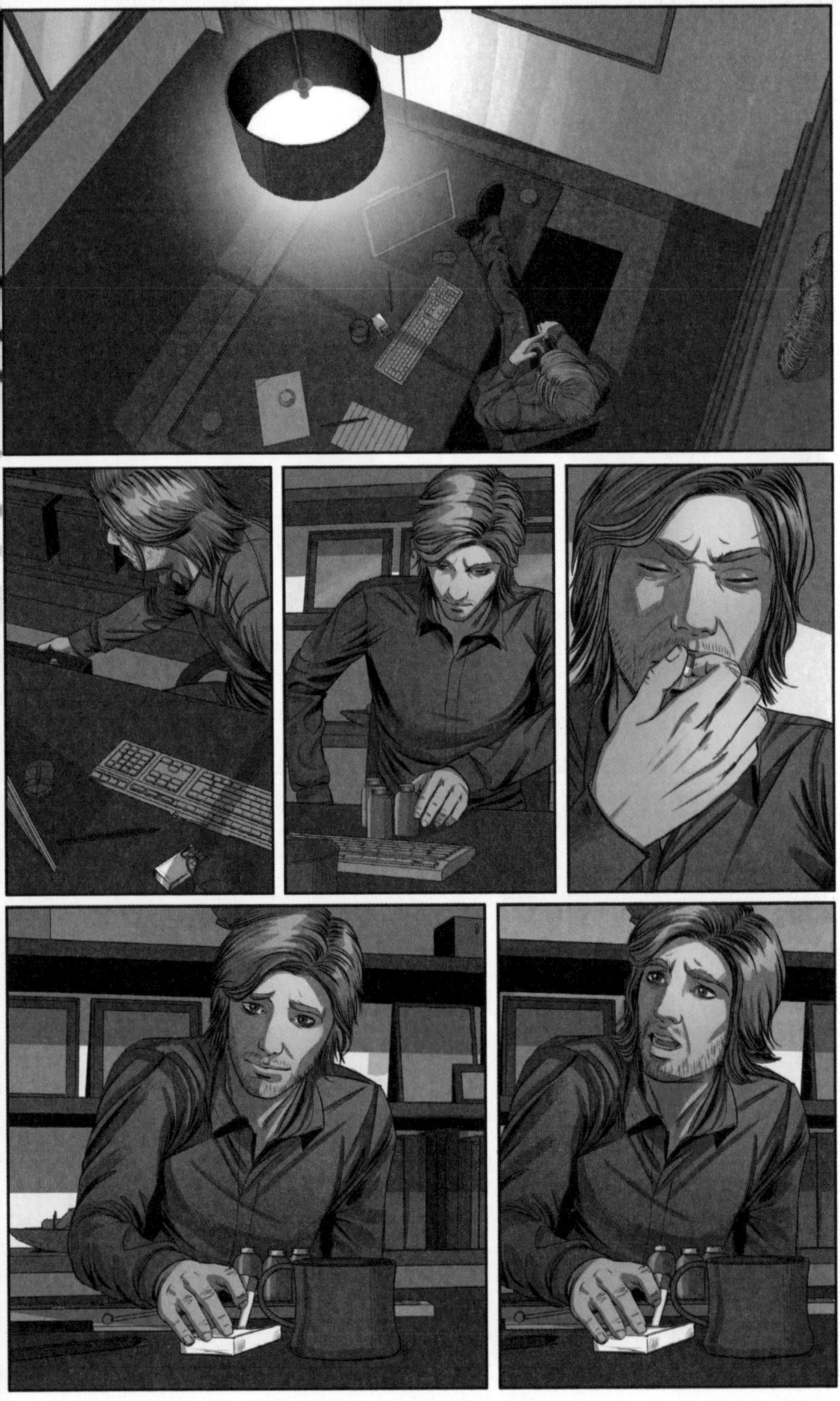

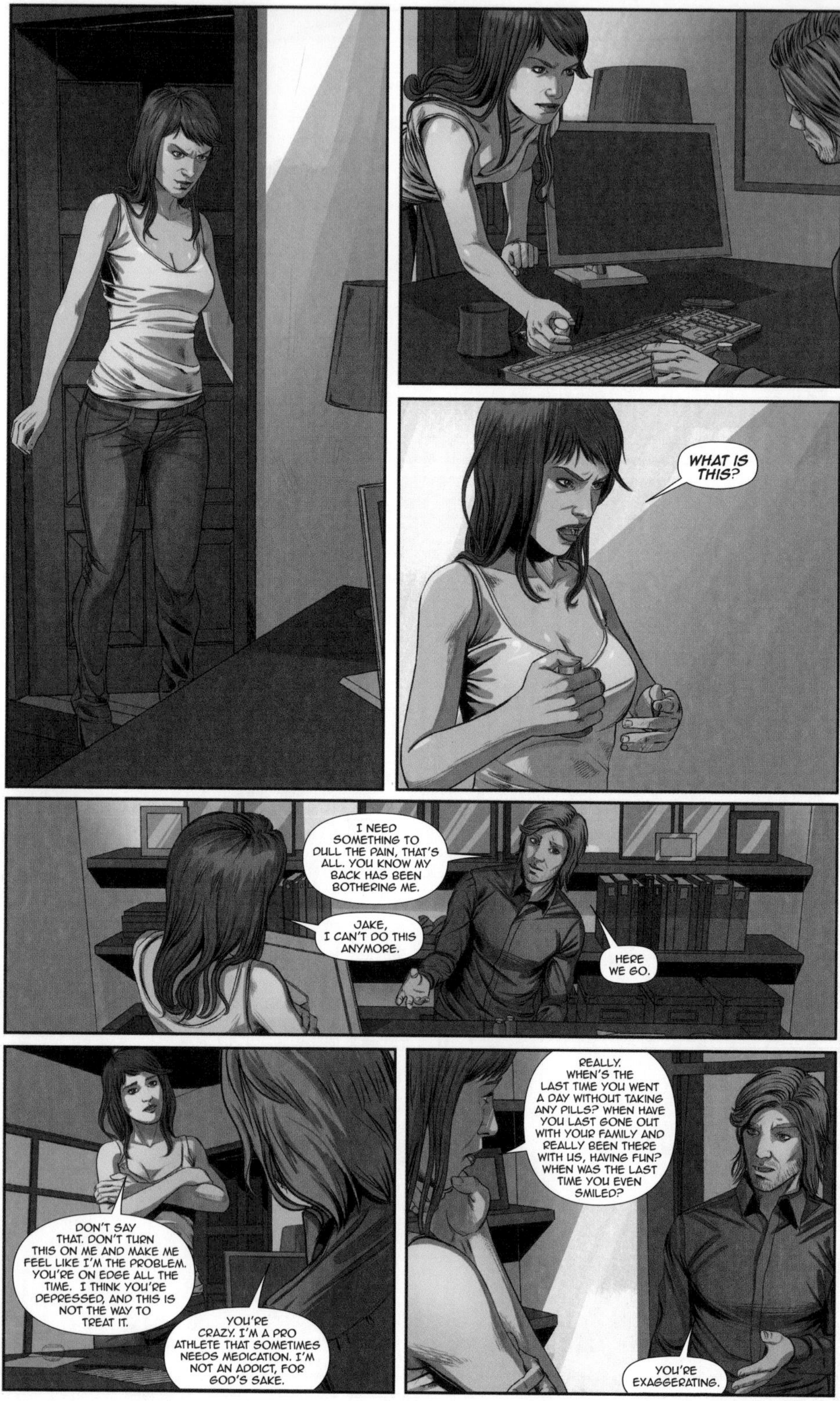
WHAT IS THIS?
I NEED SOMETHING TO DULL THE PAIN, THAT'S ALL. YOU KNOW MY BACK HAS BEEN BOTHERING ME.
JAKE, I CAN'T DO THIS ANYMORE.
HERE WE GO.
DON'T SAY THAT. DON'T TURN THIS ON ME AND MAKE ME FEEL LIKE I'M THE PROBLEM. YOU'RE ON EDGE ALL THE TIME. I THINK YOU'RE DEPRESSED, AND THIS IS NOT THE WAY TO TREAT IT.
YOU'RE CRAZY. I'M A PRO ATHLETE THAT SOMETIMES NEEDS MEDICATION. I'M NOT AN ADDICT, FOR GOD'S SAKE.
REALLY. WHEN'S THE LAST TIME YOU WENT A DAY WITHOUT TAKING ANY PILLS? WHEN HAVE YOU LAST GONE OUT WITH YOUR FAMILY AND REALLY BEEN THERE WITH US, HAVING FUN? WHEN WAS THE LAST TIME YOU EVEN SMILED?
YOU'RE EXAGGERATING.

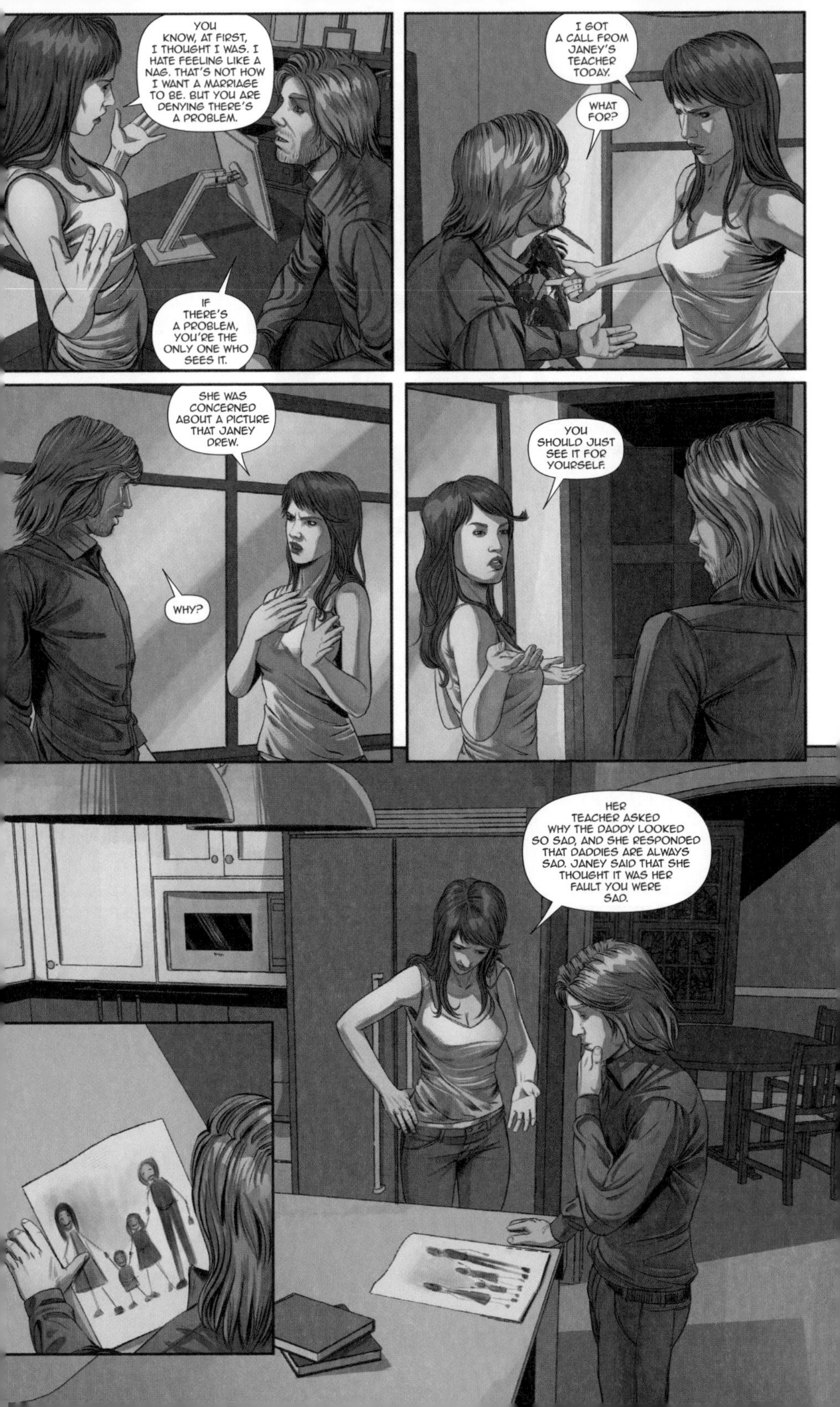
YOU KNOW, AT FIRST, I THOUGHT I WAS. I HATE FEELING LIKE A NAG. THAT'S NOT HOW I WANT A MARRIAGE TO BE. BUT YOU ARE DENYING THERE'S A PROBLEM.
IF THERE'S A PROBLEM, YOU'RE THE ONLY ONE WHO SEES IT.
I GOT A CALL FROM JANEY'S TEACHER TODAY.
WHAT FOR?
SHE WAS CONCERNED ABOUT A PICTURE THAT JANEY DREW.
WHY?
YOU SHOULD JUST SEE IT FOR YOURSELF.
HER TEACHER ASKED WHY THE DADDY LOOKED SO SAD, AND SHE RESPONDED THAT DADDIES ARE ALWAYS SAD. JANEY SAID THAT SHE THOUGHT IT WAS HER FAULT YOU WERE SAD.

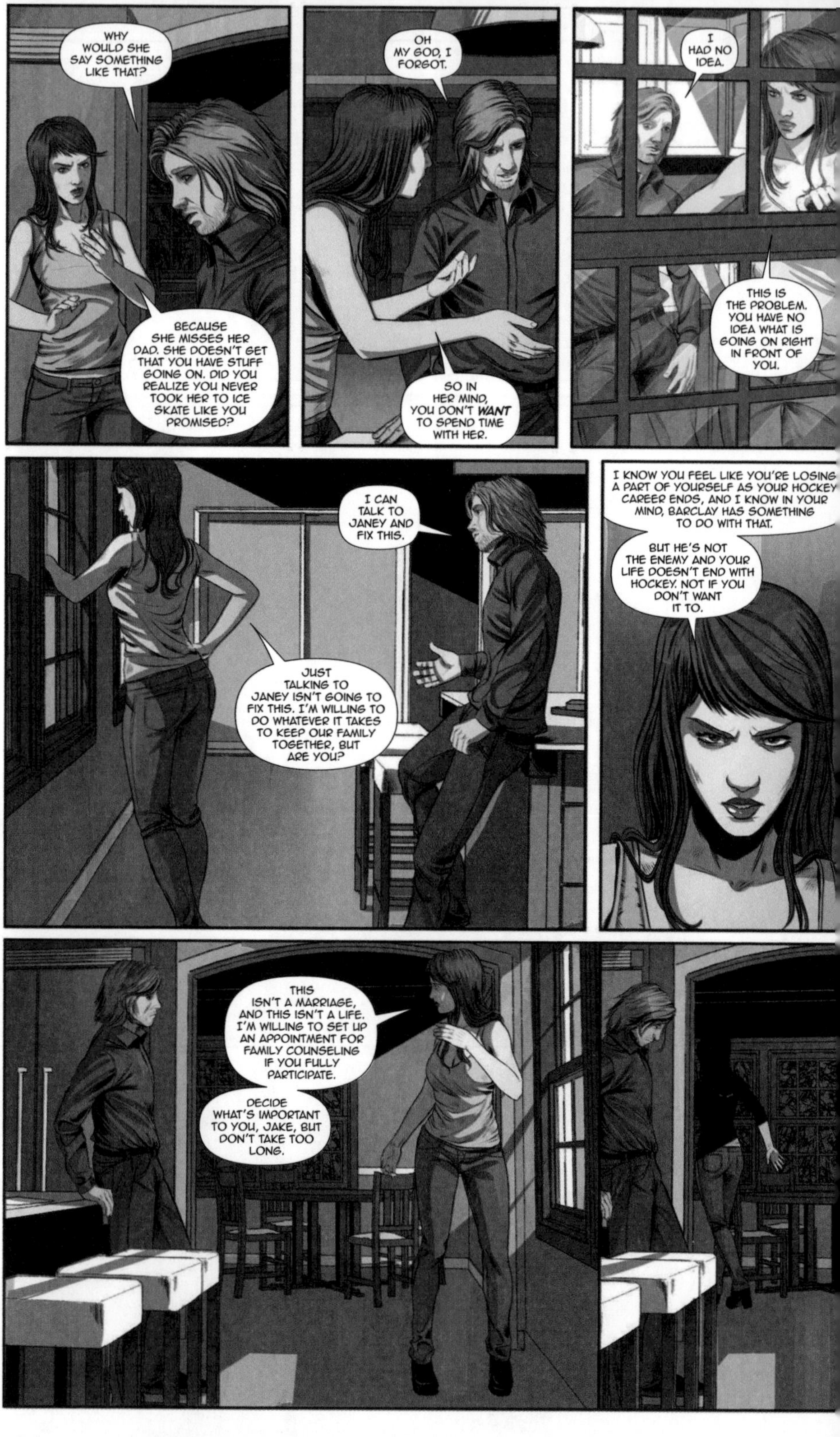
WHY WOULD SHE SAY SOMETHING LIKE THAT?
BECAUSE SHE MISSES HER DAD. SHE DOESN'T GET THAT YOU HAVE STUFF GOING ON. DID YOU REALIZE YOU NEVER TOOK HER TO ICE SKATE LIKE YOU PROMISED?
OH MY GOD, I FORGOT.
SO IN HER MIND, YOU DON'T *WANT* TO SPEND TIME WITH HER.
I HAD NO IDEA.
THIS IS THE PROBLEM. YOU HAVE NO IDEA WHAT IS GOING ON RIGHT IN FRONT OF YOU.
I CAN TALK TO JANEY AND FIX THIS.
JUST TALKING TO JANEY ISN'T GOING TO FIX THIS. I'M WILLING TO DO WHATEVER IT TAKES TO KEEP OUR FAMILY TOGETHER, BUT ARE YOU?
I KNOW YOU FEEL LIKE YOU'RE LOSING A PART OF YOURSELF AS YOUR HOCKEY CAREER ENDS, AND I KNOW IN YOUR MIND, BARCLAY HAS SOMETHING TO DO WITH THAT.
BUT HE'S NOT THE ENEMY AND YOUR LIFE DOESN'T END WITH HOCKEY. NOT IF YOU DON'T WANT IT TO.
THIS ISN'T A MARRIAGE, AND THIS ISN'T A LIFE. I'M WILLING TO SET UP AN APPOINTMENT FOR FAMILY COUNSELING IF YOU FULLY PARTICIPATE.
DECIDE WHAT'S IMPORTANT TO YOU, JAKE, BUT DON'T TAKE TOO LONG.

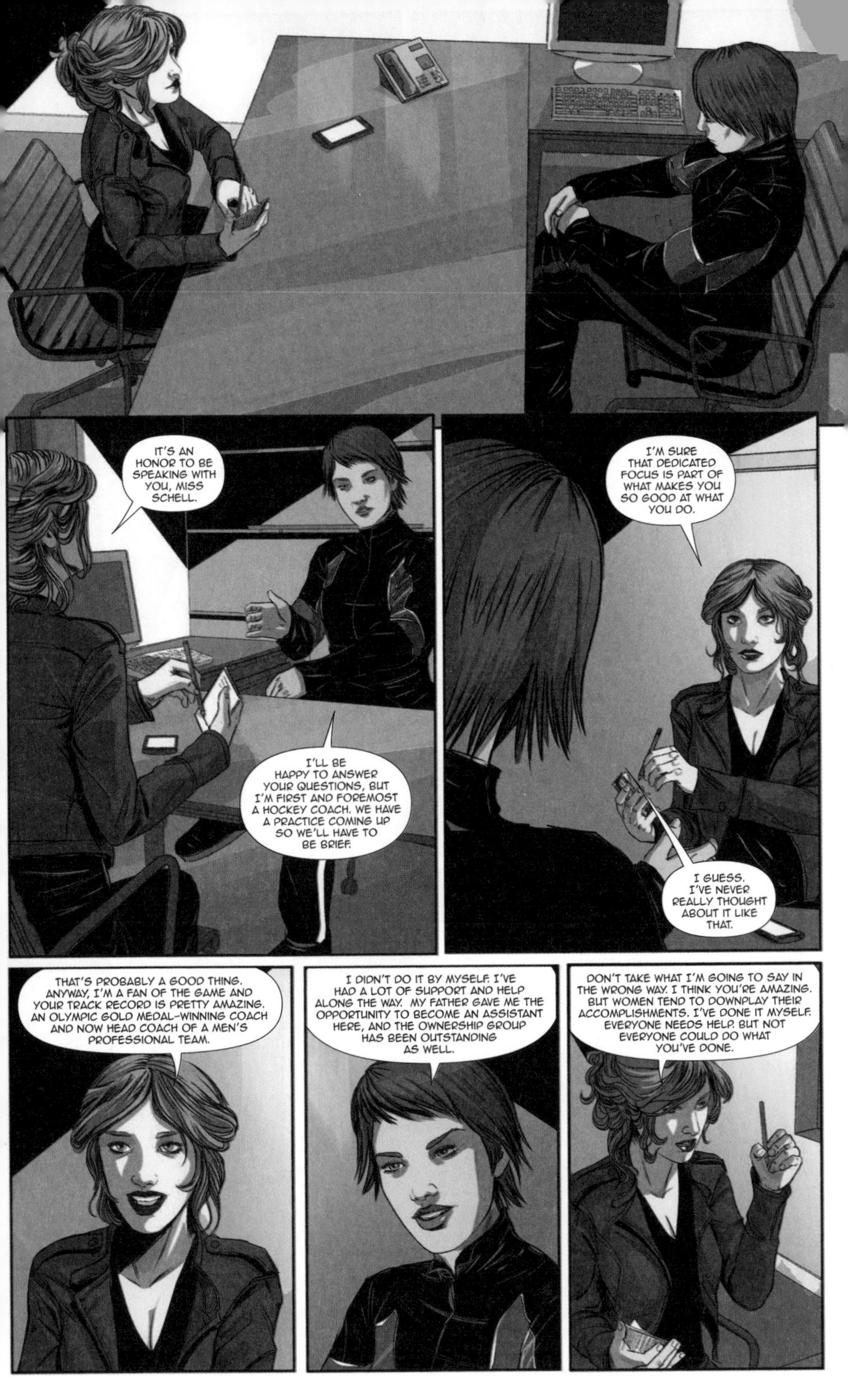
IT'S AN HONOR TO BE SPEAKING WITH YOU, MISS SCHELL.
I'LL BE HAPPY TO ANSWER YOUR QUESTIONS, BUT I'M FIRST AND FOREMOST A HOCKEY COACH. WE HAVE A PRACTICE COMING UP SO WE'LL HAVE TO BE BRIEF.
I'M SURE THAT DEDICATED FOCUS IS PART OF WHAT MAKES YOU SO GOOD AT WHAT YOU DO.
I GUESS. I'VE NEVER REALLY THOUGHT ABOUT IT LIKE THAT.
THAT'S PROBABLY A GOOD THING. ANYWAY, I'M A FAN OF THE GAME AND YOUR TRACK RECORD IS PRETTY AMAZING. AN OLYMPIC GOLD MEDAL-WINNING COACH AND NOW HEAD COACH OF A MEN'S PROFESSIONAL TEAM.
I DIDN'T DO IT BY MYSELF. I'VE HAD A LOT OF SUPPORT AND HELP ALONG THE WAY. MY FATHER GAVE ME THE OPPORTUNITY TO BECOME AN ASSISTANT HERE, AND THE OWNERSHIP GROUP HAS BEEN OUTSTANDING AS WELL.
DON'T TAKE WHAT I'M GOING TO SAY IN THE WRONG WAY. I THINK YOU'RE AMAZING. BUT WOMEN TEND TO DOWNPLAY THEIR ACCOMPLISHMENTS. I'VE DONE IT MYSELF. EVERYONE NEEDS HELP. BUT NOT EVERYONE COULD DO WHAT YOU'VE DONE.

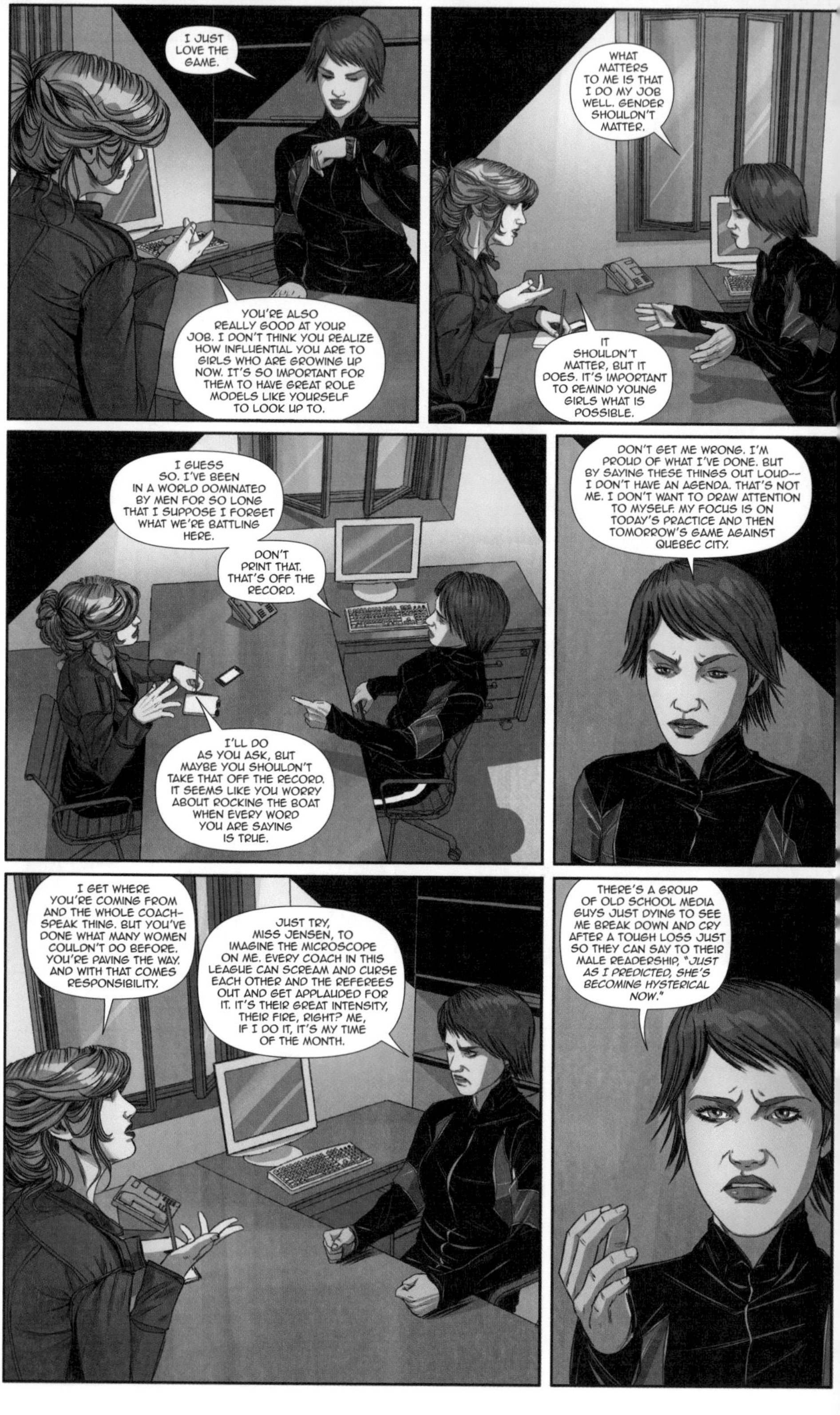
I JUST LOVE THE GAME.
YOU'RE ALSO REALLY GOOD AT YOUR JOB. I DON'T THINK YOU REALIZE HOW INFLUENTIAL YOU ARE TO GIRLS WHO ARE GROWING UP NOW. IT'S SO IMPORTANT FOR THEM TO HAVE GREAT ROLE MODELS LIKE YOURSELF TO LOOK UP TO.
WHAT MATTERS TO ME IS THAT I DO MY JOB WELL. GENDER SHOULDN'T MATTER.
IT SHOULDN'T MATTER, BUT IT DOES. IT'S IMPORTANT TO REMIND YOUNG GIRLS WHAT IS POSSIBLE.
I GUESS SO. I'VE BEEN IN A WORLD DOMINATED BY MEN FOR SO LONG THAT I SUPPOSE I FORGET WHAT WE'RE BATTLING HERE.
DON'T PRINT THAT. THAT'S OFF THE RECORD.
I'LL DO AS YOU ASK, BUT MAYBE YOU SHOULDN'T TAKE THAT OFF THE RECORD. IT SEEMS LIKE YOU WORRY ABOUT ROCKING THE BOAT WHEN EVERY WORD YOU ARE SAYING IS TRUE.
DON'T GET ME WRONG. I'M PROUD OF WHAT I'VE DONE. BUT BY SAYING THESE THINGS OUT LOUD-- I DON'T HAVE AN AGENDA. THAT'S NOT ME. I DON'T WANT TO DRAW ATTENTION TO MYSELF. MY FOCUS IS ON TODAY'S PRACTICE AND THEN TOMORROW'S GAME AGAINST QUEBEC CITY.
I GET WHERE YOU'RE COMING FROM AND THE WHOLE COACH-SPEAK THING. BUT YOU'VE DONE WHAT MANY WOMEN COULDN'T DO BEFORE. YOU'RE PAVING THE WAY. AND WITH THAT COMES RESPONSIBILITY.
JUST TRY, MISS JENSEN, TO IMAGINE THE MICROSCOPE ON ME. EVERY COACH IN THIS LEAGUE CAN SCREAM AND CURSE EACH OTHER AND THE REFEREES OUT AND GET APPLAUDED FOR IT. IT'S THEIR GREAT INTENSITY, THEIR FIRE, RIGHT? ME, IF I DO IT, IT'S MY TIME OF THE MONTH.
THERE'S A GROUP OF OLD SCHOOL MEDIA GUYS JUST DYING TO SEE ME BREAK DOWN AND CRY AFTER A TOUGH LOSS JUST SO THEY CAN SAY TO THEIR MALE READERSHIP, "JUST AS I PREDICTED, SHE'S BECOMING HYSTERICAL NOW."

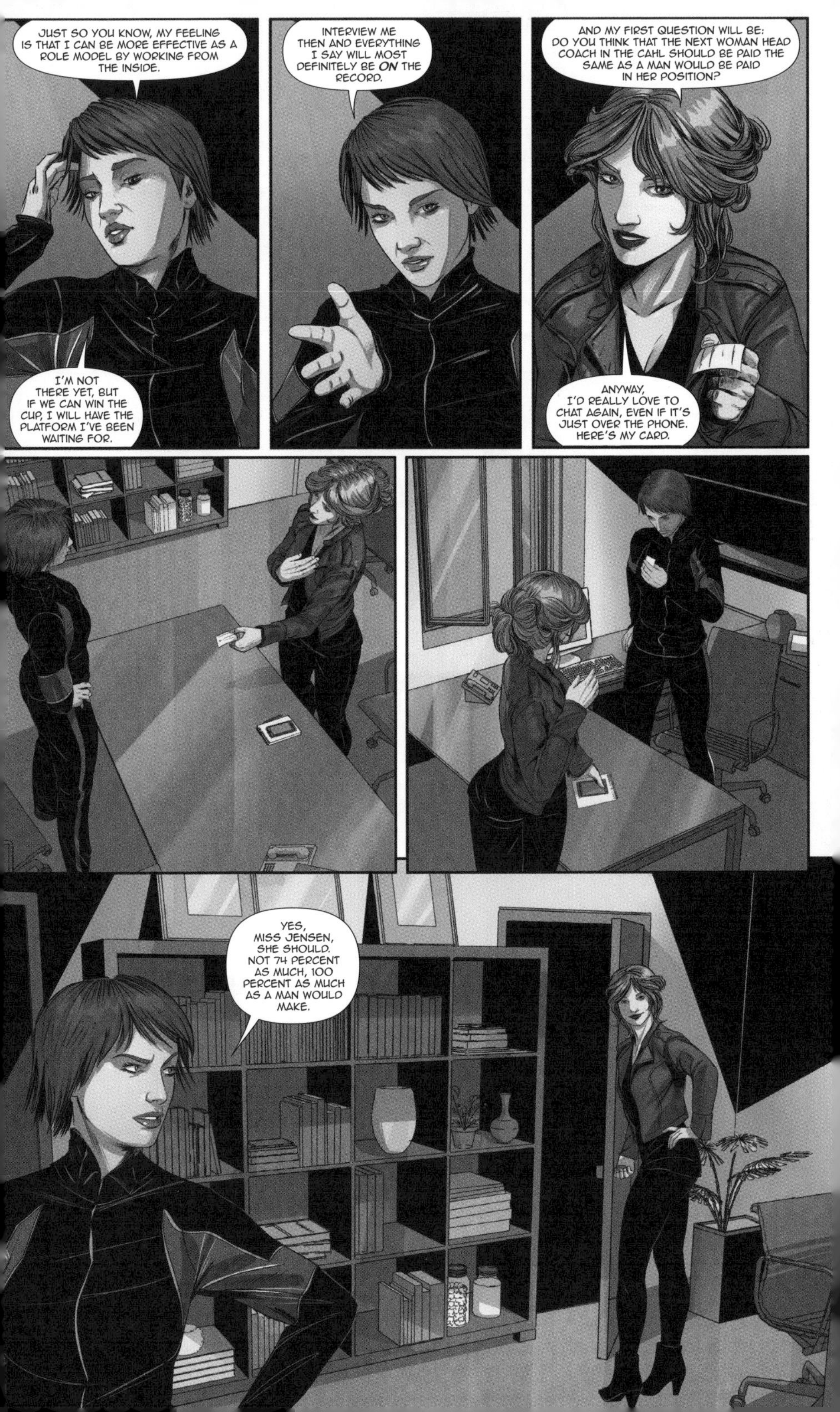
JUST SO YOU KNOW, MY FEELING IS THAT I CAN BE MORE EFFECTIVE AS A ROLE MODEL BY WORKING FROM THE INSIDE.
I'M NOT THERE YET, BUT IF WE CAN WIN THE CUP, I WILL HAVE THE PLATFORM I'VE BEEN WAITING FOR.
INTERVIEW ME THEN AND EVERYTHING I SAY WILL MOST DEFINITELY BE ***ON*** THE RECORD.
AND MY FIRST QUESTION WILL BE: DO YOU THINK THAT THE NEXT WOMAN HEAD COACH IN THE CAHL SHOULD BE PAID THE SAME AS A MAN WOULD BE PAID IN HER POSITION?
ANYWAY, I'D REALLY LOVE TO CHAT AGAIN, EVEN IF IT'S JUST OVER THE PHONE. HERE'S MY CARD.
YES, MISS JENSEN, SHE SHOULD. NOT 74 PERCENT AS MUCH, 100 PERCENT AS MUCH AS A MAN WOULD MAKE.

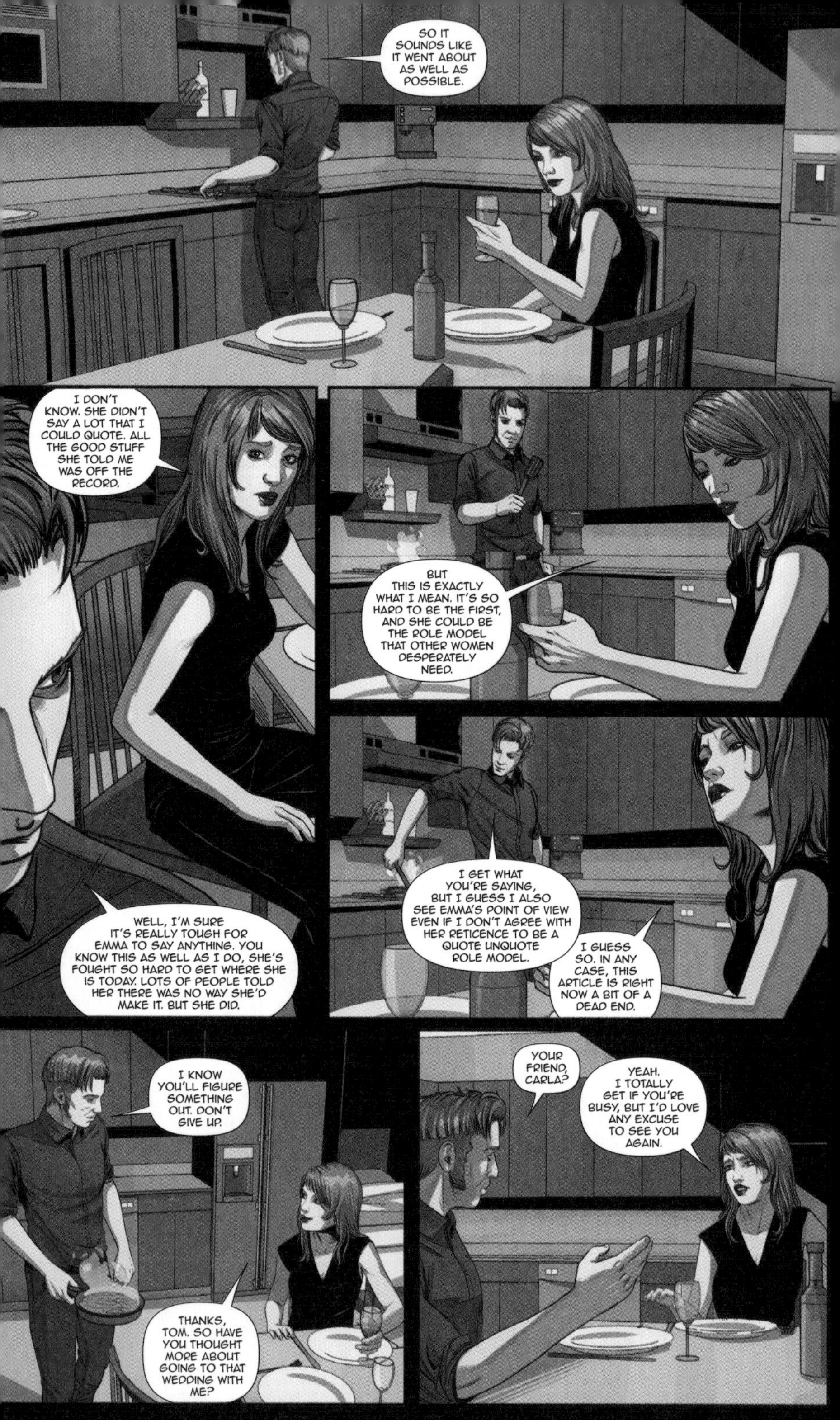
SO IT SOUNDS LIKE IT WENT ABOUT AS WELL AS POSSIBLE.
I DON'T KNOW. SHE DIDN'T SAY A LOT THAT I COULD QUOTE. ALL THE GOOD STUFF SHE TOLD ME WAS OFF THE RECORD.
WELL, I'M SURE IT'S REALLY TOUGH FOR EMMA TO SAY ANYTHING. YOU KNOW THIS AS WELL AS I DO, SHE'S FOUGHT SO HARD TO GET WHERE SHE IS TODAY. LOTS OF PEOPLE TOLD HER THERE WAS NO WAY SHE'D MAKE IT. BUT SHE DID.
BUT THIS IS EXACTLY WHAT I MEAN. IT'S SO HARD TO BE THE FIRST, AND SHE COULD BE THE ROLE MODEL THAT OTHER WOMEN DESPERATELY NEED.
I GET WHAT YOU'RE SAYING, BUT I GUESS I ALSO SEE EMMA'S POINT OF VIEW EVEN IF I DON'T AGREE WITH HER RETICENCE TO BE A QUOTE UNQUOTE ROLE MODEL.
I GUESS SO. IN ANY CASE, THIS ARTICLE IS RIGHT NOW A BIT OF A DEAD END.
I KNOW YOU'LL FIGURE SOMETHING OUT. DON'T GIVE UP.
THANKS, TOM. SO HAVE YOU THOUGHT MORE ABOUT GOING TO THAT WEDDING WITH ME?
YOUR FRIEND, CARLA?
YEAH. I TOTALLY GET IF YOU'RE BUSY, BUT I'D LOVE ANY EXCUSE TO SEE YOU AGAIN.

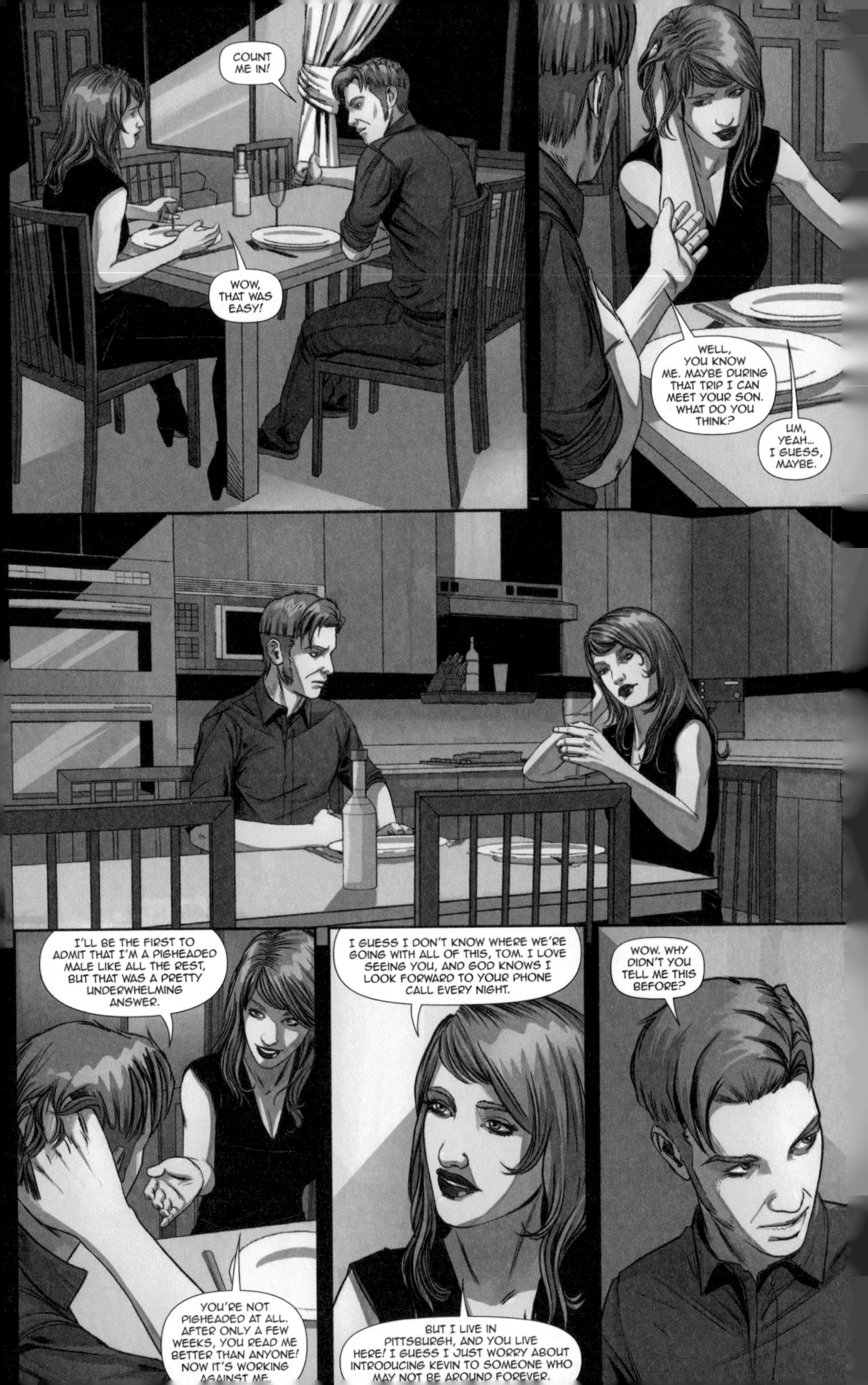
COUNT ME IN!
WOW, THAT WAS EASY!
WELL, YOU KNOW ME. MAYBE DURING THAT TRIP I CAN MEET YOUR SON. WHAT DO YOU THINK?
UM, YEAH... I GUESS, MAYBE.
I'LL BE THE FIRST TO ADMIT THAT I'M A PIGHEADED MALE LIKE ALL THE REST, BUT THAT WAS A PRETTY UNDERWHELMING ANSWER.
YOU'RE NOT PIGHEADED AT ALL. AFTER ONLY A FEW WEEKS, YOU READ ME BETTER THAN ANYONE! NOW IT'S WORKING AGAINST ME.
I GUESS I DON'T KNOW WHERE WE'RE GOING WITH ALL OF THIS, TOM. I LOVE SEEING YOU, AND GOD KNOWS I LOOK FORWARD TO YOUR PHONE CALL EVERY NIGHT.
BUT I LIVE IN PITTSBURGH, AND YOU LIVE HERE! I GUESS I JUST WORRY ABOUT INTRODUCING KEVIN TO SOMEONE WHO MAY NOT BE AROUND FOREVER.
WOW. WHY DIDN'T YOU TELL ME THIS BEFORE?

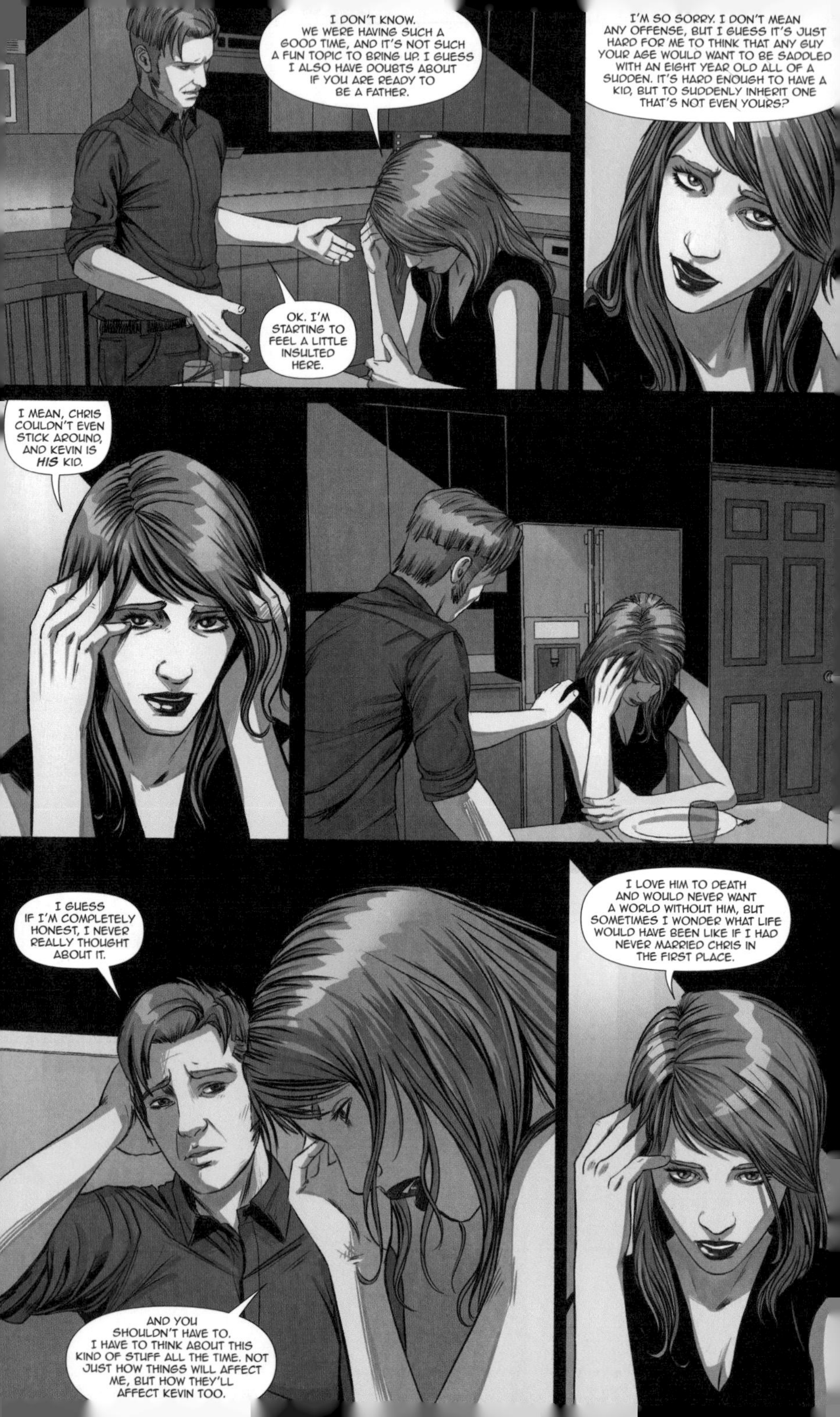
I DON'T KNOW. WE WERE HAVING SUCH A GOOD TIME, AND IT'S NOT SUCH A FUN TOPIC TO BRING UP. I GUESS I ALSO HAVE DOUBTS ABOUT IF YOU ARE READY TO BE A FATHER.
OK. I'M STARTING TO FEEL A LITTLE INSULTED HERE.
I'M SO SORRY. I DON'T MEAN ANY OFFENSE, BUT I GUESS IT'S JUST HARD FOR ME TO THINK THAT ANY GUY YOUR AGE WOULD WANT TO BE SADDLED WITH AN EIGHT YEAR OLD ALL OF A SUDDEN. IT'S HARD ENOUGH TO HAVE A KID, BUT TO SUDDENLY INHERIT ONE THAT'S NOT EVEN YOURS?
I MEAN, CHRIS COULDN'T EVEN STICK AROUND, AND KEVIN IS *HIS* KID.
I GUESS IF I'M COMPLETELY HONEST, I NEVER REALLY THOUGHT ABOUT IT.
AND YOU SHOULDN'T HAVE TO. I HAVE TO THINK ABOUT THIS KIND OF STUFF ALL THE TIME. NOT JUST HOW THINGS WILL AFFECT ME, BUT HOW THEY'LL AFFECT KEVIN TOO.
I LOVE HIM TO DEATH AND WOULD NEVER WANT A WORLD WITHOUT HIM, BUT SOMETIMES I WONDER WHAT LIFE WOULD HAVE BEEN LIKE IF I HAD NEVER MARRIED CHRIS IN THE FIRST PLACE.

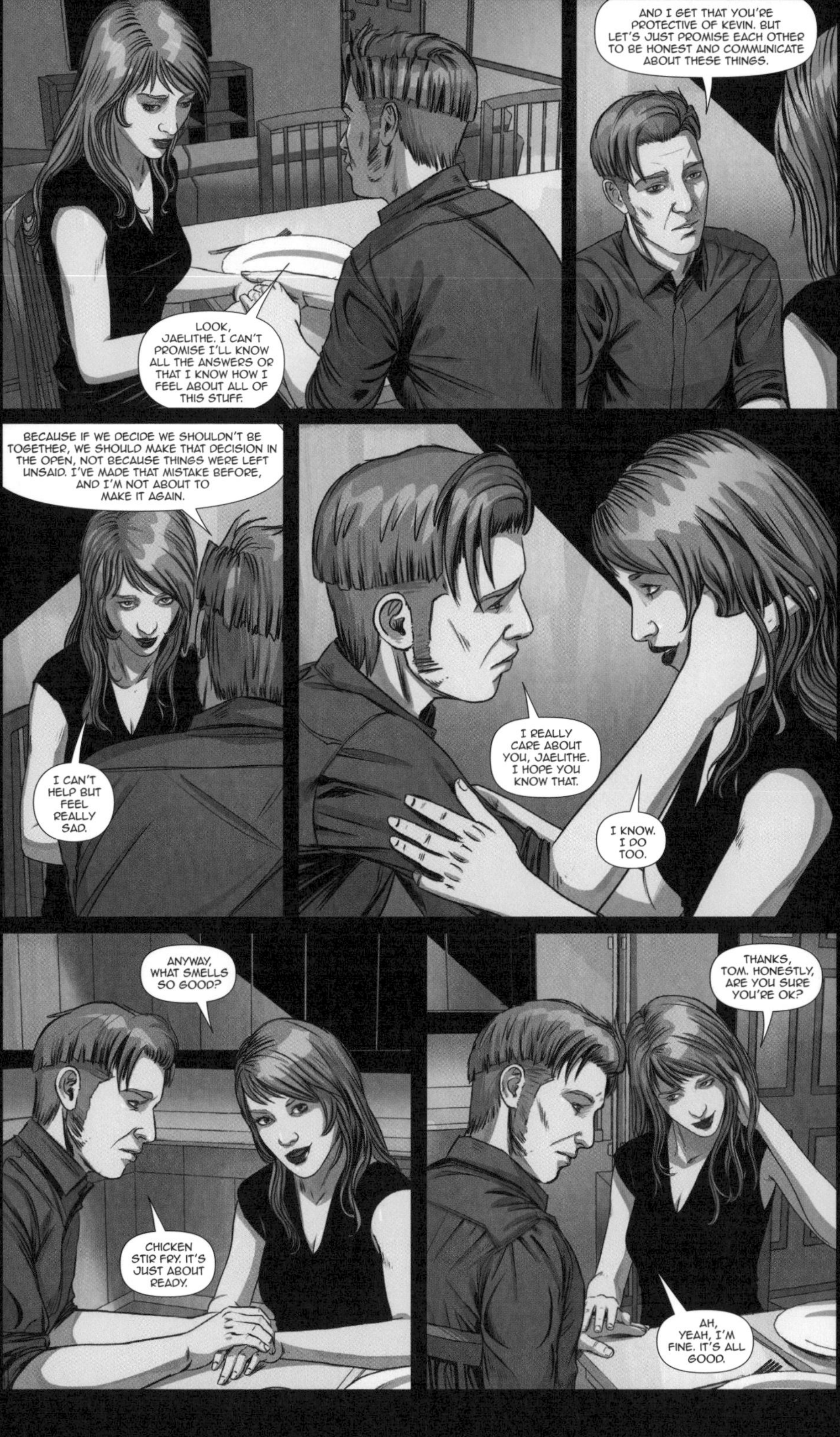
LOOK, JAELITHE. I CAN'T PROMISE I'LL KNOW ALL THE ANSWERS OR THAT I KNOW HOW I FEEL ABOUT ALL OF THIS STUFF.
AND I GET THAT YOU'RE PROTECTIVE OF KEVIN. BUT LET'S JUST PROMISE EACH OTHER TO BE HONEST AND COMMUNICATE ABOUT THESE THINGS.
BECAUSE IF WE DECIDE WE SHOULDN'T BE TOGETHER, WE SHOULD MAKE THAT DECISION IN THE OPEN, NOT BECAUSE THINGS WERE LEFT UNSAID. I'VE MADE THAT MISTAKE BEFORE, AND I'M NOT ABOUT TO MAKE IT AGAIN.
I CAN'T HELP BUT FEEL REALLY SAD.
I REALLY CARE ABOUT YOU, JAELITHE. I HOPE YOU KNOW THAT.
I KNOW. I DO TOO.
ANYWAY, WHAT SMELLS SO GOOD?
CHICKEN STIR FRY. IT'S JUST ABOUT READY.
THANKS, TOM. HONESTLY, ARE YOU SURE YOU'RE OK?
AH, YEAH, I'M FINE. IT'S ALL GOOD.

CHAPTER 8
FALLING IN REVERSE

RECOMMENDED LISTENING:

"THE DRUG IN ME IS YOU"
FALLING IN REVERSE

"GET OLDER"
MATTHEW SWEET

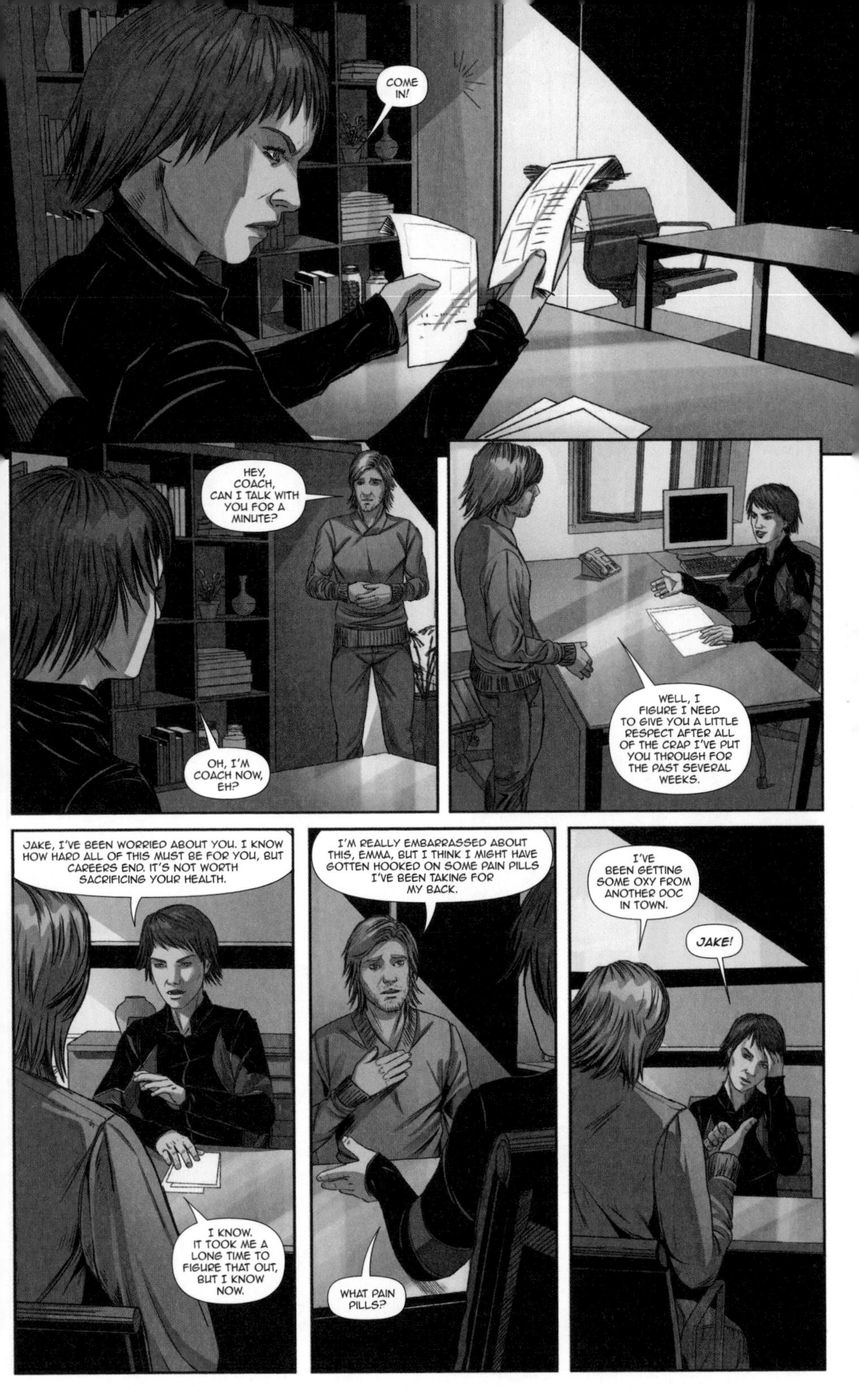
COME IN!
HEY, COACH, CAN I TALK WITH YOU FOR A MINUTE?
OH, I'M COACH NOW, EH?
WELL, I FIGURE I NEED TO GIVE YOU A LITTLE RESPECT AFTER ALL OF THE CRAP I'VE PUT YOU THROUGH FOR THE PAST SEVERAL WEEKS.
JAKE, I'VE BEEN WORRIED ABOUT YOU. I KNOW HOW HARD ALL OF THIS MUST BE FOR YOU, BUT CAREERS END. IT'S NOT WORTH SACRIFICING YOUR HEALTH.
I KNOW. IT TOOK ME A LONG TIME TO FIGURE THAT OUT, BUT I KNOW NOW.
I'M REALLY EMBARRASSED ABOUT THIS, EMMA, BUT I THINK I MIGHT HAVE GOTTEN HOOKED ON SOME PAIN PILLS I'VE BEEN TAKING FOR MY BACK.
WHAT PAIN PILLS?
I'VE BEEN GETTING SOME OXY FROM ANOTHER DOC IN TOWN.
JAKE!

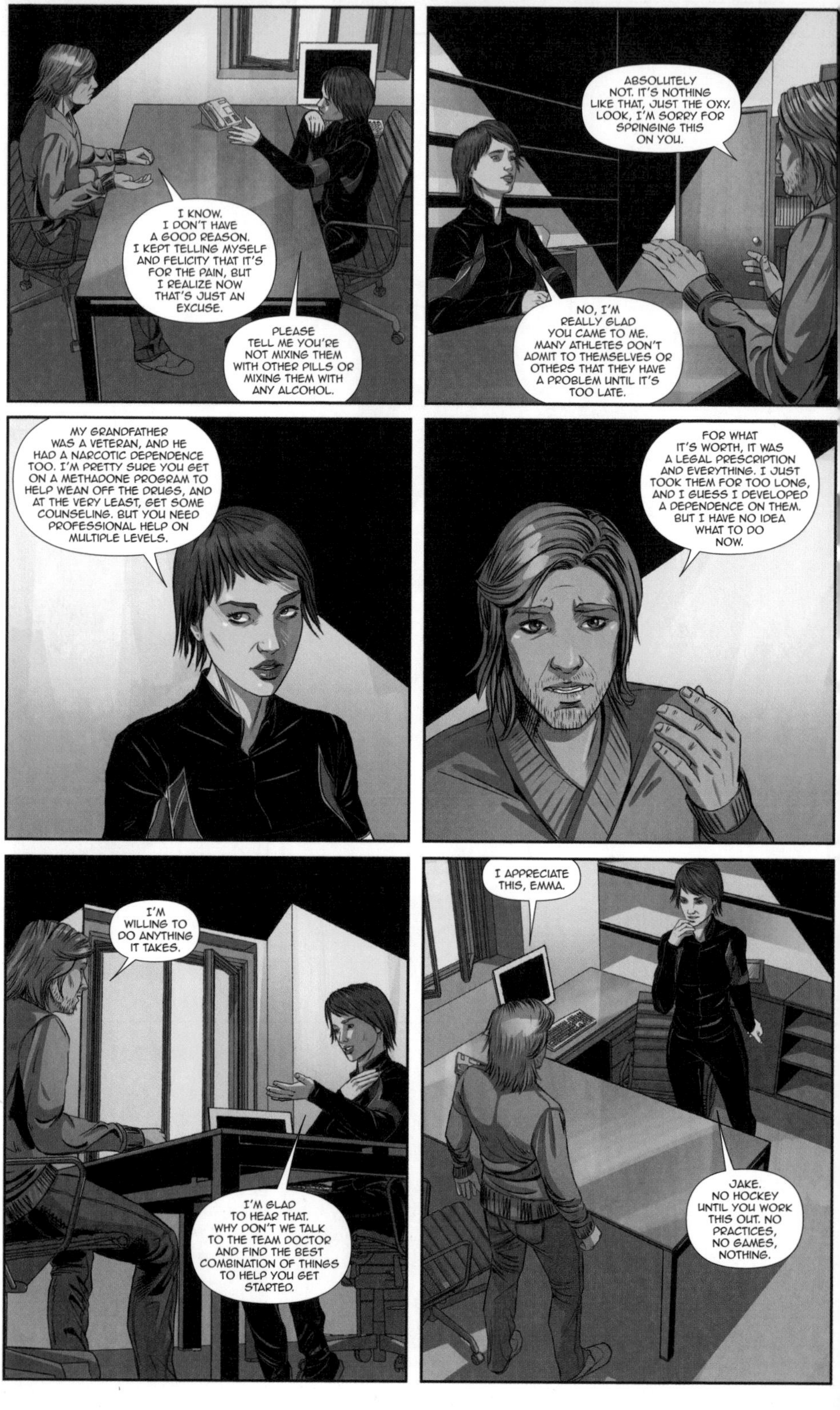
I KNOW. I DON'T HAVE A GOOD REASON. I KEPT TELLING MYSELF AND FELICITY THAT IT'S FOR THE PAIN, BUT I REALIZE NOW THAT'S JUST AN EXCUSE.
PLEASE TELL ME YOU'RE NOT MIXING THEM WITH OTHER PILLS OR MIXING THEM WITH ANY ALCOHOL.
ABSOLUTELY NOT. IT'S NOTHING LIKE THAT, JUST THE OXY. LOOK, I'M SORRY FOR SPRINGING THIS ON YOU.
NO, I'M REALLY GLAD YOU CAME TO ME. MANY ATHLETES DON'T ADMIT TO THEMSELVES OR OTHERS THAT THEY HAVE A PROBLEM UNTIL IT'S TOO LATE.
MY GRANDFATHER WAS A VETERAN, AND HE HAD A NARCOTIC DEPENDENCE TOO. I'M PRETTY SURE YOU GET ON A METHADONE PROGRAM TO HELP WEAN OFF THE DRUGS, AND AT THE VERY LEAST, GET SOME COUNSELING. BUT YOU NEED PROFESSIONAL HELP ON MULTIPLE LEVELS.
FOR WHAT IT'S WORTH, IT WAS A LEGAL PRESCRIPTION AND EVERYTHING. I JUST TOOK THEM FOR TOO LONG, AND I GUESS I DEVELOPED A DEPENDENCE ON THEM. BUT I HAVE NO IDEA WHAT TO DO NOW.
I'M WILLING TO DO ANYTHING IT TAKES.
I'M GLAD TO HEAR THAT. WHY DON'T WE TALK TO THE TEAM DOCTOR AND FIND THE BEST COMBINATION OF THINGS TO HELP YOU GET STARTED.
I APPRECIATE THIS, EMMA.
JAKE. NO HOCKEY UNTIL YOU WORK THIS OUT. NO PRACTICES, NO GAMES, NOTHING.

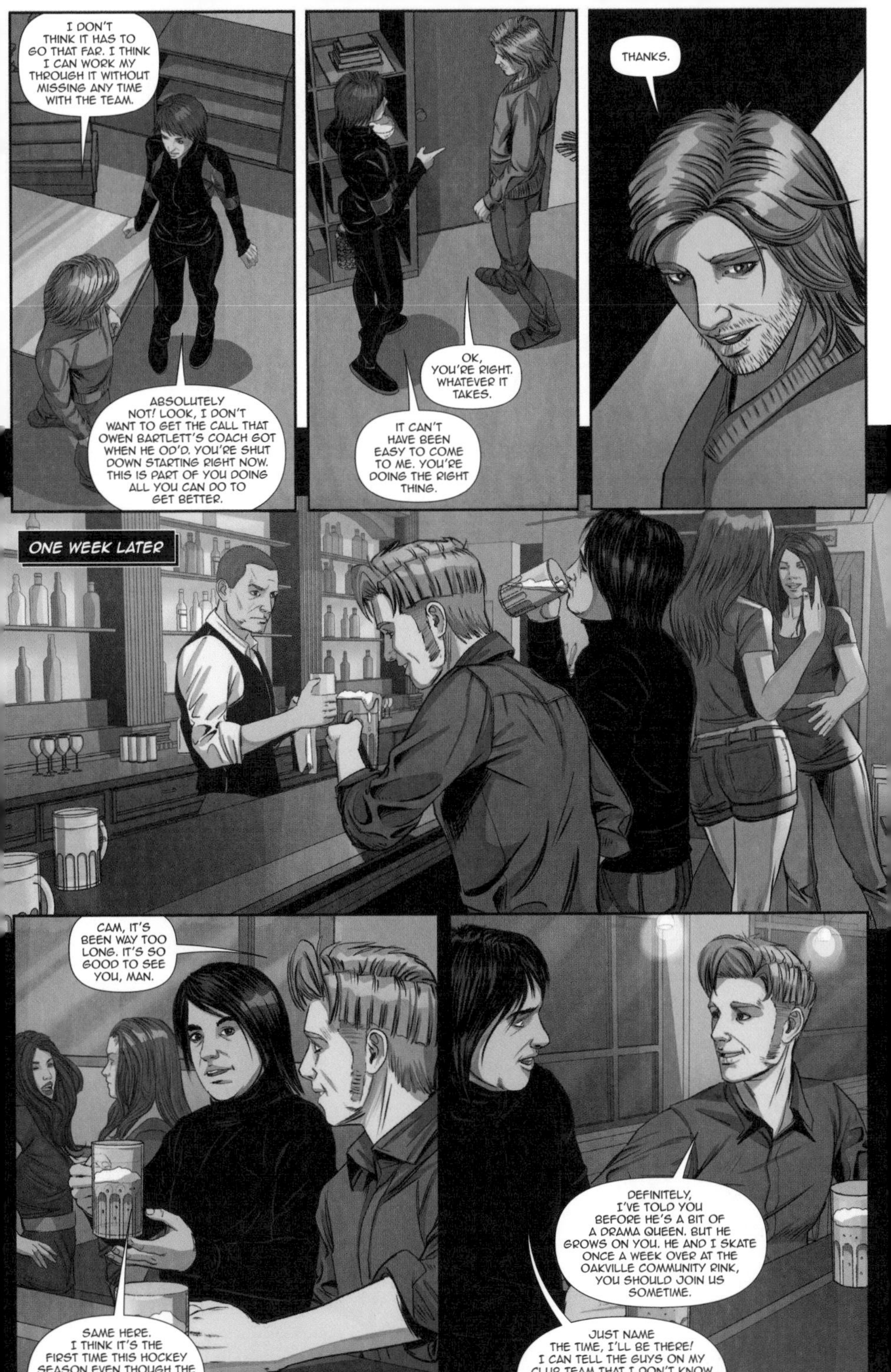
I DON'T THINK IT HAS TO GO THAT FAR. I THINK I CAN WORK MY THROUGH IT WITHOUT MISSING ANY TIME WITH THE TEAM.
ABSOLUTELY NOT! LOOK, I DON'T WANT TO GET THE CALL THAT OWEN BARTLETT'S COACH GOT WHEN HE OD'D. YOU'RE SHUT DOWN STARTING RIGHT NOW. THIS IS PART OF YOU DOING ALL YOU CAN DO TO GET BETTER.
OK, YOU'RE RIGHT. WHATEVER IT TAKES.
IT CAN'T HAVE BEEN EASY TO COME TO ME. YOU'RE DOING THE RIGHT THING.
THANKS.
ONE WEEK LATER
CAM, IT'S BEEN WAY TOO LONG. IT'S SO GOOD TO SEE YOU, MAN.
SAME HERE. I THINK IT'S THE FIRST TIME THIS HOCKEY SEASON EVEN THOUGH THE SEASON'S ALMOST OVER. I GUESS JACOBSON KEEPS YOU RUNNING AROUND A LOT.
DEFINITELY, I'VE TOLD YOU BEFORE HE'S A BIT OF A DRAMA QUEEN. BUT HE GROWS ON YOU. HE AND I SKATE ONCE A WEEK OVER AT THE OAKVILLE COMMUNITY RINK, YOU SHOULD JOIN US SOMETIME.
JUST NAME THE TIME, I'LL BE THERE! I CAN TELL THE GUYS ON MY CLUB TEAM THAT I DON'T KNOW IF I'LL BE ABLE TO SUIT UP WITH THEM ANYMORE AFTER HAVING WORKED OUT WITH JACOBSON!

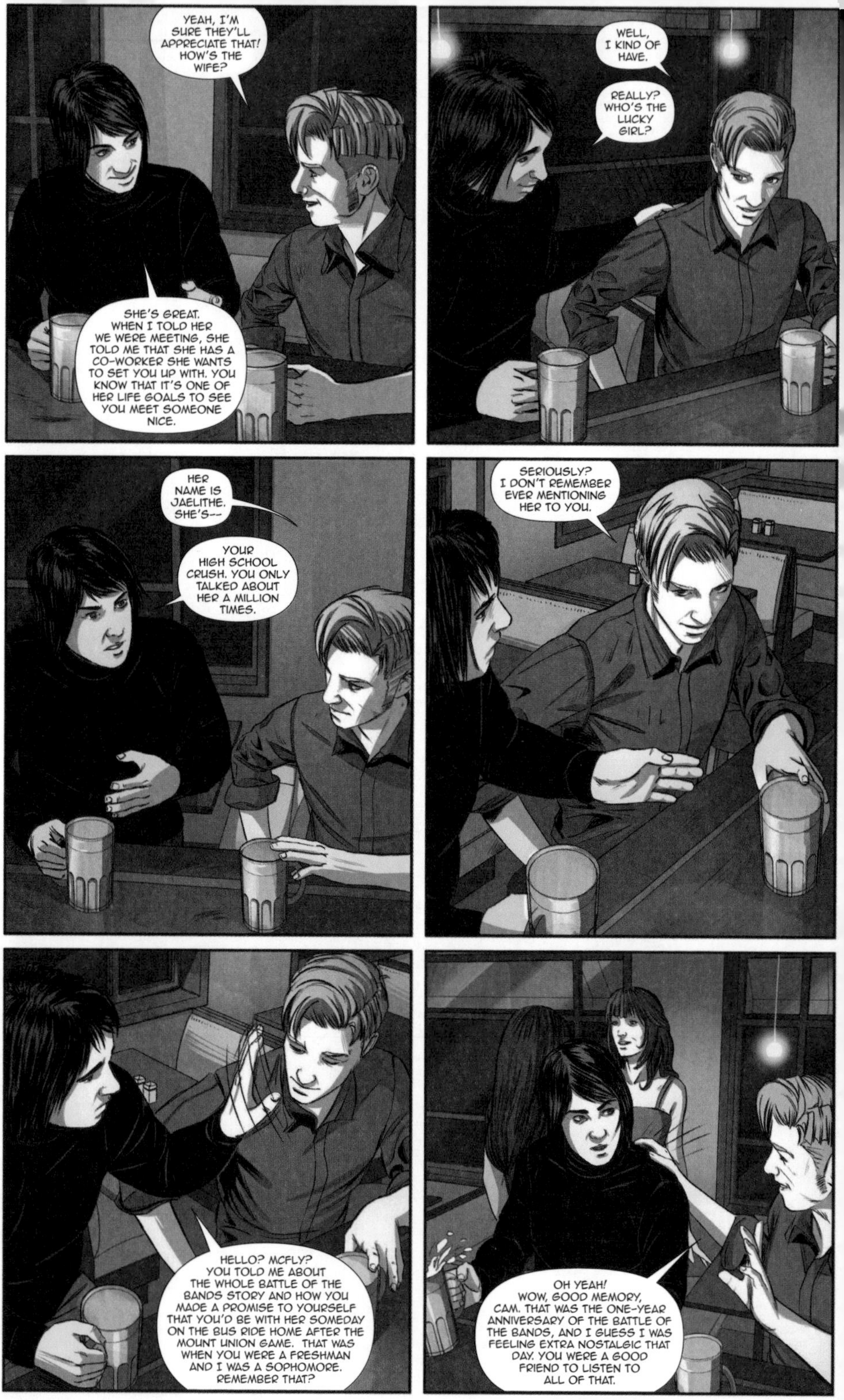
YEAH, I'M SURE THEY'LL APPRECIATE THAT! HOW'S THE WIFE?
SHE'S GREAT. WHEN I TOLD HER WE WERE MEETING, SHE TOLD ME THAT SHE HAS A CO-WORKER SHE WANTS TO SET YOU UP WITH. YOU KNOW THAT IT'S ONE OF HER LIFE GOALS TO SEE YOU MEET SOMEONE NICE.
WELL, I KIND OF HAVE.
REALLY? WHO'S THE LUCKY GIRL?
HER NAME IS JAELITHE. SHE'S--
YOUR HIGH SCHOOL CRUSH. YOU ONLY TALKED ABOUT HER A MILLION TIMES.
SERIOUSLY? I DON'T REMEMBER EVER MENTIONING HER TO YOU.
HELLO? MCFLY? YOU TOLD ME ABOUT THE WHOLE BATTLE OF THE BANDS STORY AND HOW YOU MADE A PROMISE TO YOURSELF THAT YOU'D BE WITH HER SOMEDAY ON THE BUS RIDE HOME AFTER THE MOUNT UNION GAME. THAT WAS WHEN YOU WERE A FRESHMAN AND I WAS A SOPHOMORE. REMEMBER THAT?
OH YEAH! WOW, GOOD MEMORY, CAM. THAT WAS THE ONE-YEAR ANNIVERSARY OF THE BATTLE OF THE BANDS, AND I GUESS I WAS FEELING EXTRA NOSTALGIC THAT DAY. YOU WERE A GOOD FRIEND TO LISTEN TO ALL OF THAT.

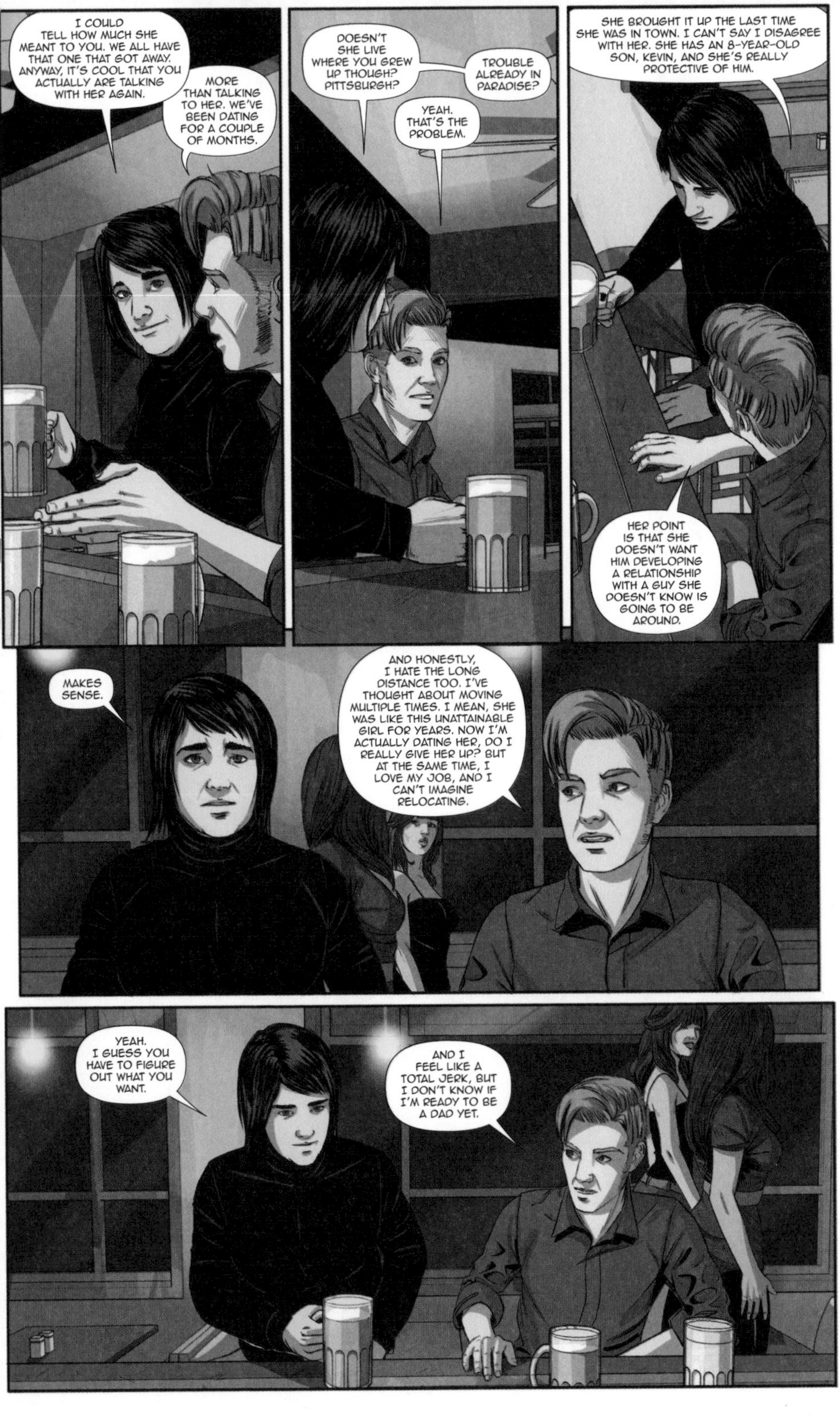

I COULD TELL HOW MUCH SHE MEANT TO YOU. WE ALL HAVE THAT ONE THAT GOT AWAY. ANYWAY, IT'S COOL THAT YOU ACTUALLY ARE TALKING WITH HER AGAIN.
MORE THAN TALKING TO HER. WE'VE BEEN DATING FOR A COUPLE OF MONTHS.
DOESN'T SHE LIVE WHERE YOU GREW UP THOUGH? PITTSBURGH?
TROUBLE ALREADY IN PARADISE?
YEAH. THAT'S THE PROBLEM.
SHE BROUGHT IT UP THE LAST TIME SHE WAS IN TOWN. I CAN'T SAY I DISAGREE WITH HER. SHE HAS AN 8-YEAR-OLD SON, KEVIN, AND SHE'S REALLY PROTECTIVE OF HIM.
HER POINT IS THAT SHE DOESN'T WANT HIM DEVELOPING A RELATIONSHIP WITH A GUY SHE DOESN'T KNOW IS GOING TO BE AROUND.
MAKES SENSE.
AND HONESTLY, I HATE THE LONG DISTANCE TOO. I'VE THOUGHT ABOUT MOVING MULTIPLE TIMES. I MEAN, SHE WAS LIKE THIS UNATTAINABLE GIRL FOR YEARS. NOW I'M ACTUALLY DATING HER, DO I REALLY GIVE HER UP? BUT AT THE SAME TIME, I LOVE MY JOB, AND I CAN'T IMAGINE RELOCATING.
YEAH. I GUESS YOU HAVE TO FIGURE OUT WHAT YOU WANT.
AND I FEEL LIKE A TOTAL JERK, BUT I DON'T KNOW IF I'M READY TO BE A DAD YET.

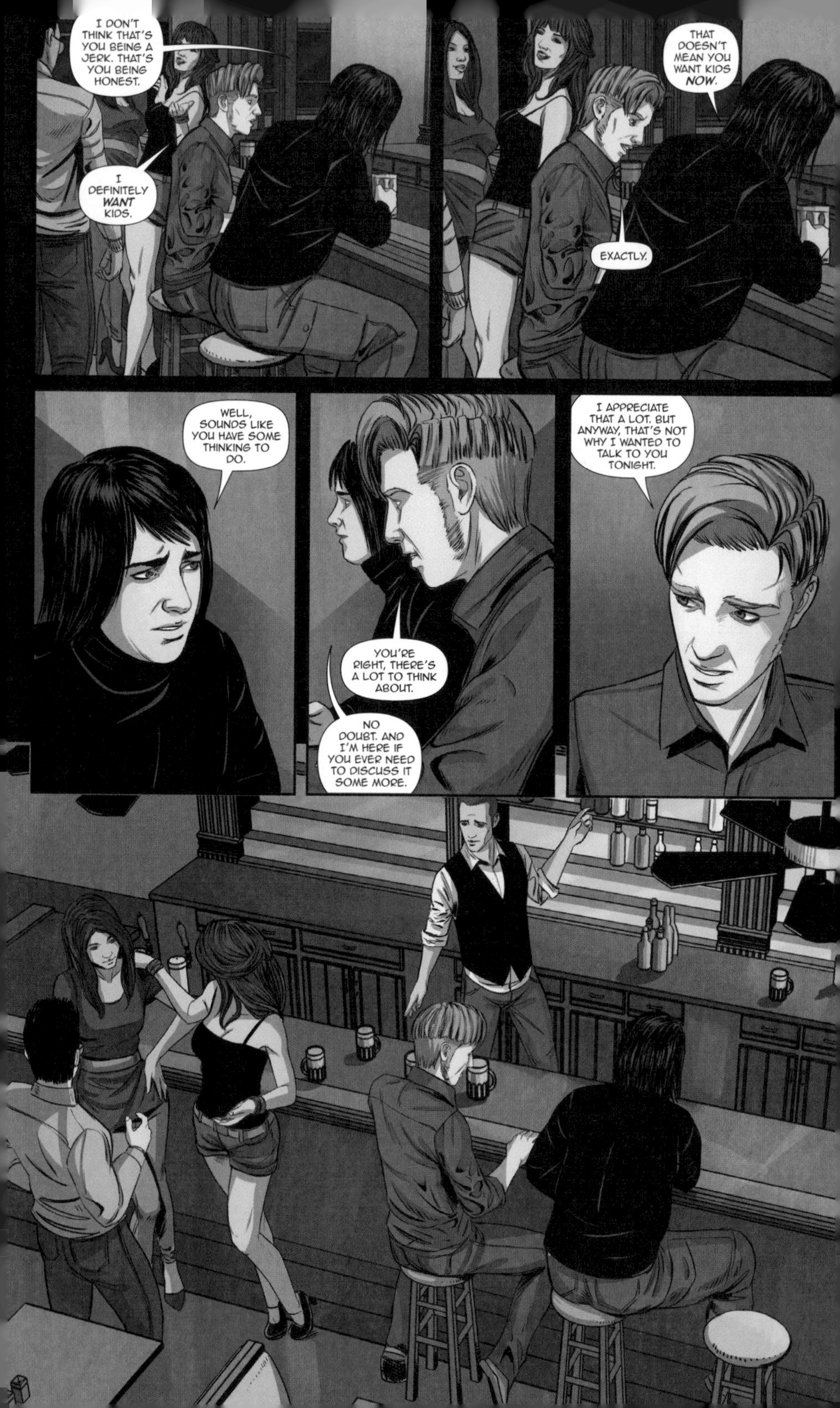
I DON'T THINK THAT'S YOU BEING A JERK. THAT'S YOU BEING HONEST.
I DEFINITELY *WANT* KIDS.
THAT DOESN'T MEAN YOU WANT KIDS *NOW*.
EXACTLY.
WELL, SOUNDS LIKE YOU HAVE SOME THINKING TO DO.
YOU'RE RIGHT, THERE'S A LOT TO THINK ABOUT.
NO DOUBT. AND I'M HERE IF YOU EVER NEED TO DISCUSS IT SOME MORE.
I APPRECIATE THAT A LOT. BUT ANYWAY, THAT'S NOT WHY I WANTED TO TALK TO YOU TONIGHT.

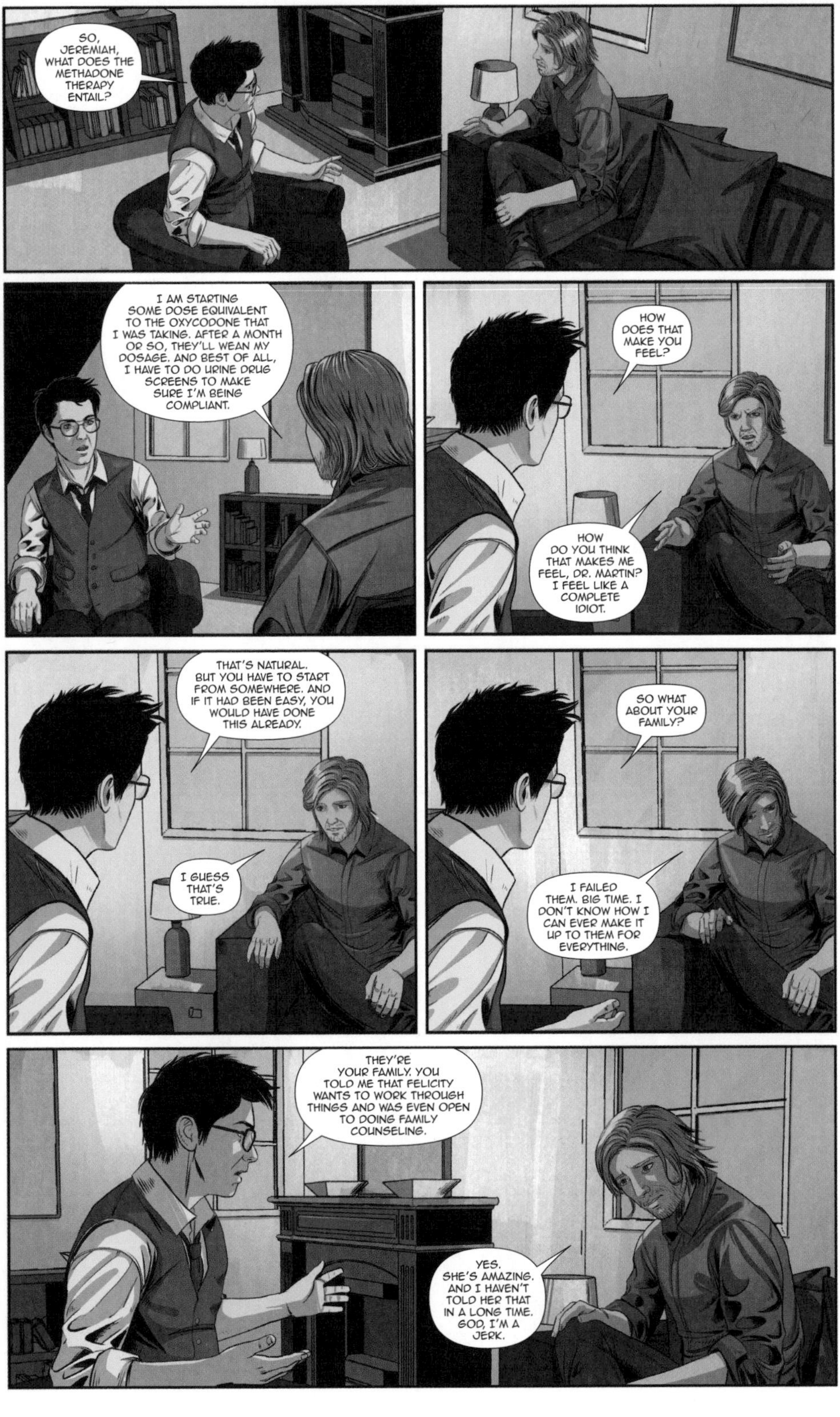
SO, JEREMIAH, WHAT DOES THE METHADONE THERAPY ENTAIL?
I AM STARTING SOME DOSE EQUIVALENT TO THE OXYCODONE THAT I WAS TAKING. AFTER A MONTH OR SO, THEY'LL WEAN MY DOSAGE. AND BEST OF ALL, I HAVE TO DO URINE DRUG SCREENS TO MAKE SURE I'M BEING COMPLIANT.
HOW DOES THAT MAKE YOU FEEL?
HOW DO YOU THINK THAT MAKES ME FEEL, DR. MARTIN? I FEEL LIKE A COMPLETE IDIOT.
THAT'S NATURAL. BUT YOU HAVE TO START FROM SOMEWHERE. AND IF IT HAD BEEN EASY, YOU WOULD HAVE DONE THIS ALREADY.
I GUESS THAT'S TRUE.
SO WHAT ABOUT YOUR FAMILY?
I FAILED THEM. BIG TIME. I DON'T KNOW HOW I CAN EVER MAKE IT UP TO THEM FOR EVERYTHING.
THEY'RE YOUR FAMILY. YOU TOLD ME THAT FELICITY WANTS TO WORK THROUGH THINGS AND WAS EVEN OPEN TO DOING FAMILY COUNSELING.
YES. SHE'S AMAZING. AND I HAVEN'T TOLD HER THAT IN A LONG TIME. GOD, I'M A JERK.

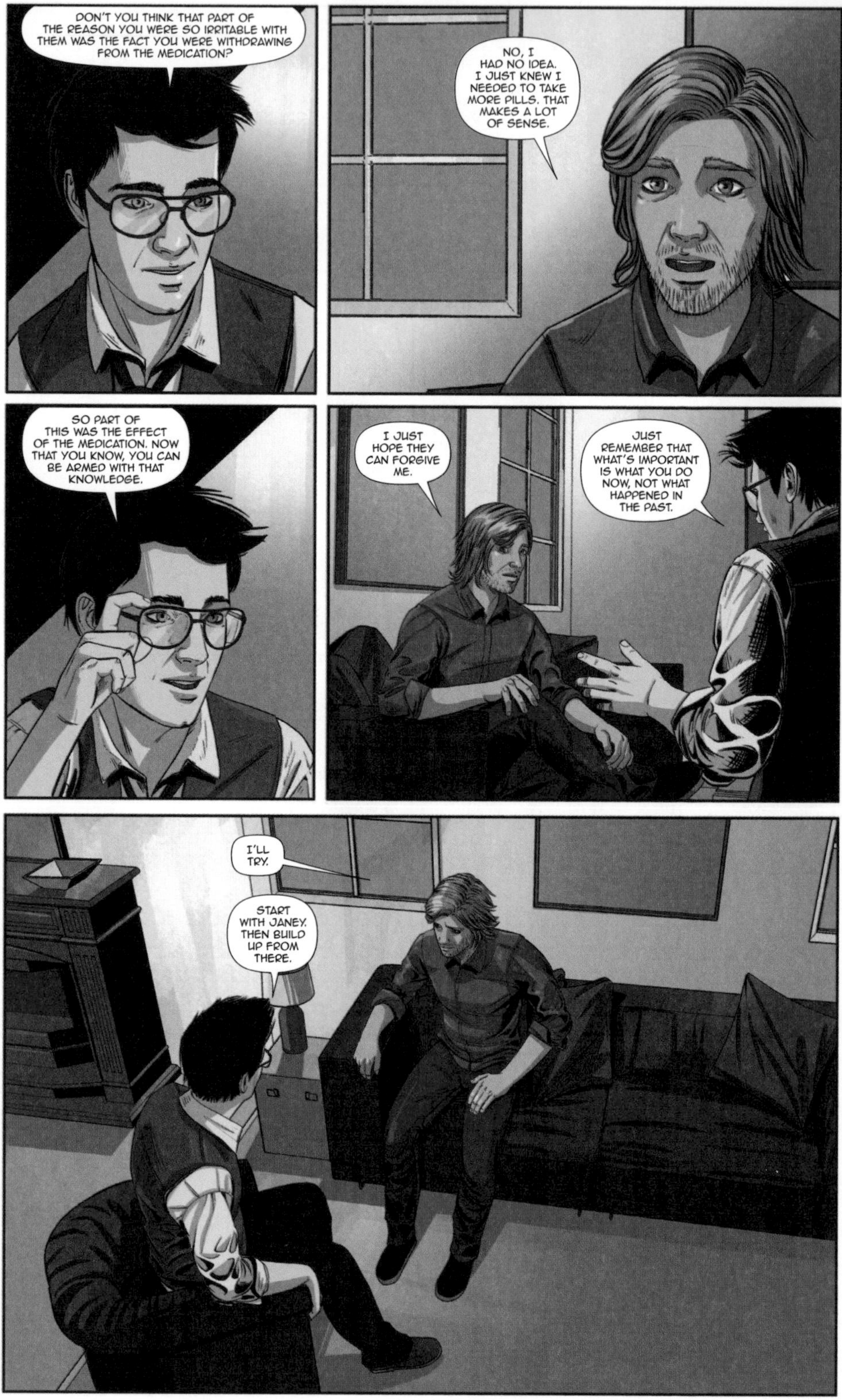
DON'T YOU THINK THAT PART OF THE REASON YOU WERE SO IRRITABLE WITH THEM WAS THE FACT YOU WERE WITHDRAWING FROM THE MEDICATION?
NO, I HAD NO IDEA. I JUST KNEW I NEEDED TO TAKE MORE PILLS. THAT MAKES A LOT OF SENSE.
SO PART OF THIS WAS THE EFFECT OF THE MEDICATION. NOW THAT YOU KNOW, YOU CAN BE ARMED WITH THAT KNOWLEDGE.
I JUST HOPE THEY CAN FORGIVE ME.
JUST REMEMBER THAT WHAT'S IMPORTANT IS WHAT YOU DO NOW, NOT WHAT HAPPENED IN THE PAST.
I'LL TRY.
START WITH JANEY. THEN BUILD UP FROM THERE.

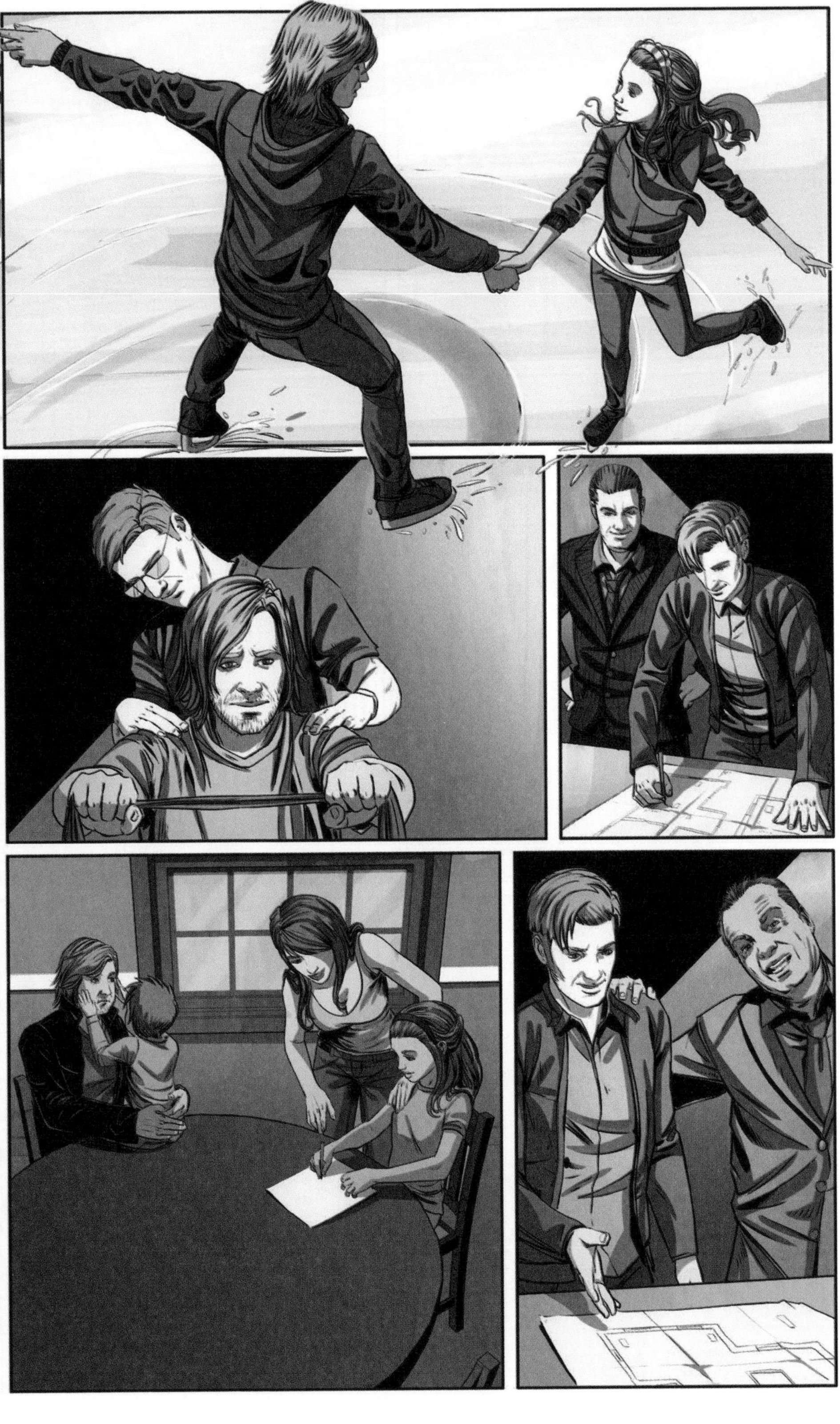

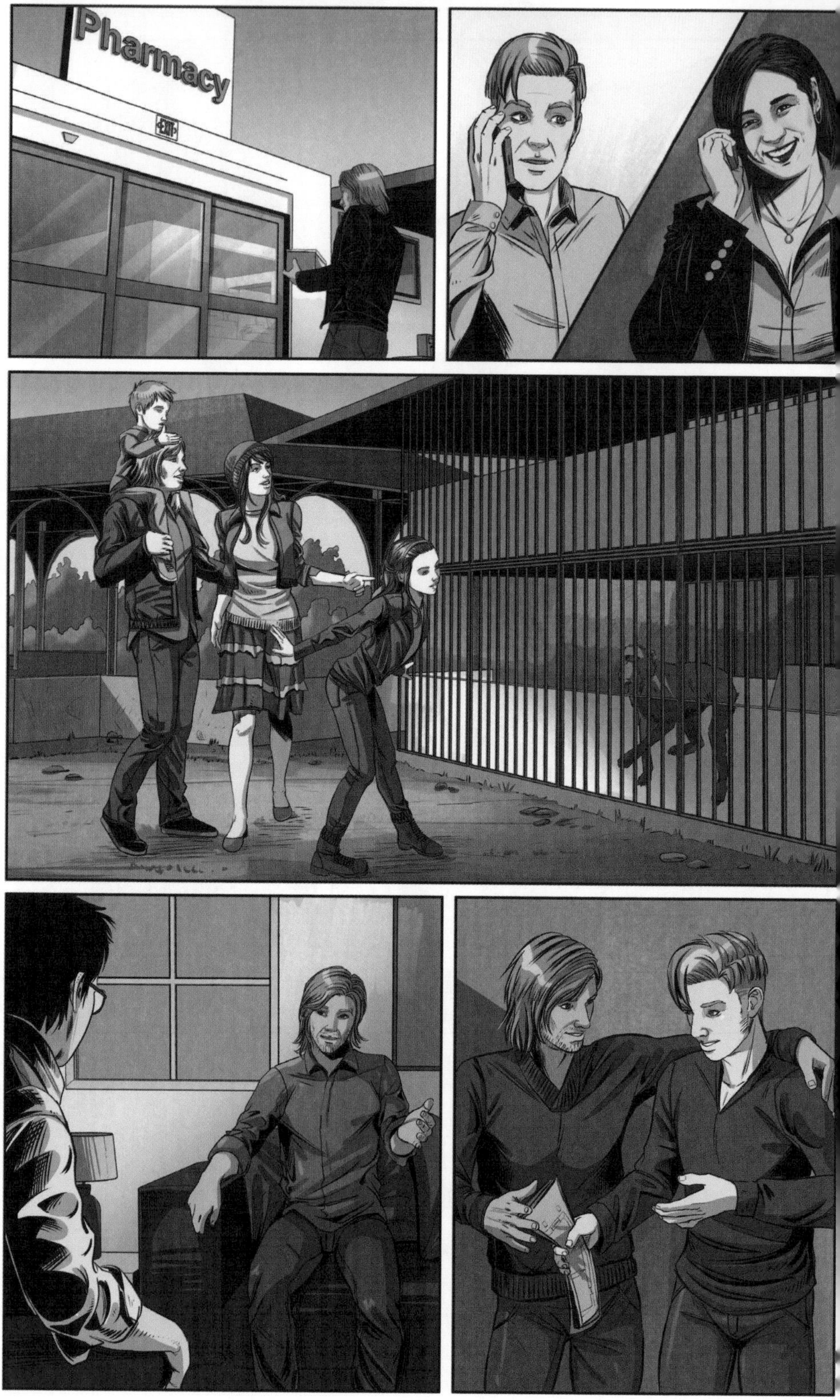
Pharmacy
EXIT

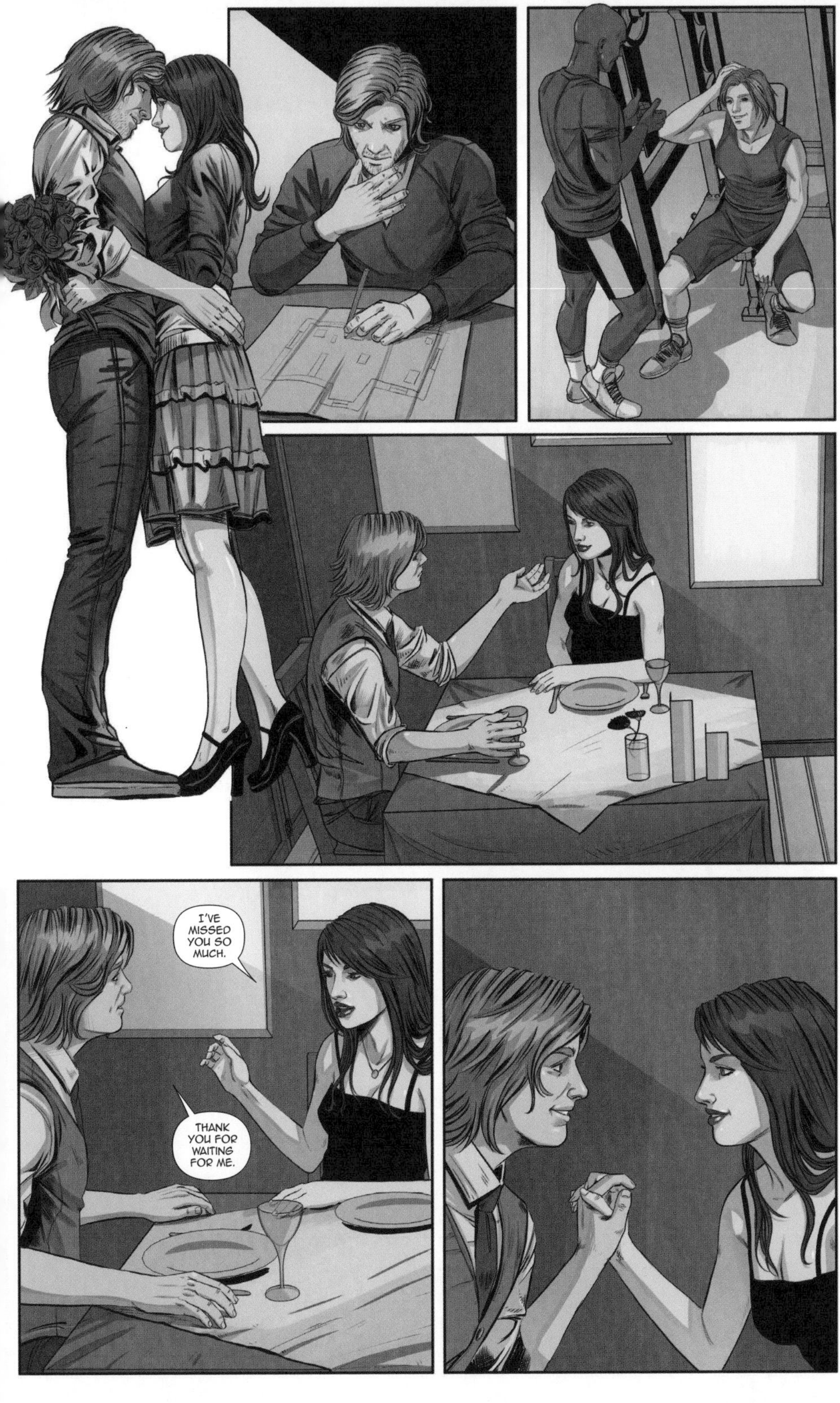
I'VE MISSED YOU SO MUCH.
THANK YOU FOR WAITING FOR ME.

CHAPTER 9

LOVE SICK/PROMISES BROKEN

RECOMMENDED LISTENING:

"SHOOTING STAR"
BOB DYLAN

"NEVER GOING BACK AGAIN"
FLEETWOOD MAC
(OR LINDSEY BUCKINGHAM
SOLO LIVE ACOUSTIC VERSION)

BONUS TRACKS

"LOVE SICK"
BOB DYLAN

"PROMISES BROKEN"
SOUL ASYLUM

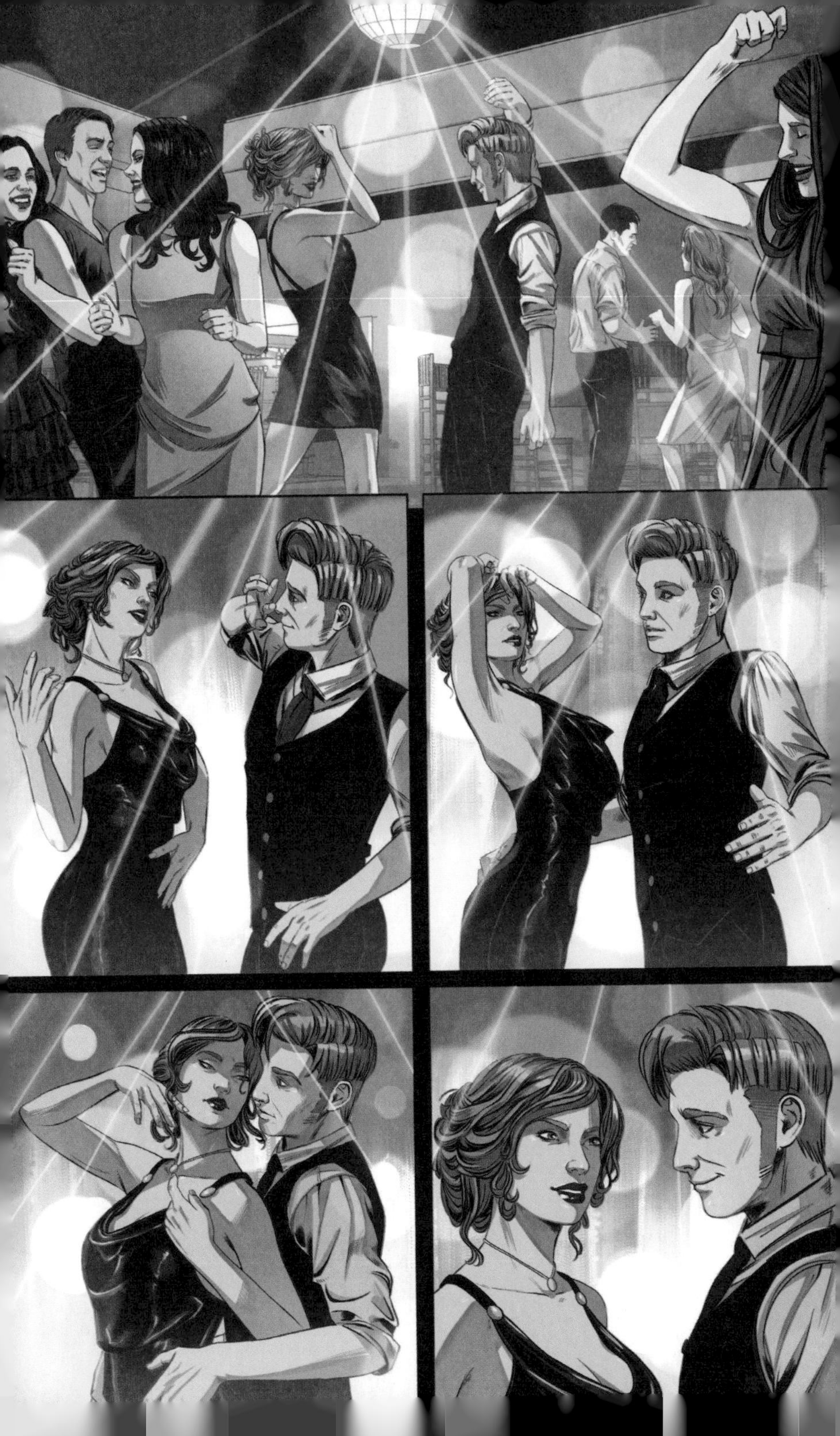

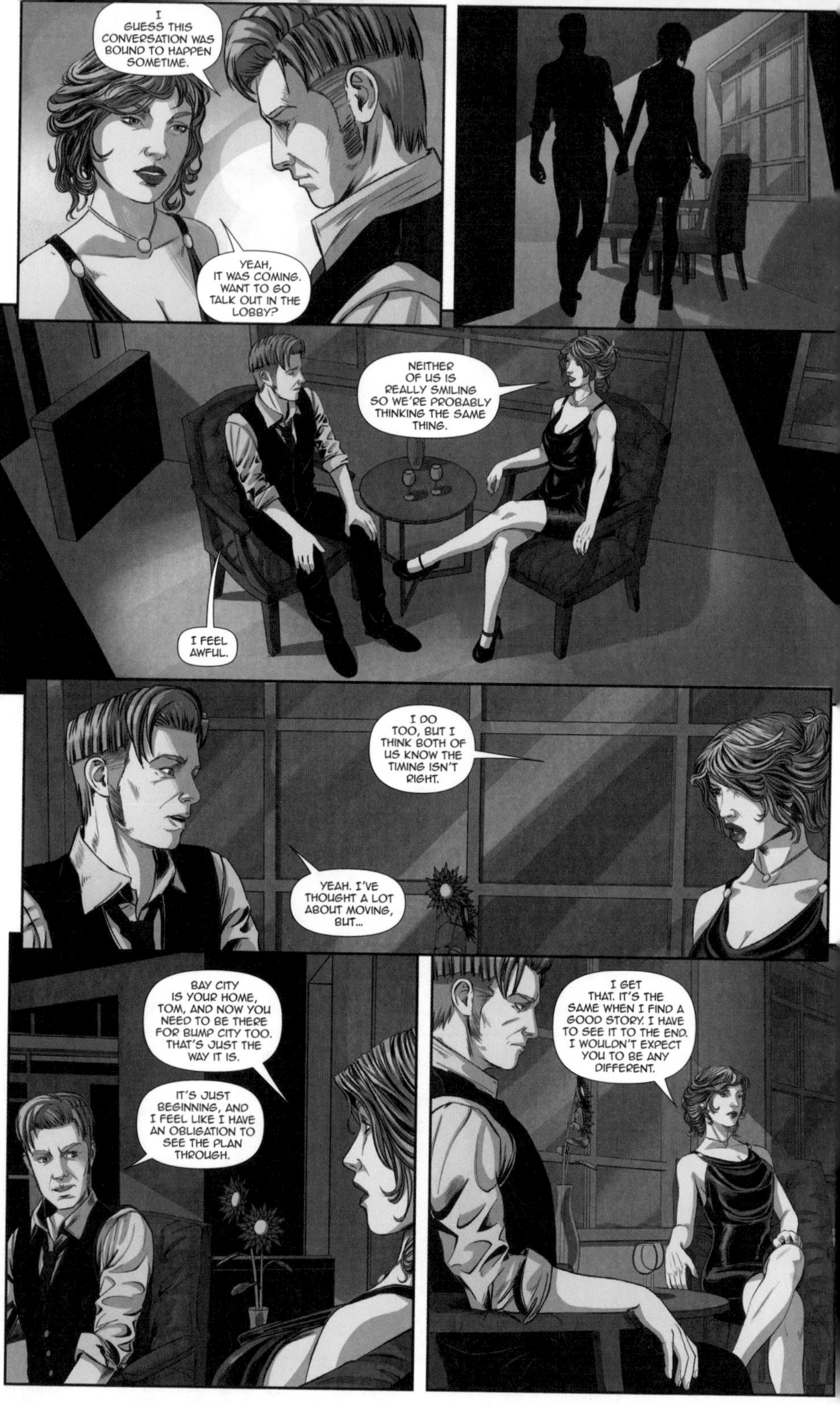
I GUESS THIS CONVERSATION WAS BOUND TO HAPPEN SOMETIME.
YEAH, IT WAS COMING. WANT TO GO TALK OUT IN THE LOBBY?
NEITHER OF US IS REALLY SMILING SO WE'RE PROBABLY THINKING THE SAME THING.
I FEEL AWFUL.
I DO TOO, BUT I THINK BOTH OF US KNOW THE TIMING ISN'T RIGHT.
YEAH. I'VE THOUGHT A LOT ABOUT MOVING, BUT...
BAY CITY IS YOUR HOME, TOM, AND NOW YOU NEED TO BE THERE FOR BUMP CITY TOO. THAT'S JUST THE WAY IT IS.
IT'S JUST BEGINNING, AND I FEEL LIKE I HAVE AN OBLIGATION TO SEE THE PLAN THROUGH.
I GET THAT. IT'S THE SAME WHEN I FIND A GOOD STORY. I HAVE TO SEE IT TO THE END. I WOULDN'T EXPECT YOU TO BE ANY DIFFERENT.

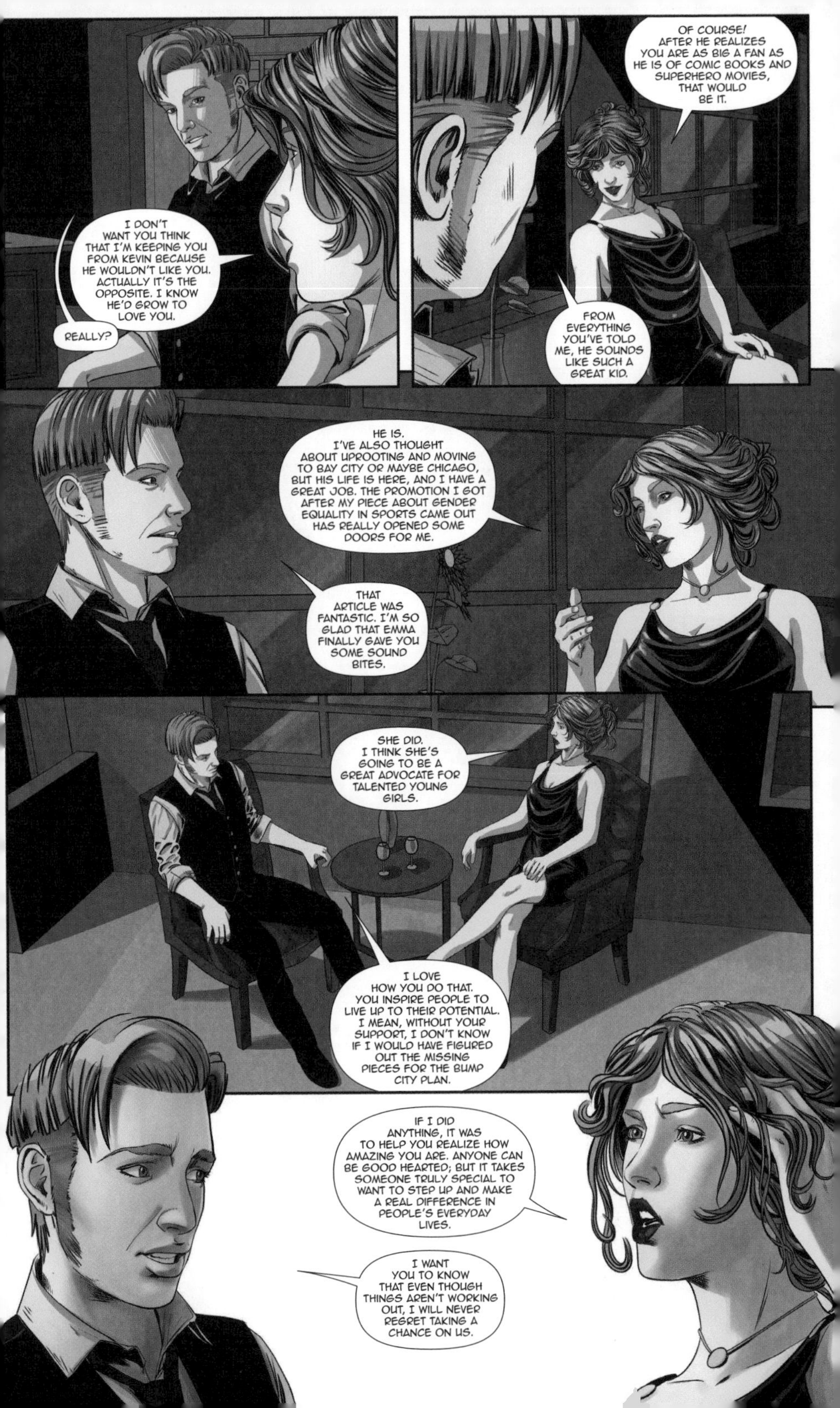
I DON'T WANT YOU THINK THAT I'M KEEPING YOU FROM KEVIN BECAUSE HE WOULDN'T LIKE YOU. ACTUALLY IT'S THE OPPOSITE. I KNOW HE'D GROW TO LOVE YOU.
REALLY?
OF COURSE! AFTER HE REALIZES YOU ARE AS BIG A FAN AS HE IS OF COMIC BOOKS AND SUPERHERO MOVIES, THAT WOULD BE IT.
FROM EVERYTHING YOU'VE TOLD ME, HE SOUNDS LIKE SUCH A GREAT KID.
HE IS. I'VE ALSO THOUGHT ABOUT UPROOTING AND MOVING TO BAY CITY OR MAYBE CHICAGO, BUT HIS LIFE IS HERE, AND I HAVE A GREAT JOB. THE PROMOTION I GOT AFTER MY PIECE ABOUT GENDER EQUALITY IN SPORTS CAME OUT HAS REALLY OPENED SOME DOORS FOR ME.
THAT ARTICLE WAS FANTASTIC. I'M SO GLAD THAT EMMA FINALLY GAVE YOU SOME SOUND BITES.
SHE DID. I THINK SHE'S GOING TO BE A GREAT ADVOCATE FOR TALENTED YOUNG GIRLS.
I LOVE HOW YOU DO THAT. YOU INSPIRE PEOPLE TO LIVE UP TO THEIR POTENTIAL. I MEAN, WITHOUT YOUR SUPPORT, I DON'T KNOW IF I WOULD HAVE FIGURED OUT THE MISSING PIECES FOR THE BUMP CITY PLAN.
IF I DID ANYTHING, IT WAS TO HELP YOU REALIZE HOW AMAZING YOU ARE. ANYONE CAN BE GOOD HEARTED; BUT IT TAKES SOMEONE TRULY SPECIAL TO WANT TO STEP UP AND MAKE A REAL DIFFERENCE IN PEOPLE'S EVERYDAY LIVES.
I WANT YOU TO KNOW THAT EVEN THOUGH THINGS AREN'T WORKING OUT, I WILL NEVER REGRET TAKING A CHANCE ON US.

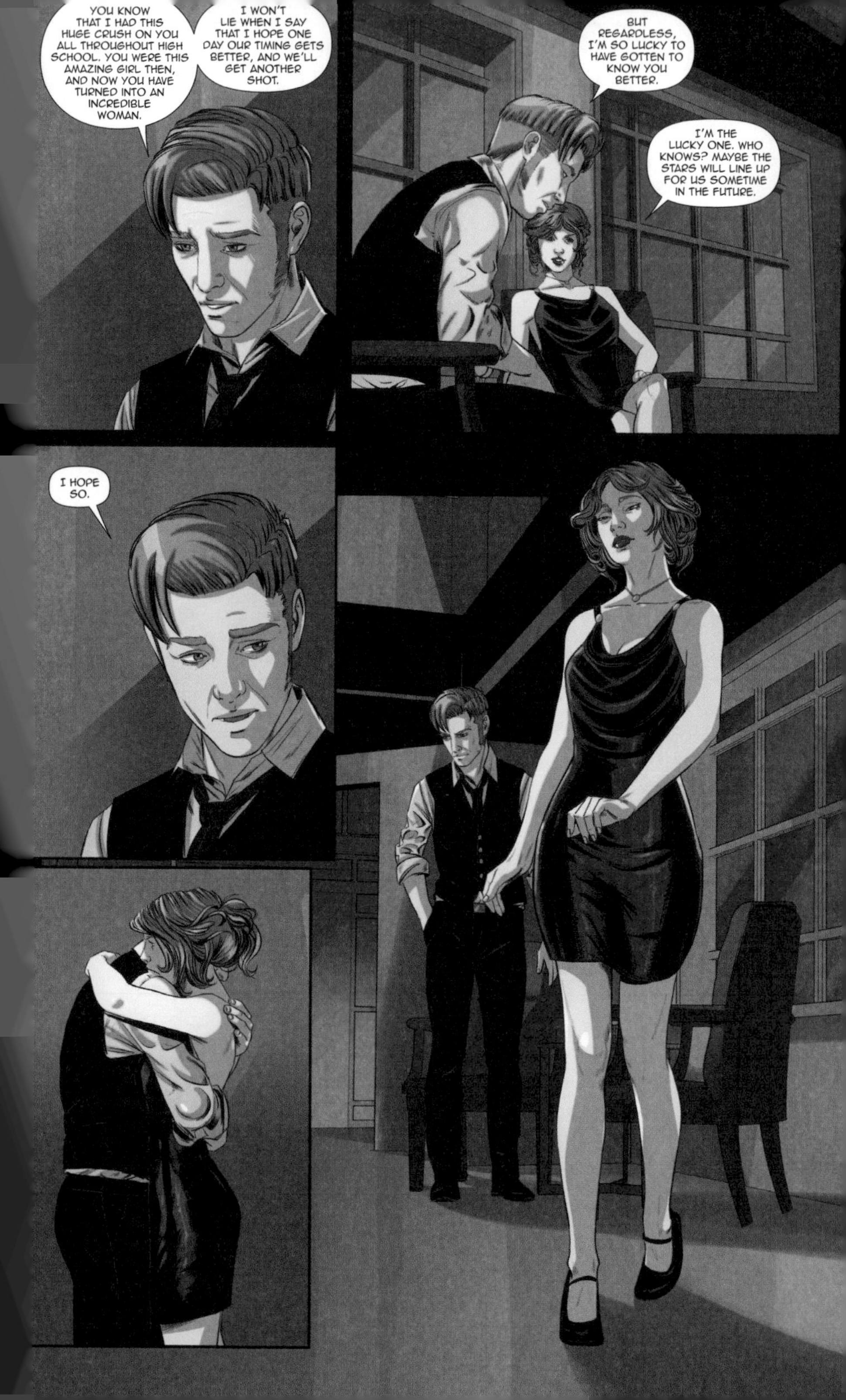
YOU KNOW THAT I HAD THIS HUGE CRUSH ON YOU ALL THROUGHOUT HIGH SCHOOL. YOU WERE THIS AMAZING GIRL THEN, AND NOW YOU HAVE TURNED INTO AN INCREDIBLE WOMAN.
I WON'T LIE WHEN I SAY THAT I HOPE ONE DAY OUR TIMING GETS BETTER, AND WE'LL GET ANOTHER SHOT.
BUT REGARDLESS, I'M SO LUCKY TO HAVE GOTTEN TO KNOW YOU BETTER.
I'M THE LUCKY ONE. WHO KNOWS? MAYBE THE STARS WILL LINE UP FOR US SOMETIME IN THE FUTURE.
I HOPE SO.

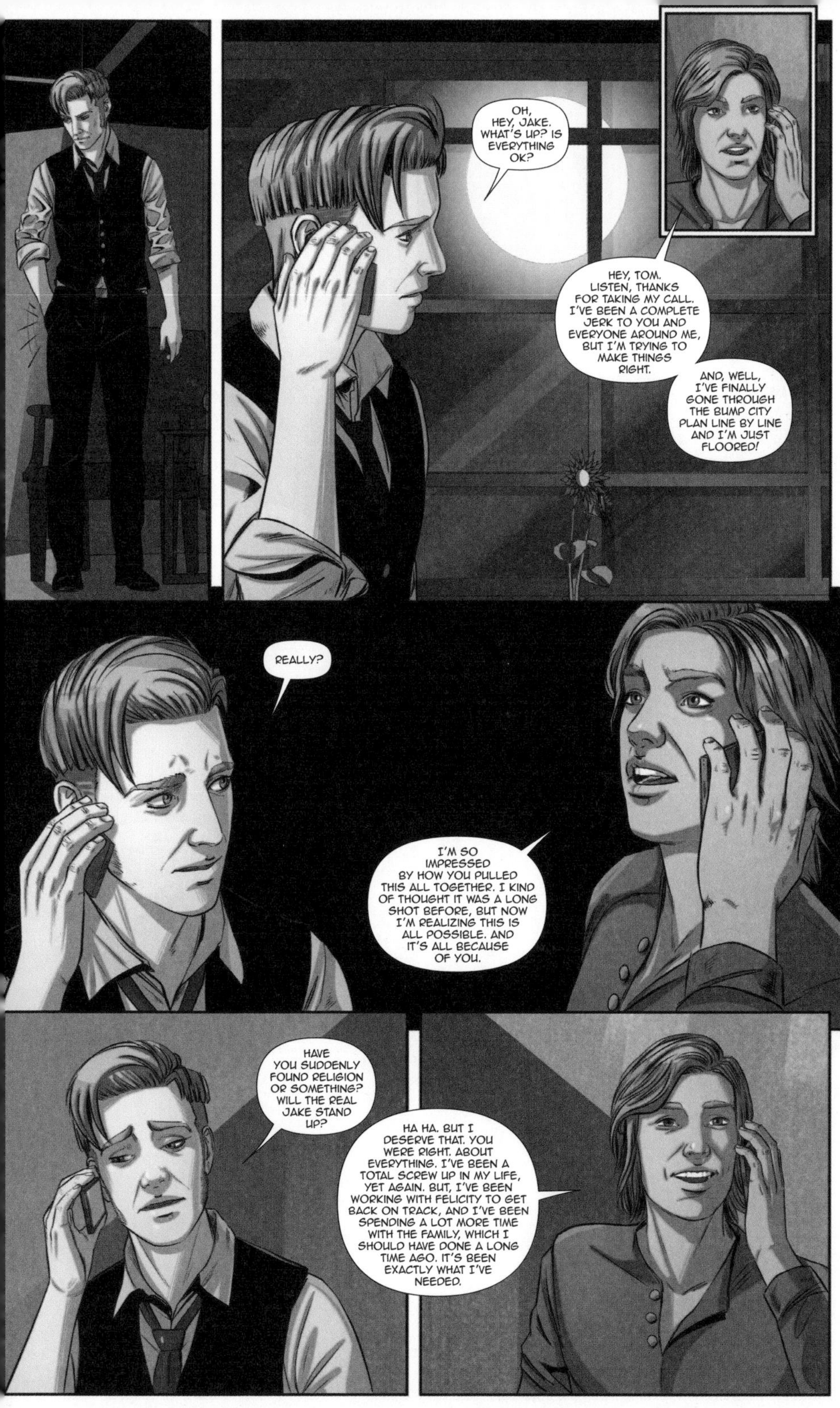
OH, HEY, JAKE. WHAT'S UP? IS EVERYTHING OK?
HEY, TOM. LISTEN, THANKS FOR TAKING MY CALL. I'VE BEEN A COMPLETE JERK TO YOU AND EVERYONE AROUND ME, BUT I'M TRYING TO MAKE THINGS RIGHT.
AND, WELL, I'VE FINALLY GONE THROUGH THE BUMP CITY PLAN LINE BY LINE AND I'M JUST FLOORED!
REALLY?
I'M SO IMPRESSED BY HOW YOU PULLED THIS ALL TOGETHER. I KIND OF THOUGHT IT WAS A LONG SHOT BEFORE, BUT NOW I'M REALIZING THIS IS ALL POSSIBLE. AND IT'S ALL BECAUSE OF YOU.
HAVE YOU SUDDENLY FOUND RELIGION OR SOMETHING? WILL THE REAL JAKE STAND UP?
HA HA. BUT I DESERVE THAT. YOU WERE RIGHT. ABOUT EVERYTHING. I'VE BEEN A TOTAL SCREW UP IN MY LIFE, YET AGAIN. BUT, I'VE BEEN WORKING WITH FELICITY TO GET BACK ON TRACK, AND I'VE BEEN SPENDING A LOT MORE TIME WITH THE FAMILY, WHICH I SHOULD HAVE DONE A LONG TIME AGO. IT'S BEEN EXACTLY WHAT I'VE NEEDED.

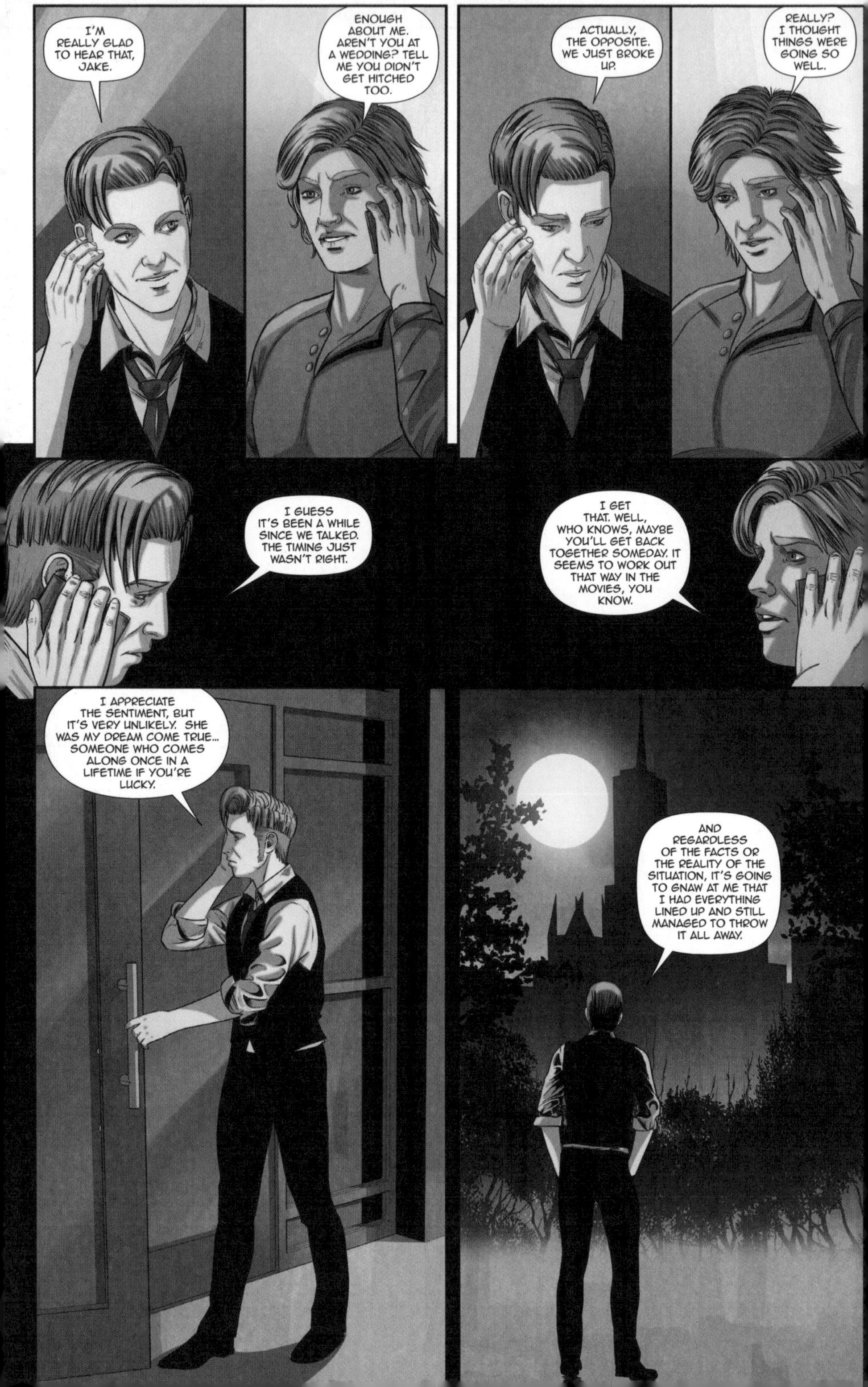
I'M REALLY GLAD TO HEAR THAT, JAKE.
ENOUGH ABOUT ME. AREN'T YOU AT A WEDDING? TELL ME YOU DIDN'T GET HITCHED TOO.
ACTUALLY, THE OPPOSITE. WE JUST BROKE UP.
REALLY? I THOUGHT THINGS WERE GOING SO WELL.
I GUESS IT'S BEEN A WHILE SINCE WE TALKED. THE TIMING JUST WASN'T RIGHT.
I GET THAT. WELL, WHO KNOWS, MAYBE YOU'LL GET BACK TOGETHER SOMEDAY. IT SEEMS TO WORK OUT THAT WAY IN THE MOVIES, YOU KNOW.
I APPRECIATE THE SENTIMENT, BUT IT'S VERY UNLIKELY. SHE WAS MY DREAM COME TRUE... SOMEONE WHO COMES ALONG ONCE IN A LIFETIME IF YOU'RE LUCKY.
AND REGARDLESS OF THE FACTS OR THE REALITY OF THE SITUATION, IT'S GOING TO GNAW AT ME THAT I HAD EVERYTHING LINED UP AND STILL MANAGED TO THROW IT ALL AWAY.

CHAPTER 10
TICK TOCK, PART 2

RECOMMENDED LISTENING:

"HO HEY"
THE LUMINEERS

"KEEP THE CAR RUNNING"
ARCADE FIRE

"UNE ANNEE SANS LUMIERE"
ARCADE FIRE

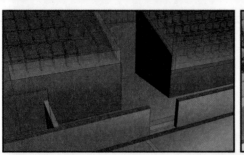

YOU WERE PRETTY EVASIVE ON THE PHONE. YOU'RE NOT GOING TO MURDER ME AND THEN BURY ME UNDER THE RINK, ARE YOU?

OK, I DESERVE THAT. I APPRECIATE YOU FOR COMING OUT HERE WITH NO NOTICE. I DIDN'T WANT TO GO INTO IT OVER THE PHONE BECAUSE I DO MY BEST THINKING AND SPEAKING ON THE ICE.

BEFORE WE START, I WANTED TO TELL YOU SOMETHING.

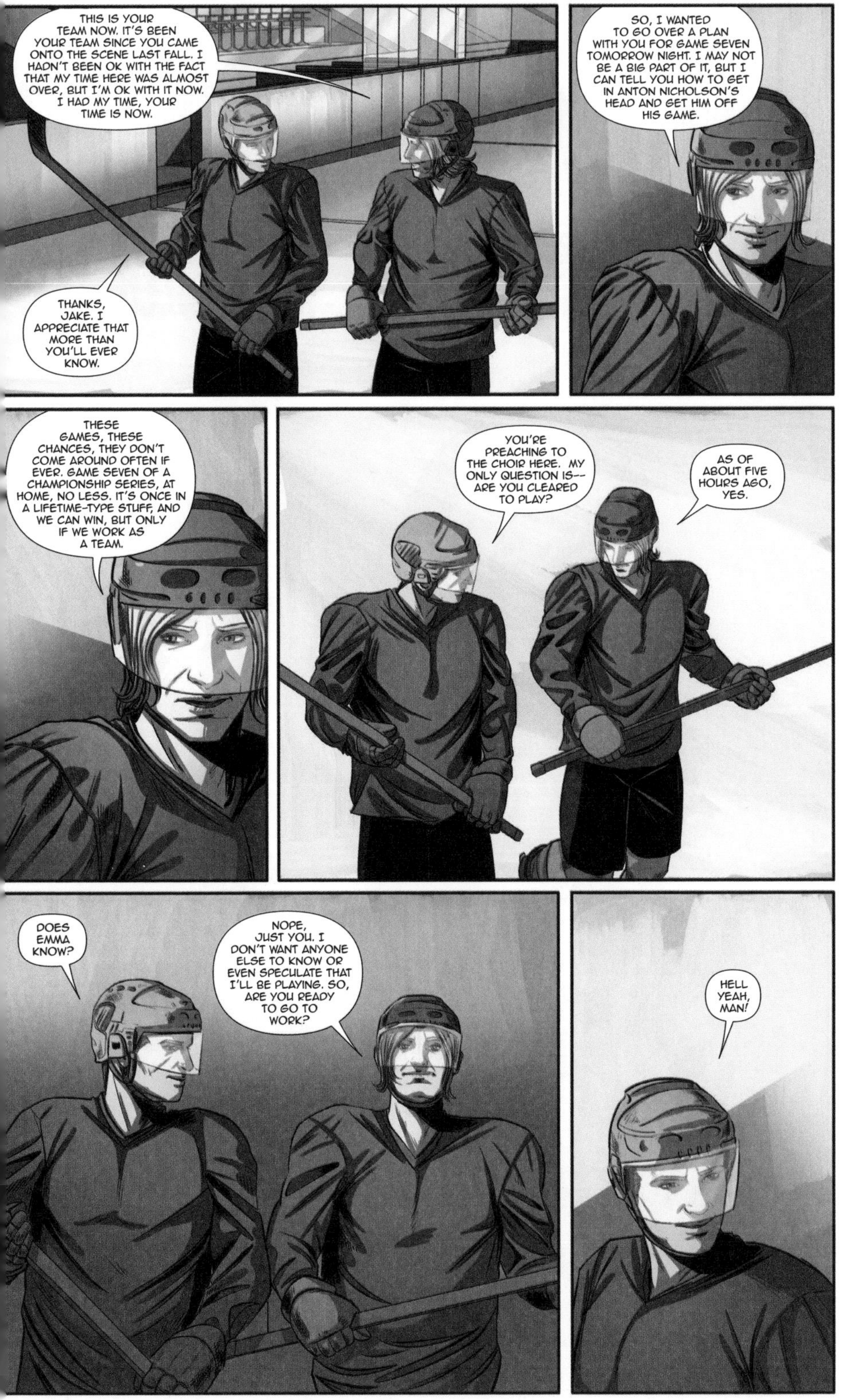
THIS IS YOUR TEAM NOW. IT'S BEEN YOUR TEAM SINCE YOU CAME ONTO THE SCENE LAST FALL. I HADN'T BEEN OK WITH THE FACT THAT MY TIME HERE WAS ALMOST OVER, BUT I'M OK WITH IT NOW. I HAD MY TIME, YOUR TIME IS NOW.
THANKS, JAKE. I APPRECIATE THAT MORE THAN YOU'LL EVER KNOW.
SO, I WANTED TO GO OVER A PLAN WITH YOU FOR GAME SEVEN TOMORROW NIGHT. I MAY NOT BE A BIG PART OF IT, BUT I CAN TELL YOU HOW TO GET IN ANTON NICHOLSON'S HEAD AND GET HIM OFF HIS GAME.
THESE GAMES, THESE CHANCES, THEY DON'T COME AROUND OFTEN IF EVER. GAME SEVEN OF A CHAMPIONSHIP SERIES, AT HOME, NO LESS. IT'S ONCE IN A LIFETIME-TYPE STUFF, AND WE CAN WIN, BUT ONLY IF WE WORK AS A TEAM.
YOU'RE PREACHING TO THE CHOIR HERE. MY ONLY QUESTION IS-- ARE YOU CLEARED TO PLAY?
AS OF ABOUT FIVE HOURS AGO, YES.
DOES EMMA KNOW?
NOPE, JUST YOU. I DON'T WANT ANYONE ELSE TO KNOW OR EVEN SPECULATE THAT I'LL BE PLAYING. SO, ARE YOU READY TO GO TO WORK?
HELL YEAH, MAN!

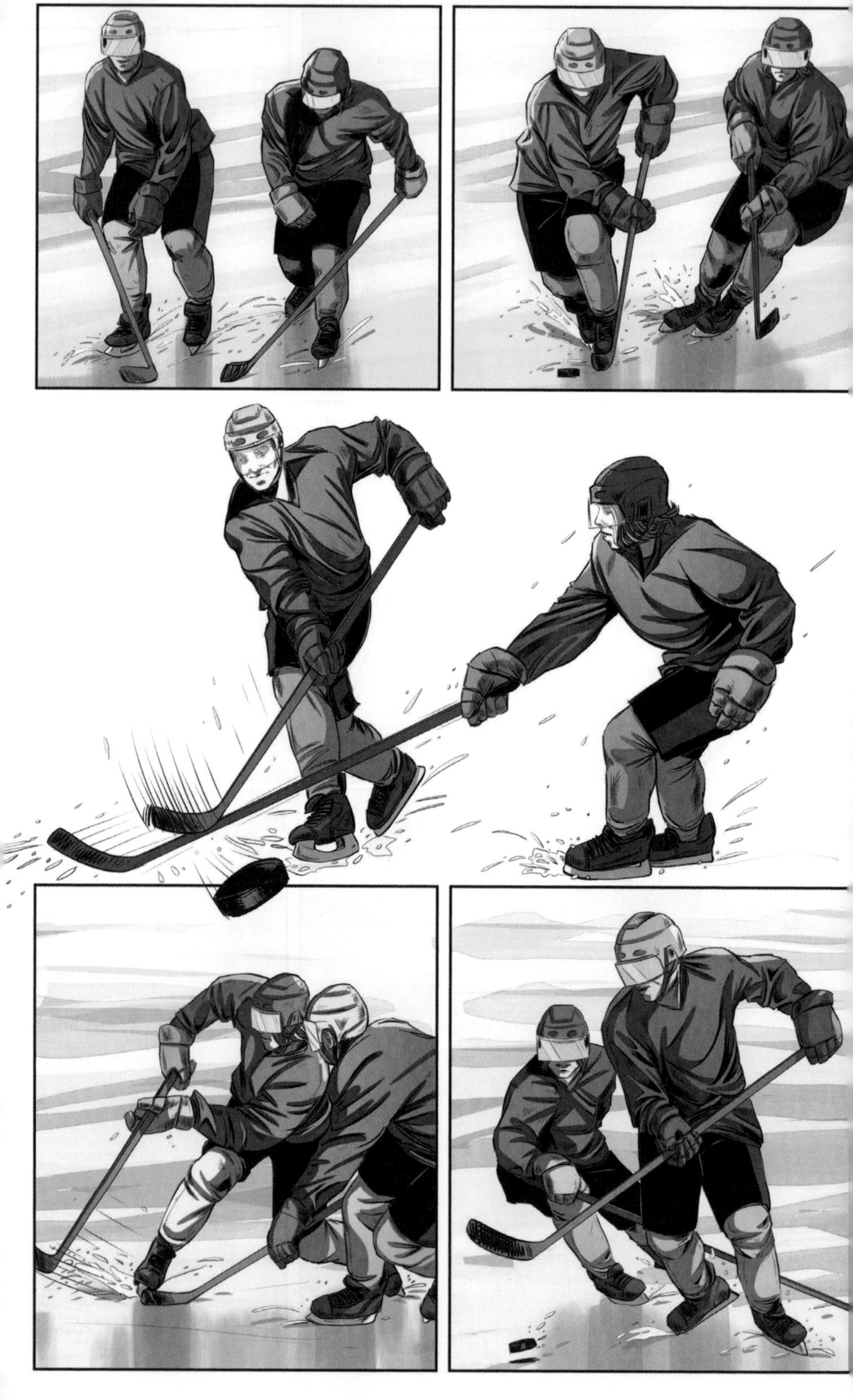

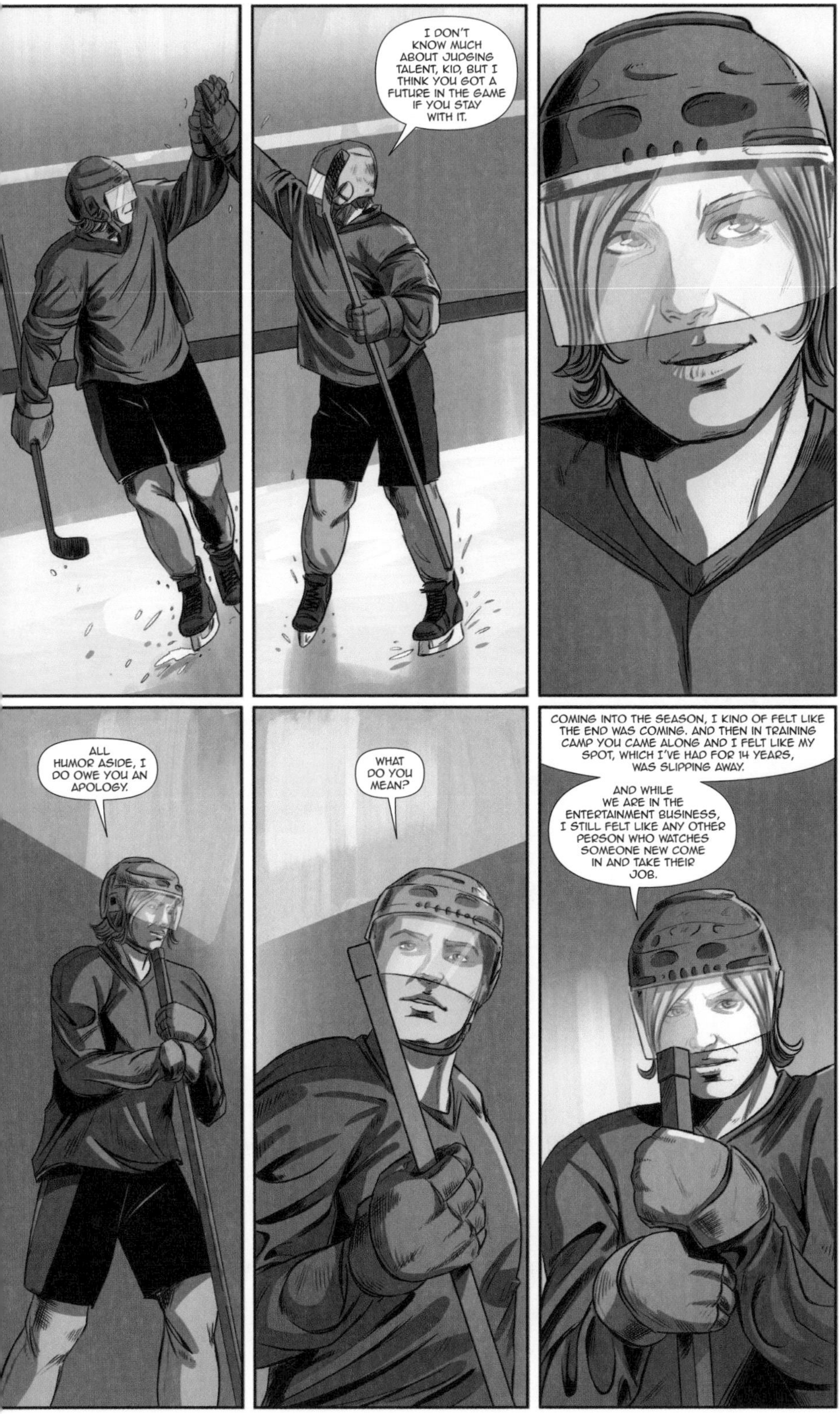

I DON'T KNOW MUCH ABOUT JUDGING TALENT, KID, BUT I THINK YOU GOT A FUTURE IN THE GAME IF YOU STAY WITH IT.
ALL HUMOR ASIDE, I DO OWE YOU AN APOLOGY.
WHAT DO YOU MEAN?
COMING INTO THE SEASON, I KIND OF FELT LIKE THE END WAS COMING. AND THEN IN TRAINING CAMP YOU CAME ALONG AND I FELT LIKE MY SPOT, WHICH I'VE HAD FOR 14 YEARS, WAS SLIPPING AWAY.
AND WHILE WE ARE IN THE ENTERTAINMENT BUSINESS, I STILL FELT LIKE ANY OTHER PERSON WHO WATCHES SOMEONE NEW COME IN AND TAKE THEIR JOB.

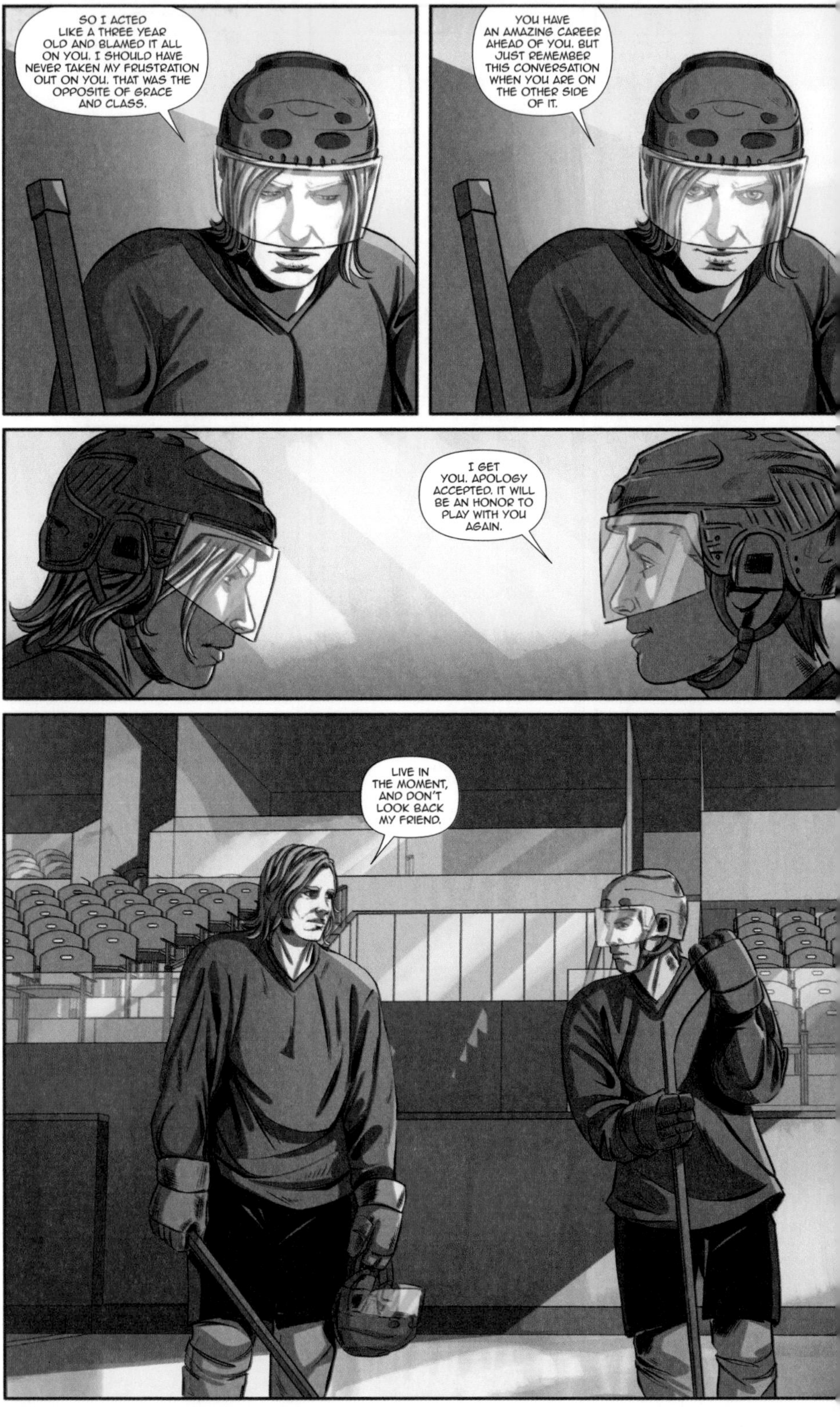
SO I ACTED LIKE A THREE YEAR OLD AND BLAMED IT ALL ON YOU. I SHOULD HAVE NEVER TAKEN MY FRUSTRATION OUT ON YOU. THAT WAS THE OPPOSITE OF GRACE AND CLASS.
YOU HAVE AN AMAZING CAREER AHEAD OF YOU. BUT JUST REMEMBER THIS CONVERSATION WHEN YOU ARE ON THE OTHER SIDE OF IT.
I GET YOU. APOLOGY ACCEPTED. IT WILL BE AN HONOR TO PLAY WITH YOU AGAIN.
LIVE IN THE MOMENT, AND DON'T LOOK BACK MY FRIEND.

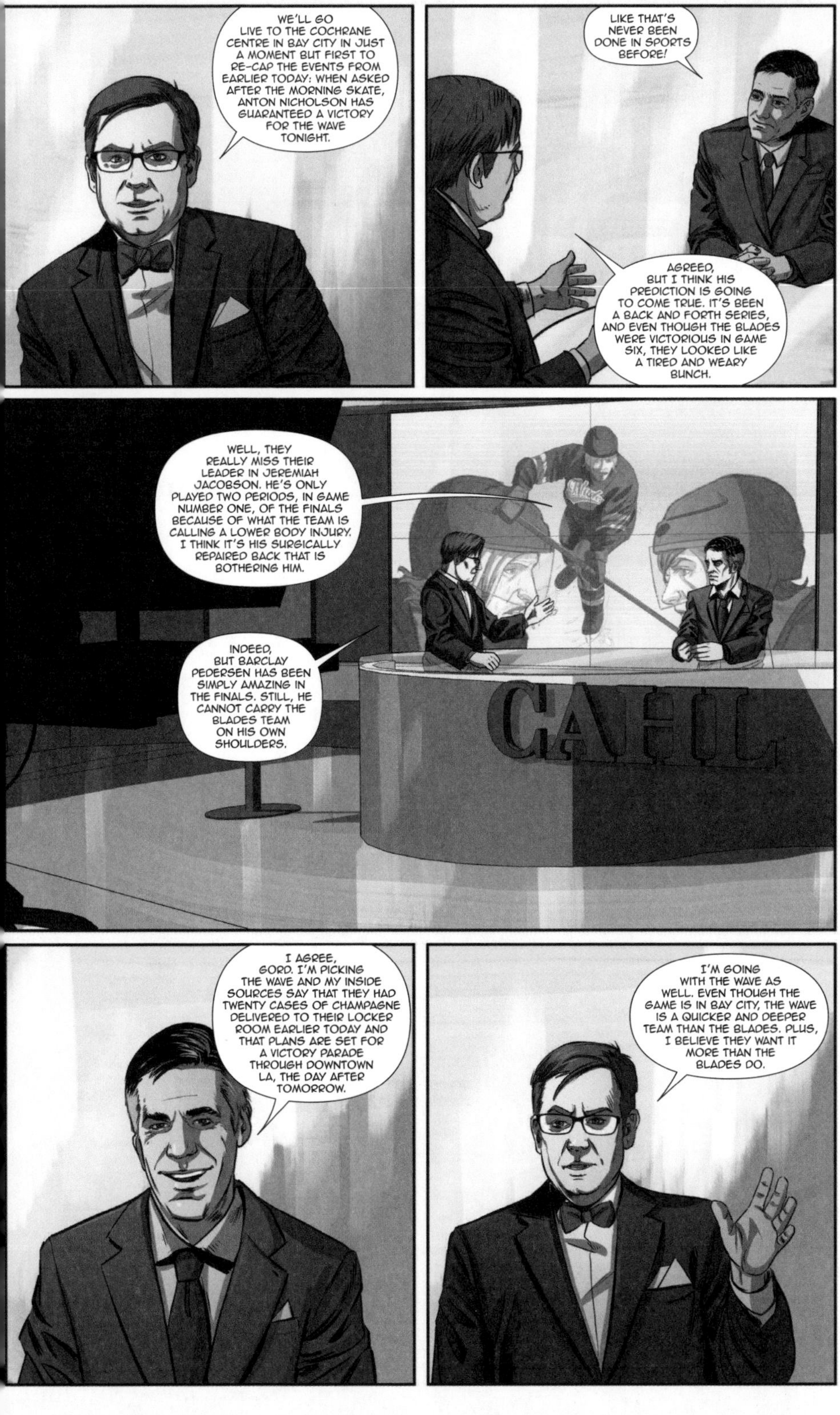
WE'LL GO LIVE TO THE COCHRANE CENTRE IN BAY CITY IN JUST A MOMENT BUT FIRST TO RE-CAP THE EVENTS FROM EARLIER TODAY: WHEN ASKED AFTER THE MORNING SKATE, ANTON NICHOLSON HAS GUARANTEED A VICTORY FOR THE WAVE TONIGHT.
LIKE THAT'S NEVER BEEN DONE IN SPORTS BEFORE!
AGREED, BUT I THINK HIS PREDICTION IS GOING TO COME TRUE. IT'S BEEN A BACK AND FORTH SERIES, AND EVEN THOUGH THE BLADES WERE VICTORIOUS IN GAME SIX, THEY LOOKED LIKE A TIRED AND WEARY BUNCH.
WELL, THEY REALLY MISS THEIR LEADER IN JEREMIAH JACOBSON. HE'S ONLY PLAYED TWO PERIODS, IN GAME NUMBER ONE, OF THE FINALS BECAUSE OF WHAT THE TEAM IS CALLING A LOWER BODY INJURY. I THINK IT'S HIS SURGICALLY REPAIRED BACK THAT IS BOTHERING HIM.
INDEED, BUT BARCLAY PEDERSEN HAS BEEN SIMPLY AMAZING IN THE FINALS. STILL, HE CANNOT CARRY THE BLADES TEAM ON HIS OWN SHOULDERS.
CAHL
I AGREE, GORD. I'M PICKING THE WAVE AND MY INSIDE SOURCES SAY THAT THEY HAD TWENTY CASES OF CHAMPAGNE DELIVERED TO THEIR LOCKER ROOM EARLIER TODAY AND THAT PLANS ARE SET FOR A VICTORY PARADE THROUGH DOWNTOWN LA, THE DAY AFTER TOMORROW.
I'M GOING WITH THE WAVE AS WELL. EVEN THOUGH THE GAME IS IN BAY CITY, THE WAVE IS A QUICKER AND DEEPER TEAM THAN THE BLADES. PLUS, I BELIEVE THEY WANT IT MORE THAN THE BLADES DO.

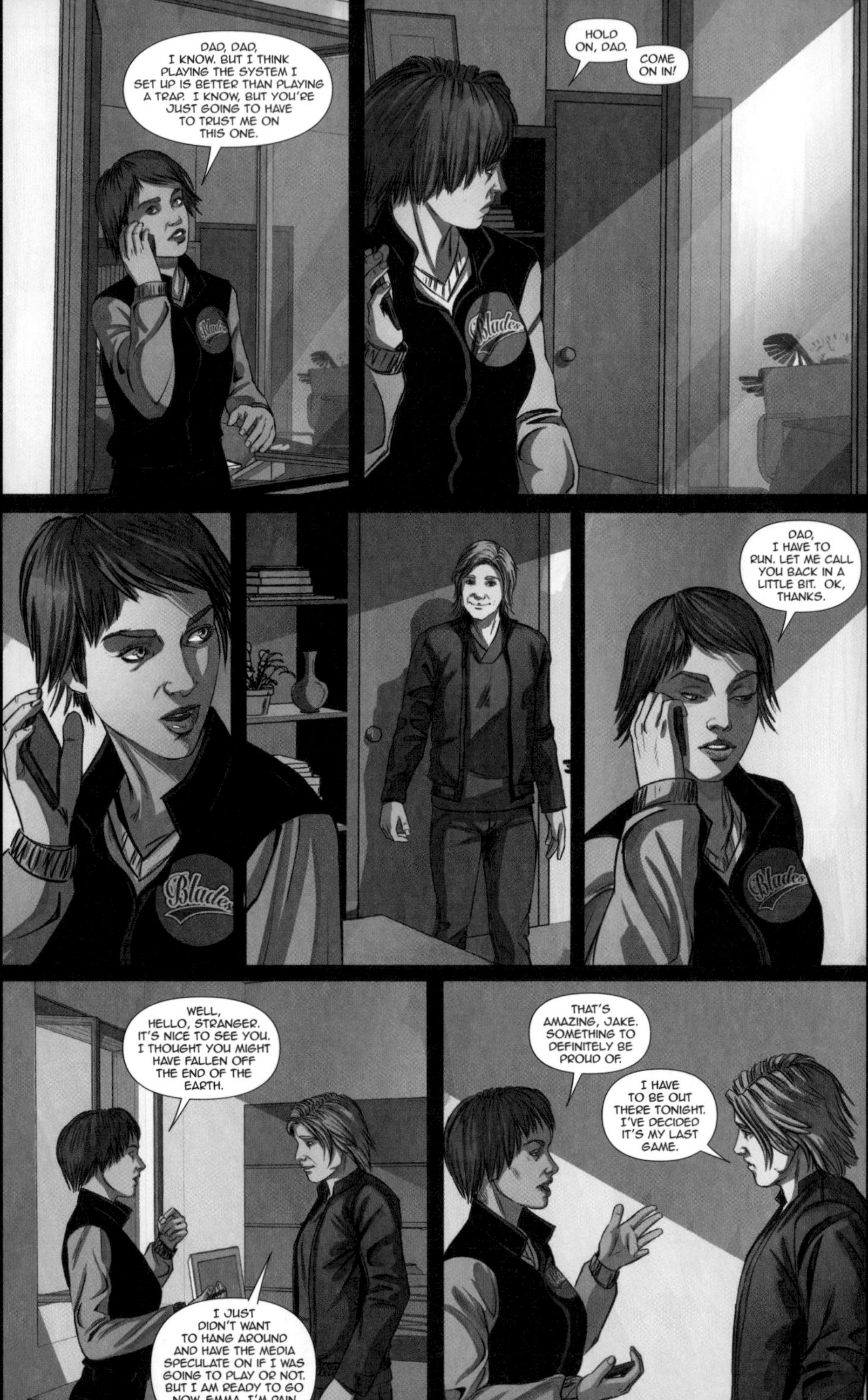
DAD, DAD, I KNOW. BUT I THINK PLAYING THE SYSTEM I SET UP IS BETTER THAN PLAYING A TRAP. I KNOW, BUT YOU'RE JUST GOING TO HAVE TO TRUST ME ON THIS ONE.
Blades
HOLD ON, DAD.
COME ON IN!
Blades
Blades
DAD, I HAVE TO RUN. LET ME CALL YOU BACK IN A LITTLE BIT. OK, THANKS.
Blades
WELL, HELLO, STRANGER. IT'S NICE TO SEE YOU. I THOUGHT YOU MIGHT HAVE FALLEN OFF THE END OF THE EARTH.
I JUST DIDN'T WANT TO HANG AROUND AND HAVE THE MEDIA SPECULATE ON IF I WAS GOING TO PLAY OR NOT. BUT I AM READY TO GO NOW, EMMA. I'M PAIN FREE AND PILL FREE.
THAT'S AMAZING, JAKE. SOMETHING TO DEFINITELY BE PROUD OF.
I HAVE TO BE OUT THERE TONIGHT. I'VE DECIDED IT'S MY LAST GAME.

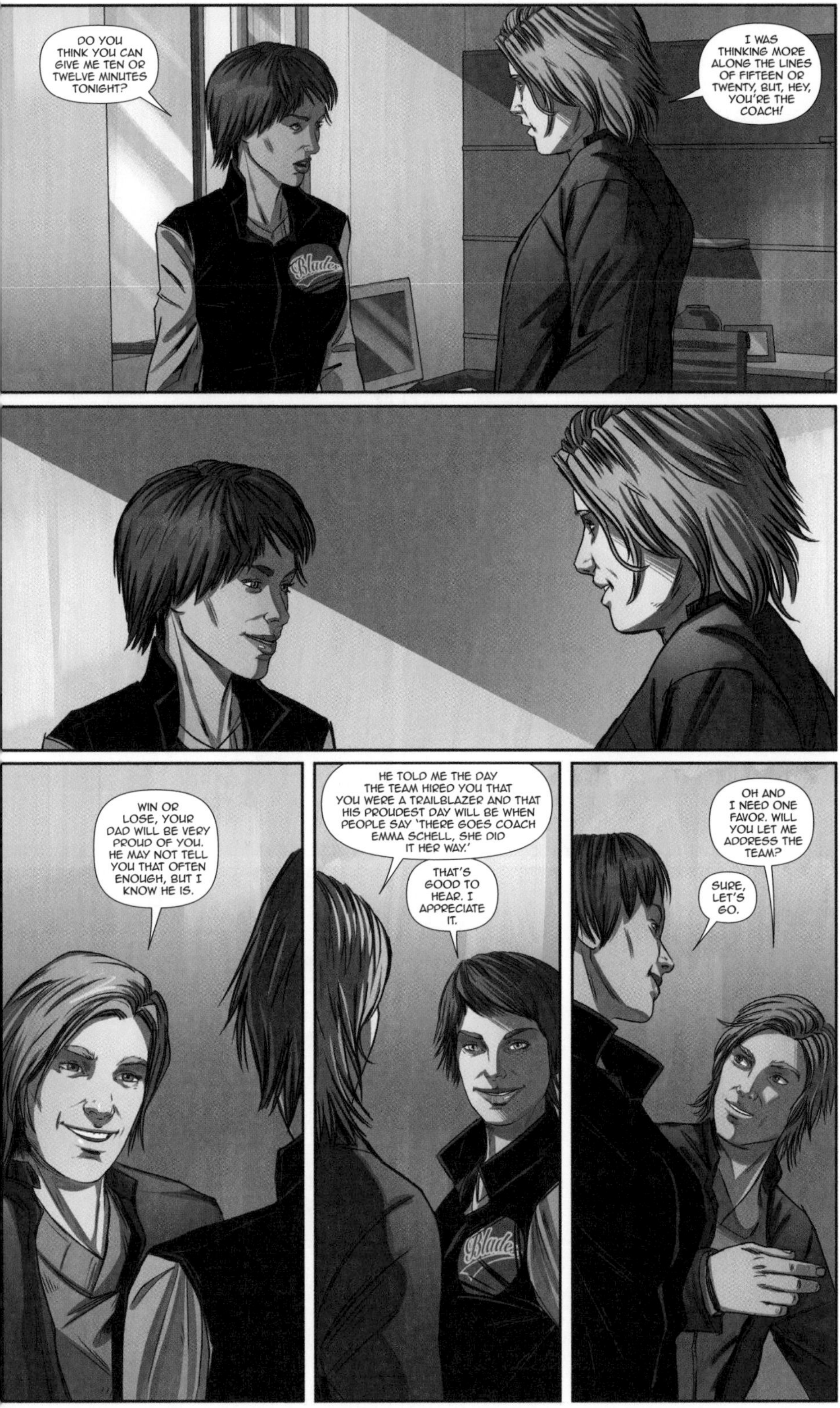
DO YOU THINK YOU CAN GIVE ME TEN OR TWELVE MINUTES TONIGHT?
I WAS THINKING MORE ALONG THE LINES OF FIFTEEN OR TWENTY, BUT, HEY, YOU'RE THE COACH!
WIN OR LOSE, YOUR DAD WILL BE VERY PROUD OF YOU. HE MAY NOT TELL YOU THAT OFTEN ENOUGH, BUT I KNOW HE IS.
HE TOLD ME THE DAY THE TEAM HIRED YOU THAT YOU WERE A TRAILBLAZER AND THAT HIS PROUDEST DAY WILL BE WHEN PEOPLE SAY 'THERE GOES COACH EMMA SCHELL, SHE DID IT HER WAY.'
THAT'S GOOD TO HEAR. I APPRECIATE IT.
OH AND I NEED ONE FAVOR. WILL YOU LET ME ADDRESS THE TEAM?
SURE, LET'S GO.

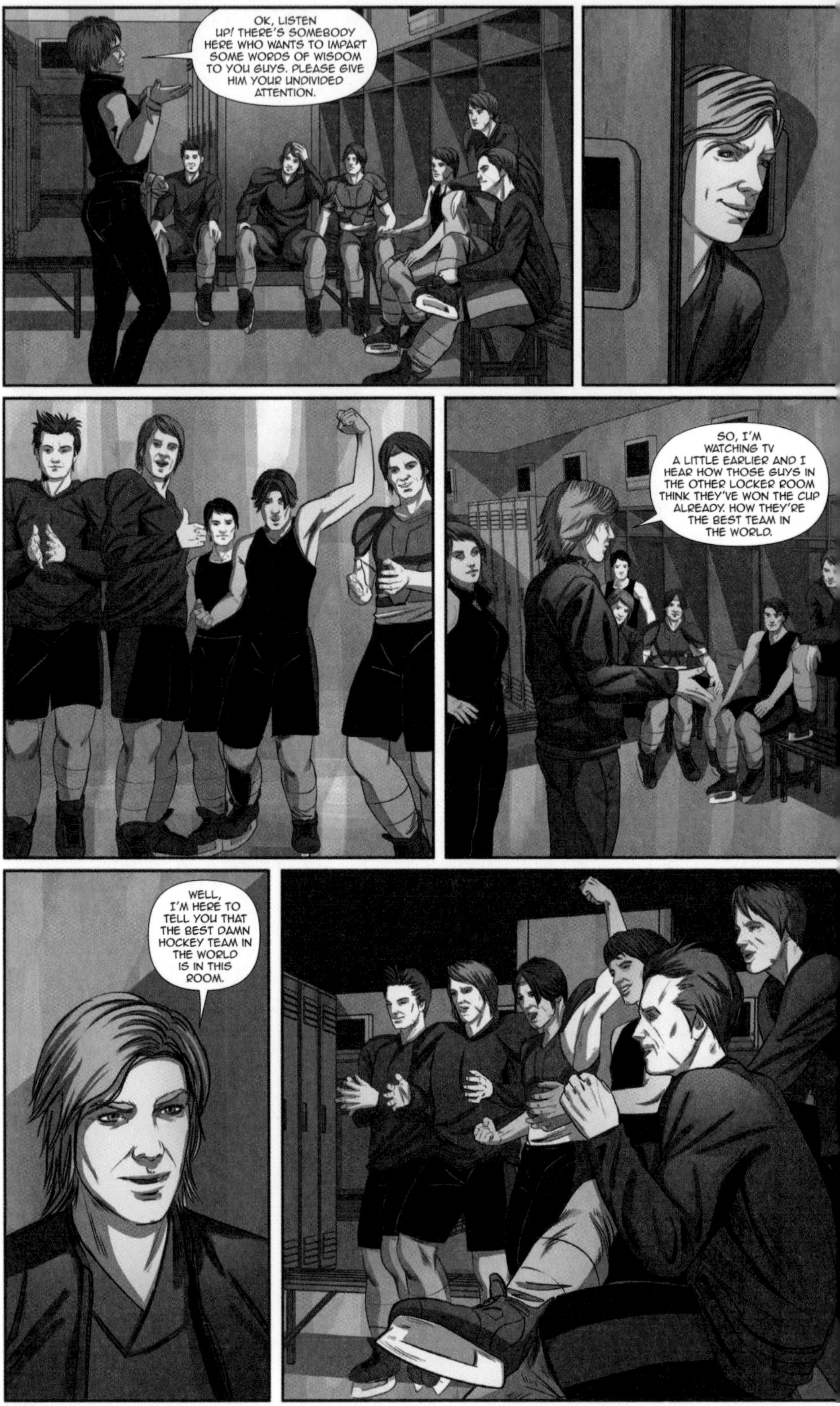
OK, LISTEN UP! THERE'S SOMEBODY HERE WHO WANTS TO IMPART SOME WORDS OF WISDOM TO YOU GUYS. PLEASE GIVE HIM YOUR UNDIVIDED ATTENTION.
SO, I'M WATCHING TV A LITTLE EARLIER AND I HEAR HOW THOSE GUYS IN THE OTHER LOCKER ROOM THINK THEY'VE WON THE CUP ALREADY. HOW THEY'RE THE BEST TEAM IN THE WORLD.
WELL, I'M HERE TO TELL YOU THAT THE BEST DAMN HOCKEY TEAM IN THE WORLD IS IN THIS ROOM.

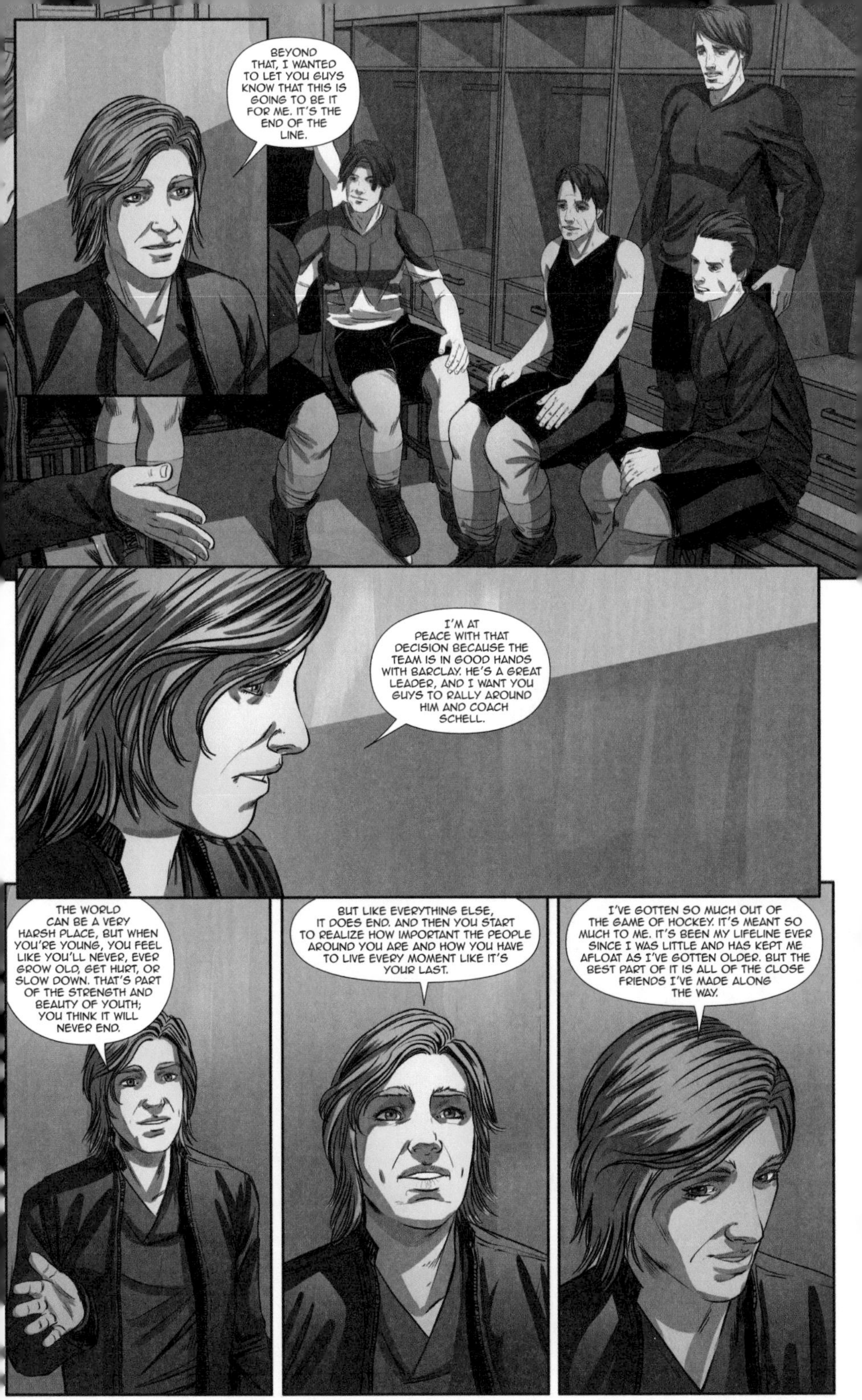
BEYOND THAT, I WANTED TO LET YOU GUYS KNOW THAT THIS IS GOING TO BE IT FOR ME. IT'S THE END OF THE LINE.
I'M AT PEACE WITH THAT DECISION BECAUSE THE TEAM IS IN GOOD HANDS WITH BARCLAY. HE'S A GREAT LEADER, AND I WANT YOU GUYS TO RALLY AROUND HIM AND COACH SCHELL.
THE WORLD CAN BE A VERY HARSH PLACE, BUT WHEN YOU'RE YOUNG, YOU FEEL LIKE YOU'LL NEVER, EVER GROW OLD, GET HURT, OR SLOW DOWN. THAT'S PART OF THE STRENGTH AND BEAUTY OF YOUTH; YOU THINK IT WILL NEVER END.
BUT LIKE EVERYTHING ELSE, IT DOES END. AND THEN YOU START TO REALIZE HOW IMPORTANT THE PEOPLE AROUND YOU ARE AND HOW YOU HAVE TO LIVE EVERY MOMENT LIKE IT'S YOUR LAST.
I'VE GOTTEN SO MUCH OUT OF THE GAME OF HOCKEY. IT'S MEANT SO MUCH TO ME. IT'S BEEN MY LIFELINE EVER SINCE I WAS LITTLE AND HAS KEPT ME AFLOAT AS I'VE GOTTEN OLDER. BUT THE BEST PART OF IT IS ALL OF THE CLOSE FRIENDS I'VE MADE ALONG THE WAY.

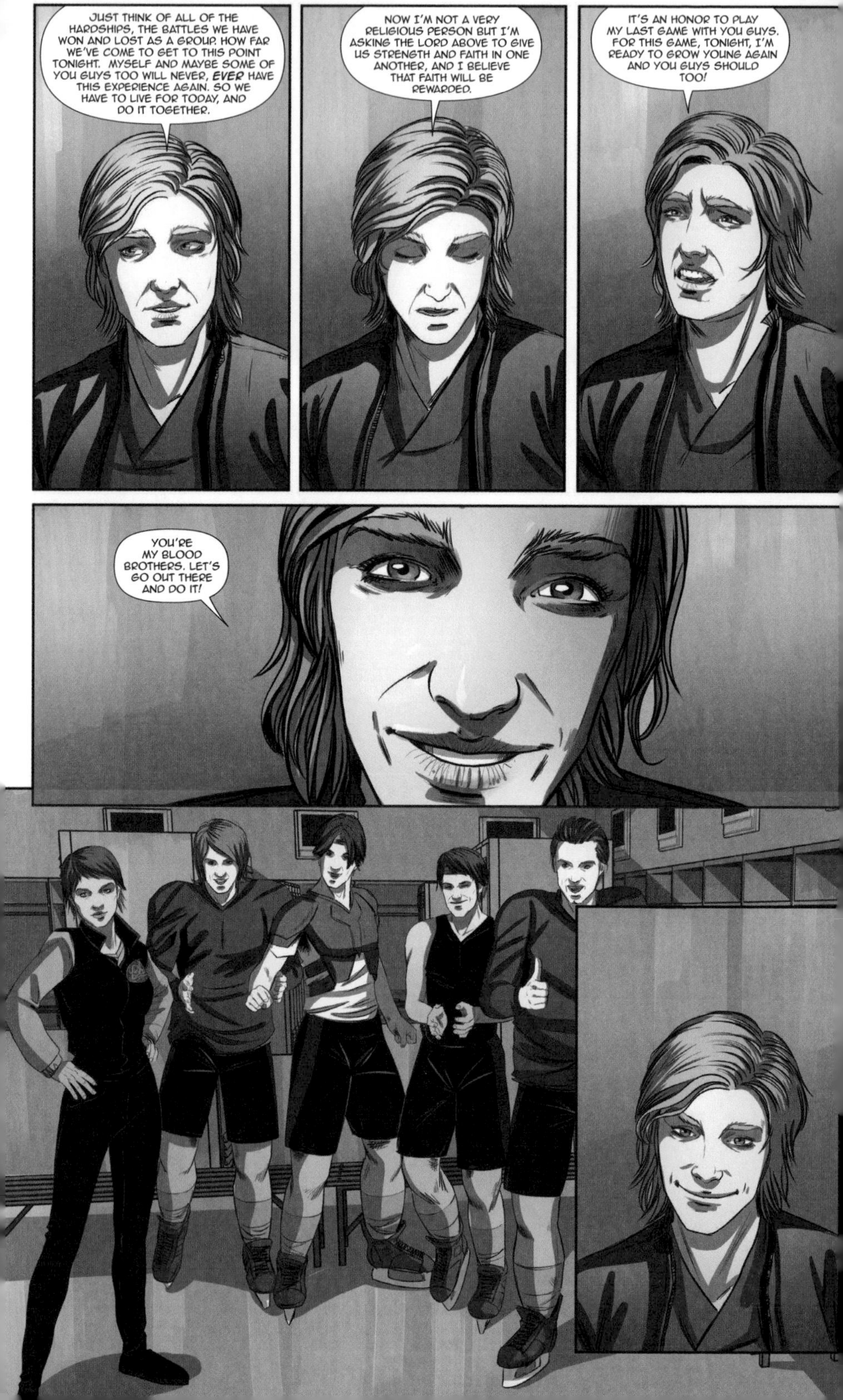
JUST THINK OF ALL OF THE HARDSHIPS, THE BATTLES WE HAVE WON AND LOST AS A GROUP. HOW FAR WE'VE COME TO GET TO THIS POINT TONIGHT. MYSELF AND MAYBE SOME OF YOU GUYS TOO WILL NEVER, EVER HAVE THIS EXPERIENCE AGAIN. SO WE HAVE TO LIVE FOR TODAY, AND DO IT TOGETHER.
NOW I'M NOT A VERY RELIGIOUS PERSON BUT I'M ASKING THE LORD ABOVE TO GIVE US STRENGTH AND FAITH IN ONE ANOTHER, AND I BELIEVE THAT FAITH WILL BE REWARDED.
IT'S AN HONOR TO PLAY MY LAST GAME WITH YOU GUYS. FOR THIS GAME, TONIGHT, I'M READY TO GROW YOUNG AGAIN AND YOU GUYS SHOULD TOO!
YOU'RE MY BLOOD BROTHERS. LET'S GO OUT THERE AND DO IT!

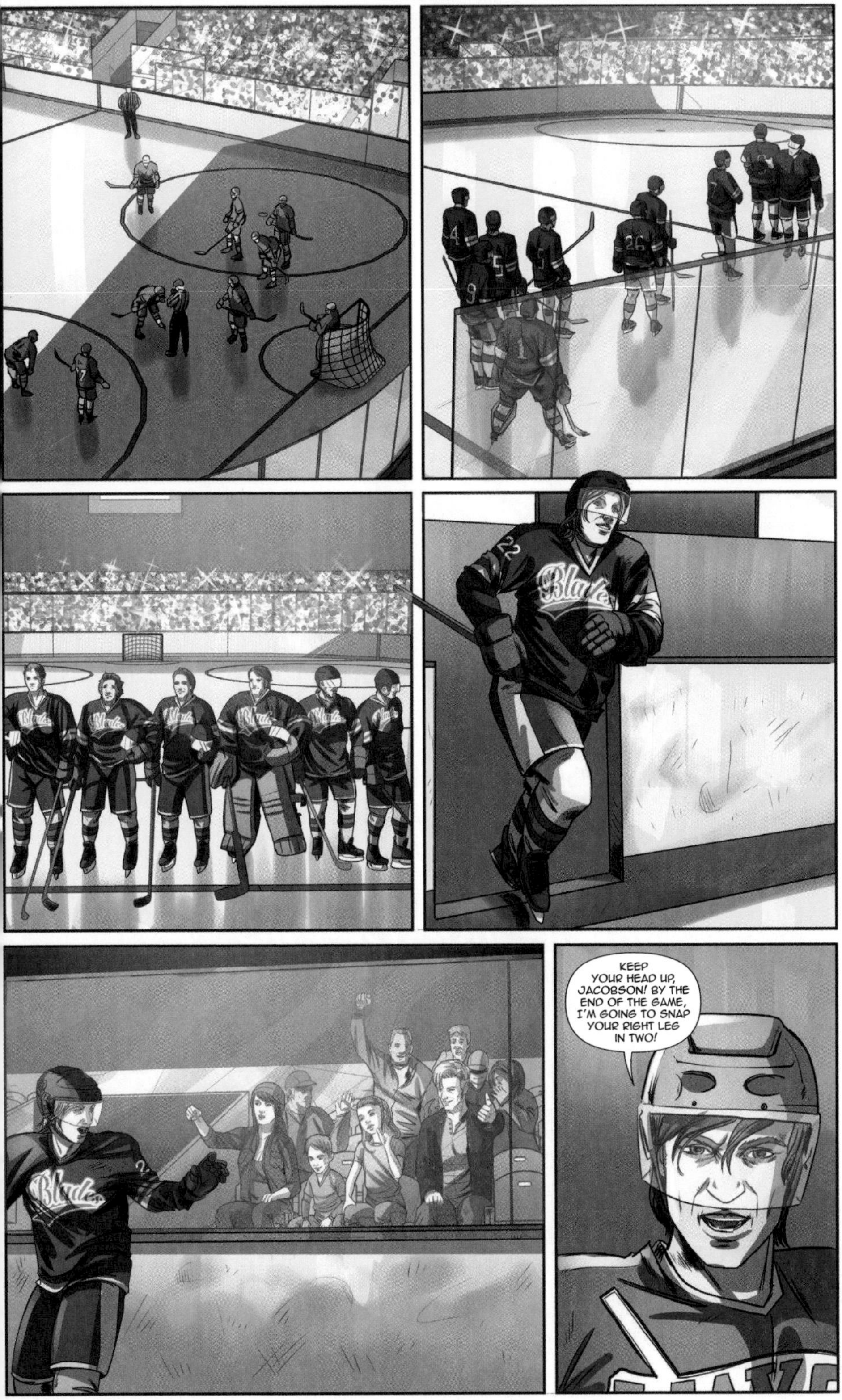
KEEP YOUR HEAD UP, JACOBSON! BY THE END OF THE GAME, I'M GOING TO SNAP YOUR RIGHT LEG IN TWO!

CHAPTER 11
LONG LIVE JEREMIAH JACOBSON

RECOMMENDED LISTENING:

"A FEW MINUTES
OF SILENCE"
PAUL WESTERBERG

"DUDE INCREDIBLE"
SHELLAC

"VICTORY DAY"
TOM COCHRANE AND RED RIDER

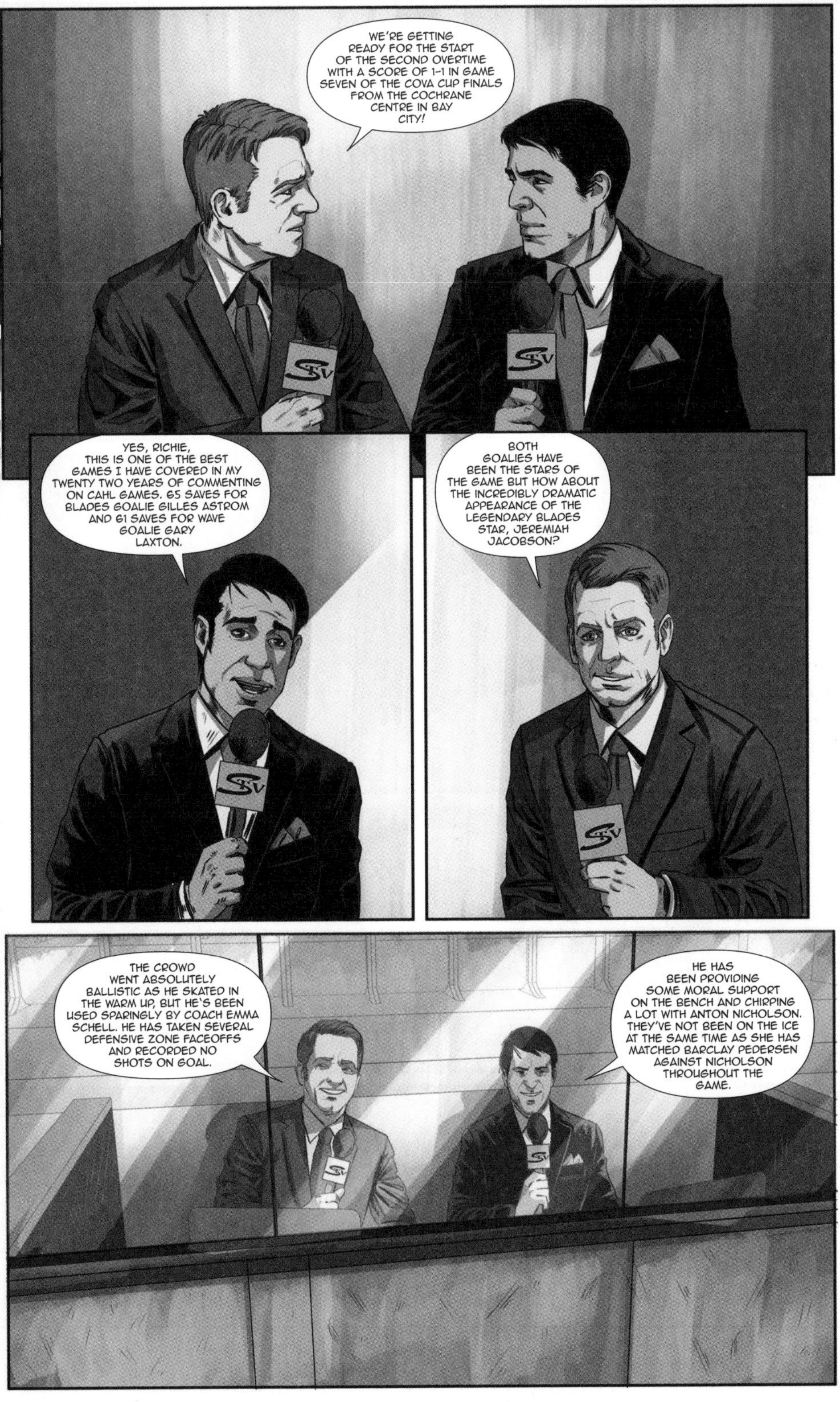
WE'RE GETTING READY FOR THE START OF THE SECOND OVERTIME WITH A SCORE OF 1-1 IN GAME SEVEN OF THE COVA CUP FINALS FROM THE COCHRANE CENTRE IN BAY CITY!
YES, RICHIE, THIS IS ONE OF THE BEST GAMES I HAVE COVERED IN MY TWENTY TWO YEARS OF COMMENTING ON CAHL GAMES. 65 SAVES FOR BLADES GOALIE GILLES ASTROM AND 61 SAVES FOR WAVE GOALIE GARY LAXTON.
BOTH GOALIES HAVE BEEN THE STARS OF THE GAME BUT HOW ABOUT THE INCREDIBLY DRAMATIC APPEARANCE OF THE LEGENDARY BLADES STAR, JEREMIAH JACOBSON?
THE CROWD WENT ABSOLUTELY BALLISTIC AS HE SKATED IN THE WARM UP, BUT HE'S BEEN USED SPARINGLY BY COACH EMMA SCHELL. HE HAS TAKEN SEVERAL DEFENSIVE ZONE FACEOFFS AND RECORDED NO SHOTS ON GOAL.
HE HAS BEEN PROVIDING SOME MORAL SUPPORT ON THE BENCH AND CHIRPING A LOT WITH ANTON NICHOLSON. THEY'VE NOT BEEN ON THE ICE AT THE SAME TIME AS SHE HAS MATCHED BARCLAY PEDERSEN AGAINST NICHOLSON THROUGHOUT THE GAME.

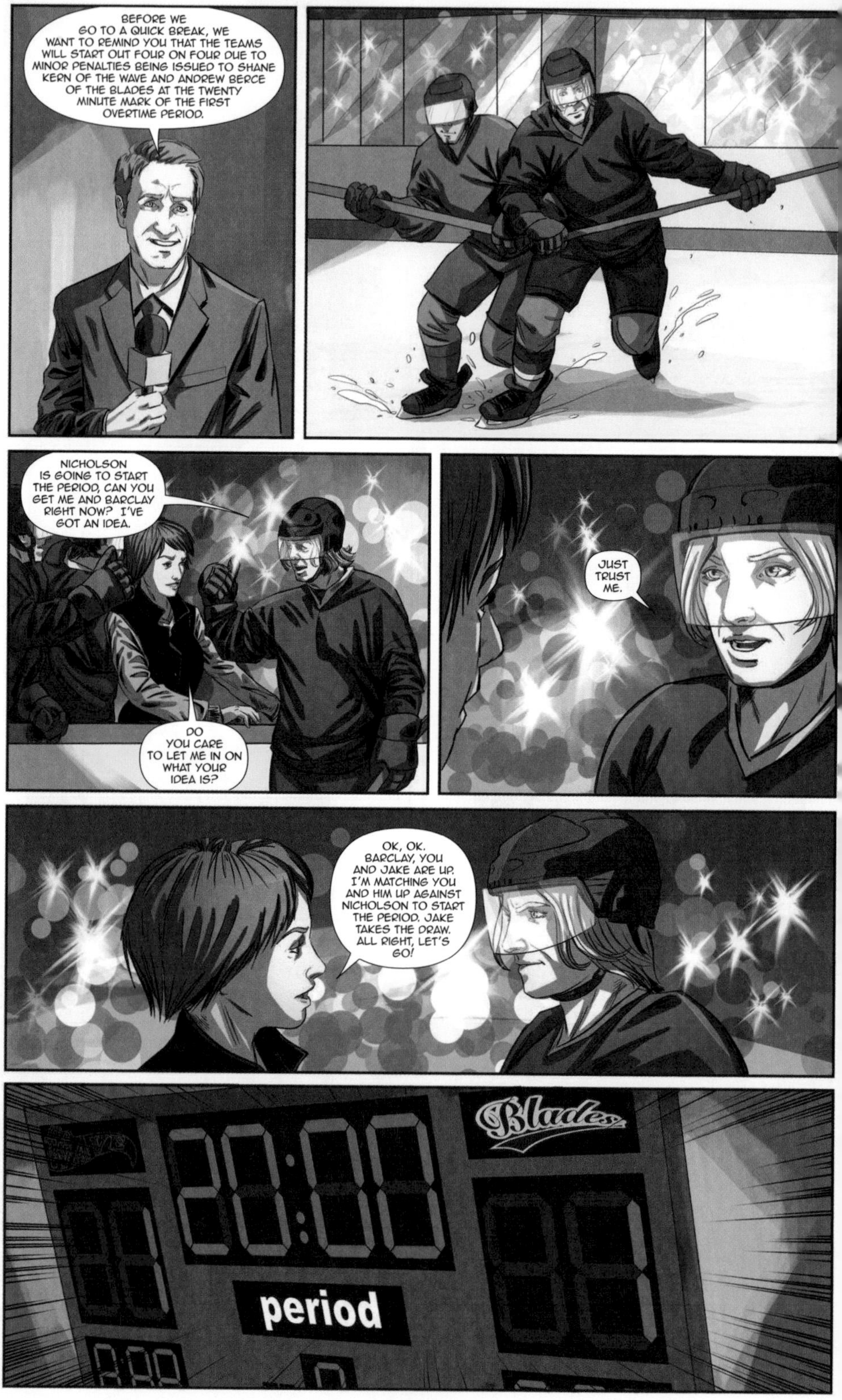
BEFORE WE GO TO A QUICK BREAK, WE WANT TO REMIND YOU THAT THE TEAMS WILL START OUT FOUR ON FOUR DUE TO MINOR PENALTIES BEING ISSUED TO SHANE KERN OF THE WAVE AND ANDREW BERCE OF THE BLADES AT THE TWENTY MINUTE MARK OF THE FIRST OVERTIME PERIOD.
NICHOLSON IS GOING TO START THE PERIOD, CAN YOU GET ME AND BARCLAY RIGHT NOW? I'VE GOT AN IDEA.
DO YOU CARE TO LET ME IN ON WHAT YOUR IDEA IS?
JUST TRUST ME.
OK, OK. BARCLAY, YOU AND JAKE ARE UP. I'M MATCHING YOU AND HIM UP AGAINST NICHOLSON TO START THE PERIOD. JAKE TAKES THE DRAW. ALL RIGHT, LET'S GO!
Blades
period

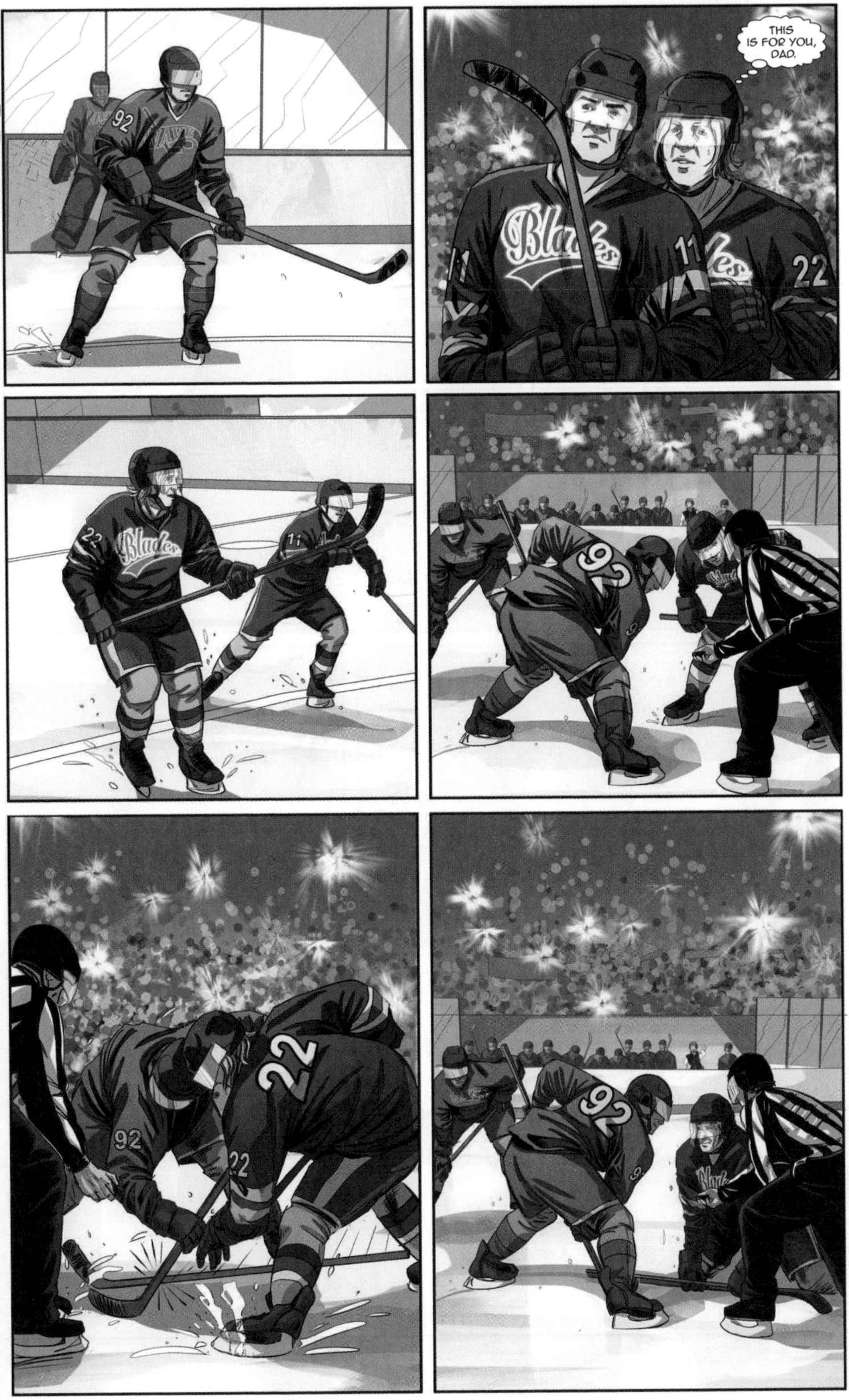
THIS IS FOR YOU, DAD.

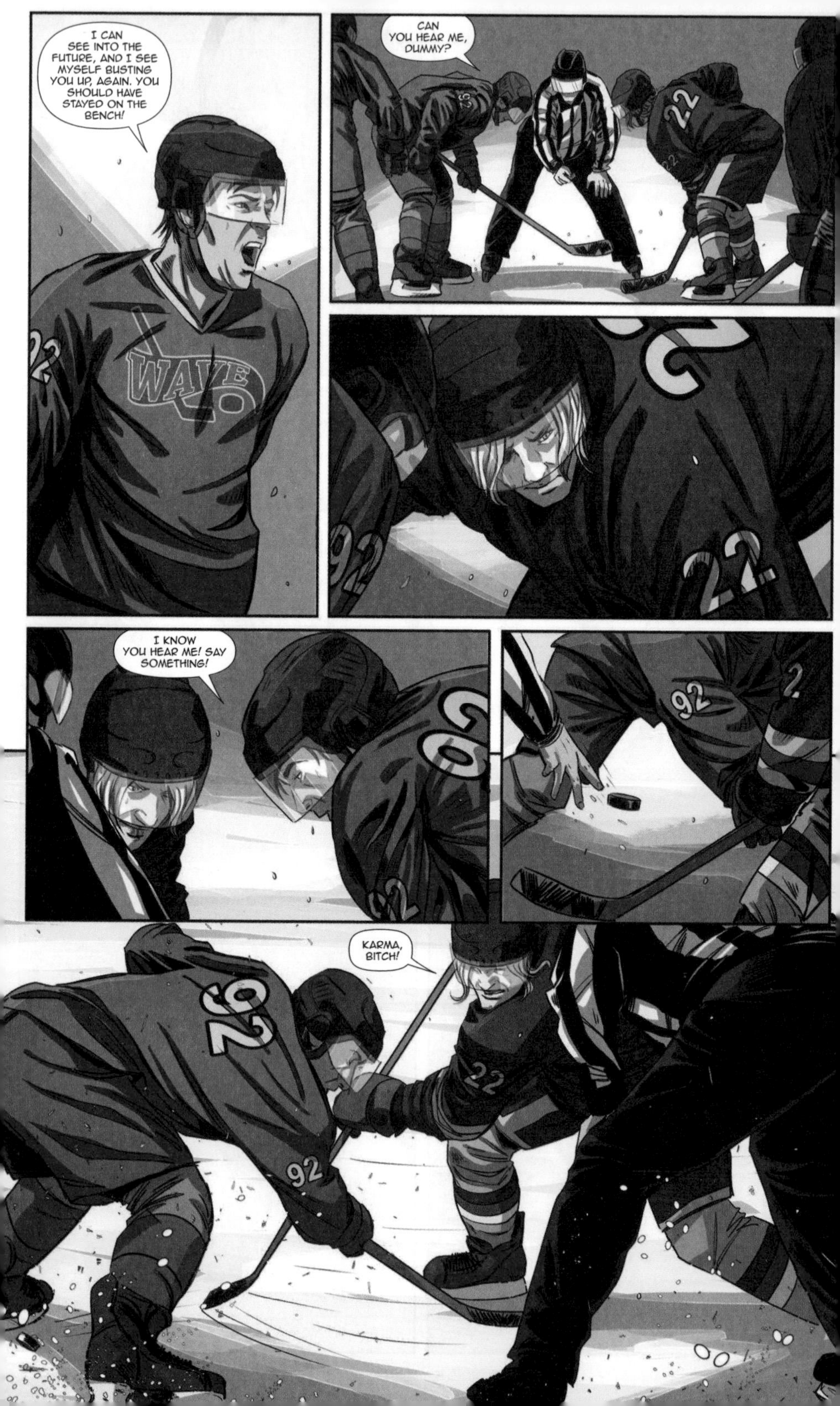
I CAN SEE INTO THE FUTURE, AND I SEE MYSELF BUSTING YOU UP, AGAIN. YOU SHOULD HAVE STAYED ON THE BENCH!
WAVE
22
CAN YOU HEAR ME, DUMMY?
92
22
22
92
22
I KNOW YOU HEAR ME! SAY SOMETHING!
92
92
KARMA, BITCH!
92
22
92

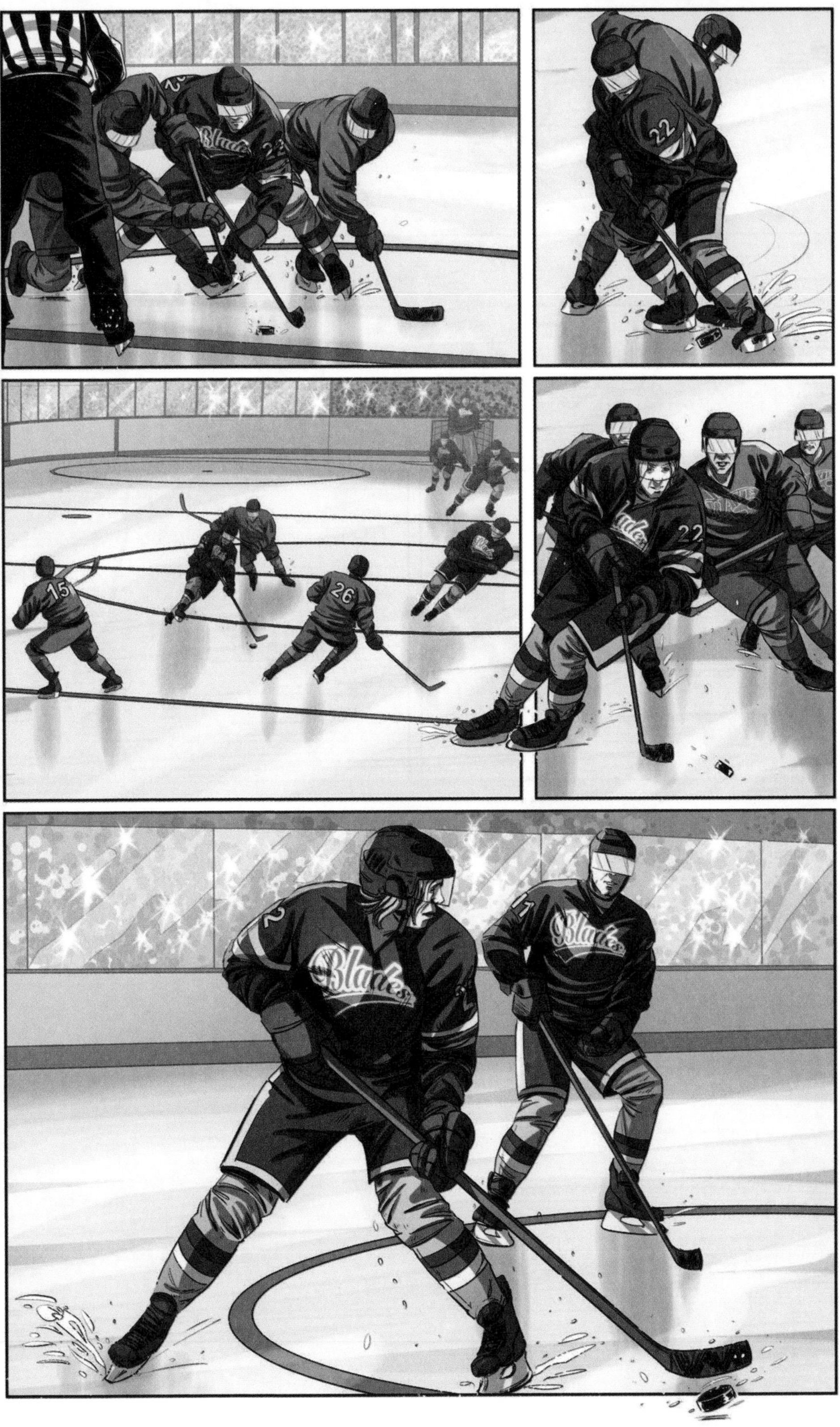
Blades
22
22
15
26
22
Blades
Blades

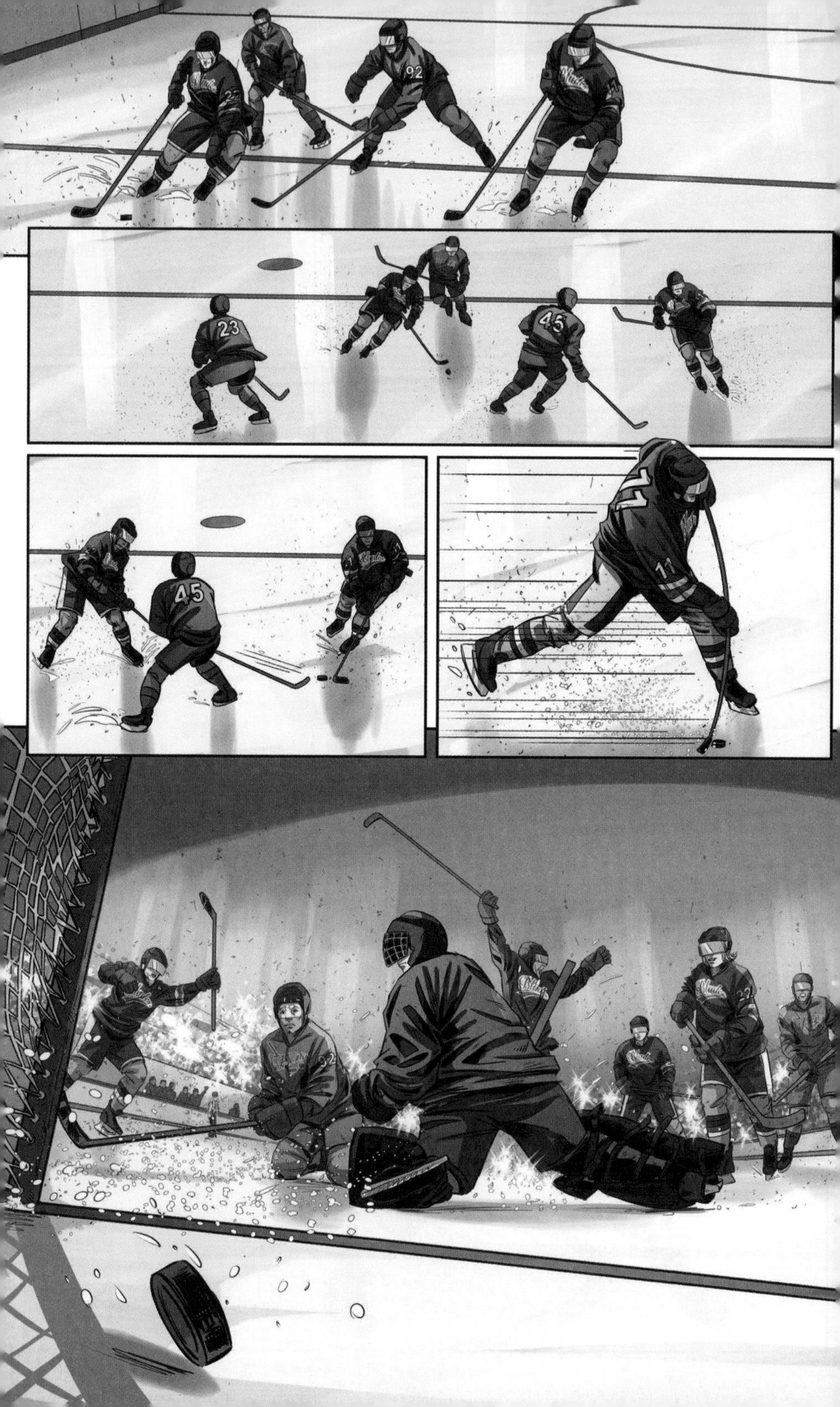

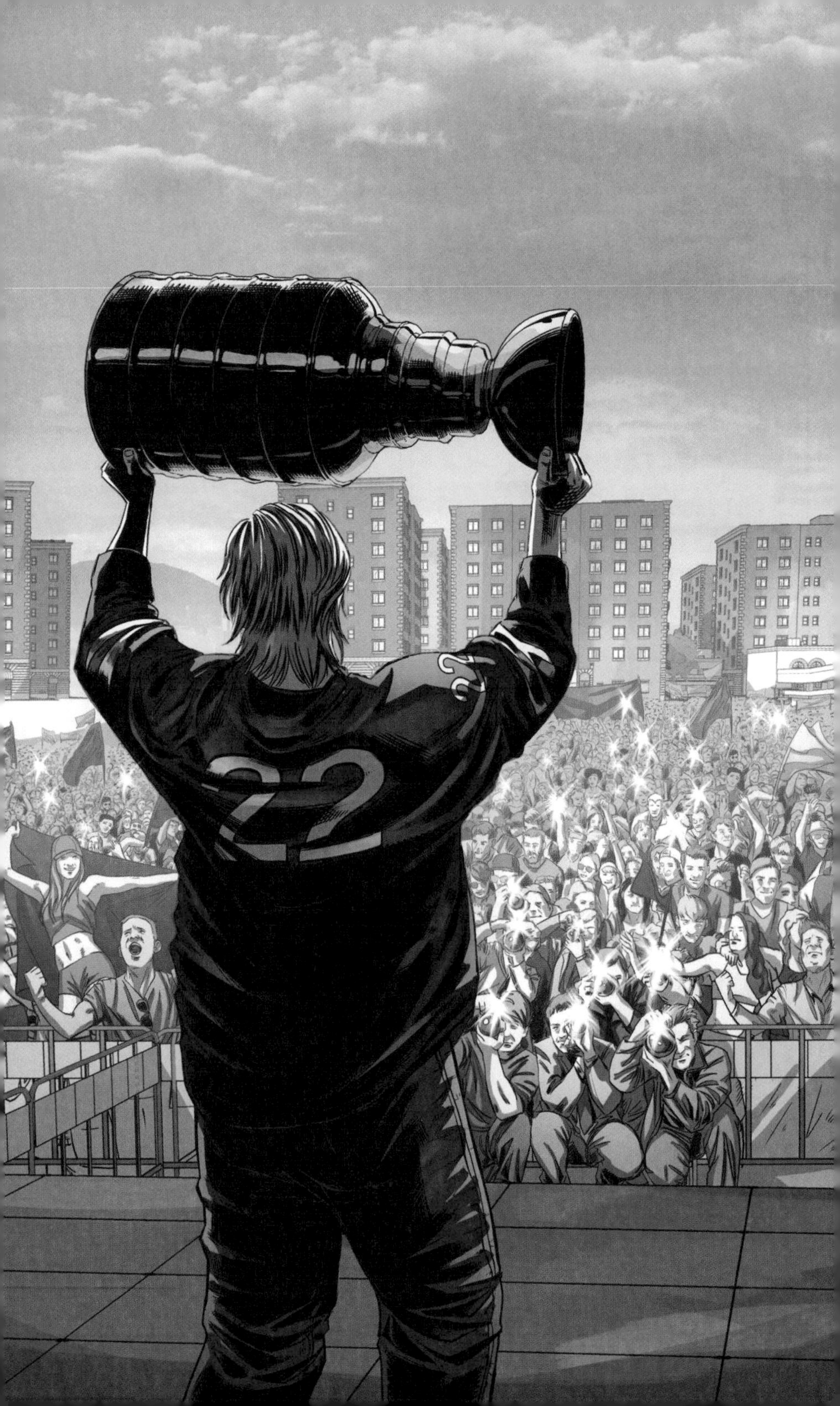
22

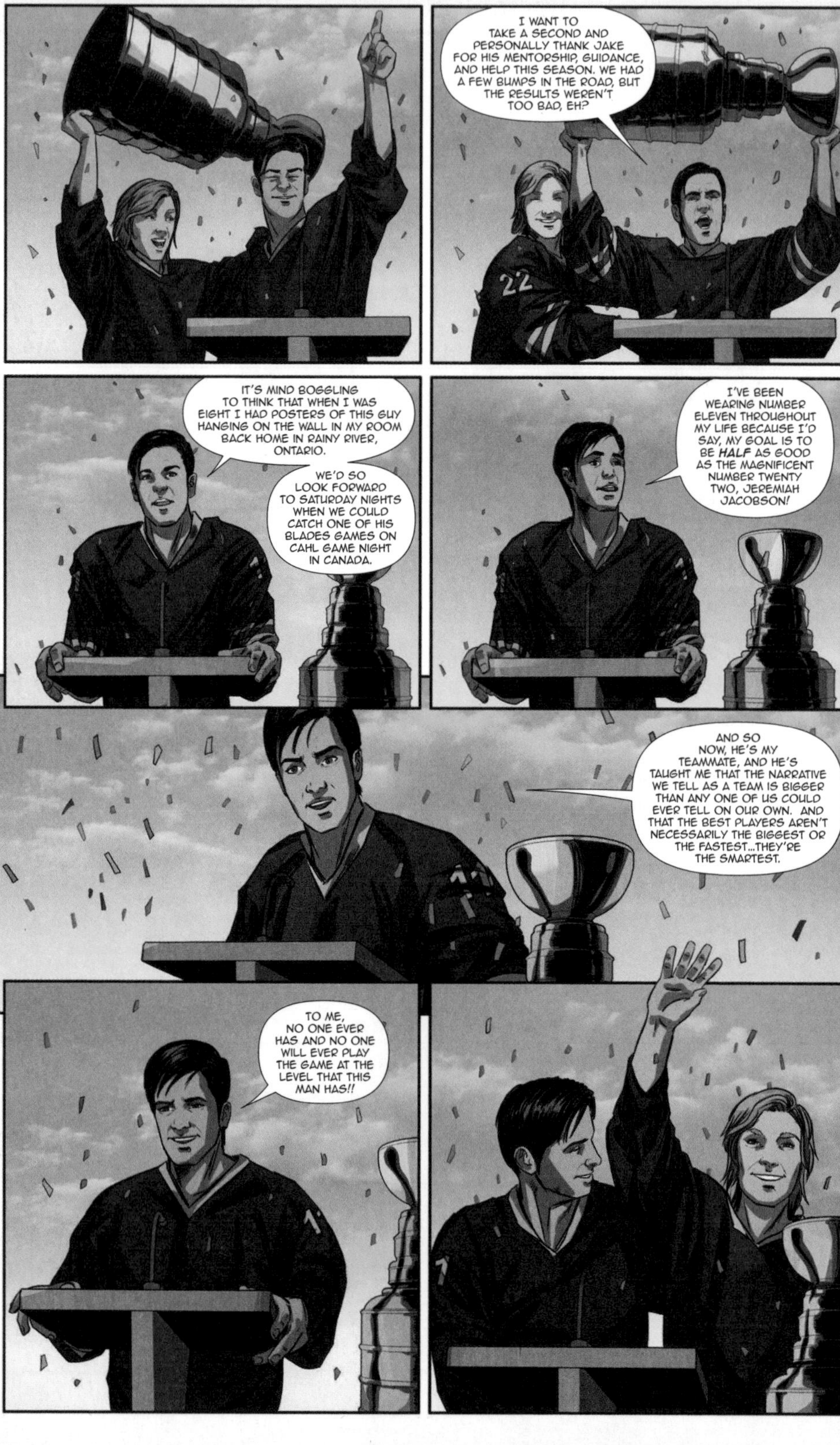
I WANT TO TAKE A SECOND AND PERSONALLY THANK JAKE FOR HIS MENTORSHIP, GUIDANCE, AND HELP THIS SEASON. WE HAD A FEW BUMPS IN THE ROAD, BUT THE RESULTS WEREN'T TOO BAD, EH?
IT'S MIND BOGGLING TO THINK THAT WHEN I WAS EIGHT I HAD POSTERS OF THIS GUY HANGING ON THE WALL IN MY ROOM BACK HOME IN RAINY RIVER, ONTARIO.
WE'D SO LOOK FORWARD TO SATURDAY NIGHTS WHEN WE COULD CATCH ONE OF HIS BLADES GAMES ON CAHL GAME NIGHT IN CANADA.
I'VE BEEN WEARING NUMBER ELEVEN THROUGHOUT MY LIFE BECAUSE I'D SAY, MY GOAL IS TO BE ***HALF*** AS GOOD AS THE MAGNIFICENT NUMBER TWENTY TWO, JEREMIAH JACOBSON!
AND SO NOW, HE'S MY TEAMMATE, AND HE'S TAUGHT ME THAT THE NARRATIVE WE TELL AS A TEAM IS BIGGER THAN ANY ONE OF US COULD EVER TELL ON OUR OWN. AND THAT THE BEST PLAYERS AREN'T NECESSARILY THE BIGGEST OR THE FASTEST...THEY'RE THE SMARTEST.
TO ME, NO ONE EVER HAS AND NO ONE WILL EVER PLAY THE GAME AT THE LEVEL THAT THIS MAN HAS!!

CHAPTER 12
FOREVER FRIENDS

RECOMMENDED LISTENING:

"BACKSTREETS"
BRUCE SPRINGSTEEN & THE E STREET BAND

"THE NEXT LIFE"
TOM COCHRANE AND RED RIDER

"MEADOWS"
JOE WALSH

"GIVE A LITTLE BIT"
SUPERTRAMP

"GOOD RIDDANCE
(TIME OF YOUR LIFE)"
GREEN DAY

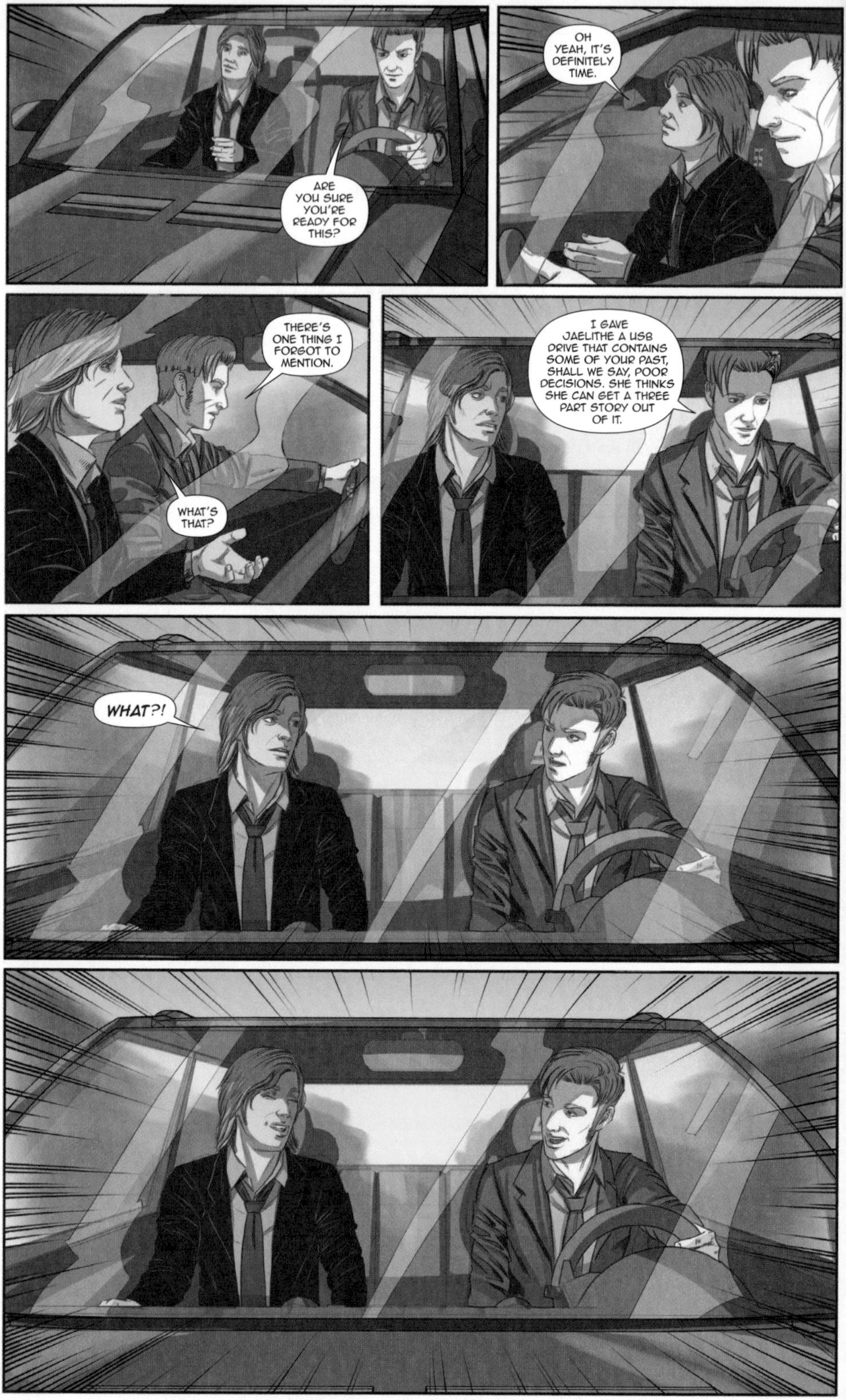
ARE YOU SURE YOU'RE READY FOR THIS?
OH YEAH, IT'S DEFINITELY TIME.
THERE'S ONE THING I FORGOT TO MENTION.
WHAT'S THAT?
I GAVE JAELITHE A USB DRIVE THAT CONTAINS SOME OF YOUR PAST, SHALL WE SAY, POOR DECISIONS. SHE THINKS SHE CAN GET A THREE PART STORY OUT OF IT.
WHAT?!

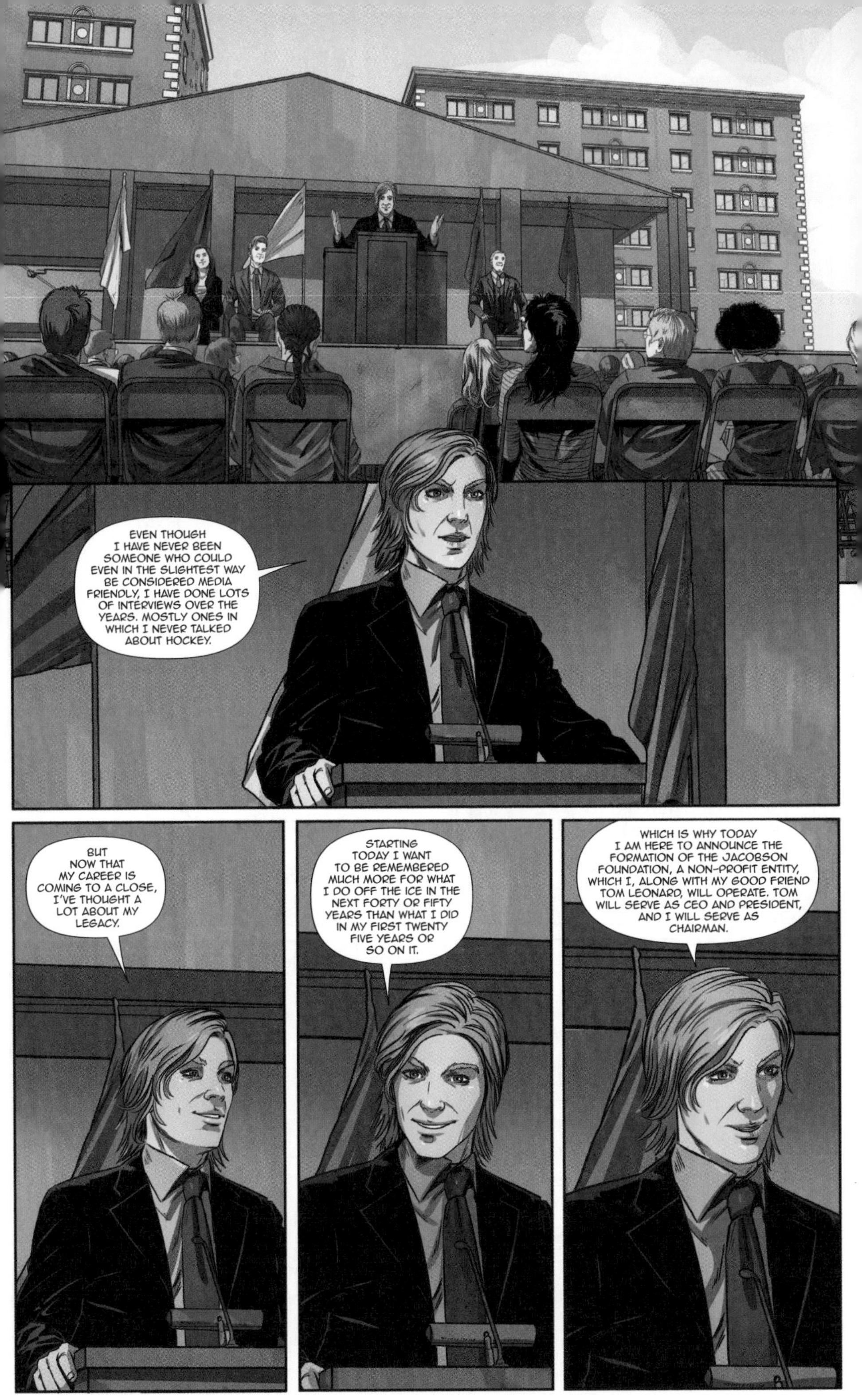
EVEN THOUGH I HAVE NEVER BEEN SOMEONE WHO COULD EVEN IN THE SLIGHTEST WAY BE CONSIDERED MEDIA FRIENDLY, I HAVE DONE LOTS OF INTERVIEWS OVER THE YEARS. MOSTLY ONES IN WHICH I NEVER TALKED ABOUT HOCKEY.
BUT NOW THAT MY CAREER IS COMING TO A CLOSE, I'VE THOUGHT A LOT ABOUT MY LEGACY.
STARTING TODAY I WANT TO BE REMEMBERED MUCH MORE FOR WHAT I DO OFF THE ICE IN THE NEXT FORTY OR FIFTY YEARS THAN WHAT I DID IN MY FIRST TWENTY FIVE YEARS OR SO ON IT.
WHICH IS WHY TODAY I AM HERE TO ANNOUNCE THE FORMATION OF THE JACOBSON FOUNDATION, A NON-PROFIT ENTITY, WHICH I, ALONG WITH MY GOOD FRIEND TOM LEONARD, WILL OPERATE. TOM WILL SERVE AS CEO AND PRESIDENT, AND I WILL SERVE AS CHAIRMAN.

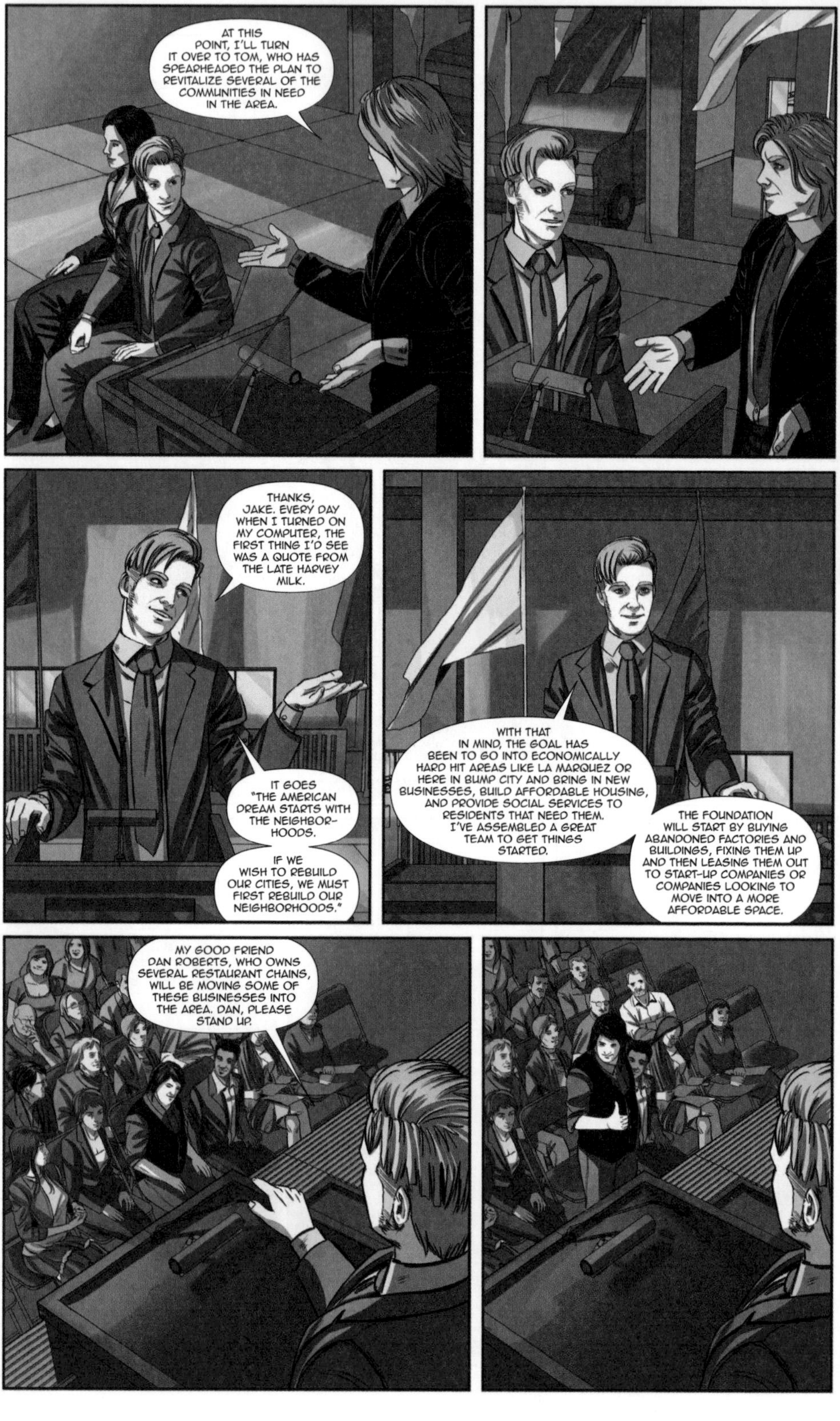
AT THIS POINT, I'LL TURN IT OVER TO TOM, WHO HAS SPEARHEADED THE PLAN TO REVITALIZE SEVERAL OF THE COMMUNITIES IN NEED IN THE AREA.
THANKS, JAKE. EVERY DAY WHEN I TURNED ON MY COMPUTER, THE FIRST THING I'D SEE WAS A QUOTE FROM THE LATE HARVEY MILK.
IT GOES "THE AMERICAN DREAM STARTS WITH THE NEIGHBOR-HOODS.
IF WE WISH TO REBUILD OUR CITIES, WE MUST FIRST REBUILD OUR NEIGHBORHOODS."
WITH THAT IN MIND, THE GOAL HAS BEEN TO GO INTO ECONOMICALLY HARD HIT AREAS LIKE LA MARQUEZ OR HERE IN BUMP CITY AND BRING IN NEW BUSINESSES, BUILD AFFORDABLE HOUSING, AND PROVIDE SOCIAL SERVICES TO RESIDENTS THAT NEED THEM. I'VE ASSEMBLED A GREAT TEAM TO GET THINGS STARTED.
THE FOUNDATION WILL START BY BUYING ABANDONED FACTORIES AND BUILDINGS, FIXING THEM UP AND THEN LEASING THEM OUT TO START-UP COMPANIES OR COMPANIES LOOKING TO MOVE INTO A MORE AFFORDABLE SPACE.
MY GOOD FRIEND DAN ROBERTS, WHO OWNS SEVERAL RESTAURANT CHAINS, WILL BE MOVING SOME OF THESE BUSINESSES INTO THE AREA. DAN, PLEASE STAND UP.

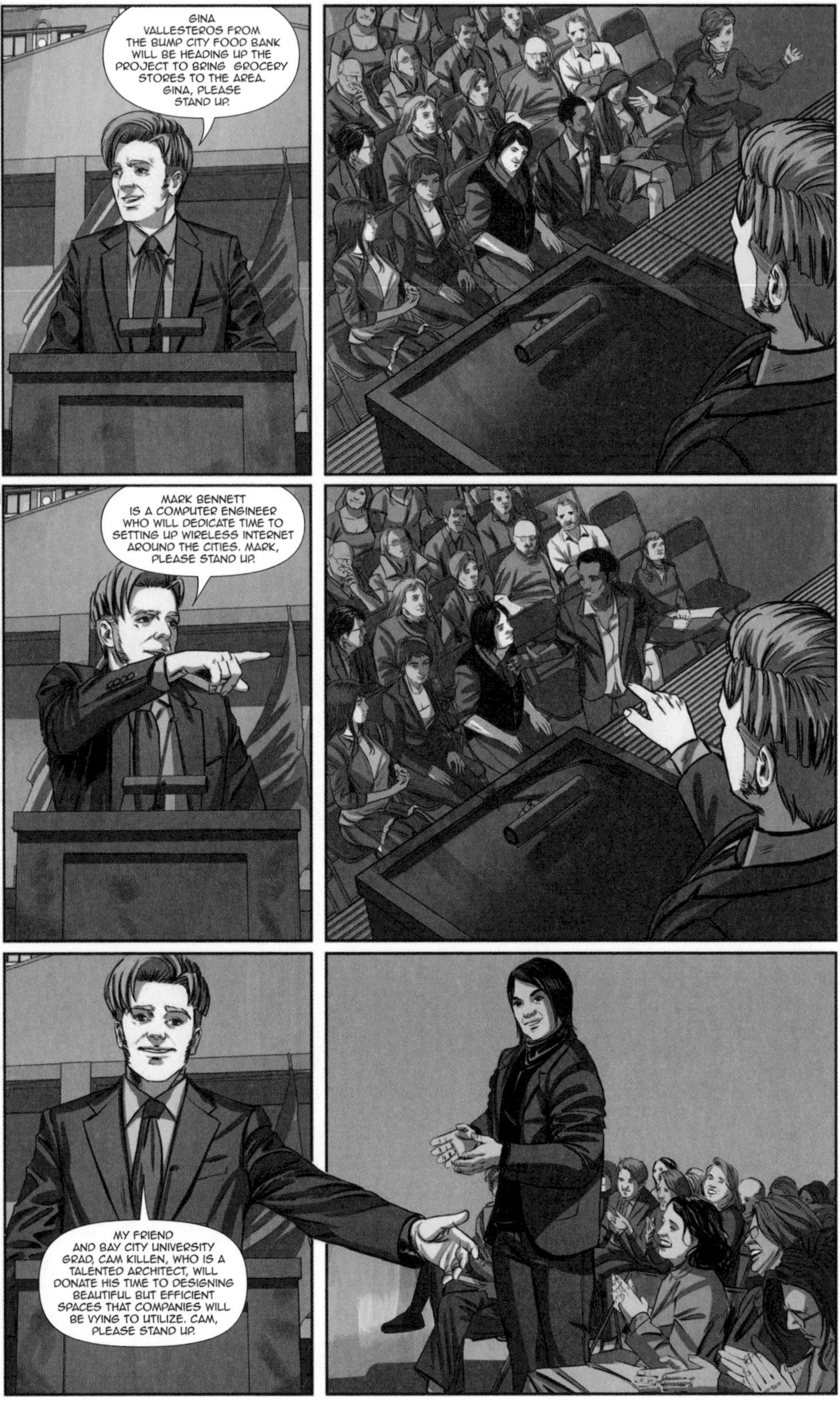
GINA VALLESTEROS FROM THE BUMP CITY FOOD BANK WILL BE HEADING UP THE PROJECT TO BRING GROCERY STORES TO THE AREA. GINA, PLEASE STAND UP.
MARK BENNETT IS A COMPUTER ENGINEER WHO WILL DEDICATE TIME TO SETTING UP WIRELESS INTERNET AROUND THE CITIES. MARK, PLEASE STAND UP.
MY FRIEND AND BAY CITY UNIVERSITY GRAD, CAM KILLEN, WHO IS A TALENTED ARCHITECT, WILL DONATE HIS TIME TO DESIGNING BEAUTIFUL BUT EFFICIENT SPACES THAT COMPANIES WILL BE VYING TO UTILIZE. CAM, PLEASE STAND UP.

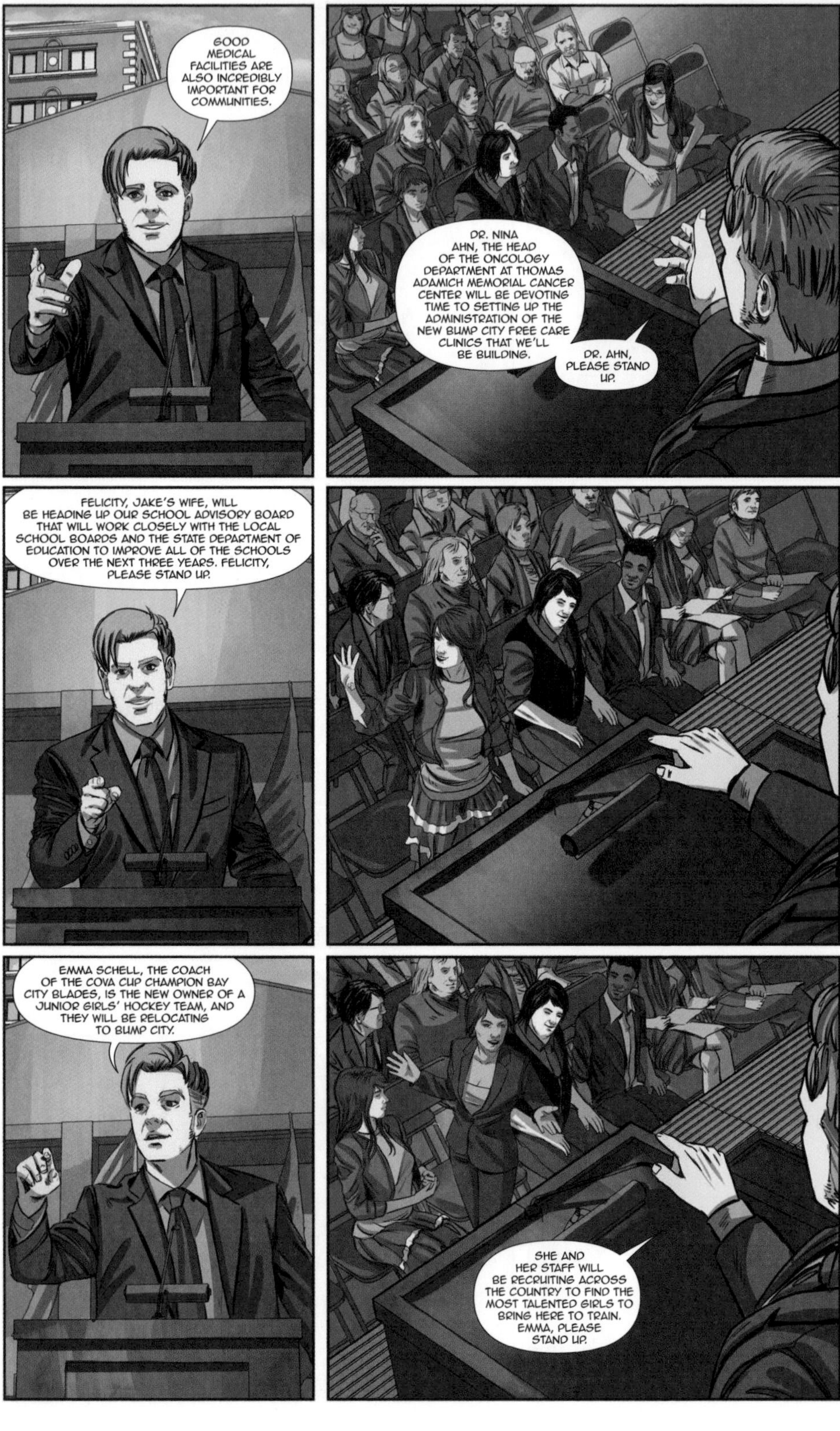
GOOD MEDICAL FACILITIES ARE ALSO INCREDIBLY IMPORTANT FOR COMMUNITIES.
DR. NINA AHN, THE HEAD OF THE ONCOLOGY DEPARTMENT AT THOMAS ADAMICH MEMORIAL CANCER CENTER WILL BE DEVOTING TIME TO SETTING UP THE ADMINISTRATION OF THE NEW BUMP CITY FREE CARE CLINICS THAT WE'LL BE BUILDING.
DR. AHN, PLEASE STAND UP.
FELICITY, JAKE'S WIFE, WILL BE HEADING UP OUR SCHOOL ADVISORY BOARD THAT WILL WORK CLOSELY WITH THE LOCAL SCHOOL BOARDS AND THE STATE DEPARTMENT OF EDUCATION TO IMPROVE ALL OF THE SCHOOLS OVER THE NEXT THREE YEARS. FELICITY, PLEASE STAND UP.
EMMA SCHELL, THE COACH OF THE COVA CUP CHAMPION BAY CITY BLADES, IS THE NEW OWNER OF A JUNIOR GIRLS' HOCKEY TEAM, AND THEY WILL BE RELOCATING TO BUMP CITY.
SHE AND HER STAFF WILL BE RECRUITING ACROSS THE COUNTRY TO FIND THE MOST TALENTED GIRLS TO BRING HERE TO TRAIN. EMMA, PLEASE STAND UP.

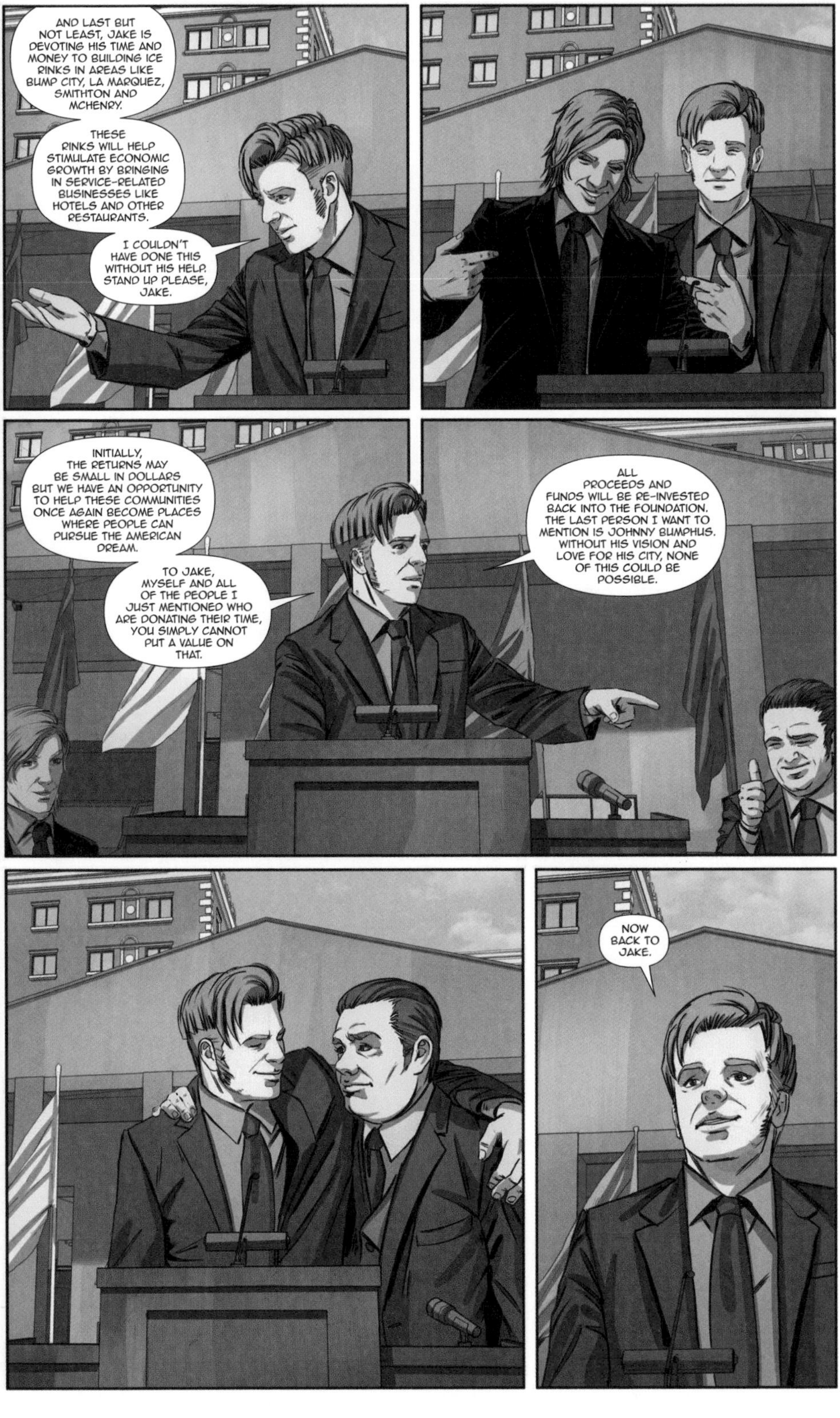
AND LAST BUT NOT LEAST, JAKE IS DEVOTING HIS TIME AND MONEY TO BUILDING ICE RINKS IN AREAS LIKE BUMP CITY, LA MARQUEZ, SMITHTON AND MCHENRY.
THESE RINKS WILL HELP STIMULATE ECONOMIC GROWTH BY BRINGING IN SERVICE-RELATED BUSINESSES LIKE HOTELS AND OTHER RESTAURANTS.
I COULDN'T HAVE DONE THIS WITHOUT HIS HELP. STAND UP PLEASE, JAKE.
INITIALLY, THE RETURNS MAY BE SMALL IN DOLLARS BUT WE HAVE AN OPPORTUNITY TO HELP THESE COMMUNITIES ONCE AGAIN BECOME PLACES WHERE PEOPLE CAN PURSUE THE AMERICAN DREAM.
TO JAKE, MYSELF AND ALL OF THE PEOPLE I JUST MENTIONED WHO ARE DONATING THEIR TIME, YOU SIMPLY CANNOT PUT A VALUE ON THAT.
ALL PROCEEDS AND FUNDS WILL BE RE-INVESTED BACK INTO THE FOUNDATION. THE LAST PERSON I WANT TO MENTION IS JOHNNY BUMPHUS. WITHOUT HIS VISION AND LOVE FOR HIS CITY, NONE OF THIS COULD BE POSSIBLE.
NOW BACK TO JAKE.

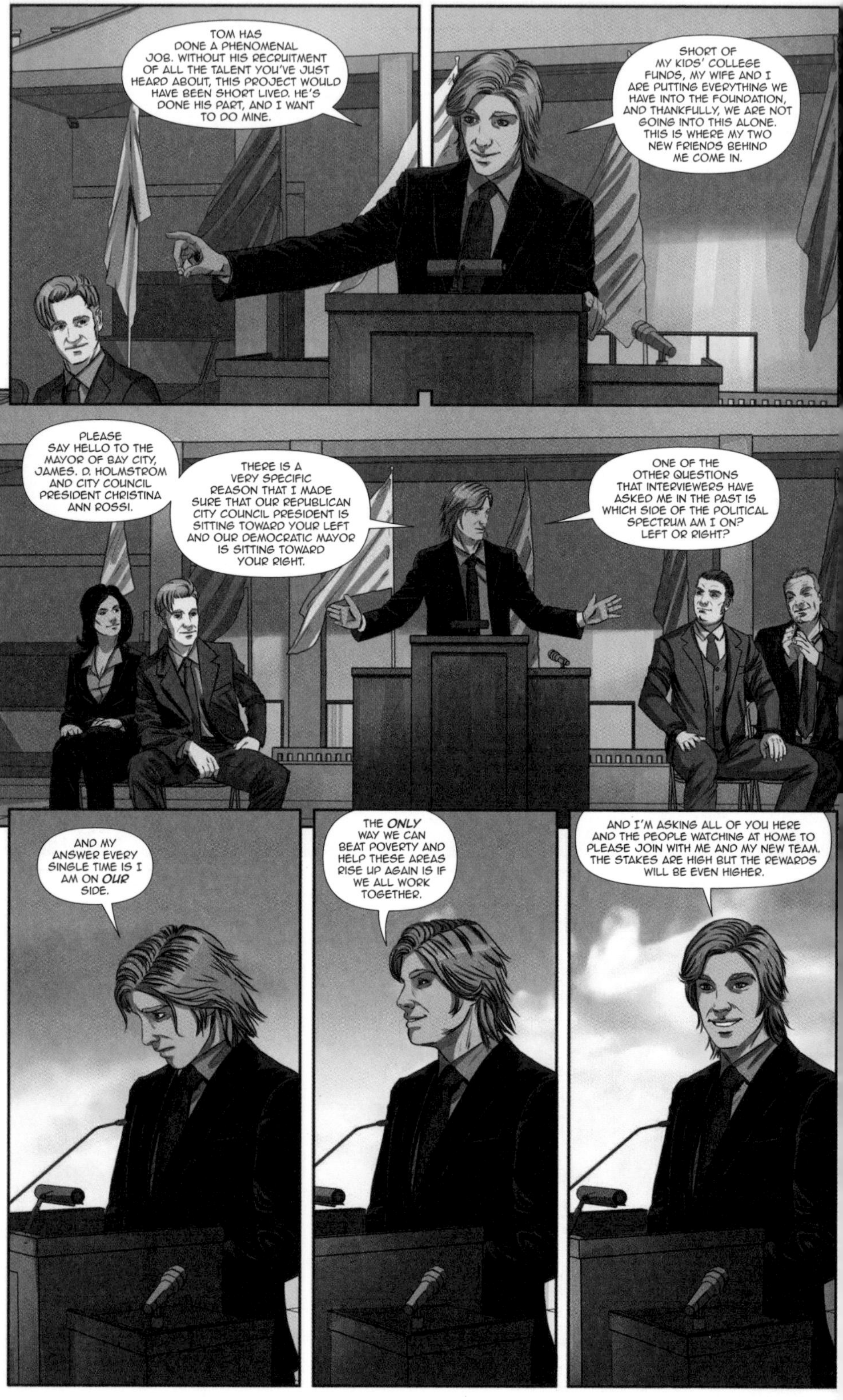
TOM HAS DONE A PHENOMENAL JOB. WITHOUT HIS RECRUITMENT OF ALL THE TALENT YOU'VE JUST HEARD ABOUT, THIS PROJECT WOULD HAVE BEEN SHORT LIVED. HE'S DONE HIS PART, AND I WANT TO DO MINE.
SHORT OF MY KIDS' COLLEGE FUNDS, MY WIFE AND I ARE PUTTING EVERYTHING WE HAVE INTO THE FOUNDATION, AND THANKFULLY, WE ARE NOT GOING INTO THIS ALONE. THIS IS WHERE MY TWO NEW FRIENDS BEHIND ME COME IN.
PLEASE SAY HELLO TO THE MAYOR OF BAY CITY, JAMES. D. HOLMSTROM AND CITY COUNCIL PRESIDENT CHRISTINA ANN ROSSI.
THERE IS A VERY SPECIFIC REASON THAT I MADE SURE THAT OUR REPUBLICAN CITY COUNCIL PRESIDENT IS SITTING TOWARD YOUR LEFT AND OUR DEMOCRATIC MAYOR IS SITTING TOWARD YOUR RIGHT.
ONE OF THE OTHER QUESTIONS THAT INTERVIEWERS HAVE ASKED ME IN THE PAST IS WHICH SIDE OF THE POLITICAL SPECTRUM AM I ON? LEFT OR RIGHT?
AND MY ANSWER EVERY SINGLE TIME IS I AM ON *OUR* SIDE.
THE *ONLY* WAY WE CAN BEAT POVERTY AND HELP THESE AREAS RISE UP AGAIN IS IF WE ALL WORK TOGETHER.
AND I'M ASKING ALL OF YOU HERE AND THE PEOPLE WATCHING AT HOME TO PLEASE JOIN WITH ME AND MY NEW TEAM. THE STAKES ARE HIGH BUT THE REWARDS WILL BE EVEN HIGHER.

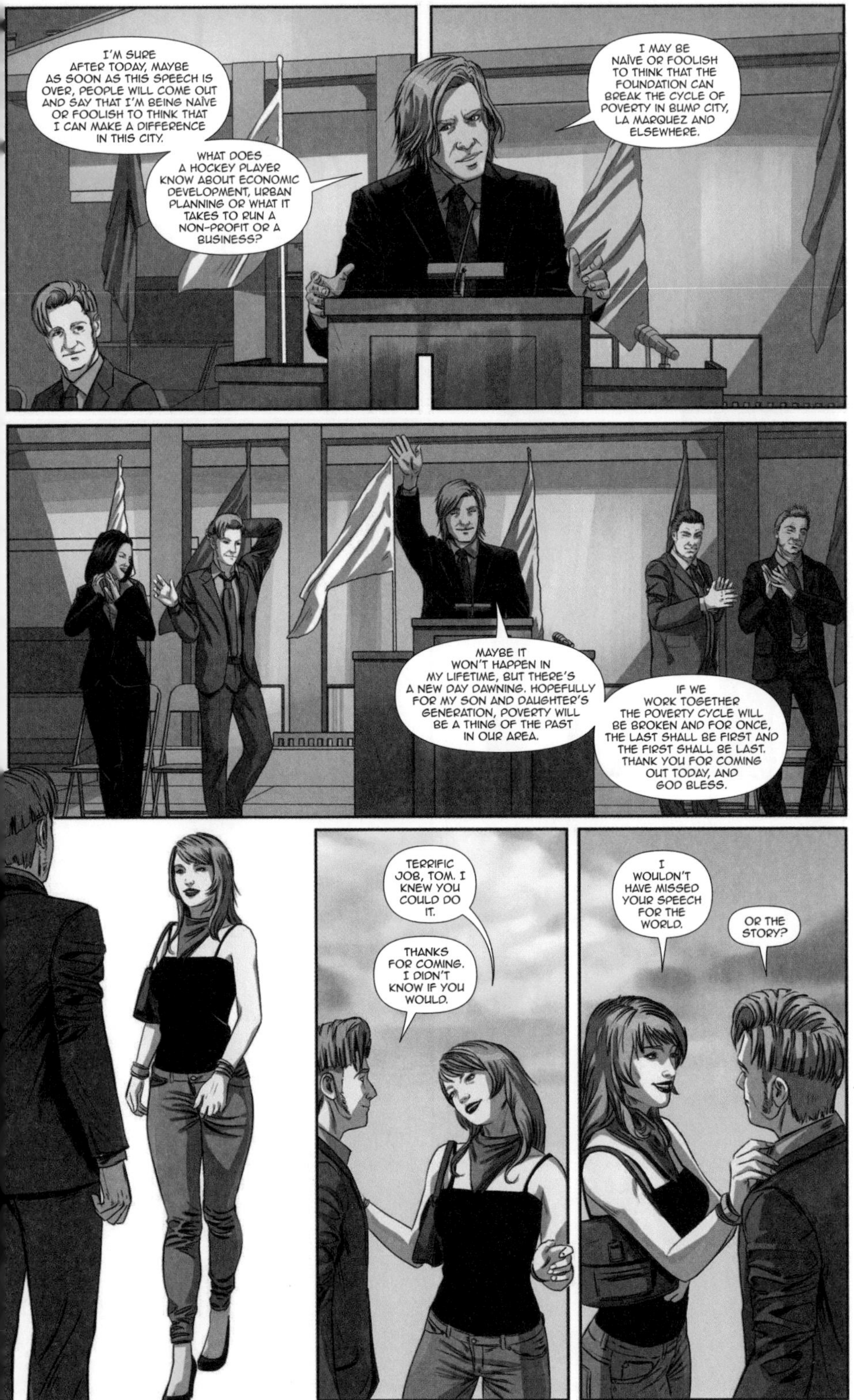
I'M SURE AFTER TODAY, MAYBE AS SOON AS THIS SPEECH IS OVER, PEOPLE WILL COME OUT AND SAY THAT I'M BEING NAÏVE OR FOOLISH TO THINK THAT I CAN MAKE A DIFFERENCE IN THIS CITY.
WHAT DOES A HOCKEY PLAYER KNOW ABOUT ECONOMIC DEVELOPMENT, URBAN PLANNING OR WHAT IT TAKES TO RUN A NON-PROFIT OR A BUSINESS?
I MAY BE NAÏVE OR FOOLISH TO THINK THAT THE FOUNDATION CAN BREAK THE CYCLE OF POVERTY IN BUMP CITY, LA MARQUEZ AND ELSEWHERE.
MAYBE IT WON'T HAPPEN IN MY LIFETIME, BUT THERE'S A NEW DAY DAWNING. HOPEFULLY FOR MY SON AND DAUGHTER'S GENERATION, POVERTY WILL BE A THING OF THE PAST IN OUR AREA.
IF WE WORK TOGETHER THE POVERTY CYCLE WILL BE BROKEN AND FOR ONCE, THE LAST SHALL BE FIRST AND THE FIRST SHALL BE LAST. THANK YOU FOR COMING OUT TODAY, AND GOD BLESS.
TERRIFIC JOB, TOM. I KNEW YOU COULD DO IT.
THANKS FOR COMING. I DIDN'T KNOW IF YOU WOULD.
I WOULDN'T HAVE MISSED YOUR SPEECH FOR THE WORLD.
OR THE STORY?

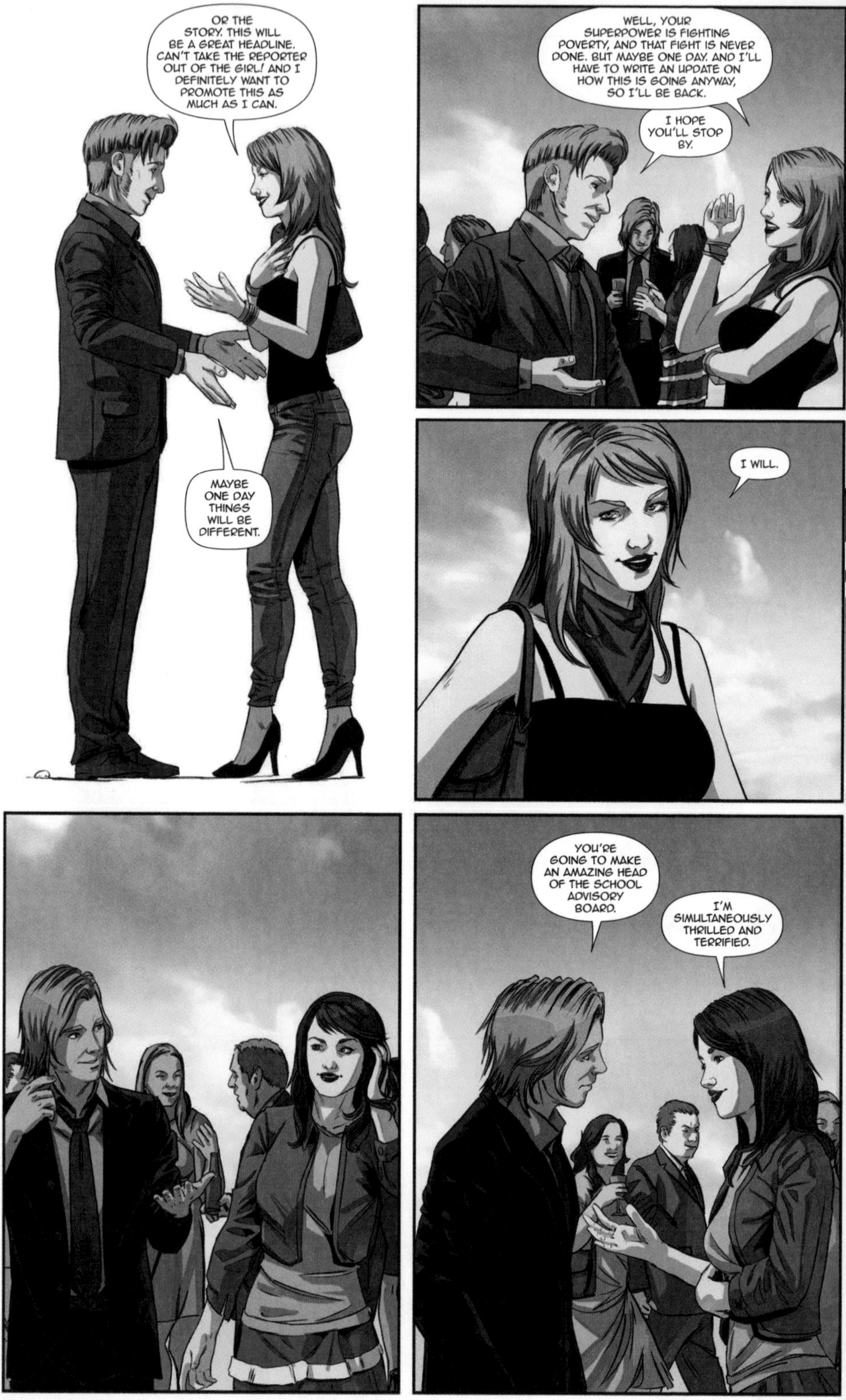
OR THE STORY. THIS WILL BE A GREAT HEADLINE. CAN'T TAKE THE REPORTER OUT OF THE GIRL! AND I DEFINITELY WANT TO PROMOTE THIS AS MUCH AS I CAN.
MAYBE ONE DAY THINGS WILL BE DIFFERENT.
WELL, YOUR SUPERPOWER IS FIGHTING POVERTY, AND THAT FIGHT IS NEVER DONE. BUT MAYBE ONE DAY. AND I'LL HAVE TO WRITE AN UPDATE ON HOW THIS IS GOING ANYWAY, SO I'LL BE BACK.
I HOPE YOU'LL STOP BY.
I WILL.
YOU'RE GOING TO MAKE AN AMAZING HEAD OF THE SCHOOL ADVISORY BOARD.
I'M SIMULTANEOUSLY THRILLED AND TERRIFIED.

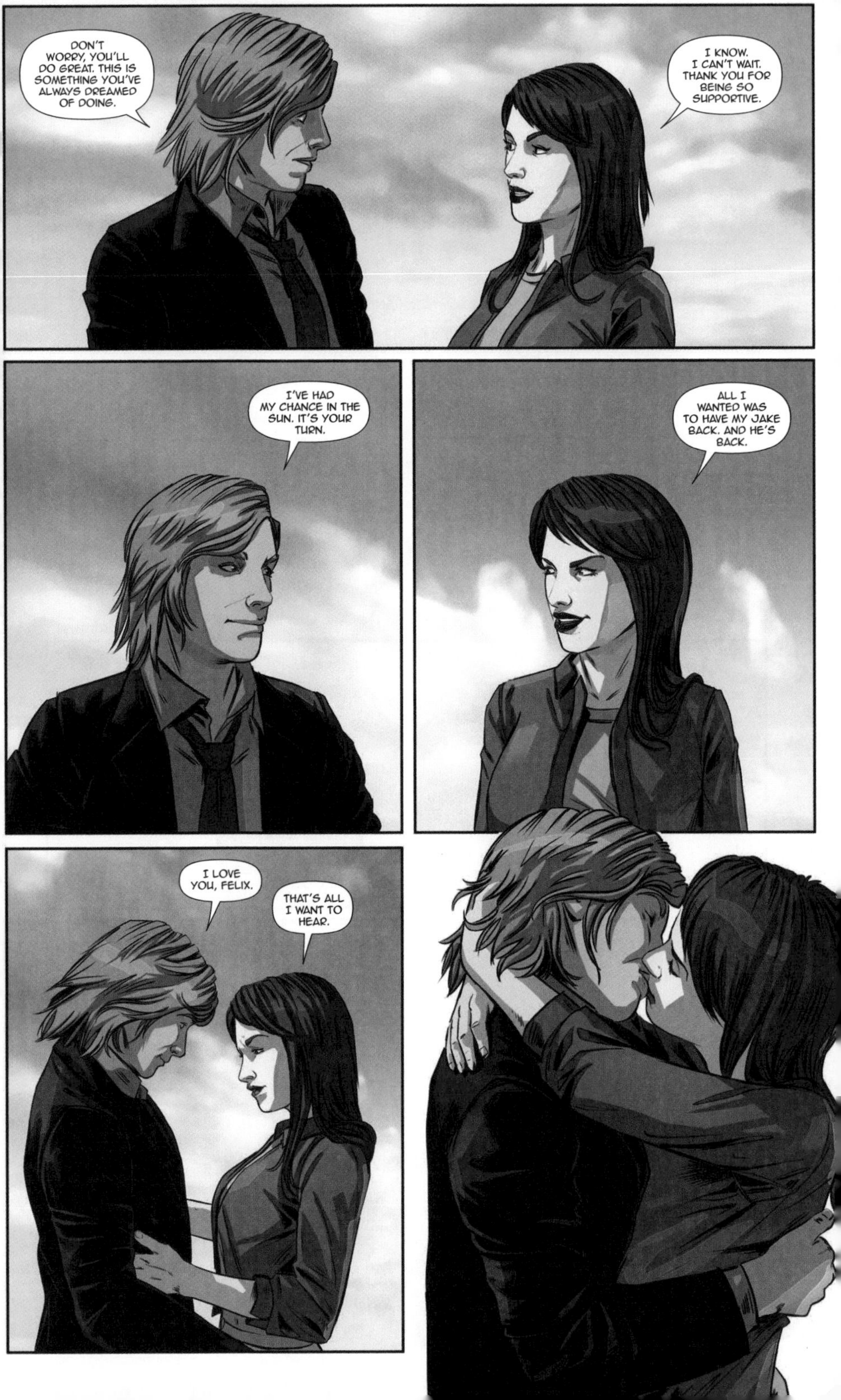
DON'T WORRY, YOU'LL DO GREAT. THIS IS SOMETHING YOU'VE ALWAYS DREAMED OF DOING.
I KNOW. I CAN'T WAIT. THANK YOU FOR BEING SO SUPPORTIVE.
I'VE HAD MY CHANCE IN THE SUN. IT'S YOUR TURN.
ALL I WANTED WAS TO HAVE MY JAKE BACK. AND HE'S BACK.
I LOVE YOU, FELIX.
THAT'S ALL I WANT TO HEAR.

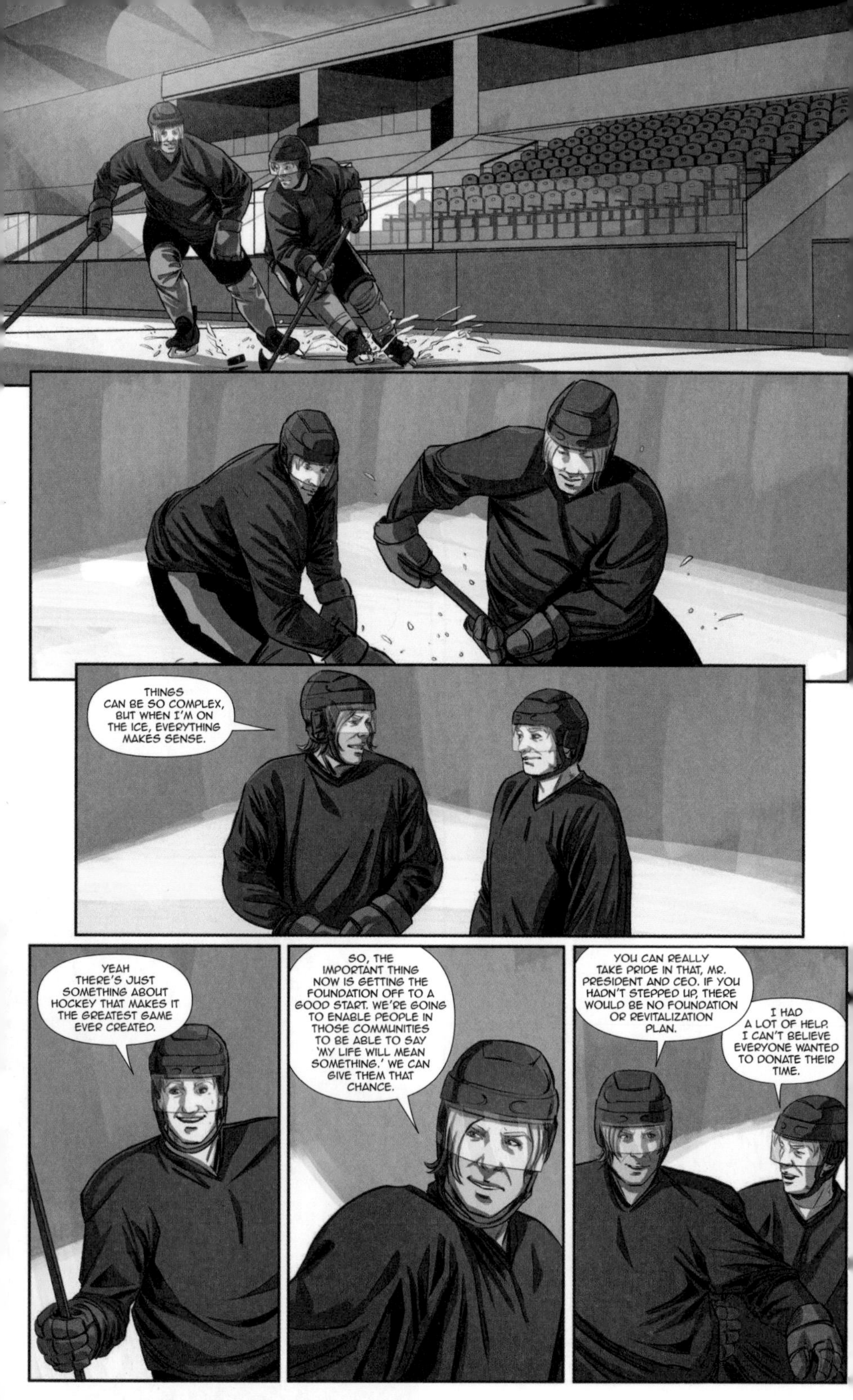
THINGS CAN BE SO COMPLEX, BUT WHEN I'M ON THE ICE, EVERYTHING MAKES SENSE.
YEAH THERE'S JUST SOMETHING ABOUT HOCKEY THAT MAKES IT THE GREATEST GAME EVER CREATED.
SO, THE IMPORTANT THING NOW IS GETTING THE FOUNDATION OFF TO A GOOD START. WE'RE GOING TO ENABLE PEOPLE IN THOSE COMMUNITIES TO BE ABLE TO SAY 'MY LIFE WILL MEAN SOMETHING.' WE CAN GIVE THEM THAT CHANCE.
YOU CAN REALLY TAKE PRIDE IN THAT, MR. PRESIDENT AND CEO. IF YOU HADN'T STEPPED UP, THERE WOULD BE NO FOUNDATION OR REVITALIZATION PLAN.
I HAD A LOT OF HELP. I CAN'T BELIEVE EVERYONE WANTED TO DONATE THEIR TIME.

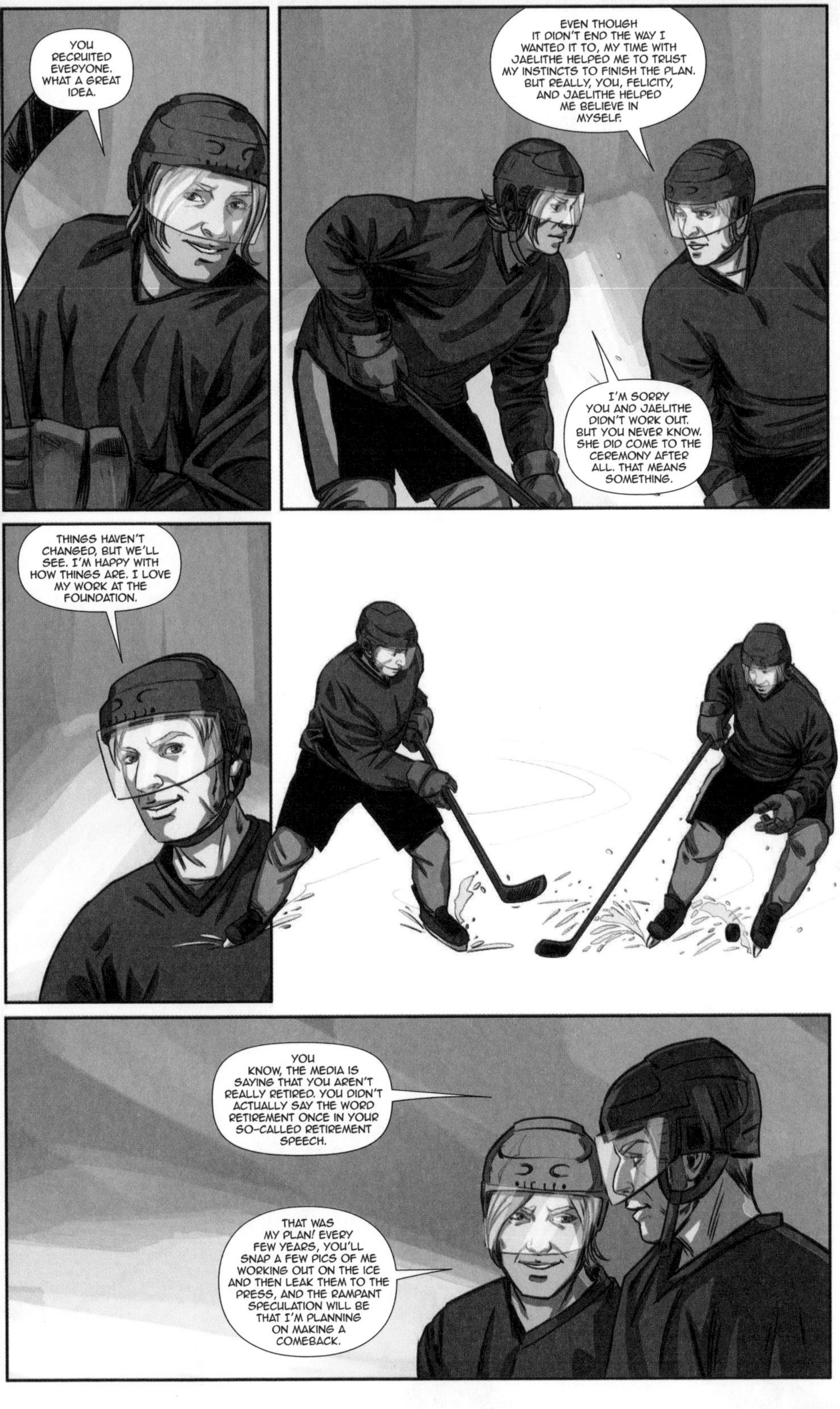
YOU RECRUITED EVERYONE. WHAT A GREAT IDEA.
EVEN THOUGH IT DIDN'T END THE WAY I WANTED IT TO, MY TIME WITH JAELITHE HELPED ME TO TRUST MY INSTINCTS TO FINISH THE PLAN. BUT REALLY, YOU, FELICITY, AND JAELITHE HELPED ME BELIEVE IN MYSELF.
I'M SORRY YOU AND JAELITHE DIDN'T WORK OUT. BUT YOU NEVER KNOW. SHE DID COME TO THE CEREMONY AFTER ALL. THAT MEANS SOMETHING.
THINGS HAVEN'T CHANGED, BUT WE'LL SEE. I'M HAPPY WITH HOW THINGS ARE. I LOVE MY WORK AT THE FOUNDATION.
YOU KNOW, THE MEDIA IS SAYING THAT YOU AREN'T REALLY RETIRED. YOU DIDN'T ACTUALLY SAY THE WORD RETIREMENT ONCE IN YOUR SO-CALLED RETIREMENT SPEECH.
THAT WAS MY PLAN! EVERY FEW YEARS, YOU'LL SNAP A FEW PICS OF ME WORKING OUT ON THE ICE AND THEN LEAK THEM TO THE PRESS, AND THE RAMPANT SPECULATION WILL BE THAT I'M PLANNING ON MAKING A COMEBACK.

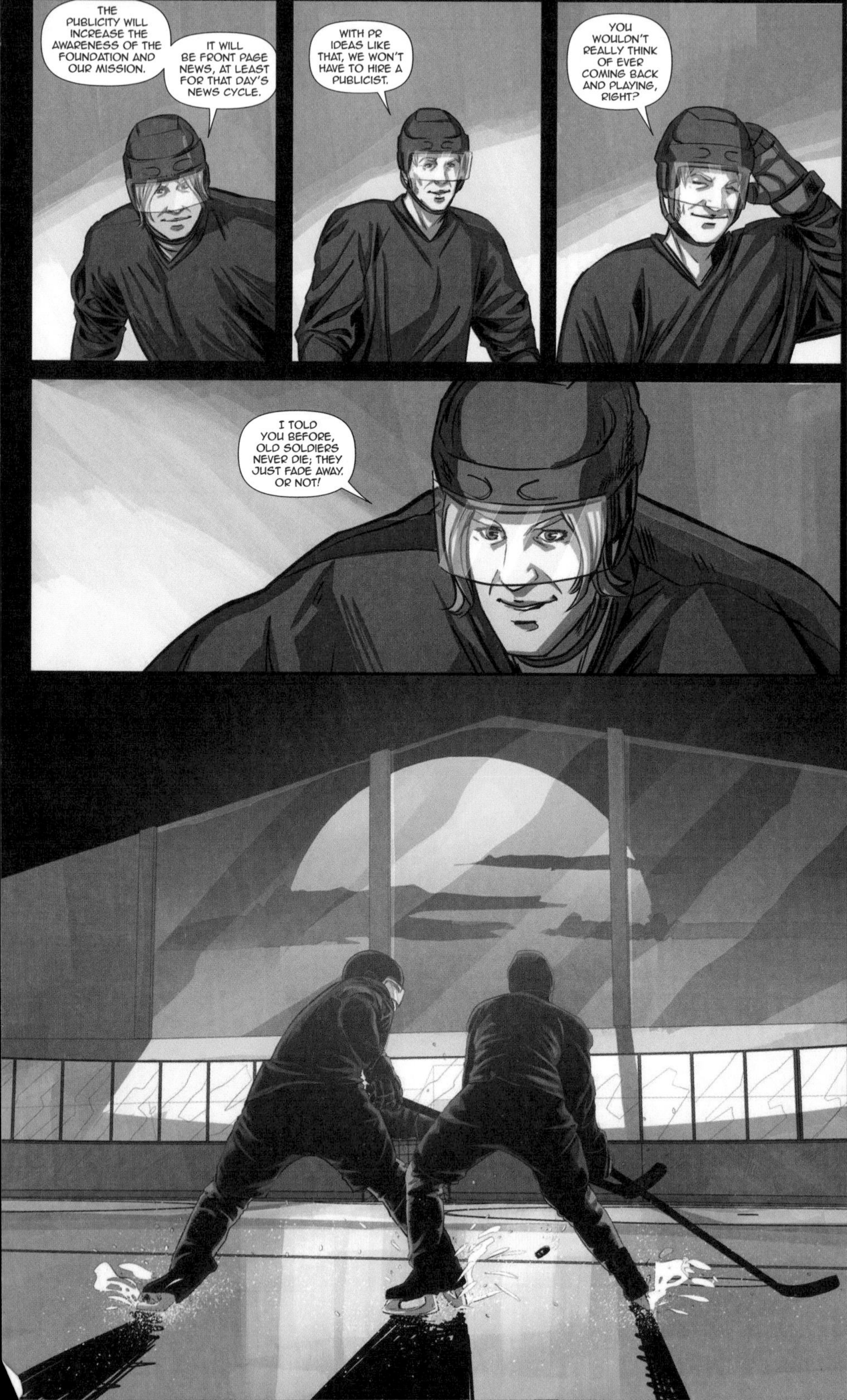
THE PUBLICITY WILL INCREASE THE AWARENESS OF THE FOUNDATION AND OUR MISSION.
IT WILL BE FRONT PAGE NEWS, AT LEAST FOR THAT DAY'S NEWS CYCLE.
WITH PR IDEAS LIKE THAT, WE WON'T HAVE TO HIRE A PUBLICIST.
YOU WOULDN'T REALLY THINK OF EVER COMING BACK AND PLAYING, RIGHT?
I TOLD YOU BEFORE, OLD SOLDIERS NEVER DIE; THEY JUST FADE AWAY. OR NOT!

[redacted]

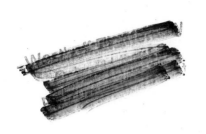